Urban Nightmares

Urban Nightmares

The Media, the Right, and the Moral Panic over the City

Steve Macek

University of Minnesota Press
Minneapolis • London

The section of chapter 5 on David Fincher's *Seven* was first published, in somewhat different form, in *College Literature* 26, no. 1 (Winter 1999): 73–90; reprinted here with permission.

Published by the University of Minnesota Press
111 Third Avenue South, Suite 290
Minneapolis, MN 55401-2520
http://www.upress.umn.edu

Library of Congress Cataloging-in-Publication Data

Macek, Steve, 1965–
    Urban nightmares : the media, the right, and the moral panic over the city / Steve Macek.
    p. cm.
    Includes bibliographical references and index.
    ISBN-13: 978-0-8166-4360-8 (hc : alk. paper)
    ISBN-10: 0-8166-4360-1 (hc : alk. paper)
    ISBN-13: 978-0-8166-4361-5 (pb : alk. paper)
    ISBN-10: 0-8166-4361-X (pb : alk. paper)
    1. Cities and towns—United States—Public opinion. 2. Inner cities—United States. 3. Cities and towns in mass media. 4. Urban policy—United States. 5. Fear of crime—United States. I. Title.
    HT123.M14 2006
    307.76′0973—dc22
                                                            2006004278

Printed in the United States of America on acid-free paper

The University of Minnesota is an equal-opportunity educator and employer.

12 11 10 09 08 07   10 9 8 7 6 5 4 3 2

Contents

A Landscape of Fear

The cancer of fear has taken over. We have government by fear.
We have a fear economy. We have a landscape of fear. We have a
mass media that sells it.

—William Upski Wimsatt, "The Fear Economy," *Adbusters*

To put it crudely, the "moral panic" appears to us to be one of the
principal forms of ideological consciousness by means of which a
"silent majority" is won over to the support of increasingly coercive measures on the part of the state, and lends its legitimacy to a
"more than usual" exercise of control.

—Stuart Hall et al., *Policing the Crisis*

Two *Time* magazine covers from the early 1990s reflect what many contemporary observers agreed was a growing climate of apprehension surrounding the American city. The first, for the September 17, 1990, issue,
features a painting of a dark New York City composed entirely of hive-
like apartment buildings, adult bookstores, X-rated film theaters, and
looming skyscrapers (see Figure 1). In the windows of these buildings
can be seen silhouettes of people fighting, crying, brandishing knives,
shooting up drugs, and holding pistols to their heads; on the streets, the
illustration shows someone being mugged, a bum drinking while sprawled
out on the sidewalk, a hooker plying her trade, and a police car pulling
over a motorist. "The Rotting of The Big Apple" reads the headline hovering over this dismal scene, and the related feature story inside reveals
breathlessly that "frightened residents now wonder if Gotham's trea-
sures are worth the hassle—and the risk" (Attinger 1990, 36). The story
goes on to cite a 1990 Time/CNN poll that found that 78 percent of

New York City residents feel the city is dirty, 73 percent say it is a dangerous place to live, and 59 percent would rather live somewhere else (39–40).

The second cover, for the April 19, 1993, issue of the magazine, boasts a foreboding rendition of Los Angeles at night painted in the same style (see Figure 2). Appropriately, there are no skyscrapers in this landscape, only highway overpasses and the flat architecture of the strip mall. But, as with the cover about New York City's decline, all manner of criminal mischief is depicted taking place on L.A.'s broad thoroughfares and silhouetted against the windows of its buildings: guys pointing guns at each other, people being robbed, drug deals being made, and so on. In the distance, at the foot of the Hollywood hills, fires burn (no doubt an allusion to the fires started during the so-called Rodney King riots of 1992). "Los Angeles: Is the City of Angels Going to Hell?" asks the headline. The accompanying story is full of bad news about L.A., which is described as living "in the grip of racial tension, red ink and cynicism" (Lacayo 1993, 28). Together the two *Time* covers (along with the feature stories they announce) paint a picture of the nation's cities as violent and out of control, as populated by murderers, muggers, drug addicts, and lowlifes, as places where the rules of normal, decent behavior no longer apply.

Time magazine was hardly alone in its bleak portrayal of urban reality during the 1980s and 1990s. Television news programs and "reality" police shows like the Fox network's *Cops* presented a similarly scary picture of inner-city neighborhoods overrun with crime and vice. So did fictional television dramas like *NYPD Blue* and *Homicide*. Hollywood films like *Batman* (1989) and *Seven* (1995) projected creepy images of dark, dilapidated cities incubating every conceivable evil. Syndicated columnists George Will and John Leo regularly bemoaned the mounting horrors of urban life in their columns. Talk shows routinely debated how awful things in the urban core had become and argued over the reasons for the decline. Intellectuals worried that the disorder and violence of America's postindustrial slums signaled the impending collapse of civilization itself. From feature-length films to 30-second television commercials, from newspaper editorials to best-selling books, representations of "the city as nightmare" circulated through every arena of the media.

The anxious mood surrounding the American metropolis showed up in national opinion polls as well. For example, one 1991 *Newsweek/ NBC* poll found that fully 88 percent of the nation saw cities in negative terms and 42 percent identified crime and drugs as the urban core's biggest problems (Morganthau and McCormick 1991, 42). Anxiety about the spread of urban lawlessness drove millions to move to "gated communities," to invest in home security systems, and to support punitive "crime-fighting" legislation like the so-called Clinton Crime Bill that passed through Congress in 1994. Indeed, it could be argued that hysteria about urban violence and degeneracy became a defining feature of every level of American politics in the late 1980s and throughout the 1990s. In 1993, in the wake of the Rodney King riots, Richard Riordan, a white Republican, was elected mayor of heavily Democratic and decidedly multicultural Los Angeles by selling himself as "Tough Enough to Turn L.A. Around" and pledging to hire three thousand new police officers to patrol the city's neighborhoods (Davis 1993, 49). A few months later, law-and-order crusader and former prosecutor Rudolph Giuliani was elected mayor of New York after promising to wage a "10- to 15-year war on crime" and swearing that he would take Manhattan's streets back from homeless "squeegee men" (Kambler 1994, 44). Even as such conservative politicians celebrated those aspects of big city life that appealed to tourists and affluent professionals (gentrification, revitalized downtowns, new entertainment districts, upscale museums, pro sports teams), they consistently demonized and denigrated the legions of urbanites who were indigent or working class. At the national level, every president from Ronald Reagan (1980–88) to Bill Clinton (1992–2000) scored political points and boosted his approval ratings by denouncing promiscuous ghetto "welfare queens," announcing a commitment to wage a "war on drugs" centered on minority neighborhoods, or by ostentatiously putting hundreds of thousands of new cops on the streets to combat youth gangs.

The political ramifications of all this divisiveness can be traced in

Figure 1. *Time* cover, September 17, 1990. Art by Roger Brown.

Figure 2. *Time* cover, April 19, 1993. Art by Roger Brown.

the dismal history of urban and social policy in the years since Reagan first ascended to the presidency. During the Reagan era and after, mainstream politicians and the largely middle-class, largely suburban voting public turned decisively against aid to cities and their neediest inhabitants. Federal subsidies, upon which many big city governments depended to balance their budgets, were slashed (Dreier et al. 2001). Funding for public housing construction was cut (Clay 1992). Welfare—alleged to be a driving force behind the malaise of the ghetto underclass—was "reformed" out of existence (Albelda and Withorn 2002). Meanwhile, federal and state spending on police and prisons soared as Congress and state legislatures squandered scarce tax dollars to combat the looming inner-city crime threat (Garland 2001, 167–92; see also Parenti 1999). Penalties for graffiti writing, drinking in public, and other petty crimes associated with urban public space were stiffened and rigorously enforced by newly aggressive metropolitan police departments (McArdle 2001). And in one downtown after another, homeless people who dared to venture into areas where they might come into contact with the affluent and privileged were systematically targeted for harassment and arrest (Mitchell 1995).

Everywhere one looked in American culture during the 1980s and '90s there were symptoms of a heightened sensitivity to the menace of the postindustrial metropolis and its residents. Everywhere there was alarm about the city's moral decline and rampant criminality. In the minds of many Americans, economically depressed urban centers like Philadelphia, Baltimore, St. Louis, and Detroit had become vast landscapes of fear, seen as teetering on the verge of an impending apocalypse or already smoldering in ruins. In short, for much of our recent history, the United States has been in the throes of what sociologists and media theorists call a "moral panic" (or, more precisely, a series of closely related, overlapping moral panics) directed at the country's big cities and at their black and Latino inhabitants.

This book seeks to explain how and why this happened. It explicates the social, political, economic, and cultural conditions that initially gave rise to the panic over the city. It identifies which social actors promoted alarm over conditions in the urban core for what political ends. It underscores the role of "experts" and policy discourse in legitimating this climate of apprehension. And, most important, it explores the role played by the mass media—from the news to Hollywood films to advertising—in inflating the perceived menace of the postindustrial metropolis and legitimating the right's "law-and-order" remedies for the nation's urban ills.

From Panic to Hegemony

Outbursts of cultural anxiety like the one inspired by the urban crisis of the '80s and '90s are a common feature of the cultures of advanced industrialized nations. Since the mid-1970s, such waves of fear have been theorized using the concept of the "moral panic." Broadly speaking, a moral panic can be defined as any sudden upsurge of public concern over, or alarm about, a condition or group socially defined as "threatening" or "dangerous." Sociologists and cultural studies scholars have written about moral panics surrounding Mods (Cohen 1972), punk rockers (Hebdige 1979), AIDS sufferers (Watney 1987), mugging (Hall et al. 1978), subway graffiti (Austin 2002), and "random violence" (Best 1999). The concept was first used extensively by Stanley Cohen in his study of the way politicians, police, and the media responded to a series of pitched street battles between Mods and Rockers, rival youth subcultures, in late 1960s Britain. "Societies appear to be subject, every now and then, to periods of moral panic," Cohen observed. "A condition, episode, person or group of persons emerges to become defined as a threat to societal values and interests; its nature is presented in a stylized and stereotypical fashion by the mass media; the moral barricades are manned by editors, bishops, politicians and other right-thinking people; socially accredited experts pronounce their diagnoses and solutions; ways of coping are evolved or . . . resorted to" (Cohen 1972, 9). As we shall see, the upsurge of concern over the city in '80s and '90s America followed a trajectory very similar to the one Cohen outlines.

For Cohen, a moral panic always involves a sudden rise in popular fear about a social group perceived to be threatening or deviant; it also involves increased hostility toward that group, such that they come to be seen as "folk devils," embodiments of evil. The "folk devils" created by this increased hostility become the target of a "moral crusade" led by politicians, intellectuals, and others who amplify the fears surrounding the "devils" in the process of proposing explanations of and solutions to the threat they allegedly pose. The mass media are especially crucial to this process as it is circulation through the media that gives elite diagnoses and interpretations of the threatening group influence and social weight. Cohen and just about everyone else who has studied moral panics insist that the fears generated are almost always "disproportionate" in the sense that the perceived threat is typically more grave than "is warranted by a realistic appraisal" (Thompson 1998, 9). Moreover, moral panics are not automatic or spontaneous responses on the part of experts or the public to objective social conditions; the problems and threats they address are problematic and threatening by virtue of being socially and culturally defined that way. In other words, the deviant, threatening, or troubling objects of a panic are social constructions, produced by particular social agents in particular contexts for specific purposes. This is especially true of the panic over the city that permeated American culture in the '80s and '90s, which was directed at what turns out to be a very carefully fabricated and grossly inflated "threat": an urban underclass of working-class blacks and Latinos thought to be so deviant, murderous, and immoral as to constitute a serious danger to the nation's security and well-being.

Scholars disagree about why such sudden waves of fear occur as well as about the political interests they serve. Marxist and post-Marxist analysts of moral panics often interpret them as a means by which social elites create convenient scapegoats (black muggers, punk rockers, homosexuals) for social ills like crime, poverty, and the destabilization of family relationships that are structurally generated by the unjust organization of the social system itself. A paradigmatic example of such an analysis is *Policing the Crisis* (1978) by Stuart Hall and his colleagues at the Center for Contemporary Cultural Studies in Birmingham. The book examines the politics of the "mugging" scare that swept through Britain in the early 1970s. According to Hall and his co-authors, that panic was manufactured by elites to divert attention from a deepening crisis of British capitalism and as a response to an "exhaustion" of public consent to the country's crumbling social democratic state. On their argument, crusading politicians and judges fanned fears about black street crime in London and other large cities to the point where mugging came to stand for everything that had gone wrong in British society. As framed by these hysterical fears, mugging became "the *signifier* of the crisis in the urban colonies" (Hall et al. 1978, 3) and by defining its meaning in this grandiose manner, the moral crusaders shored up support for "law and order" and for expanding the coercive powers of the state. In short, Hall and company's analysis shows how the panic over mugging "functioned as a mechanism for the construction of an authoritarian consensus, a conservative backlash" (viii), a backlash that not long after became the ideological foundation of ultraconservative politician Margaret Thatcher's rise to power. As the argument delineated in this book shows, the approach pioneered in *Policing the Crisis* can be fruitfully applied to the task of deciphering the origins, meaning, and politics of the panic over the moral decline of the U.S. city in the '80s and '90s.

As I argue at length in the chapters to come, that panic is best understood as an ideologically conservative reaction to the extreme racial and economic polarization of America's large metropolitan areas. Since the 1970s, the socioeconomic gap between the country's affluent (usually white) suburbs and increasingly isolated, ever more impoverished, black and Latino inner cities has widened dramatically. The escalating climate of fear surrounding the postindustrial city analyzed in *Urban Nightmares* was a demagogic, politically regressive, often racist response to these developments on the part of elite opinion-makers, one that filtered down to and infected the general public, particularly the suburban middle class. The panic over the city was promoted, at least in part, by a culturally authoritative "discourse on the urban crisis"— generated by a small army of right-wing politicians, pundits, policy analysts, and intellectuals—that blamed the urban minority poor for the deprivation and social isolation they were forced to endure and inflated the danger they posed to the rest of American society. In the work of reactionary social commentators like Charles Murray and William Bennett, the menacing inner city of the 1980s and '90s was transformed into a symbol and "ideological conductor" for a broader set of social concerns; indeed, the specter of the out-of-control central city crystallized middle-class anxieties about the transformation of the family, drug use, street crime, race relations, and the quality of public education in ways that consistently legitimated conservative positions on these issues. The panic—and the popularity of the alarmist discourse on America's cities that sustained it—thus coincided with and helped to consolidate the rightward drift of U.S. politics since the early 1980s. Like the mugging scare in 1970s Britain, the scare over the cities in late-twentieth-century America helped secure popular consent to a punitive, even mean-spirited, politics, one that subjected urban working-class communities to increased policing while at the same time depriving them of government income support and social services.

On my account, media representations of the postindustrial American city during this period for the most part reproduced and validated the right's discourse on the urban crisis while amplifying the suburban middle-class fears the discourse helped to generate. Television and print news organizations covered urban issues in ways consonant with the prevailing panic over the moral decline of the cities. Mainstream films invariably depicted the urban landscape as terrifying and crime-filled, confirmed suburbia's racist fantasies about ghetto culture, and embraced conservative mystifications (and exaggerations) of the cities' problems. Even advertising mobilized fears of a perilous urban realm to sell a variety of products (cars, home security systems, personal computers), strengthening those fears in the process. The treatment of the central city by the media, right-wing intellectuals, and politicians from the early 1980s onward thus combined to produce a wave of popular alarm over the city that, in turn, was used as the pretext for a campaign to "get tough" on the city's poorest, most oppressed residents. Needless to say, the consequences of all this anti-urban hysteria for America's metropolitan centers have been and continue to be disastrous.

The Flow of the Argument

The argument synopsized above is fleshed out in the six chapters that make up the body of *Urban Nightmares*. As I have already noted, the rising spiral of public concern over conditions in the city in the 1980s and '90s was initially occasioned by a set of interlocking demographic and economic changes that dramatically transformed American cities and their suburbs in the postwar era. Chapter 1 describes the historical trajectory of these changes. In the years following World War II, middle-class flight to the suburbs, the ghettoization of the African American population, and the restructuring of the American economy together produced an escalating crisis of joblessness, destitution, and collapsing social institutions in many of America's inner cities. This crisis reached its zenith in the 1970s and persisted through the last two decades of the twentieth century. At the same time, the processes of economic and demographic change drove the growth of affluent white suburbs marked by an intensely private, home-centered culture and attitudes toward the city that range from indifference to open antipathy. In the resulting, socially polarized metropolitan landscape, representations of cities as "landscapes of fear" and of their residents as inherently threatening flourished.

Central to my argument is the idea that the panic over inner-city pathology and chaos has been structured and informed by a conservative discourse that consistently blamed the victims of the urban crisis for their plight and constructed the central city as an object of middle-class fear. Chapter 2 locates the roots of this discourse in Victorian attitudes toward the slums and in the long tradition of American anti-urbanism. It then moves on to trace the emergence of several important themes of the discourse in the right-wing cognoscenti's response to the inner-city riots and civil rights protests of the 1960s. The right's interpretation of the urban upheavals of that turbulent decade, I argue, revived Victorian, moralistic notions about poverty and urban criminality while pandering to burgeoning white fears of an angry black ghetto. Chapter 3 examines how reactionary theorizing about urban problems finally became hegemonic during the Reagan, Bush, and Clinton years. It shows how the right's theories elided the real causes of those problems, and looks at the way the ideologically charged concept of the "urban underclass" shaped urban and social policy debates to the great detriment of people of color and the working class. In particular, it analyzes how the central texts of this discourse—such as Charles Murray's *Losing Ground* (1984) and William Bennett, John DiIulio, and John Walters's *Body Count* (1996)—made sense of urban disorder, poverty, and street crime in ways that insulated the dominant social order from criticism. The chapter concludes with a review of the various political and ideological functions of the conservative discourse on the postindustrial city, stressing how it has helped to consolidate white, middle-class suburban support for the right's punitive "law-and-order" agenda.

One of the more striking aspects of American media culture during the last two decades of the twentieth century was the degree to which it was permeated by images of the U.S. city as a zone of apocalyptic social decay, wanton violence, and depravity. Such representations encoded the reigning conservative understanding of the urban crisis and gave visceral, terrifying form to suburban middle-class anxieties. Without them, there would have been no moral panic. For this reason, the remaining three chapters of the book focus in one way or another on the media's representations of the postindustrial city. Others have written penetrating analyses of the dubious politics of recent media representations of contemporary American cities. I cite two particularly insightful books on the subject—*Voices of Decline* (1993) by Robert Beauregard and *Cracked Coverage* (1994) by Jimmie Reeves and Richard Campbell—quite often in the course of this study. Nevertheless, these works confine their examination of media discourse exclusively to the news media (and in the case of Beauregard's book, to the increasingly anachronistic print news media). This is a mistake in my view, in part because the news media are no longer as popular or as influential as they once were and in part because it is not this or that isolated text but the ideological themes that are repeated across various media (ads, films, news shows) that have genuine social impact. Hence, in my own analysis of the media's treatment of the postindustrial city I cast a broader net, examining the ways television news, advertising, and popular film all contributed to the rising spiral of public concern over the city's moral decay.

Chapter 4 of this study looks at mainstream journalism's role in popularizing and legitimating the dominant, conservative view of urban problems. I first discuss the mainstream news media's tendency to reflect elite perspectives on the social world and point out its crucial role in generating (and sustaining) moral panics. Then, drawing on research conducted at the *Vanderbilt Television News Archive*, I show how network TV news coverage of cities and of the urban poor from the late 1980s to the mid-1990s consistently promoted conservative interpretations of their troubles. My analysis documents the degree to which television news fixated on underclass deviance and misbehavior to the exclusion of other, arguably more important, stories about the city. It shows how this coverage privileged the voices of right-wing commentators and law-and-order politicians. It also examines the ways in which the sometimes gory, sometimes lurid footage of the inner city featured on television news provided persuasive "visible evidence" for their arguments.

In chapter 5 I go on to dissect the ways suburban fears and reactionary ideologies were articulated in the bleak, apprehensive vision of urban life projected by mainstream commercial films during the Bush and Clinton years. In yuppie horror films like *Judgment Night* (1993) and *Eye for an Eye* (1996), dark detective thrillers like *Seven* (1995), comic-book inspired blockbusters like *Batman* (1989) and *The Crow* (1994), dystopian science fiction movies like *Escape from L.A.* (1996) and *Mimic* (1997), and "social problem" pictures like *Dangerous Minds* (1996), Hollywood repeatedly invoked (and justified) the prevailing moral panic over urban life. Such films have helped to elaborate a collection of alarmist, anti-urban tropes and stereotypes that echo those employed in the dominant political and journalistic discourse about American cities and their inhabitants. The centerpiece of this chapter is a close reading of David Fincher's harrowing neo-noir slasher film, *Seven*, which seeks to establish that its nightmarish vision of the city both embodies conservative, suburban paranoia and is entirely symptomatic of recent Hollywood treatments of urban life.

Chapter 6 explores the relationship of the panic over the urban crisis to that ubiquitous yet often-overlooked aspect of media culture: advertising. Just as television news stories and Hollywood films have played to and reinforced ideologically laden middle-class fears of the city, a significant amount of television and print advertising has promoted paranoia about urban space and a corresponding fetishism of private life. I demonstrate this by surveying the use of anti-urban anxieties to sell everything from personal computers to home security systems to sport utility vehicles. Advertising too, this chapter contends, has added to public concerns about the dangers and moral decay of the postindustrial city.

As is the case with any work of political and cultural analysis, the arguments sketched out in *Urban Nightmares* have political as well as scholarly implications. In order to put the book's arguments into proper perspective, I spell out what those political implications are. Thus, in the conclusion, I briefly assess the future of urban paranoia and assay the prospects for a progressive alternative to the politics of panic, one concerned with promoting democracy and social justice for the cities and suburbs alike.

For far too long now, the right has seized on popular anxieties about the postindustrial metropolis as a pretext for "getting tough" on America's poor, dismantling the social welfare state, and cutting aid to central cities. Putting an end to these relentless attacks on the wellbeing of our cities and their residents will require, among other things, a sustained struggle to combat and dispel this climate of panic. *Urban Nightmares* is offered as a modest contribution to that effort.

CHAPTER 1

The Origins of the Crisis: Race, Class, and the Inner City

The anxiety over deteriorating social and moral conditions in America's cities that seized the public imagination in the late 1980s and '90s did not materialize *ex nihilo*. Rather, the escalating urban paranoia of this period was a confused response to a set of interlocking demographic, economic, and social changes that polarized our metropolitan regions along lines of race and class. In the postwar era, the mostly white upper and middle class largely abandoned the central cities for the suburban fringe and with them went many of the businesses that were once the foundation of vibrant downtown economies. At the same time, the nation's poor—particularly the Latino and African American poor—became concentrated in the deteriorating inner-city neighborhoods being left behind. By the 1980s and '90s, virtually all big U.S. cities suffered from higher rates of joblessness, poverty, and crime than their suburbs and a number of declining metropolitan centers in the North and Midwest found themselves locked into a more or less permanent state of crisis. Indeed, by that point, the dramatic expansion of what geographer Paul Knox calls "the landscapes of the excluded"—blighted, segregated slums housing the destitute, the homeless, and the chronically unemployed— had arguably become the defining feature of American urbanization (Knox 1993). It was at precisely this juncture that the city and its problems became the focus of intense, sometimes hysterical, public concern.

As I demonstrate at great length later in the book, the prevailing discourse on the urban crisis in the '80s and '90s ultimately served conservative political interests and legitimated the regressive social policies they favored. As imagined by right-wing intellectuals, mainstream politicians, and the major media, the inner cities had become nightmare zones of crime and pathology and out-of-control urban populations were largely to blame. The geographical and cultural distance separating ghetto residents from white suburbanites predisposed the latter to accept such representations at face value. And the fears these representations tapped into stemmed, at least in part, from a middle-class suburban culture marked by racism, privatism, anti-urbanism, and extreme individualism. Of course, there was more than a kernel of truth in depictions of the city as frightening and dangerous; as we shall see, the squalor and economic hopelessness endured by those trapped in our blighted urban centers has been and continues to be truly horrifying. The problem is that such depictions obscured the causes and distorted the meaning of the inner city's troubles in ways that actually served to perpetuate them. A reaction to the structural economic and social problems of the postindustrial metropolis, the media-induced panic over urban disorder ultimately worked to stigmatize and "other" an already disadvantaged and unfairly marginalized urban working class, deepening and hardening the city/suburb divide in the process.

In order to understand why conditions in the urban core during the '80s and '90s provoked such alarm, and why the dominant discourse on those realities took on the ideological complexion it did, we must first review the facts about the economic and demographic trends that have so dramatically reshaped our metropolitan areas in the past fifty years.

Marxist urban theorists (Harvey 1989; Gordon 1984), social historians (Sugrue 1996; Jackson 1985), and others studying the contemporary American city (Wilson 1996, 1987) have offered various explanations for the relative decline of the central city and the social polarization of metropolitan areas that culminated in the crisis of the 1980s and '90s. Some stress the play of economic or market forces. Some point to the impact of space-conquering technologies like the telephone and the automobile. Others highlight the role of government housing and transportation policy. Still others point to race and race relations as central to the shaping of the postindustrial metropolis. In the synoptic account delineated below, I emphasize three factors most scholars agree have been decisive: first, the suburbanization of business and manufacturing along with the postwar suburban exodus of much of the white population; second, the so-called Great Migration of America's black population from the rural South to the urban North and the persistent segregation and marginalization of the northern black population in inner-city ghettos; and, third, the restructuring of the American economy and its disastrous impact on the wages and economic prospects of American workers, particularly those left behind in large central cities.

I leave it to the urban theorists to debate which of these trends were "determining in the last instance" and which mere epiphenomena. My claim is simply that these three tendencies together were primarily responsible for the fact that our central cities by the '80s and '90s had become disproportionately poor, of color, and saddled with a host of seemingly intractable social problems while at the same time our mostly white suburbs emerged as largely privatized places of relative affluence. After sketching out how suburbanization, ghettoization, and economic restructuring combined to produce the social and economic collapse of our once-prosperous cities, I briefly turn my attention to the distinctive suburban political culture that grew up in response to the balkanization of the metropolitan region and to the role played by the media within it. This account will lay the groundwork for my later examination of the way discourses about the postindustrial city fueled middle-class urban paranoia and the rise of "law-and-order" politics directed against impoverished city residents.

Suburbanization and the Fate of the Metropolis

Most commentators agree that the source of many of the inner city's current problems can be traced to the most striking and distinctive feature of American urbanization in the twentieth century: the migration of huge segments of the urban population (and much of the nation's economic activity) from the cities to the suburbs, that zone of low-density settlement sprawling out for miles beyond the city's borders. At the turn of the nineteenth century, only 10 percent of the nation's citizens lived in a handful of suburbs, mostly surrounding large industrial cities (Ashton 1984, 64). By 1920, shortly after the majority of Americans became urban, suburbs were growing faster than the cities they surrounded. By 1990, 45 percent of the U.S. population were classified by the Census Bureau as "suburban dwellers" (Fishman 1990, 27) and, perhaps even more importantly, by 1992 suburbanites were casting a clear majority of votes in presidential and statewide elections (Thomas 1998; Edsall and Edsall 1992; Schneider 1992). In 2000, according to the census, 52 percent of all Americans, and 73 percent of the white population, resided in the suburbs (Simon and Cannon 2001, 16; Frey 2001, 1). By the close of the twentieth century, observers agreed, suburbia had eclipsed the cities to become the setting and center of much of the country's political and economic life. The story of how this happened has been told many times and I will not belabor the details here (for a more complete account see Archer 2004; Ashton 1984; Fishman 1987; Jackson 1985; Judd and Swanstrom 1994; Lazare 2001). However, I do want to briefly survey the overall trajectory of suburbanization and highlight the deleterious effects it has had on the urban core.

During the nineteenth century, most suburbs of American cities were enclaves for the nation's wealthy elite who moved there to avoid the noise, pollution, and crime of the big cities while remaining close enough to the city-based businesses and industries they owned to actively manage them. Llewellyn Park—a picturesque development in the New Jersey hills overlooking New York City that became home to Thomas Edison and other captains of industry—was typical of this sort of elite suburb (Jackson 1985, 76–79). Accessible only by prohibitively expensive trains (and steam ferries), places like Llewellyn Park (or Philadelphia's Main Line) were socially and racially homogenous "bourgeois utopias"—to use Robert Fishman's phrase—that affirmed "leisure, family life and union with nature" and consciously excluded the boisterous public life and working-class culture of the cities (Fishman 1987, 4). Ever since, as architectural historian John Archer has observed, "suburban planning and design have been substantially informed by ideologies of individualism, privatism and the nuclear family" (Archer 2004, 1271). By the end of the nineteenth century, falling rail fares and the spread of streetcars brought these "bourgeois utopias" and their family-centered lifestyles within reach of more and more upper-middle-class professionals. Yet, the rail and streetcar suburbs continued to be economically dependent on their neighboring central cities and frequently were legally annexed by and incorporated into those cities after a few years of independent existence. All of this began to change during the 1920s.

While every innovation in transportation technology has left its imprint on the shape of the nation's urban agglomerations, the automobile has had an impact that would be difficult to underestimate. The shift to an automobile-centered system of transportation allowed for much greater and more diffuse dispersal of the population than had the old train, bus, and streetcar system. In the first two decades of the twentieth century, only the well-to-do owned cars and the automobile had only a minor impact on the structure of American cities. But during the 1920s, automobile ownership exploded, with registrations soaring from 9 million in 1920 to more than 26 million in 1930 (Kay 1997, 170). The rising number of cars, in turn, paved the way for an unprecedented suburban boom. In the 1920s, the suburban population grew at a rate of over 46 percent, more than double the growth rate of the central city population (see Table 1). Some suburban communities—like Grosse Point outside Detroit and Elmwood Park outside of Chicago—grew by more than 700 percent (Jackson 1985, 176). And though the suburban growth rate slowed considerably during the Great Depression and World War II, it has consistently outpaced the rate of central-city growth for more than eight decades now.

This relentless deconcentration of the nation's population was abetted by federal policies that aimed to put every American family— or at least every white American family—into its own single-family home and that actively discriminated against the inner cities. During the 1930s, Congress and the president passed a series of laws that had the effect of creating cheap credit for home buyers that later helped to spur suburban expansion dramatically. For instance, the federally instituted Home Owners Loan Corporation (HOLC) "refinanced tens of thousands of mortgages in danger of default or foreclosure" on a long-term basis (Jackson 1985, 196). Another Depression-era creation, the Federal Housing Administration (FHA), insured long-term, low-interest mortgages made by private lenders for home purchases and made it possible for home buyers to purchase a home with a very small down payment (204). Together with a Veteran's Administration (VA) program that subsidized the mortgages for those who had fought in World War II, these measures made available the funds necessary to meet the escalating housing needs of the post–World War II years. However, HOLC, and later the FHA and VA, refused to underwrite loans for housing units in the older, ethnically heterogeneous neighborhoods of the inner cities. For instance, in 1966, at a time when whole suburbs were being built overnight with government-sponsored loans, the mostly black city of Camden, New Jersey, failed to receive a single FHA-backed mortgage (Massey and Denton 1993, 55). As historian Kenneth Jackson notes, "the main beneficiary of the $119 billion in FHA mortgage insurance issued in the first four decades of FHA operation was suburbia, where almost half of all housing could claim FHA or VA financing" (215).

Table 1. Increases in Metropolitan Area Population Expressed as Percent Growth, 1910–2000

Years	Central City	Suburbs
1910–20	25.2	32
1920–30	20.9	46.4
1930–40	4.4	13.6
1940–50	14	35.9
1950–60	10.7	48.6
1960–70	6.4	26.8
1970–80	0.1	18.2
1980–90	2.3	12.3
1990–2000	9.7	16.6

Sources: For data from 1910 to 1990, Judd and Swanstrom 1994, 184–85 and 188–89; for data from 1990 to 2000, U.S. Census Bureau, *2000 Census.*

In the wake of World War II, the pace of suburbanization accelerated as never before, fueled by hordes of demobilized veterans eager to
settle down and raise families in suburban single-family homes pur-
chased with government-backed mortgages. From 1940 to 1950, the
suburban population increased at a rate of 35 percent (compared to a
rate of 14 percent for the cities) and, from 1950 to 1960, the rate of
suburban growth rose to over 48 percent (see Table 1). But even these
numbers understate the explosiveness of suburbia's rise. Between 1950
and 1970, the suburban population shot from 36 to 74 million (Jackson 1985, 283). Housing starts climbed from just 142,000 in 1944 to
1,952,000 in 1950 and "in every year from 1947 through 1964 the number of housing starts topped the 1,200,000 mark" (Teaford 1986, 100).
Nothing symbolized the rise of the new "mass suburb" better than the
construction of Levittown, New York, at the time the largest private housing development in American history. The company that built Levittown—Levitt and Sons—applied pre-fabricated elements, standardized
designs, and the techniques of mass production to the construction of a
suburban community on 4,000 acres of Long Island farmland (Jackson
1985, 234–38). The houses they built were standardized, cookie-cutter
affairs, and, at the height of production, Levitt was putting up an amaz-
ing thirty houses a day (235). By the time Levittown was finished, the
development boasted more than 17,400 houses and 82,000 residents
(235). The Levitts and the legions of developers who copied their suc-
cesses depended on the easy credit made possible by the VA and FHA to
facilitate the sale of all those homes.

The federal government's contribution to suburbanization did not
end with its lavish backing for mortgages. During the war, the War Production Board invested the vast majority of its military dollars in the
suburbs, thus strengthening the already-suburban character of manufacturing (Lazare 2001, 192). The Housing Act of 1949 authorized a
series of misnamed "urban renewal" projects that leveled many allegedly
"blighted" inner-city, working-class neighborhoods, creating severe shortages of affordable housing in the cities as a result (Hall 1988, 227–34).
In 1956, President Eisenhower signed an act establishing the interstate

highway system, "the greatest peacetime public works project in the history of the world" (Kay 1997, 231). Under the terms of the act, the federal government would provide states with 90 percent of the cost of building 41,000 miles of highway, amounting to some $50 billion annually (231). Between 1975 and 1995, the government invested $1.15 trillion in roads and highways but only $187 billion in mass transit (Dreier et al. 2001, 105). In so doing, Washington was effectively underwriting suburbia's automobile-centered way of life. In addition, with increases in federal income tax rates, the mortgage interest deduction "blossomed into a major asset, not just for the affluent but for a growing portion of the middle class. Not only could middle-class Americans not afford to rent but, thanks to the complicated array of carrots and sticks that the tax code represented, they could not afford *not* to pump more and more of their wealth into real estate" (Lazare 2001, 183). In short, throughout the period of the postwar suburban boom, government policy encouraged families to abandon the cities for the greener pastures of the newly constructed subdivisions.[1] And leave they did.

The consequences of suburbanization for the central cities were dire. To begin with, from the late 1940s on, the populations of many of the nation's largest cities dwindled or grew at anemic rates. Eleven of the twelve largest cities in 1950 lost population in the following decade (Teaford 1986, 109). The decline accelerated in the '60s and '70s with manufacturing cities like St. Louis, Cleveland, and Detroit hemorrhaging more than 20 percent of their population in the '70s alone (Judd and Swanstrom 1994, 188). As Table 2 documents, many of the country's biggest urban centers—Philadelphia, Detroit, Baltimore, St. Louis, and Washington, D.C.—continued to suffer massive losses well into the '80s and '90s. Only Sun Belt cities like Houston, Dallas, Nashville, Phoenix, and Los Angeles—laid out like suburbs to begin with and organized around the automobile—experienced sustained growth during the postwar years. Yet even in the booming cities of the South and West, suburban populations typically grew as fast as those at the core (Judd and Swanstrom 1994, 190).

The families leaving the metropolitan centers for the suburbs in

Table 2. Population Changes in Selected Large Central Cities, 1950–2000

City	1950	1960	1970	1980	1990	2000
New York City	7,891,957	7,781,984	7,894,862	7,071,639	7,323,564	8,008,278
Chicago	3,620,962	3,550,404	3,366,957	3,005,072	2,783,726	2,896,016
Philadelphia	2,071,605	2,002,512	1,948,609	1,688,210	1,585,577	1,517,550
Los Angeles	1,970,358	2,479,015	2,816,061	2,969,850	3,485,398	3,694,820
Detroit	1,849,568	1,670,144	1,511,482	1,203,339	1,027,974	951,270
Baltimore	949,708	939,024	905,759	787,775	736,014	651,154
Cleveland	914,808	876,050	750,903	573,822	505,616	478,403
St. Louis	856,796	750,026	622,236	453,085	396,685	348,189
Washington, D.C.	802,178	763,956	756,510	638,333	606,900	572,059
Boston	801,444	697,197	641,071	562,994	574,283	589,141

Sources: For data from 1950 to 1970, U.S. Bureau of the Census, *Censuses of Population* 1950–1970; for 1970 to 2000, census data drawn from the State of the Cities Database, U.S. Department of Housing and Urban Development, http://socds.huduser.org/Census/Census_java.html.

the postwar decades were disproportionately middle class. When they left, so did the department stores, shops, and other retail outlets that depended on their patronage, resulting in a wholesale collapse of downtown shopping and entertainment districts. From 1950 on, the retail sales volumes for central cities plummeted, even as overall consumer spending increased. Between 1948 and 1958, sales in downtown Philadelphia declined by 5 percent while retail in the city's suburbs rose by 70 percent (Teaford 1986, 111). Even larger declines in downtown retail volume were recorded in Detroit (27 percent), Milwaukee (16 percent), and Los Angeles (19 percent) (Hannigan 1998, 33). The departure of the middle class also sucked the life out of the cities' once-thriving entertainment and cultural industries. Late-nineteenth- and early-twentieth-century cities offered their residents a rich collection of conveniently located, relatively affordable "public amusements" such as theaters, parks, movie palaces, professional sports teams, bars, amusement parks, and dance halls (Nasaw 1993). Such amenities were sorely missed by the families who settled in subdivisions like Levittown. The rapid dissemination of television (between 1950 and 1960, the proportion of American families owning a TV set rose from 9 percent to 90 percent) helped to alleviate the cultural isolation that was one of the main disadvantages of suburban living (Baughman 1992, 30, 41). Competition from TV, in turn, drained away the audience for central-city theaters, music halls, professional sports teams, and pubs. "Film going declined catastrophically in the 1950s," Kenneth Fox has observed. "Theaters, amusement parks and other forms of 'live' entertainment suffered as well. Bars and taverns experienced declining patronage, and for patrons who remained behind an important attraction was being able to watch TV away from home and family" (Fox 1985, 67). By the early 1970s, downtowns across the country had begun to empty out and "die" at night after the last commuters went home.

After several decades of steady economic and demographic decline, a number of larger metropolitan centers—notably New York, Chicago, San Francisco, Seattle, and Boston—finally enjoyed something of a renaissance in the 1990s, and for the first time in many years experienced an influx of new residents. Indeed, according to one Fannie Mae study, in the 1990s "many older industrial cities . . . rebounded considerably from the traumatic population losses of the 1970s," most either growing again or at least losing population at substantially reduced rates (Simmons and Lang 2001, 1). Much of this revival was centered in and around newly gentrified neighborhoods and revitalized downtown entertainment districts catering to young urban professionals, affluent out-of-town tourists, and middle-class suburbanites (areas that consciously excluded less well-off urban residents). Yet the "urban turnaround" of the '90s failed to arrest, much less reverse, the decline of cities like Milwaukee, Cleveland, Washington, D.C., Baltimore, or Philadelphia. Moreover, though big metropolitan centers like Chicago and New York began to grow again in the 1990s, the suburban population nationwide still grew at twice the rate of the population in the central cities (U.S. Bureau of the Census 2000). As had been the case for over half a century, the suburbs, especially the outer-ring suburbs, remained the engines of the nation's economic and demographic growth. Most of the average metropolitan area's wealthy and middle-class families made their homes there and such areas continued to capture the lion's share of newly created jobs and income. Perhaps even more importantly, the vast disparities in wealth and income separating the cities and the suburbs—which will be examined in some depth later in this chapter—remained entrenched throughout the '90s (Logan 2002, 1). And inner-city neighborhoods in the 1990s continued to house a disproportionate share of the nation's (overwhelmingly minority) poor and unemployed and to suffer from a disproportionate share of social ills like drug abuse and crime.

But to talk about suburbanization and its effects on U.S. cities in race-neutral terms is to tell only half, or less than half, the story of what has happened to our urban centers. Suburbanization and the ensuing balkanization of our metropolitan areas had and continues to have pronounced racial overtones. A disproportionate number of the families leaving the cities at the height of the postwar exodus were of European descent. During the 1950s alone, the white population of New York City declined by 7 percent, Chicago's declined 13 percent, and Philadelphia's by 13 percent (Teaford 1986, 115). In the period from 1960 to 1977, it is estimated that U.S. central cities lost some 4 million white residents (Lipsitz 1998, 7). White flight from the cities helped to precipitate many of the urban problems that so alarmed the observers of the '80s and '90s; at the same time, entrenched racist attitudes toward inner-city minority communities structured the socially dominant perceptions of those problems. Indeed, it is hard to imagine the panic over the cities that gripped the public in the '80s and '90s taking hold absent the crucial dimension of race.

Black Migration, Ghettoization, and the Othering of the Inner City

Historian Kenneth Jackson has remarked that "[n]o discussion of the settlement patterns of the American people can ignore the overriding significance of race" (Jackson 1985, 289). This is something of an under-statement. Among the events that left their imprint on American cities in the twentieth century, few have been as sweeping or as rapid as the sharp demographic shifts that transformed the racial and ethnic make-up of the cities' populations. Easily the most important of these demo-graphic shifts were what is often referred to as the Great Migrations of African Americans from the rural South to the urban industrial centers of the North that took place from 1920 to 1970. These migrations, cou-pled with a rigid system of racial segregation in housing, gave rise to the vast black ghettos that so many conservative pundits and commentators identify as the main source of the nation's urban ills. The emergence and spread of such segregated black enclaves gave white middle-class fami-lies further reason to abandon the cities. To understand the roots of the urban crisis then, one must grasp how and why the African Ameri-can population in the United States became so urbanized and so unfairly ghettoized.

For some fifty years following the conclusion of the Civil War, the vast majority of former African American slaves and their descendents continued to reside in the South. In fact, in 1910, 89 percent of the country's 10 million black citizens lived there, most toiling away at the same menial, agricultural jobs that black slaves had performed before emancipation (Thernstrom and Thernstrom 1997, 54). The outbreak of World War I cut off immigration from Europe and created a severe labor shortage in the industrial zones of the North, forcing factory owners for the first time to hire blacks in sizable numbers. Between 1914 and 1920, almost half a million blacks left the South to take advantage of the new opportunities; another 750,000 followed by the end of the '20s (Jones 1992, 213). This outflow of African Americans marked the first Great Migration and it was during this period that large black communities established themselves in cities like New York, Cleveland, Detroit, and Chicago. This wave of migration slowed during the Depression and historians date it as ending in 1930 (even though southern blacks continued to travel north in lesser numbers throughout the ensuing decade).

Roughly ten years later, industry's rising demand for labor power during World War II and the modernization of southern agriculture initiated a second, more dramatic Great Migration, one that would last some thirty years. Between 1940 and 1960, a wave of more than 3 million southern blacks moved north and, between 1960 and 1970, they were joined by another 1.4 million (Thernstrom and Thernstrom 1997, 79). Most of these migrants settled in the large cities of the Northeast and Midwest, filling the inner-city neighborhoods being vacated by white families leaving for the suburbs. In the process, they transformed the social fabric of the nation's big urban centers (see Table 3).

In 1940, blacks made up less than 10 percent of the population of Chicago, Detroit, and Cleveland; by 1970, they accounted for over 30 percent of the population of those cities. In 1940, only 49 percent of African Americans lived in cities (as compared to 57 percent of whites); by 1970, 81 percent of African Americans were urban dwellers (while only 72 percent of whites lived in metro areas) (Thernstrom and Thernstrom 1997, 80). In the space of just thirty years, black Americans became the most urbanized ethnic group in the country (and an integral segment of the urban industrial proletariat). By the 1990s, after decades of white flight, African Americans constituted at least half of the population in cities like Detroit, Newark, Washington, D.C., and Baltimore and were a sizable minority of the population of most other major urban centers (Hacker 1992, 229).

Initially at least, migration north had salutary effects on the fortunes of African Americans that can only be hinted at here. Blacks who made their way to places like Detroit and Chicago were liberated from the legal subordination they endured in the South, earned considerably more than their southern counterparts, attended better schools, could exercise their right to vote, and even became players in local politics. Yet, for all this, the African Americans flowing into northern industrial cities faced a white backlash that took the form of violent protests against blacks who moved into white neighborhoods as well as the more common response of "white flight" from neighborhoods in the process of becoming integrated. White resistance to residential integration—whether "fight" or "flight"—forced blacks arriving in northern industrial cities to live in rigidly circumscribed, racially homogenous, and often very poor enclaves, and this resistance only hardened over the course of the Great Migrations (Sugrue 1996; Lipsitz 1998; Massey and Denton 1993).

Table 3. Percentage of Black Population for Selected Cities, 1940–90

City	1940	1950	1960	1970	1980	1990
New York City	6.1	9.8	13.9	21.1	24.0	28.7
Chicago	8.2	14.1	22.8	32.7	39.5	39.1
Los Angeles	4.2	10.7	13.5	17.9	16.7	14.0
Philadelphia	13.0	18.3	26.4	33.6	37.5	39.8
Detroit	9.2	16.4	28.8	43.7	62.6	75.7
Baltimore	19.3	23.8	34.7	46.4	54.4	59.2
Cleveland	9.6	16.3	28.6	38.3	43.4	46.6
St. Louis	13.3	18.0	28.6	40.9	45.2	47.5
Washington, D.C.	N/A	35.4	54.8	71.1	69.7	65.8
Boston	3.1	5.3	9.0	16.3	21.7	25.6

Sources: For data from 1950 to 1970, U.S. Bureau of the Census, *Censuses of Population* 1950–1970; for 1970 to 1990, census data drawn from the State of the Cities Database, U.S. Department of Housing and Urban Development, http://socds.huduser.org/ Census/Census_java.html.

In their groundbreaking book *American Apartheid: Segregation and the Making of the Underclass* (1993), Douglas Massey and Nancy Denton document the ongoing segregation of blacks and the construction of ever more isolated black ghettos throughout the industrial North in the years from 1910 to 1970. They use several different statistical indices to measure the extent of racial segregation in American cities over time. The most important of these measures is the index of dissimilarity, which gauges how evenly a particular population is spread among different neighborhoods (or census tracts) in a given city (20). On a scale where 100 equals complete segregation and 0 equals complete integration, Massey and Denton found that the average index of dissimilarity for seven large northern cities rose from 59 in 1910 to 89 in 1940 (31). Essentially, this means that by 1940, 89 percent of the black population in these cities would have had to move in order to achieve perfect integration. Another of Massey and Denton's indices, the index of isolation, measures "the extent to which blacks live among other blacks" by looking at the percentage of blacks living in the census tract of the average African American (65). According to their calculations, at the turn of the century the average African American resident of a typical northern city lived in a neighborhood that was less than 8 percent black but by 1930 that same resident lived in a neighborhood that was almost 30 percent black (24).

By the end of World War II, the institution of the ghetto—a homogeneously black residential area bounded by a widely recognized "color line"—was firmly in place not just in northern cities but in cities around the country. The massive influx of black immigrants during the postwar years did little to change the harsh realities of segregation. Instead of breaking down the walls of the ghetto, the southern black migrants who arrived in the cities during the so-called second Great Migration expanded the ghetto's size and its isolation from the rest of the city. Indeed, the rapid white suburbanization that took place from the 1950s through the 1970s merely shifted residential apartheid from a neighborhood to a metropolitan scale, creating the now-classic pattern of "a chocolate city with vanilla suburbs" all over the country (Massey and Denton 1993, 67–74). Moreover, while the civil rights struggle of the 1950s and '60s did improve many facets of African American life for the better, it did virtually nothing to address the problem of residential segregation. Thus, "in the three decades after 1940, black-white segregation remained high and virtually constant, [the index of dissimilarity] averaging over 85 at all times in all regions" (46). The most recent figures Massey and Denton cite, for 1980, show that progress toward racial integration in housing between 1960 and 1980 was so gradual and so minimal as to be insignificant. They report that the average index of dissimilarity for blacks in major northern cities was 80.1 in 1980 and the average African American resident of those cities lived in a census tract that was 66 percent black (64). Measured segregation was even higher than the national average in older industrial cities like Gary (90.6), Chicago (87.8), and Cleveland (87.5) (64).

Massey and Denton's statistics demonstrate unequivocally that by 1980 the vast majority of African Americans were still experiencing shockingly high degrees of residential segregation from whites. Even more troubling is the fact that a sizable proportion of the urban dwelling black population were living under conditions best described as "hyper-segregated":

[O]ne third of all African Americans in the United States live under conditions of intense racial segregation. They are unambiguously among the nation's most spatially isolated and geographically secluded people, suffering extreme segregation across multiple dimensions simultaneously. Black Americans in these metropolitan areas live within large, contiguous settlements of densely inhabited neighborhoods that are packed tightly around the urban core. In plain terms, they live in ghettos. (Massey and Denton 1993, 77)

It is important to recognize that not all African Americans are trapped in ghettos or even reside in cities. Between 1990 and 2000, the proportion of black residents of metropolitan areas living in the suburbs rose by 38 percent (Logan 2002, 1). However, "in general black suburbs are located near city limits and are often the result of the 'spillover' of black urban enclaves into suburban municipalities" (Pattillo-McCoy 1999, 24). As Mary Pattillo-McCoy's book *Black Picket Fences* amply documents, even solidly middle-class black communities typically exist in such close social and spatial proximity to the ghetto that their residents find it impossible to escape the ghetto's characteristic ills (joblessness, violent crime, the underground drug economy) (6). Of course, intense racial segregation by itself didn't render the metropolitan core unlivable or precipitate the urban crisis of the '80s and '90s. But the expansion of the ghetto (and the concurrent acceleration of white flight) coincided with changes in the American economy that hit the fortunes of large cities and their minority working-class inhabitants especially hard. And this shift had the effect of amplifying the already formidable socio-economic problems caused by the intense racial segregation of our metropolitan areas.

The Political Economy and Geography of Widening Social Inequality

Since the 1960s, the United States—like many other advanced capitalist countries—has undergone a shift from a manufacturing-based to a service or "postindustrial" economy, a shift that has undermined the economic health of many large Northeastern and Midwestern metropolitan centers and exacerbated the already stark inequalities of wealth and income separating the nation's cities and suburbs (Sassen 2000; Harvey 1989, 147–57).[2] During the '70s, '80s, and '90s, the United States lost millions of high-paying, unionized industrial jobs—disproportionately located in urban areas—as major American manufacturers relocated abroad in search of cheaper labor while those that remained behind "downsized" their workforces in order to take advantage of breakthroughs in productivity-enhancing technology (like computers and advanced telecommunications). Lay-offs, cut-backs, and plant closings became commonplace across America's industrial heartland. While the United States remained one of the world's leading producers of manufactured goods, the steady loss of factory jobs and the weakening of the nation's labor unions undermined the economic security and bargaining power of blue-collar workers lucky enough to still be employed. At the same time, employment in service industries of all kinds—often low-paid, nonunion, and insecure—expanded rapidly, generating the bulk of the new jobs in both cities and suburbs (Sassen 2000, 64–65). Coupled with suburbanization, the transition to a service economy left the central cities with rising poverty, high unemployment, restricted economic opportunity, and few resources with which to cope with their mounting social needs.

In the 1980s, the decade during which the full and devastating scope of this restructuring blossomed into public view, the U.S. economy lost 1.2 million manufacturing and mining jobs while adding 19.3 million jobs in the service sector (Mishel et al. 1999, 172). The vast majority of these new jobs (14.2 million) were clustered in the low-wage retail and personnel services sectors. This trend did not abate much in the 1990s (172). Between 1989 and 1997, the United States lost more than 630,000 factory and mining jobs while adding 2.6 million jobs in the poorly paid retail sector alone (173). The loss of manufacturing jobs, a foundation of vibrant urban economies since the mid-nineteenth century, dealt a serious blow to America's urban working class. The share of the country's central-city workforce employed in manufacturing declined from 24 percent in 1950 to 15 percent in 1990 (*Metro Futures* 1996, 3). One study discovered that in the twenty-year period between 1967 and 1987, Philadelphia lost 64 percent of its manufacturing jobs, Chicago 60 percent, New York 58 percent, and Detroit 51 percent (Kasarda 1995, 215-16). Another study found that between 1978 and 1988, seventeen large central cities with 20 percent of all 1978 factory jobs suffered 70 percent of the nation's manufacturing losses; over this ten-year span alone, the city of Milwaukee lost 30.1 percent of its industrial jobs and the city of Detroit lost 33 percent (*Metro Futures* 1996, 5). Even the relatively well-off Minneapolis–St. Paul core lost 20 percent of its manufacturing jobs during the 1980s (Orfield 1997, 4).

The disappearance of the central cities' manufacturing base helps to explain their catastrophically high levels of joblessness.[3] As Table 4 makes clear, cities have had higher rates of unemployment than their

Table 4. Urban and Suburban Unemployment Rates (Percentage of Workforce)

Year	Cities	Suburbs
All Metropolitan Areas		
1970	4.6	3.8
1980	7.1	5.6
1990	7.7	5.1
2000	7.4	4.6

Year	City	Suburbs
New York, New York		
1970	4.2	2.6
1980	7.7	4.4
1990	9.0	4.5
2000	9.6	4.1

Year	City	Suburbs
Chicago, Illinois		
1970	4.4	2.5
1980	9.8	4.8
1990	11.3	4.0
2000	10.1	4.1

Year	City	Suburbs
Los Angeles, California		
1970	6.9	5.6
1980	6.8	5.5
1990	8.3	6.7
2000	9.3	7.3

Source: Census data from the State of the Cities Database, U.S. Department of Housing and Urban Development, http://socds.huduser.org/Census/Census_java.html.

suburbs since at least the 1970s, in the case of big cities like New York and Chicago, sometimes twice as high. Suburban office parks and strip malls, not historic downtowns or central-city manufacturing zones, are now the land of economic opportunity in this country. One U.S. Department of Housing and Urban Development report found that in seventy-seven large metropolitan regions during the early 1990s, 97 percent of new businesses and 87 percent of entry-level jobs were located outside the central city (cited in Orfield 1997, 4).

Some urban workers displaced by restructuring never worked again; others were forced to take the lower-paying jobs being created in the service sector. According to one estimate, more than 57 percent of the long-term employees (with three or more years at a given job) who lost their jobs in the lay-offs of the 1980s suffered substantial financial losses as a result of lower earnings at their new jobs or significant periods of unemployment before finding a new job (Goldsmith and Blakely 1992, 65). Indeed, the shift to the "service economy" has meant that more and more workers have had to try to make ends meet on jobs that pay extremely low, even sub-poverty wages; for instance, the portion of the workforce that earned less than half the average wage grew from 12 percent in the early 1970s to 17.2 percent by 1986 (Law and Wolch 1993, 182). Nearly half of America's poor adults work an average of 40 hours a week or more (Sklar 1993, 28–29). As Schwartz and Volgy report, "[m]ore than 13 million jobs for steady, full-time workers in 1989 . . . paid less than it took to lift a family of three effectively out of poverty" (Schwartz and Volgy 1993, 192). Overall, the median weekly wage in the United States fell 12 percent between 1973 and 2000 (and this despite the fact that wages have been climbing gradually since 1997) (Collins and Yeskel 2000, 39). The average real wage for those workers with less than a high school education fell from $11.21 an hour in 1973 to a paltry $8.22 an hour in 1997, a 26 percent drop (Sassen 2000, 130).

The shift to a service economy has adversely affected the majority of waged workers in other ways as well. For instance, the difficulty of organizing unions at typical service-sector firms like McDonalds or Wal-Mart has enabled employers to impose part-time, temporary, or flexible work arrangements on rising numbers of workers. Temporary and part-time employees usually make lower wages, have fewer benefits, and, of course, have far less job security than their full-time counterparts. According to Law and Wolch, "employment in the temporary service industry has averaged an annual growth of 11 percent per year since the mid-1970s compared to 2.1 percent for all non-agricultural jobs" (Law and Wolch 1993, 170). The part-time and temporary workforce tripled between 1980 and 2000 and, as of 2000, a full 30 percent of American workers were in such work arrangements (Collins and Yeskel 2000, 23). "Today," Chuck Collins and Felice Yeskel point out, "the single biggest employer in the United States is Manpower, Inc., a temporary employment agency with 3,200 offices in fifty countries and over 560,000 workers in the United States" (109). As Saskia Sassen among others has noted, this tendency toward the "casualization" and destabilization of employment has been especially pronounced in big-city labor markets (Sassen 2000, 118–20).

The main cumulative effect of all these changes has been a massive, nearly unprecedented polarization of wealth and incomes along with a dramatic upswing in poverty. Between 1977 and 1999, the real after-tax income of the wealthiest 1 percent of U.S. households grew by 119 percent while real after-tax income declined by 3 percent for the middle 20 percent of households and by 12 percent for the poorest 20 percent of households (Collins and Yeskel 2000, 39). The ratio of family income of the top 5 percent of families to the lowest 20 percent rose from a low of 11.3 in 1973 to a record high of 19.5 in 1997 (Mishel et al. 1999, 50). The wealth gap increased as well. The share of the nation's total assets owned by the richest 1 percent of households climbed from 19.9 percent in 1976 to 40.1 percent in 1997, making it the greatest concentration of wealth in the hands of the very rich since the 1920s (264). Meanwhile, at the bottom of the financial hierarchy, the proportion of the nation's households with zero or negative net worth rose from 15.5 percent in 1983 to 18.5 percent in 1995 (Collins and Yeskel 2000, 53). As a consequence, the number of people filing for personal bankruptcy more than doubled, from 661,000 in 1990 to 1,350,000 in 1999 (19).

The ramifications of this polarization of wealth and incomes for our urban centers would be difficult, if not impossible, to overstate. In 1994, the *New York Times* reported that the income gap between the rich and poor in Manhattan had reached Third World levels: by 1990, "the top fifth of Manhattan households made 32 times as much as the bottom fifth, an average of $174,486 compared with $5,435" (Roberts 1994, 33). Even more significant was the growing inequality in income between the cities and the suburbs. The ratio of central-city per capita income to suburban per capita income in the eighty-seven largest metropolitan regions sank from 105 percent in 1960 to 87 percent in 1999 (Dreier et al. 2001, 40). A group of planners, architects, and urban historians surveyed for a study commissioned by the Fannie Mae Foundation predicted that "growing disparities of wealth" would be the most significant influence on the shape of America's cities well into the twenty-first century (Collins et al. 1999, 13).

A central repercussion of the rising joblessness and declining incomes produced by restructuring has been a marked increase in poverty, especially in central cities. The official poverty rate for the nation as a whole climbed from an all-time low of 11.1 percent in 1973 to 12.8 percent in 1989 and 13.3 percent in 1997 (spiking as high as 15 percent during the recessions of the early '80s and '90s) (Mishel et al. 1999, 280). In 1969 there were 24 million poor people in the United States; by 1983, that number had risen to 35 million and, in 1990, it stood at 32 million (Goldsmith and Blakely 1992, 30). Yet the official poverty line—based on questionable assumptions about household budgets—is widely regarded as underestimating the true extent of economic need (Dreier et al. 2001, 17). If we count the number of people earning less than one half of the median annual income as poor, then 22.3 percent of the population would have been classified as poor in 1997, significantly more than the 13.3 percent as measured by the official rate (Mishel et al. 1999, 288). Moreover, if the definition of poverty were adjusted to account for the exorbitant cost of housing and child care in large metropolitan centers like New York and Los Angeles, the poverty line for those areas would have to be set at roughly five times the official level (Dreier et al. 2001, 17).

However it is measured, indigence in this country has been on the rise since the mid-1970s and has become increasingly (and distressingly) urbanized. Historically, poverty in America has been more of a rural phenomenon than an urban one. Thanks to decades of white flight and deindustrialization, that pattern has been reversed and the city today surpasses the countryside as the nation's chief "poverty zone."

In 1959, the poverty rate for central cities was, at 18.3 percent, about half that of rural areas (which was more than 33 percent) and only moderately higher than the suburban rate of 12.2 percent (see Table 5). By 1979, the poverty rate in the cities had risen to more than double that in the suburbs and has been roughly twice the suburban rate ever since (see Table 5). The situation has been particularly dire in declining industrial centers like Chicago, Detroit, Cleveland, and St. Louis, which were burdened with poverty rates of 20 percent or higher for the better part of the '80s and '90s (U.S. Bureau of the Census, Poverty Website, http://www.census.gov/hhes/www/poverty/poverty.html, Table 3.). One study after another attests to the fact that the nation's poor population is now disproportionately concentrated in the urban core. In 1968, only 30 percent of America's poor lived in the inner city; by 1998, 42 percent did (Harris 1998, 15). One Brookings Institution report found that in 1998 a full 40 percent of the nation's welfare families lived in the counties that contain America's thirty largest cities, up from 33 percent in 1994 (cited in Meckler 1999, A1).

Table 5. Poverty Rates for Cities, Suburbs, and Rural Areas (Percentage of Population)

Year	United States	Central Cities	Suburbs	Rural Areas
1959	22.4	18.3	12.2	33.2
1969	12.1	12.7	6.8	17.9
1979	11.7	15.7	7.2	13.8
1989	12.8	18.1	8.0	15.7
1999	11.8	16.5	8.2	14.2

Sources: For data from 1959 to 1989, U.S. Bureau of the Census, Poverty Website, Table 2 in historical poverty tables; data from 1999 from State of the Cities Database, U.S. Department of Housing and Urban Development, http://socds.huduser.org/Census/Census_java.html.

As poverty rates in our metropolitan centers have climbed so have the number and population of "high-poverty" neighborhoods—census tracts in which more than 40 percent of the residents are below the poverty line—within urban areas. According to researcher Paul Jargowsky, the number of high-poverty tracts in our metropolitan areas doubled between 1970 and 1990 and the number of people living in them jumped from 4.1 million to 8 million (Jargowsky 1996, 11.). For instance, in 1970 Chicago had only 44 such high-poverty census tracts; by 1990 that figure was up to 183 (representing 12 percent of the total land area of the city) (Adams et al. 1995, 42). Even a relatively affluent urban area like Minneapolis–St. Paul has witnessed an increase in concentrated poverty; between 1970 and 1990 the number of high-poverty tracts in the Twin Cities rose from six to thirty (Adams et al. 1995, 47). The land area of our cities given over to concentrated poverty more than doubled in the '70s and '80s (Jargowsky 1996, 85). Even more frightening, the percentage of all children living in "distressed neighborhoods" in the fifty largest U.S. cities climbed from just 3 percent in 1970 to 17 percent in 1990 (Paget 1998, 2).

Predictably, the impact of the worsening concentration of poverty in cities was especially severe for African Americans, who historically have occupied the bottom of the nation's occupational ladder. The poverty rate for blacks dwelling in the central cities swelled from 18 percent in the mid-1970s to over 30 percent in the 1980s (see Table 6).

Table 6. Poverty Rates in Central Cities by Race (Percentage of Population)

Year	Central-City Whites	Central-City Blacks
1975	7.0	18.2
1980	12.1	32.3
1985	14.9	32.1
1990	14.9	32.1
1995	12.9	30.5

Sources: For data from 1975 to 1990, Goldsmith and Blakely 1992, 47; for data from 1995, U.S. Bureau of the Census 1995, Table 19 in detailed poverty tables.

Between 1970 and 1990, the number of blacks residing in high-poverty neighborhoods climbed from 2.5 million to more than 4 million, a 70 percent increase (Harris 1998, 18). Poor African Americans in the '80s and '90s were much more likely than poor whites to live in such areas (Goldsmith and Blakely 1992, 46–52).

Sociologist William Julius Wilson's book *When Work Disappears* (1996) provides a sobering picture of the escalating unemployment and economic deprivation faced by urban blacks in the last few decades of the twentieth century. Focusing on three predominately African American communities on Chicago's South Side known collectively as "Bronzeville," Wilson shows how deindustrialization and racial isolation have interacted "to produce the recent escalating rates of joblessness and problems of social organization in inner-city ghetto neighborhoods" (24). He notes that in 1950, 69 percent of all working-age Bronzeville males worked in a typical week; but by 1990 only 37 percent did (19). The men in these neighborhoods did not withdraw voluntarily from the workforce (an explanation favored by many conservative social critics). Rather, they were forced into unemployment as a consequence of economic restructuring and the fact that the decent paying, entry-level industrial jobs on which they depended disappeared from Bronzeville and working-class black neighborhoods throughout Chicago.

What happened to the once-thriving West Side black community of North Lawndale illustrates the broader transformation. In its heyday, the neighborhood was home to Western Electric and International Harvester factories that together employed 57,000 workers. The world headquarters of Sears and Roebuck was also located there, employing another 10,000 people. In the 1960s and '70s, each of these big employers closed down or relocated, triggering the flight or shuttering of countless local shops and businesses (35–36). As a consequence, Wilson writes, "after more than a quarter century of continuous deterioration, North Lawndale resembles a war zone" (34). Similar stories could be told of the impact of deindustrialization on inner-city black neighborhoods around the country.[4] Suburbanization, deindustrialization, and racial segregation have thus combined to produce what Wilson calls "a unique and growing concentration of minority residents in the most impoverished areas of the nation's metropolises" (10).

The grim economic situation in the nation's metropolitan centers has been made significantly worse by cuts in federal aid to cities, dramatic reductions in social spending, and other policy trends of the '80s and '90s. During the Reagan and Bush eras alone (1981–92), federal aid to local governments was slashed by 60 percent (Dreier et al. 2001, 127). Federal spending on new public housing dropped from $28 billion in 1977 to just $7 billion eleven years later (Clay 1992, 263). Meanwhile, shrinking welfare benefits have made it harder for the disproportionately urban recipients of public assistance to make ends meet. Between 1975 and 1996, the inflation-adjusted value of the welfare benefit for a family of three with no other income fell 40 percent (Harris 1998, 13)—and this was *before* the massive cuts implemented by the 1996 welfare reform. The economic transformation that undermined the financial security of so many urban residents, then, coincided with the willful shredding of the social safety net, leaving the de-industrializing central cities without the resources they needed to respond to a burgeoning crisis.

Trouble at the Core:
The Human Costs of Metropolitan Polarization

As the above discussion indicates, since at least the late 1980s, many of the nation's urban centers have been trapped in a destructive and self-reinforcing structural dynamic in which "[d]isinvestment by industry and the middle class feeds—and in turn responds to—concentrations of the poor, ill-educated, and the unemployable" (Zukin 1991b, 246). Indeed, in the year 2000, the federal government designated "one in eight cities as 'doubly burdened,' defined as having at least two of the following three conditions: an unemployment rate 50 percent higher than the national average, a poverty rate 20 percent or higher, and a population loss exceeding 5 percent since 1980" (Dreier et al. 2001, 16). But what distressed most observers in the '80s and '90s was not the undeniable fact that so many American cities had become so economically disadvantaged; rather, what disturbed the pundits, politicians, and reporters were the social disorders that inevitably accompanied that disadvantage.

Of these, the cities' relatively high crime rates weighed heaviest on the minds of the nation's elite opinion makers. It has long been recognized that big metropolitan centers tend to have more crime than either small towns or suburbs. One recent analysis estimates that, despite dramatic improvements during the 1990s, "central-city crime rates are still about three times those of suburbs" (Dreier et al. 2001, 83). For instance, FBI statistics show that in 1999 the nation's central cities had three times as many murders per capita as the suburbs and four times as many robberies (FBI Crime Data 2002). Moreover, between 1970 and 1995, the murder rates in sixteen of the twenty largest U.S. cities increased, even though the national murder rate remained fairly constant over the same period (Mauer 1999, 84). Low-income minority populations like those confined to the growing ghettos of large cities have tended to be overrepresented among the victims of urban violence. One study of young black males in Philadelphia during the late 1980s found that over a three-year period 40 percent "had had at least one emergency room visit for a serious violent assault" (87).

Though it attracted the most attention, rampant crime was hardly the only serious problem afflicting marginalized and disempowered urban communities during the '80s and '90s. Because they are often located near hazardous industries or toxic waste dumps, ghettos tend to be more polluted than either suburban or well-to-do urban areas (Dreier et al. 2001, 69–70; see also Harvey 1997). They also often have higher infant mortality and death rates than more affluent communities (Drier et al. 2001, 67). Throughout the 1990s, inner-city neighborhoods from New York City to Baltimore were hit by epidemics of sexually transmitted disease and tuberculosis that largely bypassed the wealthy suburbs (Stolberg 1998; Kershaw, 2002). Inner-city residents have also tended to suffer from chronic illnesses like cancer, heart disease, kidney disease, and diabetes at far higher rates and much younger ages than rest of the population (Epstein 2003). "Black youths in Harlem, central Detroit, the South Side of Chicago and Watts have about the same probability of dying by age 45 as whites nationwide do by age 65," notes *New York Times* reporter Helen Epstein, "and most of this premature death is due not to violence but to illness" (Epstein 2003, 77).

Racially and economically segregated urban school districts faced with crumbling buildings, severe teacher shortages, and budget problems unheard of in most suburbs found it extremely difficult to offer their students anything remotely resembling an adequate education during much of the post-Reagan era (Kozol 1991; Karp et al. 1997). Inner-city black and Latino neighborhoods have been so badly served by the existing public transit system that the NAACP Legal Defense Fund has sued transportation authorities in Los Angeles and other major cities for violating their residents' civil rights (Bullard and Johnson 1997). And a 1997 U.S. Conference of Mayors' study of homelessness and hunger in twenty-nine cities revealed that demand for food relief and emergency shelter space had risen every year since 1986 (U.S. Conference of Mayors 1997). In short, life in the urban core during the '80s and '90s was marked by such a spectacular accumulation of social and economic misery that it would have been surprising if the situation had failed to raise serious concerns among the general populace.

The Privileged Side of the Urban/Suburban Divide

While the poverty, unemployment, violence, and disorder documented above contributed enormously to the panic over the city that permeated public discourse in the 1980s and '90s, conditions in communities on the privileged side of the urban/suburban divide also played a role. The balkanization of our metropolitan regions has been accompanied by the formation and reproduction of a suburban middle class uniquely receptive to depictions of the city as scary, chaotic, and threatening. Marked by withdrawal from the public life into the private sphere of the family, racialized fear of urban crime and disorder, and hostility to the cities' demand for government assistance, the conservative, slightly paranoid character of "suburban middle-class culture" has long been the subject of withering criticism. Already in 1970, in his book *The Uses of Disorder*, Richard Sennett argued that suburbia was defined by "a common determination to remain inviolate, to ensure the family's security and sanctity through exclusionary measures on race, religion, class, or other 'intrusions' on a 'nice community of homes'" (Sennett 1970, 71). It was this "urge for a purified identity," Sennett claimed, that explained why the suburban establishment "reacts with such volatility to the disorders of oppressed groups in the city, and meets the hostility from below with an oppressive hand greatly out of proportion to the original challenges" (82). Sennett's insight that postwar suburbanization was a means of constructing a "purified identity" has been echoed by commentators who point out that "the suburbs helped turn Euro-Americans into 'whites'" united not by culture, language, or religion but by their shared white privilege (Lipsitz 1998, 7).

Of course, in the decades since Sennett's diagnosis, suburbia has become progressively less homogenous; by the year 2000, in fact, one quarter of the suburban population was black, Latino, or Asian-American (Logan 2001, 1). Moreover, roughly one third of the nation's satellite communities are actually poorer than the cities they abut (Dreier et al. 2001, 232). Yet among residents of better-off, disproportionately white suburbs animus toward the oppressed of the city has become, if anything, even more vituperative and entrenched. Their investment in fortifications against intrusions from urban outsiders has only gotten stronger. Their antagonism toward political initiatives perceived as benefiting impoverished and disempowered inner-city communities has become even more unyielding. These attitudes, in turn, have filtered down to the white residents of blue-collar inner-ring suburbs. Despite their growing racial and class diversity, then, the suburbs' cultural "urge for a purified identity" and corresponding fear of unruly urban Others remain. And this has made suburbia—especially white, affluent, outer-ring suburbia—particularly susceptible to the panic over the urban crisis promoted by conservative intellectuals and the media.

Suburban antagonism toward the city manifests itself first of all as an obsessive fear of urban crime. By any standard, anxiety about lawlessness—especially violent street crimes like drive-by shootings, carjackings, muggings, and assaults—was rampant in the United States during the '80s and '90s. Respondents to national opinion polls consistently ranked crime among the most important issues facing the country (Jackson and Naureckas 1994, 10). For instance, an August 1993

Time-CNN poll reported "that 59 percent of city respondents said that they worried about being a victim of crime" (Miethe 1995, 17). Moreover, the proportions of people who say they fear that they will be victimized have been rising steadily since the mid-1960s (Liska and Baccaglini 1990). One summary of several survey results found that between 42 and 52 percent of survey respondents avoided going downtown, to certain neighborhood streets, or to particular locations within their city because of fear of crime (Miethe 1995, 22). Suburbs, especially wealthy suburbs, are among the safest places in the country and yet the 1994 annual survey of affluent suburban Orange County, California, residents found that 44 percent fear becoming the victim of a crime, 39 percent fear crime in public parks, and 31 percent are afraid of crime in shopping malls (Blakely and Snyder 1997, 151). A 1996 Knight Ridder poll found that the vast majority of those polled felt safe in their own neighborhoods but 72 percent viewed the largest city in their state as a breeding ground of crime (Montgomery 1996).

Concern about the safety of city neighborhoods has been a driving force behind the dramatic rise in the number of police in New York, Los Angeles, and other metropolitan areas since the late 1960s (Platt 1995, 6). Similar concerns have also been driving explosive growth in the private security industry; in fact, the number of people employed as private security guards more than doubled in the 1980s (Corwin 1993). Yet public fears of urban violence in the '80s and '90s were completely out of proportion with the actual risks facing most Americans, particularly most middle-class suburbanites. The national rate of violent crime, according to the most accurate measurement, actually declined slightly between 1973 and 1994 (Jackson and Naureckas 1994, 11). The murder rate meanwhile has remained basically unchanged since the mid-1970s (Platt 1995, 3). In other words, the actual threat posed by "urban underclass" crime simply does not justify suburbia's paranoia. "White punitiveness," notes one researcher, "seems to be largely inexplicable in terms of one's risk profile" (Beckett 1997, 91).

As the country's population has become more suburbanized, the white middle-class impulse to escape, divest from, and cordon off the racially heterogeneous inner city has reshaped the tenor of national politics. Suburbanites emerged as a major voting bloc in the 1970s and their political clout has been rising ever since. Consider Congress. Between 1964 and 1994, there was an 18 percent decline in congressional districts with a majority of central-city voters and a 228 percent increase in majority suburban districts (Paget 1998, 6). As a consequence, suburbanites have steadily expanded their control of committee chairmanships and other leadership positions in the House. Or consider presidential politics. Already by 1980, twenty-one states with majority-suburban populations controlled 281 electoral votes, enough electoral votes to elect a president (Thomas 1998, 57). By 1992, for the very first time, suburbanites cast the majority of presidential votes (Paget 1998, 3). In the 2000 election, the urban segment of the electorate had dwindled to the point where residents of cities of over 500,000 accounted for only 9 percent of the votes cast (Dreier et al. 2001, 235). Given that the suburbs tend to vote heavily Republican, their emerging power has been a blow to the Democrats. For instance, in the pivotal 1994 House elections, Republican candidates captured 53.5 percent of the suburban vote, enough to wrest control of the Congress away from the Democrats for the first time in sixty years (239).

As the electorate has become ever more suburban, the nation's policy makers have become increasingly reluctant to spend money addressing the cities' social needs. As I have already noted, federal spending on major urban aid programs has been plummeting since the late '70s. Federal aid in 1978 accounted for 26 percent of the average city budget; by the 1990s, money from Washington covered less than 10 percent of the average city budget (Judd and Swanstrom 1994, 321). Suburban hegemony is also to blame for tepid government support of urban mass transit systems, despite the obvious needs. For instance, in 1996 an Oregon ballot measure that would have funded a light-rail line between Portland and an outlying suburb received strong support from city voters but was defeated because of massive opposition by suburban voters (Thomas 1998, 174). And suburban congressional representatives have been leading the attack on government assistance for the poor (so often concentrated in the cities) since the 1980s, culminating in the 1996 legislation that "ended welfare as we know it" (174).

Of course, the fact that suburban politicians oppose spending tax dollars on cities doesn't necessarily mean that their constituents feel the same way. Because so few people turn out to vote in most elections, and because those who do vote don't always understand what they are voting for, election returns in congressional or presidential races are at best only a rough indicator of popular ideological and policy preferences. Yet opinion polls suggest that suburbanites tend to share their representatives' conservative views and policy preferences on a range of issues linked to the problems of the postindustrial city (poverty, crime, racial injustice, etc.) Pollster G. Scott Thomas's analysis of survey data has found that suburbanites generally support a political agenda that includes cutting aid to the poor, slashing taxes, maintaining local control of education, hiking spending for highways, funding more police, and implementing strict punishment for criminals (Thomas 1998, 159). To take just one hot-button issue, a 1995 Gallup poll taken in the midst of the debate on welfare reform found that 70 percent of suburbanites but only 62 percent of city dwellers favored cutting welfare to reduce the budget deficit (168). According to polls conducted by Clinton advisor Stanley Greenberg, white, blue-collar and middle-class voters—the very population that has become so heavily suburbanized in the postwar era—tend to believe that the urban underclass lack family values and a strong work ethic and get more government aid than they deserve (Greenberg 1995). On racial issues, suburbanites gravitate toward positions traditionally espoused by conservatives, holding that African Americans who aren't successful have only themselves to blame and opposing affirmative action. Thus, suburban voters supported California's Proposition 209—an amendment that would have outlawed government-sponsored affirmative action programs—while residents of the state's big cities overwhelmingly rejected it (Thomas 1998, 176). Suburbanites as a group also tend to resent taxes. People who make more than $45,000 a year—who cluster in affluent outer-ring suburbs—are far less likely to believe they are "getting their money's worth from their federal income taxes" than are people making less than $25,000 a year (Thomas 1998, 160; Her-szehnhorn 2001). Predictably, the main institutional supporters of California's notorious Proposition 13, which capped property taxes, were suburban homeowners associations (Davis 1990, 180–86). In short, with the exception of their support for programs that aid the elderly like Medicare and Social Security, suburbanites largely oppose "big government" and favor instead a politics of extreme privatism and atomistic individualism.

This preference for the private manifests itself in other areas of suburban culture as well. Consider, for example, the proliferation of "gated communities"—residential areas enclosed by walls intended to prevent entry by nonresidents—during the 1980s and 1990s. Most such communities operate as Common Interest Developments (CIDs) in which residents collectively own the shared amenities and a private homeowners association oversees community affairs. Quite a few are equipped with private security guards and electronic security systems. Though many cities have gated developments, the vast majority are located in the suburbs (McKenzie 1994; Blakely and Snyder 1999). The population of these fortified enclaves tends to be overwhelmingly middle or upper class, white, and middle-aged or older. The primary reason their residents choose to settle in such places, according to opinion surveys, is to escape the crime, traffic, and noise of cities and ungated suburbs (Blakely and Snyder 1997, 125–43). In their book *Fortress America*, Edward Blakely and Mary Gail Snyder estimate that by 1997 the United States had approximately 20,000 gated communities with some 3 million units of housing and 8.4 million residents (Blakely and Snyder 1999, 7).

Some of the gated developments being built in the 1990s attempted to incorporate all the traditional features of city living behind their walls. An excellent example of this trend is Green Valley, Nevada, a sprawling walled suburb outside Las Vegas that is expected to have 60,000 residents by the year 2005 (Blakely and Snyder 1999, 64). In the majority of gated developments that are organized as CIDs, homeowners associations function as a kind of private government. People who buy property in such developments are forced to join the association, pay dues, and agree to abide by rules governing everything from the kinds of pets they can own to the number of visitors they can entertain. For instance, Fairbanks Ranch, an affluent gated community in Southern California, is patrolled by private security officers who enforce a speed limit set by the homeowners association and fine repeat speeders $500 and ban them from the community's streets for a month (McKenzie 1994, 16). A few gated communities have even succeeded in incorporating themselves as full-fledged municipalities. As the proportion of the population living in them has risen, gated communities have gradually become a political force to be reckoned with. In California, private homeowners associations have lobbied state legislatures for the right to deduct homeowner dues from state income taxes (Stark 1998, 67). In New Jersey, private homeowners associations in 1990 pushed legislation through the state legislature entitling their members to rebates on the property taxes they pay to support city services (68). Gated communities and the homeowners associations that rule them represent an extreme example of what former Clinton Labor Secretary Robert Reich has called "the secession of the successful," the tendency for the affluent to abandon and divest from the nation's public institutions.

That so many Americans in recent years have settled in the privatized world of gated communities no doubt contributes to the climate of fear enveloping the cities. The fact of being viewed through the bars of so many high security fences inevitably heightens the imagined menace of the metropolis and its "undesirable" populations. "The 'ecology of fear,' a pattern of separation and isolation apparent in all spheres of our society, has transformed America's urban landscape from a public realm into a series of private territories," observes Udo Greinacher. "Cities have disintegrated as people have retreated to the safety of gated compounds or homogenous suburbs" (Greinacher 1995, 183).

The culture of suburbia into which the white middle class has retreated is above all a mass-mediated or media-dependent one. In the late-twentieth-century suburb, "electronic space replaces public space" (Greinacher 1995, 176). The suburbanization of the white middle class coincided perfectly with the dissemination of television as America's preferred medium of mass communication. Indeed, as Roger Silverstone has pointed out, TV exhibits an "elective affinity" with the privatized, home-centered way of life characteristic of suburbia (Silverstone 1994, 56); that is, as a medium designed for "home consumption," it seems uniquely suited to and has helped to foster a suburban way of life organized around the cult of domesticity and withdrawal from the larger metropolitan society. As Silverstone expresses it, "television is . . . a suburban medium. It is suburban in its institutionalization as a broadcast medium. It is suburban in the form and content of its programming. It is suburban through its incorporation into the fabric of everyday life" (57). Furthermore, Margaret Morse argues, TV tends to promote an attitude of detachment and indifference toward the world beyond the screen that mirrors and reinforces the suburbanite's dislike for the threatening public realm (Morse 1990). And since the advent of television, all the media of mass communication have been retooled for private consumption— think of the way the VCR, cable television, PCs, and the Internet have privatized the experience of watching movies—and to some extent all serve to reinforce privatism and middle-class paranoia about urban space. While the mainstream mass media encourage the suburban middle class's attachment to an insular, home-centered life, they are also one of suburbia's few sources of information about life in the urban core. This dependence on the media for knowledge of the urban "Other" by itself generates a psychological distance between the suburbs and the cities. But as we shall see later in this book, this sense of distance is compounded by the fact that the stories the media tell about urban existence are often alarming or derogatory and tend to feed into and reaffirm the agoraphobic leanings of the contemporary suburban outlook.

Conclusion: Suburban Panic and the Discourse on the Urban Crisis

The growing economic disparity between American cities and suburbs in the 1980s and '90s was so dramatic that it was virtually impossible to ignore. Also impossible to ignore was the intense poverty and host of social ills that came to be concentrated in the black and Latino inner city as a direct consequence of this polarization. Many suburbanites (and virtually all of their political leaders) reacted to this deepening divide with fear and a growing unease about an urban underclass seen as criminal, degenerate, violent, and a threat to the family-oriented way of life they cherish. No doubt this reaction was at least partially rooted in suburbia's culture of privatism and anti-urbanism. And no doubt it stemmed in part from perfectly understandable concerns about the real and sometimes brutal criminality that often plagues oppressed urban communities. However, I contend that the panic over the city was neither a simple reflex of the suburban mentality nor a realistic response to a genuine threat; rather, it was created, fueled, and organized by a right-wing discourse on the "urban crisis" that supplied an ideological framework and a set of ideologically laden concepts for interpreting conditions in the inner city, one which both amplified suburban fears and gave them a decidedly reactionary spin. The majority of suburbanites—by virtue of their racial privilege, status as homeowners, and comfortable incomes—may as a group be organically inclined to support tough anti-crime policies, to hate the messiness of urban life, and to resist spending money on social services for the poor. Nevertheless, for such inclinations to be translated into meaningful political action they have to be articulated in public debate, made self-conscious, rationalized, connected to a precise political agenda, woven into the prevailing cultural climate, and given a modicum of intellectual legitimacy. This, I argue in the next two chapters, is precisely what the dominant discourse on the urban crisis and urban decline accomplished for suburbia's inchoate anxieties about the increasingly troubled postindustrial city.

CHAPTER 2

Inventing the Savage Urban Other

Blaming the Victim depends on . . . a process of identification (carried out, to be sure, in a most kindly, philanthropic and intellectual manner) whereby the victim of social problems is identified as strange, different—in other words, as a barbarian, a savage. Discovering savages, then, is an essential component of, and prerequisite to, Blaming the Victim, and the art of Savage Discovery is a core skill that must be acquired by all aspiring Victim Blamers.

—William Ryan, *Blaming the Victim*

The whole practical aim of politics is to keep the populace alarmed (and hence clamorous to be led to safety) by menacing it with an endless series of hobgoblins, most of them imaginary.

—H. L. Mencken

In the 1980s and '90s, as central-city deindustrialization and growing racial and class segregation thrust the urban poor deeper and deeper into crisis, William Ryan's "art of Savage Discovery" flourished as never before. It became, in fact, the defining feature of mainstream political and intellectual commentary on the plight of the nation's metropolitan centers. In articles, speeches, policy papers, and best-selling books, critics, social scientists, politicians, and policy analysts repeatedly traced the troubles of America's cities to the growth of an "alien, dysfunctional" inner-city minority population marked by—on neoconservative economist Isabel Sawhill's definition—"violent crime, drug abuse, teen pregnancy, illiteracy, [and] joblessness" (Sawhill 1989, 3). Labeled "the underclass" by most commentators, poor central-city residents were framed in such analyses as suffering from behavioral as well as income deficiencies. "The underclass operates outside the generally accepted boundaries of society," wrote Ken Auletta in his eponymously titled

1982 book on the subject. "They are often set apart by their 'deviant' or antisocial behavior [and] by their bad habits" (Auletta 1982, 27–28). "These poor people are different, sadly, from you and me," explained columnist Joe Klein in an article about residents of the ghetto. "They are isolated from us; they have different values" (Klein 1996, 33).

These antisocial habits, behaviors, and values—together adding up to what journalist Nicholas Lemann called "a strong self-defeating culture" (Lemann 1986b, 68)—were said to be the main cause of inner-city poverty. The neighborhoods housing the urban underclass were almost always depicted as chaotic, ruined, and repellent, the exact inverse of the orderly domestic idyll of the suburbs. For instance, as one *New York Times* reporter described it, inner-city Detroit is "a scene of weed-choked lots and gutted wooden houses landscaped with shards of broken glass where teenagers gather aimlessly and children scavenge . . . from the debris. From their porches, the remaining homeowners, mostly black, . . . can point out a half dozen crack houses" (Krans 1988, A35). Life in these neighborhoods, influential columnist George Will proclaimed in one of his screeds, is "a slow motion riot" (Will 1994b, 11A) or, as libertarian policy wonk Charles Murray characterized it, "*Lord of the Flies* writ large" (Murray 1993, A14). Indeed, right-wing pundit Dinesh D'Souza reflected an emerging mainstream consensus when he declared in his best-selling tract *The End of Racism* (1995) that "[b]ehavior that would be regarded as pathological anywhere else is considered routine, and even glamorous, in the ghetto" (16).

As imagined by the intellectual and political establishment, the implications of the underclass's inexorable growth promised to be dire, particularly for America's cities. Some commentators worried that the pathologies of the urban poor would become accepted as normal— "defining deviancy down," as Daniel Patrick Moynihan famously put it—and render the postindustrial metropolis ungovernable. Thus, columnist John Leo, writing in the July 26, 1993, issue of *U.S. News and World Report*, warned that "[c]ities are haunted by the fear that no one is really in charge, that the nominal government can't or won't keep order, that it will cede any ground and collapse any standard to avoid trouble. . . .

Menaces aren't confronted. They are adjusted to and become part of the system" (Leo 1993, 20). Others endorsed the notion that the economic decline of the central cities coupled with the suburbanization of the majority of the population would eventually render urban life itself obsolete. "Sometime in the 1980s we came to the end of our national romance with cities and the public spaces that define them," wrote Fred Siegel, an adviser to New York mayor Rudolph Giuliani. "[T]he streets . . . that once inspired our largely urban culture now too often induce fear, as even the most innocent of experiences become fraught with potential danger" (Siegel 1997, 169). On the right fringe of the political spectrum, former Secretary of Education William Bennett framed the expansion of the underclass as a portent of an impending apocalypse, arguing that "[c]urrent trends in out-of-wedlock births, crime, drug use, family decomposition, and education decline, as well as a host of other social pathologies, are incompatible with the continuation of American society as we know it. If these things continue, the republic as we know it will cease to be" (cited in Mills 1997, 32). For the Victim Blamers of the 1980s and '90s, then, the new urban "barbarians" weren't simply a danger to themselves and other inhabitants of the big city but threatened to drag the entire nation down into a new Dark Ages.

The copious outpouring of discourse on the savagery of the metropolitan centers and their residents served, and continues to serve, the interests of the regnant political establishment (dominated by conservative Republicans and "centrist" Democrats throughout the post-Reagan era). It provided ideological cover for ongoing divestment from the urban core, legitimated cuts in social welfare spending, and justified a racialized war on drugs fought against inner-city youth. It naturalized and gave coded expression to a collection of hoary derogatory stereotypes about African Americans and the poor. As Herbert Gans has pointed out, it blamed the urban poor "falsely for the ills of American society and economy, reinforces their mistreatment, increases their misery, and further discourages their moving out of poverty" (Gans 1995, 1). Perhaps most importantly, the endless public talk and theorizing about street crime, the urban crisis, and the immorality of the underclass helped to unify middle-class, white suburbanites into an "historic bloc" in support of anti-urban, law-and-order politics. As Kofi Hadjor explains, "[e]levating the problem of the underclass performs a political function for the conservative elites. It provides a succinct counterpoint against which they can mobilize White suburban opinion" (Hadjor 1995, 125). In other words, the conservatives' victim-blaming discourse on the city should be seen as part of a Gramscian struggle for hegemony, as part of a bid for "moral and philosophical leadership" over the emerging suburban majority. As such, it did more than simply reflect middle-class anxieties about the sweeping demographic, economic, and cultural shifts transforming America's urban centers; it systematized those fears, interpreted and "made sense of" them, cast them into authoritative cultural narratives and arguments supported by "empirical data," and lent them intellectual weight and credibility. And in so doing, it functioned to perpetuate and exacerbate them as well.

Yet, as I argue further on in this chapter, the string of "savage discoveries" about the alien, dysfunctional underclass that became so prevalent in the 1980s and '90s didn't materialize out of nowhere; the right's alarmist representations of the urban poor drew on and extended a long cultural tradition of animus toward cities and the urban proletariat. In fact, one of the more baffling aspects of the popularity of conservative theories about the underclass and the urban crisis more generally is that their recycling of ancient anti-urban tropes and shop-worn racist stereotypes about ghetto residents has gone so unremarked (at least outside leftist, academic circles) and been so remarkably effective.

In this chapter, I trace the historical origins of the breathless commentary on the savage "urban other" that became so hegemonic in the late-twentieth-century American culture. Beginning with a survey of late Victorian thinking about "the slums," I go on to explore the role played by Victorian-style theories about the barbarism of ghetto dwellers in the right-wing backlash against Great Society social programs and the conservative intellectual response to the inner-city riots of the 1960s. The image of the inner-city elaborated by the neoconservatives in the '60s, I argue, mobilized middle-class suburban voters behind Republican presidential candidate Richard Nixon in the 1968 election and secured their support for his brand of "law-and-order" politics. It also laid the conceptual and rhetorical foundations for the anxious public discussions surrounding urban pathology and violence that took place at the end of the twentieth century (discussions that I examine at length in chapter 3).

The Historical Precursors of
Contemporary Urban Nightmares

Fear of the city is arguably as old as civilization itself. As Jeffrey Hadden and Josef Barton have observed, the Judeo-Christian tradition shows evidence of distinctly "anti-urban underpinnings" at its very origins (Hadden and Barton 1973, 85–90). The Bible frequently treats the city as "unnatural" and an abomination in the eyes of God (witness the rough treatment by the biblical deity of such splendid cities as Babel and Sodom and Gomorrah). Even though some ancient and early modern civilizations held cities in high regard, cities have fallen further and further into disrepute as humanity has become ever more concentrated in urban areas. As geographer Yi-Fu Tuan has noted, as cities themselves grew and became more economically and culturally important, they increasingly became the focus for anxieties once attached to nature, regarded as "out of control," wild, treacherous, and malevolent (Tuan 1979, 9).

The rapid industrialization and urbanization of the eighteenth and nineteenth centuries—which led to the emergence of giant metropolitan centers like London and Paris—only exacerbated these burgeoning fears. Nineteenth-century British observers routinely described London, Manchester, and other booming industrial towns as "grotesque and lurid, labyrinthine and obscure" (Tuan 1979, 167). Commentators on nineteenth-century Paris and turn-of-the-century Berlin portrayed them in strikingly similar terms.[1] Nor were such sentiments confined to the Europeans. In their pioneering study of American attitudes toward the city, *Intellectuals Against the City*, Morton and Lucia White note that "enthusiasm for the American city has not been typical or predominant in our intellectual history. Fear has been the more common reaction" (White and White 1962, 13). They mention, as a preeminent example of this reaction, Thomas Jefferson's well-known dislike for city life. Jefferson, by his own admission, viewed "great cities as pestilential to the morals, the health and the liberties of man" (cited in White and White 1962, 28). Nor was he the only American intellectual to see things this way. The Whites go on to note that Emerson and Thoreau viewed the city as artificial and confining (39). For Melville, Hawthorne, and Poe, "the city scene was the backdrop for frightening experiences, personal defeat, icy intellectualism, heartless commercialism, miserable poverty, crime and sin, smoke and noise, dusk and loneliness" (47).

Despite the fact that cities grew rapidly in the post–Civil War era and became the command centers of the nation's wealth and political power, postwar American writers like William Dean Howells, Theodore Dreiser, Henry James, and Frank Norris essentially shared Jefferson's dismal assessment of the metropolis. Moreover, the Whites' readings of the works of philosopher John Dewey, social reformer Jane Addams, and sociologist Robert Park—thinkers rarely viewed as enemies of the city—confirm that each harbored a preference for the close-knit community life of the town and the village and disdained the impersonality and alienation of the big city. Indeed, the Whites point out, even America's most renowned architects—Frank Lloyd Wright and Louis Sullivan—expressed hostility toward the nation's great urban centers. Wright not only followed Jefferson in believing that "the city is a cancerous growth and the home of mobocracy" (White and White 1962, 194), but felt it was doomed to "inevitably decay and disappear" (197). The entire history of intellectual attitudes toward the city in the United States is a record of complaints and fears repeated and revived again and again, particularly "fears and doubts about the activities of the city mob" that "continue from Jefferson through the early twentieth century reformers and social critics" (217).

There can be little doubt that the presence of "the mob" was the aspect of the metropolis that most terrified both American and European middle-class observers and that fear of the mob's periodic rebellions formed the subtext for all the other concerns they articulated about urban life. From the beginning of the industrial age onward, elites viewed the rise of the working-class slum, and later the immigrant and black ghetto, with an apprehension bordering on hysteria. In these densely settled, often squalid, desperately impoverished neighborhoods, which could be found in every major city in the capitalist world, successive generations of bourgeois social explorers, reformers, and uplifters confronted, surveyed, and tried to come to grips with their worst nightmares: the human detritus cast off by the exploitative economic system on which their comfortable lifestyles depended. Yet, as historian Alan Mayne contends, in a very real sense the "slums are myths . . . constructions of the imagination" (Mayne 1993, 1). As such, the very term slum "subsumed the inner-most working-class districts of every city—notwithstanding their diversity of occupations, incomes, ethnic backgrounds, and household arrangements; and the variations in age, size, and labour and housing markets amongst cities—'into one all-embracing concept of an outcast society'" (2). Representations of the slums by crusading social reformers, journalists, and writers of realist fiction cast them "as a universal antithesis of urban norms" and "constructed an imagined schism between the good city and its antithesis in order to distill the essential core values of bourgeois common sense" (10). These images of "slumland" in turn functioned "to externalize society's anxieties by projecting the sources of those anxieties on to villainous other-siders" (10). As we shall see, the urban explorers of the nineteenth century established a vocabulary and a conceptual apparatus for representing the urban poor and their neighborhoods that is still very much with us, however dramatically the objective economic and social situation of both has changed in the intervening years.

In the polemics and manifestoes of nineteenth-century moralists and social reformers, texts that formed the catalyst for the first major governmental interventions in the areas of workers' housing and public health, one finds a consistent preoccupation with the socio-biological threat posed by slums and slum dwellers. Indeed, despite their philanthropic aims, the social reformers who addressed such problems as the adequacy of lower-class housing and sanitation or the epidemic of lower-class crime employed a discourse that was consistently inflected by a tone of revulsion. This was especially evident in Britain, which already by the eighteenth century had in London a crowded city of a million people and a sizable population of infrequently employed, poorly paid laborers.

The working-class neighborhoods of London and England's other big cities, in the British reformers' texts, appear as the locus of all manner of filth, scum, and contagion (which, in turn, were associated metaphorically with immorality, crime, vice, and working-class insurgency). In fact, according to the theory of urban degeneracy that enjoyed widespread support in late-nineteenth-century Britain, the deleterious influence of the slum environment stunted the mental, physical, and moral growth of its inhabitants and rendered them "hereditarily unfit" for decent jobs (see Jones 1971). As Stallybrass and White have demonstrated, in the discourse of the social reformers, the metonymic chain by which the urban poor are associated—for a variety of contingent, sociological reasons—with squalor is forever "elided with and displaced by a metaphoric language in which filth stands in for the slum-dweller: the poor *are* pigs" (Stallybrass and White 1986, 131). The popularity of the nineteenth-century theory of degeneracy, with its circular causal links between biological weakness, a dilapidated environment, and spiritual and moral decay, helped to facilitate this slippage.

For the nineteenth-century bourgeois reformers, the step from the statement "the poor are forced to live in dirt" to the statement "the poor are inherently dirty, both morally and physically" was thus a short one to take. Edwin Chadwick's bestselling *Report on an Inquiry into the Sanitary Conditions of the Laboring Populations of Great Britain* (1842) shocked polite society with its lurid account of the slums; as Chadwick described them in an update of his earlier investigation, the slums were "fever nests and seats of physical depravity" that were "also seats of moral depravity, disorder and crime" (Chadwick 1874, 274). Henry Mayhew's articles on London street folk written for the *Morning Chronicle*, and later anthologized in *London Labour and the London Poor* (1861), had as their explicit aim to expose the plight of the lower classes as "a national disgrace to us all." Be that as it may, he consistently wrote of the London poor as "beasts of the fields," "instinctless animals," and "the lowest depths of barbarism," language that distanced urban poor racially and morally from the rest of society (Morris 1994, 18). Even shriller is this description of a visit to a typical tenement by another English reformer, Andrew Mearns, written some twenty years later:

> Few who read these pages have any conception of what these pestilential human rookeries are. . . . To get to them you have to penetrate courts reeking with poisonous and malodorous gases arising from accumulations of sewage and refuse scattered in all directions and often flowing beneath your feet. . . . You have to ascend rotten staircases. . . . You have to grope your way along dark and filthy passages swarming with vermin. Then, if you are not driven back by the intolerable stench, you may gain admittance to the dens in which these thousands of beings . . . herd together. (Mearns 1883, 4)

Mearns, like Chadwick, finds an organic connection between the dilapidation of the slum dwellers' surroundings and the corruption of their moral character: "Incest is common; and no form of vice and sensuality causes surprise or attracts attention. . . . The vilest practices are looked upon with the most matter-of-fact indifference" (7). Such representations of urban degeneration and depravity, as Gareth Stedman Jones notes, "bore little relation to the real situation of the London casual poor in the late Victorian period" (Jones 1971, 151). However, they did provide "a mental landscape within which the middle class could recognize and articulate their own anxieties about urban existence"(151) and gave coded expression to elite concerns about the growing rebelliousness of London's working-class population, poor or not (281–314).

In the United States, where the vast majority of urban poor were either recent immigrants from Italy, Ireland, Russia, China, and Eastern Europe or black migrants from the South, the fin-de-siècle paranoia surrounding the slum dweller was exacerbated by pervasive nativist and racist prejudice. Social commentators consistently described immigrant ghettos as so many beachheads for a disruptive, alien take over of the American city. Robert Hunter insisted in 1904 that the slum problem was caused by "millions of foreigners [who] have established colonies in the very hearts of our urban and industrial communities" (cited in Mayne 1993, 158). Frederick Sanborn, a founder of the American Social Science Association, lamented that "this whole segment of our people—those of foreign birth or parentage—furnishes far more than its due proportion of illiteracy, poverty, insanity, infant mortality, vice and crime when compared to the native population." (Sanborn 1886, 256–57). Likewise, the *American Journal of Sociology* in 1897 announced that "large cities are great centers of social corruption and . . . degeneration" (cited in Boyer 1978, 129). In pamphlets bearing sensational titles like *The Dangerous Classes of New York* and *The Spider and the Fly; or, Tricks, Traps and Pitfalls of City Life*, journalists and reformers presented accounts of the depravity that allegedly prevailed in the immigrant neighborhoods of America's larger cities as alarming and lurid as anything ever written about the London poor (Wright 1981, 115). For instance, the *San Francisco Chronicle* charged in 1900 that if people "knew what a hotbed of disease and vice [Chinatown] is they would rise up and sweep it into the bay" (cited in Mayne 1993, 189).

More often than not, the squalor of overcrowded tenements in places like New York's Lower East Side or Chicago's Near West Side was taken as a reflection of the innate (biological and moral) corruption of their residents. "Blaming the poor for the deplorable conditions around them," writes Gwedolyn Wright, "was common" (Wright 1981, 116). Jacob Riis, whose *How the Other Half Lives* (1890) did for New York what Mayhew did for London, described New York's crowded Lower East Side slums as a place where, "shunning the light, skulks the unclean beast of dishonest idleness" (35). Rev. Josiah Strong's best-selling 1885 book, *Our Country*, vehemently denounced the foreign born for turning metropolitan areas into "tainted spots on the body-politic" (177). So did the *Chicago Herald*, which announced that "it is not abject poverty which causes such nasty and cheap living; it is simply an imported habit from Southern Italy" (cited in Wright 1981, 121). Strong's 1907 polemic *The Challenge of the City* went further, "giving his chapters such lugubrious titles as 'The Modern City as Menace to State and Nation' and quoting

Shelley's epigram: 'Hell is a city much like London'" (Boyer 1978, 189). In addition to blaming foreign immigrants for the horrors of the modern metropolis, he attacked the corrupters of the city's "moral atmosphere" (prostitutes, saloon owners, street urchins, and the like), comparing them to "vermin of an Egyptian plague" (cited in Boyer 1978, 200).

Clearly, one motive behind the nineteenth-century reformer's descent into the slums was a pervasive fear that the filth, disease, vice, and crime that they imagined festered there would spread into the homes and neighborhoods of the bourgeoisie. Christine Boyer argues that, as a rule, "Improvers . . . sought not to help those condemned to seething tenement cores but to protect the rest of society from the disorder that threatened to escape from within the city perimeter" (Boyer 1987, 18). In this, they were almost certainly responding to accepted scientific opinion about the contaminating force of blighted urban areas and their residents. One popular medical theory of the time held that cholera and other epidemics were caused by miasma—or clouds of noxious odors— hovering over the slums (see Rosenberg 1992). The germ theory of disease, which became public knowledge in 1890, also reinforced elite anxieties about the urban poor. As Ehrenreich and English note, after the germ theory revealed that disease was transmitted via human beings and the things they touched, "Americans . . . became preoccupied with germs. The reason people gave for avoiding the ghetto was not the risk of being mugged, but that of being infected with disease" (Ehrenreich and English 1973, 53). Rumors circulated that it was possible to catch syphilis and typhoid from postage stamps, hand-rolled cigars, and even paper money (53). With the much-publicized exploits of Typhoid Mary, an Irish American cook who supposedly infected countless households with typhoid, the mania for finding contagion everywhere reached a fever pitch. As Stallybrass and White point out, "'Contagion' and 'contamination' became tropes through which city life was apprehended. It was impossible for the bourgeoisie to free themselves from the taint of the 'Great Unwashed'" (Stallybrass and White 1986, 135). But in the minds of the urban reformers, and the middle-class public as a whole, disease was not the only danger the slums posed for the general populace: "As the orifices of the poor opened to contaminate bourgeois space, so in the bourgeois imagination the slums opened (particularly at night) to let forth the thief, the murderer, the prostitute, and the germs—the 'mad dogs' which could 'destroy mankind'" (133).

In addition to fostering fears of contamination, well-to-do commentators expressed concerns that immigrant slum dwellers were breeding so fast they would soon outnumber the WASP middle class. As David Ward explains, "some alarmists publicized the prospect of 'race suicide' whereby the proportionate contribution of the native-born stock to the host society would be overwhelmed by the fecundity of the newcomers" (Ward 1989, 52). A related fear expressed by a number of intellectuals, most prominently genteel American reformer Fredrick Law Olmstead, was that the city in general was "alienated from nature" and inherently unhealthy, speculating that "city people—and eventually, the whole population—would fail to reproduce itself" (cited in Hall 1988, 33).

Characterizations of slum dwellers as filthy, criminal, diseased, and immoral buttressed the ancient ideological distinction between the "worthy" and "unworthy" poor, between the poor who are victims of circumstance, and hence worthy of charity (usually widows, invalids, and children), and "paupers," whose poverty is self-induced and who are thus undeserving of aid. A classic statement of this distinction can be found in an 1877 report to the New York State Board of Charities:

> by far the greater number of paupers have reached that condition by idleness, improvidence, drunkenness, or some form of vicious indulgence. . . . [I]t is equally clear that these vices and weaknesses are very frequently, if not universally, the result of tendencies which are to a greater or lesser degree hereditary. The number of persons in our poor-houses who have been reduced to poverty by causes outside of their own acts is surprisingly small. (Hoyt 1877, 287–88)

The treatment of poverty as a moral condition has long informed public and governmental response to the plight of the "Have Nots" both in the

United States and in the rest of the capitalist world. From the notorious British Poor Laws of the eighteenth and nineteenth centuries to Aid to Families with Dependent Children in America, social programs to aid the poor have distinguished between recipients who are entitled to aid and those whose claim to public assistance is viewed with skepticism and sometimes derision. Thus, Social Security—which by the 1990s had succeeded in drastically reducing the poverty rate of America's oldest citizens—is almost universally supported by Americans across the political spectrum while "welfare" for work-age women and their children is viewed with nearly universal disdain and attacked by politicians at every turn. Suffice it to say, in the late nineteenth and early twentieth centuries, "moral definitions of poverty found support in the latest intellectual fashions: in the antebellum period, in Protestant theology; after the Civil War, in the work of Darwin and early hereditarian theory; and in the twentieth century, in eugenics" (Katz 1989, 14–15). The late Victorian idea of hereditary urban degeneracy, for example, merely substituted the Darwinian notion that the urban poor were biologically "unfit" for the older claim that they were "morally inadequate" (Jones 1971, 313); in both cases, the urban poor were framed as undeserving of public aid. And it was almost always assumed that the "undeserving" made up the bulk of the destitute, especially in the slums of large cities. This is not to say that there weren't alternative and sometimes very compelling interpretations of urban poverty available to social observers during this period. In his pioneering 1887 study of the London poor, Charles Booth found that while the poor made up some 35 percent of the city's population, those who could be classified as "undeserving" constituted less than 2 percent of the population (Hall 1988, 28). "The hordes of barbarians of whom we have heard who, coming forth from their slums, will some day overwhelm modern civilization, do not exist," he argued. "The barbarians are a very small and decreasing percentage" (Booth 1888, 305). Yet Booth's was clearly a minority view. The socially dominant interpretation of the plight of the slums saw their inhabitants quite literally as "uncivilized barbarians" and equated them, almost reflexively, with crime, vice, and deviance.

At the same time as social scientists were investigating the immorality, criminality, and improvidence of the urban poor, the literature of the epoch (from Charles Dickens and Arthur Conan Doyle to Theodore Dreiser and Stephen Crane) helped to fuel middle-class fantasies about the menace of the slums by transforming the prostitute, the hooligan, the "disease carrier," and the "criminal type," along with the dark alleyways and seedy dives they purportedly inhabited, into central fixtures on the cultural landscape. Alan Mayne notes that the boundary between the slums constructed by works of fiction like *Maggie, Girl of the Streets* and *Oliver Twist* and press accounts of actual urban neighborhoods was often nonexistent. Newspaper representations of slums were "sustained in part by incorporating easily recognizable fragments drawn from popular drama, narrative, and illustration" (Mayne 1993, 154). Whether such representations were presented as fiction or reportage, they nonetheless had a common aim of transporting the reader to "the topsy-turvy world of the slum," "a strange and liminal zone . . . in which bourgeois normalcy has been turned upside down" (163). The ultimate ideological impact of imagining the slum and the urban poor in this way—as threatening, filthy, amoral, and absolutely Other—was to transform them into objects of intense loathing and to frame their troubles as largely self-caused. As we shall see, this view of urban poverty has enjoyed several revivals since the late Victorian era.

Reading "Street Violence," Reading the Ghetto

While a strong current of anti-urban anxiety (particularly anxiety about the moral threat to "decent people" posed by the urban poor) has always lurked just beneath the surface of American culture, hyperbolic discourse on the viciousness of the cities has not always been with us. In the decades after the turn of the century, representations of working-class inner-city neighborhoods as hotbeds of barbarism were at least partially eclipsed by other, more sympathetic, depictions. During the Great Depression and the era of the New Deal, the mass mobilization of the working class pushed the structural causes of urban blight, unemployment, and poverty into popular consciousness and onto the national political agenda; at the same time, social scientists, intellectuals, urban reformers, and politicians rethought and (in some cases) repudiated punitive Victorian attitudes toward the slums. In the 1950s and early '60s, the inner-city poor, when noticed at all, were typically viewed as deserving of compassion and generous aid. Michael Harrington's 1962 book, *The Other America*, famously prompted Presidents John F. Kennedy and Lyndon B. Johnson to launch a "War on Poverty" that included dramatically expanded welfare programs, federally funded job training, medical aid to the indigent, and increased government support for low-income housing. Likewise, deteriorating conditions in the cities were seen as cause for careful government research, planning, and well-funded ameliorative action (though this high-minded concern for the city did not prevent the urban renewal schemes and downtown redevelopment projects of the era from exacerbating the very problems they were intended to solve). It is worth remembering, too, that throughout this period the federal government—under intense pressure from the civil rights movement—took increasingly bold steps to protect and expand African American civil rights, moves that benefited both hyper-oppressed black southerners and residents of northern ghettos.

To be sure, during the 1950s, as the changing demographics of northern cities heightened racial tensions there, some commentators sounded warnings of impending urban doom (see Beauregard 1993, 135–54). Rising crime rates and (to judge from the number of Hollywood films devoted to the subject) the menace of juvenile delinquency caused concern as well. In 1958, for instance, Harrison Salisbury of the *New York Times* surveyed the new Fort Greene housing project in Brooklyn and declared that "Fort Greene and projects like it spawn teenage gangs. They incubate crime. They are fiendishly contrived institutions for the debasing of family and community life to the lowest possible mean" (cited in Guinther 1996, 191). However, despite some flickers of panic over urban conditions during the 1950s, the immediate origins of the current discourse on the savage urban Other must be sought in the Republican right's political and intellectual response to the hundreds of riots that tore apart America's black inner cities from the mid-1960s through the early '70s. Outbreaks of collective violence like the Watts riot of 1965 and the burning of Detroit in 1967 focused the entire nation's attention on the crisis in the cities in a way that ordinary urban squalor and desperation could not.

As explained in chapter 1, by the mid-'60s, black migration to the urban centers of the North, white suburbanization, and deindustrialization had together begun to transform America's inner cities into reservations for the minority poor. Indeed, the strict segregation of the nation's metropolitan areas along lines of race and class was by 1965 already well entrenched. The limited economic opportunity, inadequate housing, and white hostility routinely encountered by black urbanites "led to embitterment" and widespread anger, especially among unemployed young men (Sugrue 1996, 261). This development coincided with what was arguably the high-water mark of the modern civil rights movement whose demonstrations to dismantle legal segregation in the South inspired increased militancy among activists in the North. The growing economic marginalization of an entire generation of black youth together with an increasingly militant black leadership gave rise to an escalating wave of inner-city riots and violent protests that rocked America's cities every summer from 1964 through 1972. Sparked by incidents of police brutality or by the assassination of community leaders (in particular by the 1968 murder of Martin Luther King, Jr.), these insurrections created an opportunity for ghetto residents to lash out at the immediate symbols of white oppression: the cops, white-owned businesses charging exorbitant prices, and property owned by absentee landlords. According to one estimate, there were "329 important riots in the five years between 1964 and the end of 1968, involving thousands of black rioters in 257 cities scattered around the country" (Feagin and Hahn 1973, 102). The high point of this wave of civic upheaval was the year 1967, which saw major disturbances in Detroit, Newark, Milwaukee, and Cincinnati (104). Some 18,000 people were arrested, 3,400 injured, and 82 killed as a result of these and other riots in that year's "long hot summer" (104).

The most famous—and for the white establishment, most alarming—of the decade's urban upheavals was the Watts rebellion of 1965. In

1965, Watts was a poverty-stricken, decrepit, and extremely segregated African American neighborhood located south of downtown Los Angeles. In many ways it was typical of big-city ghetto areas in the 1960s: its population had swelled thanks to a steady influx of black migrants while at the same time its jobs were being exported to the suburbs (Horne 1995, 36). On the evening of August 11, a California Highway Patrol car patrolling the outskirts of the neighborhood pulled over a young black motorist on suspicion of drunk driving. A violent confrontation ensued and soon black residents were taking to the streets to battle police. The fighting ultimately raged for five days, killing thirty-four people and injuring another thousand (3). It took 16,000 police and National Guard troops to subdue the approximately 35,000 adults who had rioted; by the time the fires died down, 4,000 of those rioters were under arrest and an estimated $200 million in property damage had been done, reducing huge swaths of the largely black and Latino sections of south-central L.A. to smoldering heaps of rubble (3). The white middle class's shock and horror at the scale of destruction in this and the other riots of the '60s helped propel Ronald Reagan into the California governor's mansion in 1966, helped Richard Nixon capture the presidency in 1968, and reverberated on the national political scene for decades to come (Horne 1995, 263–306; Edsall and Edsall 1992, 47–73).

The immediate reaction to Watts and other ghetto uprisings on the part of the national political and intellectual establishment was largely sympathetic to the plight of those caught in the slums. The reports on the causes of the riots issued by the two commissions convened by President Johnson, the National Advisory Commission on Civil Disorders and the National Commission on the Causes and Prevention of Violence, while contributing to a "sense of impending doom" surrounding the inner cities (Beauregard 1996, 219) nevertheless embraced a liberal, integrationist outlook. The National Advisory Commission (usually called the Kerner Commission after its chairman, Governor Otto Kerner of Illinois) issued a report that even radical critics agreed correctly emphasized racism as the root cause of the disturbances (Rotella 1998, 216). As Feagin and Hahn explain, in the report "[o]ppressive ghetto conditions were accented. Even 'white racism' . . . was given some attention in the assessment of causes" (Feagin and Hahn 1973, 219). Similarly, the Violence Commission acknowledged white complicity in the creation of the ghetto and urged increases in general welfare expenditures (along with improved methods of social control to prevent further outbursts of collective violence) (222).

Yet, alongside such progressive (and basically accurate) assessments of the social forces behind the riots, conservatives delineated their own alternative interpretations of conditions in the ghetto and of the causes of the riots. These interpretations pinned ultimate responsibility for the "long hot summers" of the '60s on the pathology of ghetto dwellers and the permissiveness of liberal anti-poverty programs; as David Garland puts it, right-wing politicians "blamed the shiftless poor for victimizing 'decent' society . . . and blamed the liberal elites for licensing a permissive culture and the anti-social behavior it encouraged" (Garland 2001, 97). The right's account of the burgeoning urban crisis—which conspicuously avoided mention of white racism or structural changes to the American economy—gave conservatives a distinct political advantage in appealing to an alarmed white suburban populace (Edsall and Edsall 1992). And it contained the seeds of the reactionary perspective on the cities and their problems that has dominated public conversation for the past two decades.

Barry Goldwater's failed 1964 presidential campaign, which was to set the agenda of the American right on so many issues for decades to come, anticipated one of the main leitmotifs of the ensuing conservative discourse on the city. His well-known fear-mongering about the "Communist Threat" was paralleled by equally tough rhetoric about the domestic threat posed by the urban poor. "Law and order" became his favorite slogan. Indeed, in an effort to tarnish Lyndon Johnson's signature social programs, Goldwater even tried to link riots and rising crime rates in the cities to the War on Poverty. As he put it (in a speech addressing the outbreaks of violence that rocked New York and Philadelphia during the summer of '64):

If it is entirely proper for the government to take away from some to give to others, then won't some be led to believe that they can rightfully take from anyone who has more than they? No wonder law and order has broken down, mob violence has engulfed great American cities, and our wives feel unsafe in the streets. (cited in Parenti 1999, 7)

As Christian Parenti explains, Goldwater lost his race to LBJ in 1964 but his law-and-order message began to pay dividends very soon after that. "At the heart of this new type of politics was a very old political trope: white racism and the self-fueling fear bred by it. Crime meant urban, urban meant Black, and the war on crime meant a bulwark against the increasingly political and vocal racial 'other'; by the predominately white state" (7).

In California, for instance, Ronald Reagan tapped into the "white backlash" against insurrections like Watts to defeat Democratic incumbent Edmund Brown in the 1966 gubernatorial race. On the stump, he played up the need to quash urban lawlessness and suggested that government aid programs for the urban poor merely "exchange one kind of paternalism for another" (cited in Horne 1995, 301). As governor, Reagan hammered relentlessly on the issue of law and order, declaring that "we must recover the will to make our streets safe, our cities free from violence and our campuses centers for learning rather than outrage and insurrection" (Finney 1968, 1).

But it was President Richard Nixon who arguably made the most successful political use of the street violence and civic unrest of the '60s. Early on, Nixon and his strategists realized that racial tensions and the public's fear of urban lawlessness would be central to the task of "establishing a new, non-economic polarization of the electorate" (Edsall and Edsall 1992, 98). In 1968, Nixon campaigned hard on the message that he alone could restore order to the unruly ghettos. Like Goldwater, Nixon tried to tie urban rioting and crime to Democrat-sponsored social spending and "softness" on street crime: "I say that doubling the conviction rate in this country would do more to cure crime in America than quadrupling the funds for Humphrey's war on poverty" (cited in Parenti

1999, 8). What was wrong with America's depressed and disorderly urban neighborhoods, Nixon maintained, was not a lack of resources, or miseducation, or a deficit of good jobs but a lack of strong law enforcement.[2] "The truth is we will reduce crime and violence when we enforce our laws," he argued in a September 30 speech, "and when we make it less profitable, and a lot more risky, to break them" (Kenworthy 1968, 21) Meanwhile, Nixon's vice presidential running mate, Spiro Agnew, rarely missed an opportunity to lash out at the "scum," "misfits," and "garbage" he believed were responsible for the riots and publicly lamented the "steady decline in the moral climate of the country" symbolized by ghetto crime (Franklin 1968, 74; see also Edsall and Edsall 1992, 84–85). Such rhetoric struck a cord with the white middle class, who voted disproportionately for Nixon's brand of "tough" conservatism in two successive elections (Edsall and Edsall 1992, 74–98).

The Neoconservatives and the Problem of the Ghetto

The law-and-order rhetoric of the 1960s–and the stance toward metropolitan populations that it implied–was not merely an opportunistic ploy by Republican candidates out to score political points. Nixon's and Goldwater's reading of the ghetto disturbances of the period flowed from and was informed by a new strain of conservative social theory that purported to show that flawed values and dysfunctional families, not economic disadvantage or racism, were the real causes of urban violence and misery. This emergent school of social theory, sometimes known as neoconservatism, drew on the work of legions of intellectuals, social scientists, policy researchers, and poverty experts who spent the '60s busily investigating inner-city residents for signs of deviance and incorrigible criminality. Ironically, much of the conceptual arsenal used by conservatives in their efforts to demonize the inner-city poor as undeserving or to legitimate punitive crime control policies during the '60s and after was drawn directly from the work of *liberal* social scientists and poverty researchers.

One such notion was the idea that the poor were trapped in a "culture of poverty," a set of habits and values that left them unprepared to take advantage of the economic and educational opportunities created by America's overheated postwar economy. As Michael Katz has explained, in the 1960s many liberals assumed that "dependent people were mainly helpless and passive, unable, without the leadership of liberal intellectuals, to break the cycle of deprivation and degradation that characterized their lives" (Katz 1989, 17). Thus, anthropologist Oscar Lewis famously elaborated his concept of the culture of poverty to explain the reproduction of disadvantage among destitute families in Mexico, Puerto Rico, and New York's Puerto Rican communities. He argued that poverty could be understood as "subculture . . . passed down from generation to generation along family lines" (Lewis 1968, 187). In his studies of slum communities, Lewis identified no fewer than "seventy interrelated social, economic, and psychological traits" that together comprised the culture of poverty (188). Central among these was alienation from and lack of integration into dominant social institutions like schools, trade unions, churches, and political parties. Even worse, those caught in the culture of poverty purportedly lacked stable, local organizations of their own; Lewis writes, in a particularly derogatory comparison, that "[m]ost primitive peoples have achieved a higher level of socio-cultural organization than our modern slum dwellers" (191). Another essential trait of Lewis's poverty "subculture" was a lack of "middle-class values" such as a strong work ethic and respect for marriage. In addition, he describes the family lives of people in this culture as particularly chaotic:

> On the family level the major traits of the culture of poverty are the absence of childhood as a specially prolonged and protected stage of the life cycle; early initiation into sex; free unions or consensual marriages; a relatively high incidence of the abandonment of wives and children; a trend toward mother-centered families . . . and competition for limited goods and maternal affection. (191)

All of these traits conspired to produce culturally crippled individuals who suffered from "weak ego structure," inability to defer gratification and plan for the future, and a pronounced lack of class consciousness.

Lewis estimated that some 20 percent of the people officially classified as poor in the United States could be counted as members of the poverty subculture.

While most of the characteristics Lewis enumerated simply recycle familiar, demeaning myths about the poor, he was no reactionary. He insisted that the culture he described was "both an adaptation and a reaction of the poor to their marginal position in a class-stratified, highly individuated, capitalistic society" (188) and favored government action to expand economic opportunity for the poor as "absolutely essential and of the highest priority" (199). He also claimed that socialist countries like Cuba had (or appeared to have) successfully eliminated the culture of poverty (194). However, Lewis also maintained that the culture of poverty "develops mechanisms that tend to perpetuate it" and that make it easier to overcome economic deprivation than to eliminate the culture that springs from it. Despite Lewis's noble intentions, the political enemies of the poor communities he studied quite naturally seized on this later point. As Michael Katz argues, "Lewis' definition of the culture of poverty lent itself easily to appropriation by conservatives in search of a modern academic label for the undeserving poor" (Katz 1989, 19). Perhaps the most influential group of right-wing thinkers to embrace Lewis's ideas as the key to understanding the problems of America's cities during the '60s were the so-called neoconservatives.

A loosely affiliated collection of apostate Cold War liberals and ex-socialists, the neoconservatives—a group that included such notable thinkers as Irving Kristol, Nathan Glazer, Daniel Bell, and Seymour Morton Lipset—played a disproportionately large role in defining the discourse on the urban crisis of the '60s and, more specifically, in interpreting its racial dimension. Many of the neoconservatives—like Kristol, Glazer, and Bell—were former Trotskyists whose opposition to the Soviet Union and Stalinism had gradually metamorphosed into an uncritical defense of American capitalism and liberal democratic institutions. Though mainly preoccupied with the looming threat of the Soviet "Evil Empire," during the 1960s and '70s this group shifted to the right on domestic social issues as well. They evolved "a critique of welfare state programs" rooted in something like Lewis's culture of poverty thesis and a deep antagonism toward "a 'new class' of fellow intellectuals, countercultural youth and black power movement intellectuals" (Diamond 1995, 180). In particular, they came to argue for what Nathan Glazer termed the "limits of social policy," the idea that no matter how generously the government funded social programs, there was in reality very little such measures could do to, say, correct racial injustice or economic inequality. All of this had implications for the way the neoconservatives made sense of the trends transforming the cities, particularly the worsening situation in the black ghetto. In their hands, over the course of the 1960s, "liberal notions of the culture of poverty had hardened into a conservative horror of the black poor, who were conceived as shiftless, violent and addicted to public handouts" (Ehrenreich 1990, 165). Essentially, the neoconservatives managed to revive and update late-Victorian moralistic explanations of urban disorder and poverty for the postindustrial age. Their ideas on the urban crisis were widely circulated; as Robert Beauregard notes, "such neoconservative urbanists as Irving Kristol (Henry Luce Professor of Urban Values at New York University), Roger Starr (former administrator of the NYC Housing and Development Administration) and George Sternlieb (director of Rutgers University's Center for Urban Policy Research) were interviewed frequently and quoted widely in the popular media" (Beauregard 1996, 220). By the 1980s, their views on the problems of America's cities had won the upper hand in social policy debates in Washington and beyond.

The most notorious effort to sort out, from a neoconservative point of view, what was behind the poverty, crime, and deepening despair endemic to the urban neighborhoods that rioted in the mid-'60s was the report *The Negro Family: The Case for National Action* (1965) by then–Assistant Secretary of Labor Daniel Patrick Moynihan. The document, which informed a widely reported speech by President Johnson delivered at Howard University, argued that "Negro family instability" and the absence of strong father figures from many black homes was the real obstacle to blacks' social progress. As Moynihan put it, "At the heart of the deterioration of the fabric of Negro society is the deterioration of the Negro family" (Rainwater and Yancey 1967, 51). By "deterioration," Moynihan meant primarily the increase in the number of black female-headed families and the rising number of out-of-wedlock (or, as the report termed it, "illegitimate") black births since the 1930s.

While there is no denying the hard facts Moynihan marshaled to show that the black family structure had indeed changed,[3] the centrality he assigned to this shift in explaining the problems of black America proved to be controversial, to say the least. On his view, the "matriarchal" structure of the black family lead directly to what he called "the tangle of pathology," including such problems as teen pregnancy, crime, drug use, chronic poverty, and welfare dependency. Though he admitted that the female-dominated black family had been created by slavery and later reproduced by anti-black discrimination, he nevertheless insisted that "the weakness of the [black] family structure . . . will be found to be the principal source of most aberrant, inadequate or anti-social behavior, that did not establish but now serves to perpetuate the cycle of poverty and deprivation" (Rainwater and Yancey 1967, 76). Why a matriarchal family structure should lead to "the tangle of pathology" was barely explained in the report. The closest Moynihan comes to theorizing the alleged connection is his claim that "ours is a society which presumes male leadership in private and public affairs" and, because of this, "a subculture, such as that of the Negro American, in which this is not the pattern, is placed at a distinct disadvantage" (75). One implication of this argument was, of course, that blacks would not be able to attain full equality with whites without first "strengthening their families" (by which he meant, presumably, subordinating black women and children to the rule of strong "traditional" patriarchs). As a consequence, Moynihan urged that government action to improve the plight of poor blacks focus on the effort to "strengthen the Negro family so as to enable it to raise and support its members as do other families" (93).

The ideological significance of this line of reasoning was not lost on the leadership of the civil rights movement or their allies among progressive white intellectuals. Critics quite rightly charged that Moynihan's views were a variant of Lewis's barely credible culture of poverty theory. Concentrating on black pathology and family breakdown, the critics claimed, distracted "from the unfinished job of dismantling legal discrimination" (Diamond 1995, 187). It also obscured the powerful influence of private, extralegal, and informal white racism over the life chances of African Americans of all occupations and income levels. In addition, as William Ryan argued in his classic critique of Moynihan's report, some of the "evidence" advanced for the tangle of pathology and for the uniqueness of the changes in black family structure was so deeply compromised as to be untrustworthy (see Ryan 1971).

Another controversial, and in many ways more influential, application of the "culture of poverty" thesis to the urban crisis of the 1960s was Edward Banfield's *Unheavenly City* (1968). When it first appeared, Robert Beauregard reminds us, it was a text that "could not be ignored by anyone with an interest in cities" and quickly became the focus of a fierce debate both in academia and in the popular press (Beauregard 1996, 220). A professor of urban government and director of the Model Cities program for the Nixon administration, Banfield in his book launched a two-pronged attack on progressive interpretations of the ghetto unrest and riots of the era. On the one hand, he insisted that, contrary to popular opinion, the problems of the city were less severe than usually claimed. Indeed, he maintained that a "general elevation of standards makes most urban problems appear to be getting worse when, *measured by a fixed standard*, they are getting better" (Banfield 1968, 65). On the other hand, he argued that insofar as the nation's cities were beset by crime, poverty, riots, and blight, these problems could be traced in large part to the existence of an incorrigibly pathological lower class whom he defined as essentially beyond help. On this view, as Robert Beauregard points out, "government has no ameliorative role to play" (Beauregard 1993, 207) and, indeed, the few concrete policy proposals Banfield advanced toward the end of his tract concerned strengthening the punitive, police functions of the state vis-à-vis the inner-city poor.

The Unheavenly City begins with an overview of what American urbanists and sociologists have long recognized as the "logic of metropolitan growth" (Banfield 1968, 23–44). This logic dictates that poor migrants settle first in the crowded, run-down central sections of cities (near heavy industry of some kind); they later move to better neighborhoods as they ascend the income and social scale, sometimes even fleeing the cities for the suburbs. Thus, as cities grow in population, they expand inexorably outward, with the poorest residents living in the center and the wealthiest settling on the periphery. All this is fairly standard Chicago-school urban sociology. However, after describing this generic pattern, Banfield goes on to claim that while "the logic of growth" does require "that, in general, the lowest-income people live in the oldest, highest-density, most run-down housing . . . nothing in the logic of growth says that such districts must be squalid and vicious" (45–46). To account for these horrors, he introduces a concept that accounted for much of the debate surrounding his book: the concept of "class culture." What Banfield means by class culture has nothing to do with any Marxist or established sociological notion of class; for him, class membership is not determined by income level or relationship to the means of production, or even by status and prestige. Rather, he defines class in terms of "time horizons" or degree of orientation toward the future. The higher an individual's class, Banfield contends, the greater that person's "ability to discipline [him or herself] to sacrifice present for future orientation" (47). Class-determined time horizons, he argues, give rise to distinct class cultures or "life styles" that are passed from generation to generation. In turn, these "styles of life that are learned in childhood and passed on as a kind of collective heritage operate (within limits set by the logic of growth) to give the city its characteristic form and most of its problems" (46).

The remainder of *The Unheavenly City* attempts to show that many of the problems of the '60s-era city are caused by the least future-oriented of Banfield's "classes," the lower class, which he describes in the crudest possible terms. The typical member of the lower class, he tells us, "lives from moment to moment" and is "radically improvident" as well as violent and often mentally ill (53–54); moreover, "his bodily needs (especially for sex) and his taste for 'action' take precedence over everything else" (53). The morality of this class, he remarks, is "preconventional," meaning that their actions are guided not by a sense of right and wrong but by strategic calculations about what they "can get away with" (163). Lower-class families, he goes on, are almost always female-based and the women who head them usually neglect their children (53–54). For Banfield "each class culture implies . . . a certain sort of physical environment" (59); and, as is to be expected, he provides the reader with a fairly sobering portrait of a typical lower-class slum:

> The lower-class individual lives in the slum and sees no reason to complain. He does not care how dirty and dilapidated his housing is either inside or out, nor does he mind the inadequacy of such public facilities as schools, parks and libraries; indeed, where such things exist he destroys them by acts of vandalism if he can. Features that make the slum repellent to others actually please him. (62)

The culture of the lower class as described by Banfield closely resembles Lewis's culture of poverty, as Banfield himself acknowledges. However, for Banfield, unlike Lewis, "poverty is its effect rather than its cause. . . . Extreme present-oriented-ness, not lack of income or wealth, is the principal cause of poverty in the sense of the 'culture of poverty'" (125). The postulate of a distinctive lower-class culture serves as a kind of catchall explanation; Banfield references it to explain not just central-city poverty, but also urban crime, illiteracy, and, of course, the ghetto riots. In every case, lower-class recklessness and incapacity for deferred gratification are found to be the determining factor. Thus, he interprets the Watts riots not as a (justified) response to the police brutality and racial discrimination daily faced by Watts' black residents but as an "outbreak of animal spirits" conducted by young, action-seeking, lower-class thugs "mainly for fun and profit" (196–98).

Though he maintains that his notion of class has nothing to do with race, Banfield's improvident lower class sounds suspiciously like standard racist invective about the laziness and irresponsibility of the ghetto poor. As Gerald Houseman points out, "Banfield himself often slips into the graceless and unproved accusations one has heard charged against blacks since time immemorial" (Houseman 1982, 17). In fact, in some of his subsequent writings on the lower class, Banfield speculated that lower-class tendencies might be the product of "some genetic factor," which of course constitutes further grounds for suspecting that a racist outlook underwrites his thinking about the lower class (Houseman 1982, 19). Implicit racism is not the only problem with Banfield's notion of class. As a number of commentators have noted, Banfield's thesis of classes based upon future-orientedness lacks "an empirical base" and "does not bear up under scrutiny" (21; see also Beauregard 1996). Indeed, the one attempt to test his theory found "[v]irtually no meaningful associations . . . with various social and political behaviors, no classification scheme could be developed, and the explanatory ability of the time-horizon theory was shown to be markedly inferior to the more conventional definitions and indicators of class" (Houseman 1982, 21). The lack of "future-orientedness" that purportedly shapes the behavior of Banfield's feckless lower class also characterizes the behavior of the middle and upper class (not to mention the behavior of a substantial portion of American college students). Even if one grants that some members of the urban poor comport themselves as Banfield suggests, and some certainly do, it is by no means clear that their joblessness, criminal misconduct, or family instability are the product of some culturally transmitted inability to defer gratification. Rather, "living from moment to moment"— along with all those other behaviors that middle-class commentators find so distasteful—may well be a rational adaptation to the constrained economic and social options available to economically and racially marginalized ghetto residents.[4] In short, the lower class's lack of future-orientation may simply reflect a recognition that their future prospects are, as a matter of fact, rather bleak.

Banfield's theories justified a minimalist course of government action in responding to the crisis, a strategy of "benign neglect." Given that the lower class's problems were both incorrigible and self-imposed, he maintained most programs designed to help them "were misguided and simply raised false expectations" (cited in Beauregard 1993, 204). Indeed, like so many conservatives, he insisted that social welfare programs tend to "prolong the problems and perhaps make them worse"

(256). Thus, he advised slashing most forms of social welfare (by, among other things, defining poverty and eligibility for aid according to an extremely low, fixed standard of hardship). Where Banfield's recommendations departed from rigid insistence on government indifference to the plight of the urban poor, it was in the direction of greater police control over their lives and harsher punishments for their alleged misconduct. Thus, his advice for fighting lower-class lawlessness is to:

> [I]ntensify police patrol in high-crime areas; permit the police to "stop and frisk" and to make misdemeanor arrests on probable cause. . . . Reduce drastically the time between arrest, trial and imposition of punishment. Abridge to an appropriate degree the freedom of those who in the opinion of a court are extremely likely to commit violent crimes. . . . Make it clear in advance that those who incite to riot will be severely punished. (Banfield 1968, 246)

He also notoriously called for lower-class children to be taken from their parents and placed in foster homes and suggested that the "incompetent poor" be given "intensive birth-control guidance" (246).

Naturally, this vision of an expanded police state coupled with a stripped-down welfare apparatus appealed to many conservatives (and neoconservatives) of the time, especially within the Nixon administration. Right-wing political scientist James Q. Wilson hailed *The Unheavenly City* as "the only serious intellectual book that has been written about urban problems" (Beauregard 1993, 205). Neoconservative writer Irving Kristol, meanwhile, called it "easily the most enlightened book that has been written about the 'urban crisis'" (Kristol 1970, 198). The empirical vacuousness and conceptual weakness of Banfield's interpretation of the urban crisis of the '60s did nothing to prevent his dubious ideas and policy recommendations from being widely endorsed (sometimes wholeheartedly, sometimes with reservations) by a growing army of conservative and centrist intellectuals (Beauregard 1996, 221). Indeed, his champions, like Wilson and Kristol, reiterated, extended, and refined his general line of argument in their own writings on the city and its troubles.

Take, for instance, James Q. Wilson's many interventions in the debate over "urban problems" during the '60s and '70s. In 1968, he edited a volume titled *The Metropolitan Enigma* that gathered together essays by twelve mainstream social scientists—including well-known neoconservatives like Banfield and Moynihan—on various "symptoms of the urban sickness" (as the blurb on the back cover so eloquently put it). Like Banfield, Wilson and the contributors to his collection insisted that what are often called "urban problems" are in fact a variety of "unrelated concerns" some of which don't qualify as problems at all (like poverty, which is here, as in Banfield's work, thoroughly naturalized) and some of which appear intractable (such as rising crime rates). Among the latter, the problem of the lower-class or ghetto poor loomed especially large. Significantly, both Daniel Patrick Moynihan's research on the "Negro family" as well as the chapter from Banfield's *Unheavenly City* blaming lower-class "animal spirits" for inner-city riots were included in the anthology. Wilson's afterword made clear that he found much to agree with in both authors' vision of the urban crisis. In particular, he agreed with them that "certain parts of our central cities have become human cesspools into which our worst human problems have flowed and in which, through some kind of bacterial action, a self-sustaining reaction has been created that is making matters worse" (Wilson 1968, 403). Biologically derived metaphors like the ones deployed in this passage recall the nineteenth- and early-twentieth-century city reformers' colorful discourse of pathology and operate with similar ideological import. The same terrified obsession with inner-city (black and Latino) criminality surfaces again and again in Wilson's subsequent work. Thus, in his 1975 book, *Thinking About Crime*, Wilson gives a conservative twist to the Kerner Commission's progressive conclusions by claiming that "we are becoming two societies—one affluent and worried, the other pathological and predatory" (Wilson 1975, 14). As we shall see in the next chapter, Wilson in the 1990s developed—in the form of his now-famous "broken windows" theory of crime—an influential argument for intensive policing directed at inner-city neighborhoods as a way of combating the growing underclass threat to the affluent.

Though best known as the leading standard-bearer for staunch, (neo)conservative anti-communism, and as a shameless apologist for the war in Vietnam, Irving Kristol also found time during the '60s and early '70s, at the height of his powers as a polemicist, to speak out on the "urban crisis." Like Banfield and the neoconservatives generally, he insisted that many of the problems plaguing America's cities were simply intractable (Kristol 1972a, 39–41). The economic, social, and demographic decline of the city, he argued, is the product of such irreversible trends as the collapse of the railroads and the relocation of corporate headquarters. Indeed, he contends that America, unlike Europe, has long been an "urban civilization without cities," as he put it in his eponymously titled essay on the subject (36); that is, unlike Europe, American urbanization has always been dispersed and has never united a critical mass of political, economic, financial, and cultural functions in a single, unifying center like Paris or London. The ongoing economic decline and dilapidation of the city is for him not worth worrying about, because, as a product of inexorable dynamics, nothing ultimately can be done to change it. Moreover, echoing Banfield, he claimed that "[i]t is the startling absence of values that represents the authentic 'urban crisis' of our democratic, urban nations," though here it is unclear whether he thinks this "lack" can be redressed (Kristol 1972b, 20).

What is perhaps most distinctive about Kristol's writings on the city is the degree to which they emphasized the destructive impact of so-called social engineering (as represented by the expansive government programs of Johnson's Great Society) on cities and their populations. Kristol, as Sara Diamond has explained, was and remains a proponent of "the inevitability, if not desirability, of social inequality" (Diamond 1995, 188). As such, he viewed the growing demands for social equality voiced by welfare recipients, blacks, women, and other oppressed groups during the 1960s as potentially disastrous because they raised hopes that could not (and even if they could, should not) be fulfilled. In fact, it is clear that he regards popular egalitarian desires and the movements for social justice they animate as the main symptom of and evidence for the "lack of values" he alludes to in his work. In Kristol's view, the people chiefly responsible for stirring up these destructive desires were a group he labeled "the new class": scientists, teachers, educational administrators, social workers, middle-class professionals of various sorts, journalists, lawyers, intellectuals, and academics. Indeed, as Houseman observes, "The 'new class' pops up so often in Kristol's urban vision, and in his writing generally, that it has almost become a synonym for 'evil'; it covers a host of sins" (Houseman 1982, 140). What this amorphous group supposedly shares, according to Kristol, is a set of "liberal," "permissive," "counter-cultural" attitudes coupled with an elitist disdain for ordinary American culture. And they are ambitious, obsessively so. Ultimately, Kristol sees his "new class" as engaged in an epochal struggle for political power with the business community, which it hates and envies. It is a struggle that—at least circa 1972—the "new class" seemed to be winning. Like other neoconservatives, he regarded "antipoverty measures as a scheme for New Class advancement in which the hapless poor had somehow gotten entangled" (Ehrenreich 1990, 184) and the victory of 1960s antipoverty legislation was a sign for Kristol that the "new class" was firmly ensconced in power in the nation's capital. Naturally, Kristol regarded the consequences of "new class"–initiated reforms for the American city as cataclysmic. For instance, like Banfield and Wilson, he blamed overly generous welfare payments for the break-up of the inner-city black family. The policy implications of his scattered commentary on the urban crisis were clear and in line with the positions that have been popular with conservatives since the nineteenth century: cut social spending and clamp down on ghetto troublemakers.

Ghetto Bashing Becomes a Habit

Moralizing, victim-blaming explanations for the troubles of America's inner cities in the 1960s lent credibility to Nixon's law-and-order rhetoric and legitimated the Republican's punitive response to the rioting of the decade. But the interpretation of the urban crisis proffered by Banfield and company had other advantages for conservative politicians as well. At precisely the moment when the nation's central cities were being hit hardest by white flight and deindustrialization, the neoconservatives' treatment of urban problems largely absolved middle-class suburban-ites of all responsibility for the city's decline. By connecting lower-class criminality and family breakdown to overly generous Great Society pro-grams, they justified attacks on the welfare state and helped to discredit liberalism and its legacy (Gans 1995, 99). Perhaps most importantly, neoconservative commentary on urban issues consistently stigmatized the inner city as menacing and pathological, an alarming image that divided suburbanites from city dwellers and that was frequently turned to polit-ical advantage by Nixon and a whole series of ghetto-bashing politicians after him (Edsall and Edsall 1992, chapters 8–12).

Since the 1960s, the basic approach to urban disorder, violence, and poverty articulated by Banfield and his fellow neoconservatives has come to dominate public discussion of the American city. As the next chapter documents, in the 1980s and '90s, an explosion of research about and commentary surrounding the "urban underclass" recycled and reha-bilitated earlier theorizing about urban poverty and inner-city decay as products of "dysfunctional behavior " and "defective values." The oppo-sition the neoconservatives set up between the undeserving "lower-class" poor and the culturally pure, morally upright middle class became an obsession for social scientists, politicians, and pundits trying to make sense of the postindustrial city as did the notion that this pathological population was expanding at an alarming rate. Banfield's insistence on the fundamental intractability of many of the city's problems surfaced again in conservative social thought during the Reagan era and after, this time in the form of the proposition that American cities had become (economically and technologically) obsolete and parasitical on the "self-sufficient" suburbs. Moreover, the fear of urban disorder and violence so effectively promoted by conservative thinkers against the backdrop of the Watts riots and the burning of Detroit continued to perform salient political and ideological functions for conservative politicians through-out the Reagan, Bush, and Clinton administrations, most notably by generating public enthusiasm for even more forceful repression of the urban poor.

CHAPTER 3

Catastrophe Is Now:
The Discourse on the Underclass

> The city becomes the symbol, and at times the scapegoat, for the
> destitution, alienation, oppression, decay and fears engendered by a
> flawed political economy.
>
> —Robert Beauregard, *Voices of Decline: The Postwar Fate of U.S. Cities*

As the conservative counterattack on the gains made by the civil rights
movement and other democratic mobilizations of the '60s and '70s (the
women's movement, the welfare rights struggle, and so on) gained
momentum, the demonization of the inner city became increasingly
central to right-wing thought and political strategy. Building on Banfield's theory of the "lower class," conservative intellectuals during the
Reagan, Bush, and Clinton years posited a violence-prone, amoral, self-
destructive "urban underclass" as the wellspring of all the city's problems
and attacked liberal social programs, from homeless relief to food stamps,
for normalizing their deviance and "bad behavior" (MacDonald 2000,
164). The law-and-order rhetoric and the image of the out-of-control
street thug that Nixon deployed to such powerful effect in his presidential campaigns came to dominate all public discussions of urban issues,
not just for politicians but for policy experts, social scientists, and popular commentators as well.

"The power to impose and inculcate a vision of divisions, that is,
the power to make visible and explicit social divisions that are implicit,"
sociologist Pierre Bourdieu has remarked, "is political power par ex-
cellence" (1989, 23). In the '80s and '90s, conservatives succeeded in
popularizing a vision of American society as fundamentally divided between the residents of the postindustrial slums, seen as pathological and
threatening, and the white, middle-class residents of sprawling suburban

Edge Cities, seen as normal, decent, and under siege. As this chapter demonstrates, it was a vision that served a number of vital ideological functions for the political establishment and for the unequal, increasingly authoritarian social order they sought to defend. Endlessly cited and recited in the media, the opposition between dystopian inner-cities rife with pathology and utopian (or at least comfortable and safe) suburbs fueled a climate of panic that influenced the nation's lawmakers as well as the broader public.

This chapter analyzes the organizing role played by the concept of the underclass in conservative interpretations of the postindustrial city and its discontents since 1980. I begin by discussing the way the concept informed the explosion of conservative research and commentary on disempowered inner-city communities over the past two decades and show how such commentary attempted to rehabilitate the moralistic approach to urban poverty associated with the neoconservatives (and, before them, with the Victorian social reformers). I explore the ideological function and political uses of the dominant discourse on the urban crisis and the underclass, underscoring how conservative thinking about such issues legitimated central-city poverty and racial segregation, celebrated "traditional family values," discredited the welfare state, and justified merciless repression of the recalcitrant poor. I go on to highlight the various ways the right-wing narrative about the underclass amplified the social distance between suburbanites and city dwellers and bolstered the idea—promulgated by conservative intellectuals from the Reagan era onward—that cities themselves had become obsolete. The chapter ends by assaying the impact of the right's reading of urban social problems on local and national politics and on urban policy.

The Perfect Scapegoat: Charles Murray on the Urban Poor

> We tried to provide more for the poor and produced more
> poor instead. We tried to remove the barriers to escape from
> poverty, and inadvertently built a trap.
>
> —Charles Murray, *Losing Ground*

No single thinker has exerted as much influence over the discourse surrounding the urban crisis and the "underclass" over the last two decades as self-styled libertarian social theorist Charles Murray (though it should be noted that Murray himself did not start to use the term "underclass" until the late '80s). Like Banfield and Kristol before him, Murray's widely discussed *Losing Ground* (1984) attacked liberal welfare programs for "demoralizing" the urban poor, promoting immorality and self-destructive behavior, creating disincentives to marriage, fostering dependency on government handouts, and, ultimately, impoverishing the very people they were designed to pull out of poverty. All the postindustrial city's woes, he suggested, could be traceable to a single cause: our allegedly overgenerous aid to the poor. Critic John Clarke is right when he calls the book a "tour de force" of existing New Right arguments on the "errors and effects of the expansion of public welfare in the 1960s and '70s" (Clarke 1991, 138), a brilliant summing up and repackaging of ideas associated with Moynihan, Wilson, and Banfield. Written and promoted with a $125,000 subsidy from the conservative Manhattan Institute (Lane 1985, 14), the book immediately became the Reagan administration's "bible" on social policy and basically set the terms for every congressional debate surrounding welfare or urban policy since (including the 1994–96 cycle of debates leading up to the much-heralded congressional vote to "end welfare as we know it").

Murray himself became one of the most consulted, talked about, and respected commentators on poverty, especially inner-city poverty, in the country. His opinion pieces on such subjects as the L.A. riots of 1992, ghetto crime, and the IQ of the urban poor ran (and continue to run) regularly in the *Wall Street Journal* and other newspapers of record. Television news shows turned to him as the authority (or, at least, the conservative authority) on welfare, teen mothers, and the breakdown of the black family. Syndicated columnists George Will, Charles Krauthammer, and Joe Klein quoted him frequently and enthusiastically endorsed his views. Grover Norquist, president of Americans for Tax Reform, "compares him to intellectuals like Darwin, Freud and Marx" (Stefancic and Delgado 1996, 85). Even President Clinton averred in a 1995 interview with Tom Brokaw that Murray had done the nation a service by drawing attention to the problem of "underclass" family breakdown (NBC 12/3/95). Moreover, Murray's 1994 treatise, *The Bell Curve*, co-authored with Richard Herrnstein—a book that attempted to rehabilitate the eugenic idea that racial inequality in America is traceable to hereditary differences in intelligence—received extensive coverage in *Forbes*, *Time*, and *Newsweek* and was featured on ABC's *Nightline* (Naureckas 1995).

Given the impact of Murray's *Losing Ground* on the discourse surrounding the urban crisis, its thesis, supporting claims, and empirical evidence merit close scrutiny. Murray's main line of argument is deceptively straightforward. He begins by articulating the reactionary consensus view that, by the '80s, something had gone grievously wrong with the inner-city poor. As he interprets them, the basic indicators of well-being for the poor (poverty, wages, employment, crime rate, out-of-wedlock-birthrate, etc.) improved steadily from the 1940s to the 1960s. Then, in the mid-1960s, these same indicators allegedly took a sudden turn for the worse, just as Kennedy and then Johnson began to liberalize eligibility for welfare, increase funding for medical care for the poor, and authorize millions for urban renewal. In particular, Murray notes an increase in what he calls "latent poverty" (which he defines as "the number of poor before government transfers are taken into account") (Murray 1984, 64). On Murray's statistics, latent poverty declined from 33 percent of the population in 1950 to 18.2 percent in 1968 before rising to 19 percent in 1972 and 22 percent in 1980 (64–65). At the same time, he points to a parallel rise in unemployment, particularly among African Americans. As he remarked of the trend line from 1960 to 1980, "[o]n the face of things, it would appear that large numbers of young black males stopped engaging in the fundamental process of seeking and holding jobs" (78).

Extrapolating from (and explicitly defending the findings of) the notorious Moynihan report, Murray claimed that the period immediately following the implementation of the Great Society programs also saw an upsurge in the number of single-parent black families. While the proportion of black families that consisted of husband-wife households remained constant from World War II through 1967, in 1968 that percentage slipped from 72 percent to 69 percent (in the space of one year) and then declined to 59 percent in 1980 (129–30). "A change of this magnitude," wrote Murray gravely, "is a demographic wonder, without precedent in the American experience" (130). Even though he grants that some social statistics concerning the well-being of the poor continued to improve well into the '70s—notably the official poverty rate, which only started to rise after 1974, and the high school enrollment rate, which rose steadily until 1980—Murray insists that "few could avoid recognizing that the inner cities were more violent and ravaged than ever before" (145).

As is perhaps already clear, there is nothing particularly novel or groundbreaking about any of the data or longitudinal trends Murray breathlessly reports (although, as we shall see, some of the data he cites are inaccurate and some of the trends he points to do not hold up under scrutiny); social scientists of all political stripes had been tracking most of these conditions long before Murray's book appeared on the scene. What was unique about *Losing Ground* when it first appeared—and what recommended it to the Reagan administration—was the way it linked these trends to the liberal poverty programs of the 1960s. Bluntly put, Murray posits the War on Poverty as the principal cause of the surge of "latent poverty" in the black ghetto and elsewhere from 1968 onward. By instituting an overly generous set of social programs for the poor, he argues, the federal government in the '60s effectively changed the "rules of the game" according to which the poor lived their lives, worked, had children, and planned for the future. The result was "to make it profitable for the poor to behave in the short term in ways that were destructive in the long term" (9). Welfare and the other poverty programs of the '60s had, the argument went, created for the underclass a set of perverse "incentives to fail."

Murray supports the thesis that the "violent and ravaged" situation of the inner city stems from the corrosive effects of liberal poverty-fighting measures, not by pointing to any direct evidence, but by means of a series of what he calls "thought experiments." He begins by assuming that "all, poor and non-poor alike, use the same general calculus in arriving at decisions," and that everyone is guided generally by a sense of their own rational self-interest (155). He next imagines a poor, unmarried young couple, Harold and Phyllis—recently out of high school and expecting a baby—and contrasts the options available to the pair before and after the War on Poverty. According to Murray, in 1960, prior to the new poverty programs, AFDC was stingy enough and the rules for recipients strict enough that the most attractive course of action for the hypothetical couple would be to get married and have Harold support the family by toiling away at a low-paying, menial job. By 1970, Murray claims, welfare had become generous enough and the rules for recipients liberal enough that "the old-fashioned solution of getting married and living off their earned income has become markedly inferior" (160). Under the new system of incentives, Harold and Phyllis could bring in more by living together without getting married and having Phyllis draw AFDC benefits. The apparent strength of this line of reasoning of course is that it avoids the moralistic judgments implicit in the idea of a culture of poverty. As Murray himself puts it, "There is no breakdown of the work ethic in this account of rational choices among alternatives. There is no shiftless irresponsibility. It makes no difference whether Harold is white or black. There is no need to invoke the specters of cultural pathologies or inferior upbringing" (162); at the same time, Murray stresses that if one factors in "the lower class and black cultural influences that are said to foster high illegitimacy rates and welfare dependency" then "the effects [of welfare] on behavior are multiplied" (162).

But Murray doesn't stop here. He goes on to argue that just as powerful as the disincentives to marriage and respectability built into post-'60s welfare programs are their "demoralizing effect" on the poor. Here, just a few pages after foreswearing cultural factors in his explanation for the explosion of the urban underclass, he brings them back in. Murray contends that one of the major (and he intimates, intended) consequences of the War on Poverty was "getting rid of the stigma of welfare" (182). By making it culturally acceptable for poor people to seek aid from the government, the new policies withdrew status from "the low-income, independent working family" and from "the behaviors that engender escape from poverty" (179). Ultimately, the changes in social policy made during the '60s also denied that "people are responsible for their condition" (182). This denial, Murray maintains, "has had a pernicious homogenizing effect on the status of poor people," obscuring the boundary between the undeserving and the deserving poor (186). And, he continues, by denying that people are responsible for their own actions and by rewarding people for dependency, the United States has forced all poor people to behave as abject victims. He thinks this is especially true of the black urban poor. Thus he writes that "[e]very assumption that a young black in the ghetto might make about his inability to compete with whites was nourished by social policy telling him, through the way it treated him day to day, that he was an un-responsible victim" (187). In other words, by the end of his analysis of what we now refer to as the "underclass," Murray was reiterating the same mean-spirited myths about lower-class and ghetto culture Banfield had promoted.

The policies recommended in *Losing Ground* continued the spirit of Banfield's doctrine of benign neglect and were, if anything, more radical and even more devoid of basic human decency. Many of Murray's proposals are pure libertarian/neoconservative boilerplate: he supports "vouchers" as a way of saving public schools (224) and recommends repealing all forms of affirmative action as embodying white "condescension" toward blacks (222). But some of his other recommendations promise a return to a punitive nineteenth-century–style capitalism, one without safety nets for those unfortunates who stumble in the midst of the free market's relentless struggle for survival. Thus, he would scrap "the entire federal welfare and income-support structure for working-aged persons, including AFDC, Medicaid, Food Stamps, Unemployment Insurance, Worker's Compensation, subsidized housing, disability insurance and the rest" (227–28). The upshot of such sweeping cuts, he notes approvingly, would be to leave working-age people completely at the mercy of the private labor market and force them to seek assistance from family or private charities when they couldn't find a job (228). Even a master satirist like Voltaire or Swift could hardly invent a more blatantly anti-worker, pro-business agenda. Yet it was this analysis and this set of policy prescriptions that became the blueprint for successive efforts at what was euphemistically called "welfare reform" in Washington, D.C., and in state governments throughout the '80s and '90s.

Despite its immense impact on the discourse on the urban under-class, and despite its centrality to debates surrounding welfare reform, many of *Losing Ground*'s central contentions turn out to be utterly false and its overall perspective deeply biased by a highly selective, ideologi-cally warped narrative of recent American history. As Stephanie Coontz quipped, "The phenomenal publicity and approval generated by Mur-ray's book had more to do with the way it tapped into powerful cultural myths about self-reliance and dependency than with any connection to empirical evidence" (Coontz 1992, 81).

To begin with, Murray's figures are often dubious. As Michael Katz points out, Murray gets the poverty rate wrong (the 1965 rate was twice as high as the 1980 rate) and his discussion of the rise of latent poverty is misleading since he ignores the fact that "many elderly people withdrew from the work force when Social Security benefits increased" (Katz 1989, 154). Furthermore, his famous calculations of the relative advantages of welfare versus work for his hypothetical couple are com-pletely off. According to Katz, Murray uses the most generous welfare package in the country—Pennsylvania's—as the basis for his calcula-tions. But in most of the country, "work at a minimum wage job was more profitable; in the South, minimum wage jobs often paid twice as much" (154). Moreover, his argument neglects the fact that the real value of the average welfare package fell by 20 percent during the 1970s (154). In addition, Murray dramatically understates the positive effects of gov-ernment assistance programs on the condition of the poor in the late '60s and '70s. Infant mortality rates had declined very little up until 1965 but were cut in half between 1965 and 1980 following the introduction of Medicaid (Coontz 1992, 81). Moreover, the nutrition gap between the poor and other Americans declined significantly only after the expan-sion of food stamps and the introduction of subsidized school lunches in the late '60s (81).

Even more damning for Murray's position is the lack of evidence for any sort of causal relationship between welfare, out-of-wedlock births, and the breakup of the family. AFDC was introduced a full twenty years before the rise in the number of female-headed families Murray worries about, apparently without adverse effects. And it is not clear that the rise in female-headed families since the mid-1960s has anything at all to do with the Great Society's "liberalizing" of eligibility requirements for the program. As Stephanie Coontz points out, "between 1972 and 1980, the number of children living in female-headed households rose from 14 percent to almost 20 percent, but the number in AFDC homes held constant at about 12 percent" (Coontz 1992, 82). Far from acting as an incentive for single women to get pregnant, welfare appears to have the opposite effect: women receiving AFDC are actually less likely to have children than those who aren't (83). Murray would have us believe that poverty and welfare dependency is caused by the disintegration of the family, particularly the black inner-city family, under the pressure of welfare's perverse incentives. But the collapse of the two-parent family is more properly understood as a consequence, rather than a cause, of poverty. As Coontz observes, "Two of three poor blacks living in single parent families were poor *before* their families split up" (251). Finally, the sensational claim that out-of-wedlock births "exploded" in the '70s and '80s needs to be taken with an enormous grain of salt: while the ratio of illegitimate to legitimate births rose during the period Murray studied (a fact he notes again and again in his book) the illegitimacy rate—the absolute number of illegitimate births in a given year—actually fell (O'Connor 2001, 248).

But the most problematic aspect of *Losing Ground* isn't Murray's statistical sleight-of-hand or his fraudulent correlations between welfare and this or that social disorder; rather, what is most troubling are the vital facts and broad swathes of social history he leaves out of his account. For instance, he tells the story of the soaring black unemployment and inner-city crime of the 1970s without once mentioning the Great Migrations of southern blacks to northern cities, without even alluding to the way the industrialization of agriculture displaced southern share croppers, without discussing how racist unions cut off black access to good blue-collar jobs until the courts forced them to change, without acknowledging the ongoing dynamics of racial segregation, *and* without discussing the rapid deindustrialization of the cities. Missing from his argument is any reference to the economic downturns of the '70s and '80s, declining real wages, or the changing occupational structure that has created precious few good jobs for the unskilled workforce left behind in the urban core. Furthermore, as John Clarke has argued, Murray throughout his book consistently allows statistics about black, inner-city poverty to stand in for statistics about poverty in general. "The narrative effect of this statistical device," Clarke writes, "is to 'ghettoize' poverty and its attendant demoralization within black America" (Clarke 1991, 139). That is, his choice of focus helps to obscure the realities of poverty outside the ghetto, in white America, and obscures the commonalties between urban and suburban poverty. If all of this is added to the picture, Murray's book must be reckoned not as an honest effort to comprehend what has happened to make the central cities so "ravaged and violent," but as an ideologically motivated slander directed against the urban, black poor.

Sadly, in the conservative cultural climate of the 1980s and 1990s, none of the well-documented flaws of *Losing Ground* did much damage to the public profile or influence of its author. Murray's commentary on the urban crisis continued to be widely circulated in the media and oft cited in congressional speeches. Much of this commentary built directly upon the specious reasoning deployed in *Losing Ground*. Thus, in the immediate wake of the L.A. riots of 1992, Murray was called on frequently to explicate conditions in the inner city and he seized on these opportunities to expand on his earlier analysis. For example, his contribution to a 1992 *Commentary* forum on the riots advances the thesis that "[t]he conditions in South Central Los Angeles in 1992 that produced the riots *are* importantly a product of those [social policy] reforms of a quarter-century ago" (Murray 1992, 23). Once more he repeats his accusation that '60s-era reforms in welfare policy and criminal justice tore "apart the web of status rewards and penalties that govern behavior in any community" (24), resulting in soaring rates of black illegitimacy and rising rates of black violent crime. But, he contends, even those without knowledge of these statistics could see, since the mid-1960s, "that life was deteriorating; they could see it in the abandoned buildings, the youth hanging out on the streets, and the destruction of the well-ordered black working-class neighborhoods that had once dotted inner cities" (24). And, as in *Losing Ground*, he dwells on the destructive impact of female-headed households. "[T]he underlying problem that drives so many of the other problems among the underclass" is, he writes, "children growing up without fathers and women trying to get along without husbands" (28). Having identified what he sees as the core problem of the inner city, Murray ends on a pessimistic note. None of the government-sponsored attempts to solve this problem have worked; indeed, he speculates that the social fabric of the inner city "has become so tattered that it is difficult to see any external means of restoration." The only authentic solutions he envisions were either "treating the inner city as occupied territory and its citizens as wards to be tutored and manipulated by the wise hand of the state" (30) or, his preferred remedy, eliminating all government aid to inner-city communities.

Murray was particularly visible in the debates surrounding welfare reform that occupied so much of the country's collective attention from 1993 to 1996. In a 1993 editorial in the *Wall Street Journal,* "The Coming White Underclass," Murray cautioned that the illegitimacy and pathological behavior previously identified with the ghetto had begun to "spread," disease-like, into the white population, spawning a "white underclass." In a typically alarmist paragraph, he declared that "[t]he brutal truth is that American society as a whole could survive when illegitimacy became epidemic within a comparatively small ethnic minority. It cannot survive the same epidemic among whites" (Murray 1993, A15). The solution, he urged, was to stigmatize single motherhood, eliminate economic support for financially struggling families, and make "an illegitimate birth the socially horrific act it used to be" (A15). The piece immediately became ammunition for a host of right-wing pundits in their public relations war against welfare. As Stefancic and Delgado explain, "in the following days, influential commentators like George Will, Charles Krauthammer, Michael Barone, John Leo and Joe Klein wrote about the developing white underclass, and Murray was interviewed by David Brinkley, John Stossel, and Connie Chung" (Stefancic and Delgado 1996, 85). In his interventions in favor of slashing aid to poor women and children, Murray consistently returned to the stereotyped image of black urban neighborhoods as nightmarish places populated by wanton women giving birth to children destined for lives of crime and violence. For instance, in a 1995 editorial in the *New York Times* defending the Republican welfare bill, he anxiously warned that unless welfare is eliminated (or substantially "reformed"):

> [T]he Calcutta that we already have behind the gates of the public housing projects, the Calcutta that social workers and police deal with every day, will continue to grow. Catastrophe for children in low-income communities is not five years after a Republican welfare bill. Catastrophe is now. (Murray 1995, 25A)

This sort of hyper-inflated rhetoric also crops up in Murray's most appalling "contribution" to the public discussion surrounding the problems of the so-called underclass, namely *The Bell Curve*.

Published in 1994 to a flurry of hype and controversy, *The Bell Curve: Intelligence and Class Structure in American Life*, an 845-page tome cowritten by Murray and the late psychometrician Richard Herrnstein, purports to show both that measured intelligence—otherwise known as IQ—increasingly determines people's life chances in American society and that such intelligence (or, as they sometimes call it, "general cognitive ability") is to a substantial degree hereditary. The book's explicit aim is to refute what the authors dismiss as the "ideology of equality" and to show that liberal political theory "underestimates the importance of differences that separate human beings" (532). In their view—which they attempt to back up with a plethora of statistics, charts, and graphs—a person's IQ fixes not only his or her chances for academic success but also his or her occupation, income, inclination to get married, moral sense, and respect for the law. They insinuate that little or nothing can be done to raise measured intelligence; hence, IQ becomes destiny. And, they continue, differences in group intelligence largely explain socio-economic inequalities between the races. In particular, they point to a supposedly consistent finding that whites on average score 15 points higher on IQ tests than African Americans. Indeed, Murray and Herrnstein essentially argue that the characteristic problems of the black urban underclass—poverty, welfare dependence, and criminality—may well be the result of congenital stupidity. Their statement that "going on welfare really is a dumb idea, and that is why women who are low in cognitive ability end up there" (201) is typical of the causal links they attempt to forge in this regard.

Having blamed a collective cognitive shortfall for the plight of the inner city, *The Bell Curve* proceeds to paint a harrowing picture of an apocalyptic America polarized between "cognitive elites" and the IQ-deprived underclass, one in which the underclass—by their very nature promiscuous and fertile—is breeding faster than the elite. "[D]emographic trends" write Murray and Herrnstein, are "exerting downward pressures on the distribution of cognitive ability in the United States . . . pressures [that] are strong enough to have social consequences" (342). Not surprisingly, the shape assumed by those "social consequences" is precisely the sort of urban dystopia conservatives like Murray have been trading in since the 1960s. If the growth of the underclass is not checked, Murray and Herrnstein caution, we may need "a custodial state" to keep them in line, "a high-tech and more lavish version of the Indian Reservation for some substantial minority of the nation's population, while the rest of America tries to go about its business" (526). The only hope of avoiding this nightmare scenario, the authors maintain, is to follow through on Murray's call for an end to all aid to the poor, this time for reasons that are openly eugenic. "The United States already has policies that inadvertently social-engineer who has babies, and it is encouraging the wrong women," writes Murray and his co-author. They go on to say "[w]e urge that these policies, represented by the extensive network of cash and services for low-income women who have babies, be ended" (548).

The aporias and defects of *The Bell Curve*'s position are by now so well known they need not be reviewed here. It is enough to mention that the book's central assumptions—that there is such a thing as general intelligence, that this ability is measured accurately by IQ tests, and that there are significant genetic differences between racial groups that IQ test results could feasibly be correlated with—have been refuted thoroughly and in detail many times over (see Stephen J. Gould's *Mismeasure of Man* [1981], the articles in Frazer's *Bell Curve Wars* [1995], and Giroux and Searls 1996).[1] Indeed, the very idea that there is any meaningful genetic or biological profile to our culturally constructed categories of "race" is laughable: genetic variations between individuals classified as members of a given "racial" group are always much larger than variation between such groups, sure proof that "races" are not natural categories (Gould 1981). Never once in their massive book do Murray and Herrnstein attempt to defend the proposition that our social and cultural labels for race have significant biological or genetic correlates; as such, their entire enterprise blatantly "begs the question" that it is supposed to answer.

What is left of Murray and Herrnstein's tract after the pseudo-science has been debunked is, as Adolph Reed correctly observed, "really just a compendium of reactionary prejudices" (Reed 1994, 16) or, as Jacqueline Jones quipped, "hate literature with footnotes" (Jones 1995, 93). In fact, the book relies for evidence of its most sensational race-related assertions almost exclusively on research bankrolled by the white supremacist Pioneer Fund, an organization whose founding charter commits it to "'racial betterment' and aid for people 'deemed to be descended primarily from white persons who settled in the original 13 states prior to the adoption of the Constitution of the United States'" (Naureckas 1995, 13).

Amazingly, despite its white supremacist underpinnings, *The Bell Curve* received wide coverage when it first appeared. The *New Republic* devoted an entire issue to it and the book made the cover of *Newsweek*. It was discussed on *Nightline, Primetime Live, MacNeil/Lehrer NewsHour, The McLaughlin Group,* and *All Things Considered* as well as every network television news show. To be sure, much of the discussion of the book was critical, often pointedly so. However, the very fact that its thesis was considered worthy of extended consideration indicates how well "*The Bell Curve* fits with current political agendas" (Giroux and Searls 1996,

19); its very presence in the national dialogue reflects the normalization of once marginal ultra-right-wing views. As Giroux and Searls point out, "conservative and liberal commentators such as Mickey Kaus, Rush Limbaugh, and Nathan Glazer separate themselves from the unapologetic racism of *The Bell Curve*, but support policies that are similar in their effects on the black underclass and the urban poor" (12).

The Urban Underclass and the Right-Wing Imaginary

Though he cast a very long shadow, Charles Murray was not the only right-wing intellectual whose work nourished the reigning discourse on the problems of the so-called underclass during the Reagan, Bush, and Clinton years. In his 1985 book *Beyond Entitlement: The Social Obligation of Citizenship*, Princeton professor Lawrence Mead echoed Murray's contention that welfare programs trap recipients in poverty. However, Mead went on to insist that merely cutting aid programs would not eliminate the underclass because generations of dependency had rendered the urban poor unfit to survive off the dole. Instead of simply cutting them off, he argued, a concerted government effort would be needed to break the dependent poor's sense of "entitlement," to inculcate them with a work ethic, and train them to cope in normal society. "The most vulnerable Americans need obligations, as much as rights, if they are to move as equals on the stage of American life," he writes (17). This means, first of all, that rather than blaming the market or institutional racism for their failure, "government must persuade them to blame themselves" and that poverty programs must be designed to "affirm the norms for functioning on which social order depends" (7). But even more importantly, Mead argued that the hardcore urban poor should be compelled to take even very low-paying employment. The political import of Mead's proposals is nicely summed up by the title of his edited volume, *The New Paternalism* (1997). Like Murray, Mead became a respected commentator liberally consulted on stories about welfare reform and the underclass.

Other conservative intellectuals, like Marvin Olasky, author of *The Tragedy of American Compassion* (1993), added a religious gloss to Murray's critique of the welfare system. According to Olasky, the growth of government antipoverty programs eroded traditional personal (and spiritual) relationships between the givers of charity and the recipients, relationships that allegedly helped to uplift and ennoble all parties. Things were, he insists, much better back in the 1890s when the values of work and faith guided treatment of the disadvantaged:

> The perspective from 1990 shows that the social revolution of the 1960s has not helped the poor. More women and children are abandoned and impoverished. The poor generally, and the homeless particularly are treated like zoo animals at feeding time. . . . Let's transport an able-to-work, homeless person back from the present to 1890 and ask the question, "Are you better off now than you were then?" Then he would have been asked to take some responsibility for his own life, and to help others as well, by chopping wood or cleaning up trash. Then he would have had to contact other people, whether relatives or other colleagues. Now he is free to be a "naked nomad" shuffling from meal to meal. (222–23)

Like Murray and Banfield, Olasky sees no-strings-attached aid to low-income single mothers as the driving force behind the disorder of our major cities. As he puts it in an editorial touting the Republicans' 1996 welfare reform package, "from New York to Los Angeles the grim twilight struggle of abandoning dads and psychologically dead kids is running nightly at the drive-ins and the drive-bys" (Olasky 1996, 14A). For Olasky, the only way to "renew American Compassion" is to eliminate all cash subsidy to the destitute and to trust in the power of religious charities, an approach that "emphasizes volunteers tutoring children, being big brothers or sisters and helping parents to be responsible" (14A).[2] Olasky, like Murray and Mead, can thus present Republican enemies of social spending as "being the political force with *real* sympathy for those who endured the bad system that created their poverty, who only needed help to break the 'habit of welfare,' to attain freedom from bureaucracy, and to have a chance to participate in a rejuvenated economy and revived moral order" (Withorn 1998, 139).

Following the lead of Moynihan and Murray, some conservatives and crypto-conservative "New Democrats" fixated to an even greater degree on the breakdown of the family and the collapse of "traditional family values" as responsible for just about every conceivable dimension of the urban crisis—from crime to drugs to homelessness to joblessness to welfare dependency. As Judith Stacey explains, these champions of the traditional family "argue that the presence or absence of two married, biological parents in the household is the central determinant of a child's welfare and thereby of society's welfare" and "identify fatherless families as the malignant root of escalating violence and social decay, claiming such families generate the lineage of unemployed, undomesticated, 'family-less fathers' . . . who so threaten middle-class tranquility" (Stacey 1995, 55).

David Blankenhorn, co-director of the Institute for American Values and chair of the national Fatherhood Initiative, is representative of this school of thought. In his 1995 book *Fatherless America*, he asserts that the "real" crisis in the inner city is that it is "a world largely without responsible male adults" (29), which in turn gives rise to youth poverty and violence on an epidemic scale. "Routine violence, intimidation by gangs, destruction of property, teenage childbearing, an ethos of fear and fatalism," writes Blankenhorn, "these are the defining characteristics of residential communities almost totally devoid of male authority" (229). Similarly, journalist Kay Hymowitz in a 1994 article published in the conservative *City Journal* regaled readers with descriptions of the disordered world of "the underclass teen mommy," "a culture created and ruled by children, a never–never land almost completely abandoned by fathers and, in some sad cases, by mothers as well" (Hymowitz 2000, 237). Her comrade at *City Journal*, Heather MacDonald—whose shrilly moralistic coverage of urban schools and ghetto poverty won plaudits from Republican lawmakers throughout the '90s—proposed that many, if not all, of New York City's social problems stemmed from the fact that "the two parent family is all but extinct in some neighborhoods, rendered superfluous by welfare's subsidy for illegitimacy" (MacDonald 2000, 154). MacDonald's solution to the crisis of the inner-city family was characteristically blunt: "the city," she argued, "ought to restore the distinction between the deserving and the undeserving poor" and should consider "the use of boarding-school like institutions outside the city" for children from broken homes (172). Meanwhile, Blankenhorn's laundry list of ideas for strengthening "fatherhood" and "male authority" ranged from a fairly predictable call for an overhaul of the welfare system—which, he said, "constitutes a direct economic subsidy for out-of-wedlock childbearing" (Blankenhorn 1995, 231)—to the bizarre demand that state legislatures "prohibit sperm banks and others from selling sperm to unmarried women" (233). Such proposals openly demand a reassertion of male authority in what is imagined to be "wild," female-run inner-city households and a corresponding increase in the social control of women (or, at the very least, increased control over their access to frozen sperm). As Judith Stacey has correctly observed, the decline of the male-headed family, the rise in out-of-wedlock births, and the conservative nostalgia for the strong father of yesteryear inadvertently reveal "the inequity and coercion that always lay at the vortex of the supposedly voluntary 'companionate marriage' of the 'traditional nuclear family'" (Stacey 1995, 62).

In the discourse on the urban malaise, the underclass typically appears not merely as *fatherless* and *dependent* on overly generous government handouts, but also as profoundly *amoral* and *pathological* as well. While the rigorously positivistic Murray hardly ever talks openly about anything as nebulous as the "values" and "culture" of the underclass—preferring instead to deal with the hard, quantifiable realities of "the economic disincentives to marriage" posed by welfare and statistically measurable "genetic intelligence"—most public commentary on the problem of the underclass has dwelt precisely on such things. For instance, it is a perceived decline in "traditional values" among the underclass that Mead hopes to reverse by means of his new paternalism and Blankenhorn thinks will be eliminated by a revival of fatherhood. This preoccupation with the immorality of the urban poor can be seen most clearly in right-wing writers such as Gertrude Himmelfarb, Dinesh D'Souza, Myron Magnet, and, perhaps most especially, William Bennett.

Eminent British historian Gertrude Himmelfarb, a long-time Thatcherite and the wife of Irving Kristol, is in many ways the most intellectually accomplished figure in this group. Author of several well-regarded scholarly tomes on Victorian England—including *Victorian Mind* (1968), *Poverty and Compassion: The Moral Imagination of the Late Victorians* (1992), and *The Idea of Poverty* (1983)—Himmelfarb intervened in the underclass debate with *The De-moralization of Society* (1994), her much-talked-about panegyric to Victorian values (or, as she prefers to call them, the Victorian virtues, values-talk being too relativistic in her view). For her, the Victorian ethos entails a "belief in family and home, respectability and character" (Himmelfarb 1994, 14) that is scandalously absent from contemporary American life. The bulk of the book surveys (and valorizes) the thought of Victorian moralists and the history of Victorian philanthropy, purporting to show that the elevated moral standards of the period together with its charitable institutions did wonders for the poor and working class. (For instance, she claims that the spread of Victorian values throughout British society helped reduce crime and "illegitimacy" in even the poorest neighborhoods of East London toward the end of the nineteenth century, conveniently ignoring other possible explanations for these trends.) Among other things, Himmelfarb attempts to rehabilitate the term "pauper"—Victorian shorthand for the lazy, able-bodied poor—along with the moral stigma attached to it. "Today the very word 'stigma' has become odious, whether applied to dependency, illegitimacy, addiction, or anything else," she writes. "Yet stigmas are the corollaries of values. If work, independence, responsibility, respectability are valued, then their converse must be devalued, seen as disreputable" (142). Along the way, she also throws some mean-spirited jabs at left-leaning Victorians like H. G. Wells, Havelock Ellis, Olive Schreiner, and Oscar Wilde for rejecting "respectable" morality.[3]

Toward the end of the book, Himmelfarb derives a predictable lesson from the history she has recounted. "[T]he Victorians," she writes "had the satisfaction of witnessing a significant improvement in their condition; we are confronting a considerable deterioration in ours" (222).

The cause of this deterioration? Himmelfarb blames a pervasive "demoralization" of social policy, a willful refusal to make moral distinctions in granting aid to the indigent or punishing crime that allegedly lies behind most of our pressing social problems, including those of the "underclass." "[E]ven traditional values," she argues, "require legitimation. . . . And in secular society, legitimation or illegitimation is in the hands of the dominant culture, the state and the courts" (248). For Himmelfarb, confronting the problem of the underclass requires a proactive "moral reformation" and may well involve the state "legislating morality" (248) à la Mead's new paternalism.

Another conservative writer who has made a name for himself excoriating the urban underclass for their perverse values and pathological culture is Dinesh D'Souza, former editor of the Heritage Foundation's *Policy Review* and author of *Illiberal Education* (1991), the book that launched the "Political Correctness" fracas of the early 1990s. In 1995 D'Souza weighed in on the debate about the underclass with his ponderous 722-page polemic *The End of Racism*. In it, D'Souza argues explicitly that African Americans should stop using structural racism and racial discrimination as "an excuse" for their moral and cultural "failures." Though he rejects the biologically based racism of *The Bell Curve*, he nonetheless shares Murray's vision of the black inner city as a kind of apocalyptic landscape, a lawless wasteland given over to barbarism. "The last few decades," he writes:

> have witnessed nothing less than a breakdown of civilization within the African American community. This breakdown is characterized by high rates of criminal activity, by normalization of illegitimacy, by the predominance of single-parent families, by high levels of addiction to alcohol and drugs, by a parasitic reliance on government provision, by a hostility to academic achievement, and by a scarcity of independent enterprises. (D'Souza 1995, 477)

The origins of this breakdown, he insists, are to be sought in "deficiencies not of biology but of culture" (486). For D'Souza, "black culture . . .

has a vicious, self-defeating and repellent underside that it is no longer possible to ignore or euphemize" (486). As proof of this self-defeating culture he cites the obscene lyrics of rap tunes by 2 Live Crew and quotes tales of sensational criminal behavior from the trashy biographies of notorious gang members. According to D'Souza, these "black pathologies which are so flagrant that no one can ignore them" (480) in turn justify most, if not all, white discrimination against blacks. Discrimination against African Americans in hiring, housing markets, and even the criminal justice system is, he argues, basically rational. As an example, he cites fear of black youth occupying urban space. "Everyone knows," he argues, "that young blacks are convicted of a high percentage of violent crimes, and since most Americans are highly risk-averse to crime, they have good reason to take precautions and exercise prudence" (261). Discrimination against young black men in America can only be eliminated by "getting rid of the destructive conduct of the group that forms the basis for statistically valid group distinctions" (287). Legally banning racial discrimination has proven futile, he concludes, and has encouraged members of the black underclass to adopt a "victim" mentality. He is particularly critical of the civil rights establishment "which now has a vested interest in the persistence of the ghetto, because the miseries of poor blacks are the best advertisement for continuing programs of racial preferences and set-asides" (554).

To encourage the underclass to shape up, and to force African Americans to come to grips with their "failures," D'Souza recommends that racial discrimination be made legal once more and specifically calls for the repeal of the Civil Rights Act of 1964 (544). Nowhere in the book does D' Souza grapple with the enormous body of systematic evidence that racial discrimination and other forms of white racism continue to limit the life chances of African Americans and specifically contribute to the perpetuation of the ghetto (see Lipsitz 1998). Though its publication was greeted with a firestorm of criticism, and though two well-known black conservatives considered its conclusions so patently offensive they cut off their relationships with the American Enterprise Institute as a result, the book became an instant bestseller and was reviewed in the *New York Times,* the *Wall Street Journal,* and the *New York Review of Books* (Rorty 1995; McGowan 1995; Fredrickson 1995).

Though not as well known outside conservative circles as D'Souza and Himmelfarb's works, Myron Magnet's book *The Dream and the Nightmare* (1993)—a work admired by former GOP Speaker of the House Newt Gingrich and President G. W. Bush, among others (see Scott 1997; Mitchell 2000)—also traces the problems of the contemporary American urban scene back to the defective values and pathological culture of the urban underclass. A former writer for *Fortune* magazine and editor of the Manhattan Institute's *City Journal,* Magnet focused explicitly in his book on the way in which the emergence of the underclass has transformed "the basic texture of today's American cities" (13) and offered the reader shocking descriptions of inner-city squalor and depravity that would not have appeared out of place in a nineteenth-century account of life in "slumland." "[I]n late twentieth-century American cities," he writes, "increased crime spawned by the underclass surely represents a step backward in the development of civilization" (51). Already in his introduction, he paints a picture of the postindustrial metropolis riven by "daily juxtapositions . . . so bizarre that they strain belief, however numbingly familiar they grow":

> In New York City, directly under the windows of the treasure-crammed five-million-dollar apartments that loom over glittering Fifth Avenue, for instance, sleep homeless, one and sometimes two to a park bench, haggard, usually ill, huddled in rags turned dead grey with dirt and wear. In a gentrified neighborhood across town, bustling with upper-middle-class professionals, only the thickness of brick separates a building where staid burghers have paid upwards of three quarters of a million dollars for an apartment from the squalid crack house next door. (13)

Such imagery in the work of socialists like Fredrick Engels, Jack London, or Upton Sinclair typically sets up and provides rhetorical warrants for a condemnation of capitalist society and its manifest inhumanity; in the passage above, the portrait of social contrasts is but a prelude to the condemnation of capitalism's victims.

In chronicling the "poverty and vice that pervade America's cities" (14), Magnet repeatedly seizes on and holds up the most violent and depraved street criminals as "typical" members of the underclass. Thus, he cites as "representative" of the underclass "Preston Simmons of the Bronx, known as Little Man. He rises above anonymity because he was blasted away on Thanksgiving Day 1989, by eleven bullets from a nine-millimeter automatic pistol. His age: fourteen" (40). In the portrait of Little Man that follows we learn that he was the fourth of seven "illegitimate" children, that his mother has been on welfare for two decades, that he lived in a public housing project, that he had trouble in school, that he was a drug dealer, and that he had already at the tender age of fourteen impregnated his seventeen-year-old girlfriend. However, nothing Magnet tells us humanizes Little Man or provides any grounds for empathy with his tragic plight. This tendency to demonize the underclass is carried even further in his repeated discussions of the 1989 rape of a jogger by six black youths in New York's Central Park. Again and again in *The Dream and the Nightmare*, Magnet returns to this incident as symptomatic of all that is dysfunctional about inner-city culture. The youths, he argues, "went wrong with a characteristic underclass ferocity and lack of restraint. Mischief for them wasn't hooky or drinking beer but, if the allegations are true, terrorizing their neighbors and vandalizing their homes. 'Wilding' played a big enough part in their lives, and in their culture, to require a special name" (70–71). Whether meditating on black plastic garbage bags "slashed open [by scavenging homeless people], their contents wildly strewn all over the pavement in a sickening riot of rot and disorder" (77) or discussing "welfare's unwholesome world, where young women grow middle-aged as wards of the state" (136), Magnet constructs a thoroughly nightmarish and utterly stereotypical picture of the postindustrial metropolis as a place made repugnant and unlivable by the presence of the poor and the homeless.

While Magnet's depictions of underclass pathology and street violence are certainly chilling, they are hardly novel. Similar portrayals permeate scholarly and mainstream representations of the urban crisis. However, Magnet's account of the sources of this crisis adds an interesting twist to standard complaints about the "culture of poverty": he insists that the urban poor are as much victims of the culture of wealthy liberals—the culture of the "Haves"—as they are victims of their own self-destructiveness. Specifically, he faults the middle-class cultural revolution of the 1960s for encouraging irresponsible behavior patterns—sexual promiscuity, disdain for bourgeois respectability, moral permissiveness, tolerance of drug use—that are allegedly fatal for the poor. "Poverty turned pathological," he argues, "because the new culture invented by the Haves . . . permitted, even celebrated, behavior that when poor people practice it, will imprison them inextricably in poverty" (19). A permissive, middle- and upper-class culture descended from the '60s, allegedly emphasizing personal liberation and indulgence of even the most antisocial impulses, becomes the catch-all explanation for the most disturbing aspects of the contemporary metropolis.[4]

Thus, Magnet explains the Central Park "Wilding" case by arguing that "[w]hen, doubtless following a leader gripped by a psychopathology beyond class or culture, they went crazily, catastrophically wrong, nothing in their culture pulled them up short at some intermediate atrocity instead of letting them go all the way to gang rape" (71). He goes on to suggest that "[w]hen crime flourishes as it now does in our cities, especially crime of mindless malice, it isn't because society has so oppressed people as to bend them out of their true nature and twist them into moral deformity. It is because the criminals haven't been adequately socialized" (158). He sees this failure of socialization as the fault of the morally lax culture of the '60s. Similarly, he explains the problem of homelessness by tracing it back to the de-institutionalization of the mentally ill in the 1980s and then argues that "the whole de-institutionalization debacle . . . was the direct expression of key ideas of the cultural revolution of the Haves," a revolution in which "madness came to stand as a metaphor for the whole instinctive, impulsive, irrational inner life which the Haves sought to liberate in themselves" (82). If unemployment in the urban core is high, he argues, then it is because "the culture of the Haves" taught "the children of upright black workers" to spurn their parents' work ethic as "a badge of servility and inferiority" (142).

Indeed, Magnet's fixation on cultural causes of socioeconomic "failure" is so great that he goes out of his way to repudiate Charles Murray's analysis of the urban crisis in *Losing Ground*, with its emphasis on the economic rationality of the poor and the "incentives to fail" built into the welfare system. Welfare's economic incentives to misbehave, Magnet argues, simply cannot explain the extreme pathology of the underclass. Interestingly, though, he traces the origins of the urban crisis back to the same period as Murray and roughly the same root cause: the social movements of the 1960s and the social policy changes they wrought. And many of his policy prescriptions parallel Murray's prescriptions for rooting out the inner-city's social malignancy. The United States has made, he argues "a Herculean effort to rescue the worst-off" and it has only made things worse. Thus, he concludes in Murray-esque fashion, we should "[s]top the current welfare system, stop quota-based affirmative action, stop treating criminals as justified rebels, stop letting bums expropriate public space or wrongdoers live in public housing at public expense, stop Afrocentric education in the schools" (225). In other words, roll back many of the significant social gains achieved by the civil rights, feminist, prisoner's rights, and poor people's movements, all in the name of making cities more habitable.

The Ideological Uses of the Underclass

> [U]nderclass thinking draws its force from its fundamental
> dehumanization and retrograde, ideological quarantining of
> inner-city poor people.
>
> —Adolph Reed Jr., "The Underclass as Myth and Symbol"

To say that the central ideological function of the concept of the underclass in the '80s and '90s was to justify the right's attack on social programs for the urban poor is to state the glaringly obvious. That purpose is, after all, made transparently clear in *Losing Ground*, *The Dream and the Nightmare*, *The End of Racism*, and just about every other right-wing polemic published on the subject. As Herbert Gans has noted, "the undeserving poor can be used to justify attacks on the welfare state, which makes them politically useful, directly and indirectly to conservatives" (Gans 1995, 99). The unsavory image of chaotic and depraved inner-city populations addicted to charity performs essentially the same function as it did in the nineteenth century: to discredit all but the stingiest forms of aid to the poor.

Nor is it a mystery why conservatives and the powerful economic interests they are aligned with would want the most minimal welfare system possible. As Frances Fox Piven and Richard Cloward have demonstrated, the chief reason welfare programs like the old Aid to Families with Dependent Children (now renamed Temporary Assistance for Needy Families) and Social Security exist is to regulate and manage the labor force (Piven and Cloward 1971). Historically, welfare in the United States has expanded and become more generous when unemployment and poverty are high and the disgruntled poor threaten to disrupt the smooth functioning of the economy; once order is restored, it tends to contract, denying applicants benefits and forcing them back onto the tender mercies of the labor market (xv). An expanded and generous welfare system is a boon to workers because it gives them an alternative (however unappealing) to competing with one another for jobs that can be accepted only on the employer's terms. In Piven and Cloward's formulation:

> [T]he unemployed constitute a reserve army of labor to be used by capitalists to weaken and divide the proletariat. Desperation pits the unemployed against the still-employed, thus weakening labor's bargaining power. But income security programs reduce unemployment and temper desperation. They remove millions of people from the labor market and protect millions of others from the ravages of unemployment. The consequence is to tighten labor markets and reduce fear among those still in the market and thus to strengthen workers in bargaining with employers over wages and working conditions. (Piven and Cloward 1996, 76)

So, in justifying cuts to welfare and other forms of government aid to the poor, the victim-blaming discourse on the urban crisis effectively advances capitalist class interests in keeping workers thoroughly subordinated and disciplined. The assault on the underclass and on the welfare system that one sees in the discourse on the postindustrial city should be understood in part as intellectual cover for a campaign to raise profit margins by expanding the reserve army of labor and depressing wages, a campaign that was enormously successful in the '80s and '90s. Of course, business has other reasons for favoring cuts to big government social programs: decreased social spending often translates into lower corporate taxes (and hence greater net profits). Moreover, the real estate industry approves of slashing funds for public housing programs because it means less competition for them. Discrediting "big government" and "big spending liberalism" as responses to the dilemmas facing American cities thus has multiple direct benefits for the powerful interests affiliated with the right.

But the ideological significance of the discourse on the underclass goes well beyond advancing the political and economic establishment's narrow interest in slashing welfare. Another function it performs is to reconcile the fact of rampant inner-city poverty, decay, and squalor with the seemingly incompatible idea that American capitalism is the most free, most egalitarian, and most just political and economic system history has ever known; that is, it demonstrates (or aims to demonstrate) that the existence of the postindustrial ghetto *does not undermine or invalidate* the status quo's claim to political and moral legitimacy. That deteriorating social conditions in the city could undermine that claim is an ever-present possibility. Over a hundred and fifty years ago, in the *Communist Manifesto*, Marx and Engels suggested that the "pauperization" of the working class would eventually "de-legitimate" bourgeois rule. "The modern laborer," Marx and Engels write, ". . . becomes a pauper, and pauperism develops more rapidly than population and wealth. And here it becomes evident that the bourgeoisie is unfit any longer to be the ruling class in society" (Marx and Engels 1998, 49–50). As the litany of urban social ills presented in chapter 1 shows, the basic contradiction between the wealth of the bourgeoisie and the "pauperism" of the city-dwelling working class is no less compelling today.

The conservative discourse that frames the underclass as the root cause of the urban crisis works to contain this contradiction by portraying the poverty, unemployment, and crime of the inner city and the ruination of the metropolis in general as essentially inevitable and incorrigible. In other words, it "naturalizes" present social relations and trends, making "social relations appear to have the fixed and immutable character of natural laws" (Giddens 1979, 195). This is certainly the general thrust of a book like *The Bell Curve*, which quite literally naturalizes inner-city, black poverty by treating it as a product of genetically inherited IQ. But more generally, the discourse on the urban crisis works to naturalize ghetto crime, poverty, and joblessness by framing such problems as essentially immune to government or collective action. For instance, Murray, Himmelfarb, D'Souza, and Magnet all echo classical liberal Thomas Malthus in treating poverty as constituting "a separate 'natural' condition. People are poor because they are degenerate. . . . As such, poverty is beyond institutional redress" (Smith 1990, 215). As Ruth Smith argues, the legitimacy of capitalism (or, as she calls it, "liberal society") requires that the contradiction between the smooth operating of the market and the want of the poor be erased; and to do that, the system's apologists attribute to its victims a "disorderly nature" that prevents them from realizing the benefits of participation in the free market (225). What else is the theory of the underclass but a theory about the *disorderly nature* of the ghetto poor?

An equally important operation performed by the copious right-wing commentary on the underclass is to reinforce the central underlying premises of the nation's dominant ideology, that constellation of "ruling ideas" that—as Marx and Engels point out—"are in every epoch the ideas of the ruling classes" (Marx and Engels 1998, 67). In the United States, this ruling ideology revolves around individualism and a neoliberal cult of the free market, on the one hand, and the normativity of the white, heterosexual, patriarchal family, on the other. The core beliefs of the individualist, neoliberal strand of this outlook are plain enough: the idea that that government governs best that governs least, disdain for civic organizations and the public realm, belief in the near sacredness of private property, antagonism toward any restrictions on the workings of the "free market," the equation of freedom with the freedom to buy and sell, elevation of the individual and individual rights over society and collective obligations, shameless consumerism, celebration of the Protestant "work ethic" (in theory if not in practice), and a Horatio Algeresque faith in America as a meritocratic "land of opportunity." They comprise, in short, that set of beliefs that Robert Bellah and his colleagues studied in *Habits of the Heart* (1985), that Herbert Gans dissected in *Middle American Individualism* (1988), and that Barbara Ehrenreich essayed in *Fear of Falling* (1989) (see also Frank 2000). Often, this extreme individualism and free market fundamentalism is coupled with a sentimental, almost maudlin veneration of the white, patriarchal nuclear family—one in which men are breadwinners and women are confined to the home—as the bedrock of American social life and the model against which to measure all other familial arrangements; paradoxically, this remains the case even today, when the great majority of U.S. families, even the great majority of politically conservative U.S. families, emphatically do not match the ideological norm.

In any case, it is easy to see how the right-wing discourse on the urban underclass works to bolster both main strands of the nation's ruling ideology. Murray, Magnet, and other right-wing commentators on the inner-city's problems offer an endless series of arguments in favor of less government, the free market, and individual effort as the solution to all social afflictions. Their portrayal of the urban poor as shiftless and lazy implies that the suburban and affluent are the opposite—responsible and hard-working; presenting urban decline and the plight of the inner-city residents as self-inflicted reinforces "individualism." "If the poor can be imagined to be lazy" writes Herbert Gans, "they help reaffirm the 'Protestant work ethic'" (Gans 1995, 96). At the same time, commentators like Murray, Himmelfarb, and Blankenhorn harken back nostalgically to the allegedly endangered nuclear family as the foundation of what they imagine were the safer, more orderly cities of the 1940s and '50s.[5] The hysterical rhetoric that pervades the right's analysis of the underclass family and the fears such demagoguery evokes are predicated on the valorization of the male-headed nuclear family as a "haven in a heartless world," a privileged zone of safety divorced from the menacing city. This characterization of the so-called traditional family has always been, to a significant degree, a patriarchal fiction (Coontz 1992; Stacey 1995; Cloud 1998), yet by framing the family arrangements of the urban poor as somehow deviant the fiction can be preserved and perpetuated.

Another important ideological feature of the discourse on the underclass (and one related to its reinforcement of atomistic individualism) is the way it mystifies the structural political-economic dynamics behind inner-city poverty, teen pregnancy, and urban decline by blaming these phenomena on the defective morals and pathological behavior of the urban poor themselves. The squalor and disorder of the central cities is presented not as an effect of the "free market" but as a dysfunction of the individuals living there. As Kofi Hadjor has pointed out with regard to the underclass debate, "[a] central attraction of the 'underclass' concept from the conservative point of view is that it separates poverty from its social causes" (Hadjor 1995, 147). The prevailing discourse on the misery of the cities either obscures or downplays deindustrialization as a factor driving urban economic dislocation and black family breakdown. And it does the same with nearly every other structural social or economic cause of the urban crisis: it fails to acknowledge the proliferation of temporary, low-wage work (and the disappearance of living-wage jobs) that has accompanied the rise of the service sector economy in most major cities; it ignores the past and continued red-lining of inner-city neighborhoods by banks, federal mortgage programs, and insurance companies that restricts the urban poor's access to capital for business and denies them loans to buy homes; it refuses to acknowledge the gross disparity in funding between urban and suburban school districts that consigns inner-city kids to second- and third-class educations; it diverts attention from the housing industry's failure to provide affordable housing (especially in inner cities) and from government policies that allow central-city roads and mass transit systems to rot.

By focusing on the aberrant behavior and pathological culture of a small (and unrepresentative) group of inner-city blacks to the exclusion of the structural causes of urban poverty and disorder, the right's discourse effectively redefines systemic social problems—poverty, inner-city decay, rampant drug abuse, teen pregnancy, etc.—as problems of individual immorality. As Herbert Gans has explained, the logical implication of the dominant view of inner-city hardship is that "if people were without the moral and other deficiencies that make them poor, there might be no poverty; and if the jobless were not lazy there would be virtually no unemployment" (Gans 1995, 91). That this sort of explanation fails to explain dramatic increases in joblessness like those experienced in this country during the Great Depression should be obvious. No sane person would attempt to explain the worldwide depression of the 1930s by reference to a sudden explosion in "bad values," a rise in the number of broken families, or a sudden, cataclysmic drop-off in the "work ethic." Yet this is precisely how the increasing poverty and joblessness of American cities suffering deindustrialization and federal divestment have been theorized by proponents of the underclass theory.

Incidentally, this willful ignorance of structural economic realities extends to the right's understanding of middle-class privilege as well. Though they are forever comparing the urban underclass unfavorably to an implicitly suburban middle America, writers like Murray and Magnet somehow manage to overlook the considerable structural advantages underwriting the suburbanite's comfortable lifestyle: the tax dollars funding suburban roads and highways; their government-backed mortgages; the mortgage interest deduction that lowers their income taxes; their well-funded school districts; the federal money subsidizing suburban economic development, and so on. Indeed, according to one estimate, "in 1991, about half of all federal entitlements went to households with incomes over $30,000" (Males 1995, 14). As critic Dana Cloud points out in her analysis of the right's "family values" rhetoric, one key motive for their personalizing of the causes of material success and failure is "the privatization of social experience and responsibility" which dislocates "collective, political anxiety, discussion and action into less threatening, private venues" (Cloud 1998, 411). This privatization in turn imposes severe limits on the sorts of antipoverty measures that can be considered as plausible or within the realm of possibility, effectively confining policy discussions "to the problem of welfare rather the problems of political economy and work" (O'Connor 2001, 15). American capitalism and American society as a whole are thus absolved of any responsibility for the collapse of downtown economies, the blighting of inner-city neighborhoods, and the joblessness confronting the urban working class; in the ideological illogic of the discourse, these dismal socio-economic trends can only be reversed if their victims straighten up and take personal responsibility for themselves and their communities.

Finally, in keeping with the implicit idealism of mainstream American ideology, the dominant discourse on the urban poor in the '80s and '90s assumed that "most behavior is caused by the holding and practicing of values, with good behavior resulting from good values and bad behavior from bad values" (Gans 1995, 83). Thus, the imagined or observed misbehavior of the underclass is said to be the result of "hedonistic, 1960s values," "moral poverty," or some other moral/spiritual defect. Yet, as a matter of fact, the values of the urban poor are not all that different from those of more middle-class Americans. Take the issue of the underclass's supposed lack of family values. As Stephanie Coontz explains, "black women overwhelmingly report a preference for raising children in a two-parent family," a fact that reveals "the description of the ghetto as an alien nation, with totally different family values" to be "a gross exaggeration"(Coontz 1992, 248). Or take the poor's willingness to work. If one counts off-the-books employment, nearly half of all welfare recipients (who are, remember, virtually all women with young children) work, hardly evidence of chronic laziness (Gans 1995, 70). Locating the origins of social ills in the flawed values of degenerate individuals, especially when such values are not observed but merely deduced from overt behaviors, bolsters the idealist illusion that the "realm of consciousness" (values, ideas, morals, etc.) determines people's concrete historical existence rather than vice versa. Indeed, this general ideological impact of the concept of the underclass is inseparable from its other, more specific political and ideological purposes.

A "Criminogenic" Environment: The Inner City as Hobbesian State-of-Nature

America is a ticking crime bomb.

—William Bennett, John DiIulio, and John Walters,
Body Count (1996)

The conservative discourse on the underclass and the urban crisis, then, performed a number of functions for the right in the '80s and '90s: it mystified the sources of our most pressing urban problems, naturalized the misery of the inner city, and legitimated racist attacks on welfare and aid to the poor. But in many ways more significant than any of this was the fact that the right's discourse (quite consciously) promoted the terrifying figment of city neighborhoods ruled by armies of bloodthirsty criminals, a specter that, in turn, was used to justify a draconian police crackdown on "urban lawlessness" that helped to criminalize an entire generation of urban youth. Nowhere is the relationship between underclass theorizing and the promotion of law-and-order politics more evident than in the work of leading Republican ideologue William Bennett.

Like Charles Murray, William Bennett spent the better part of the '80s and '90s championing the idea that the troubles of the postindustrial city were caused by the decline of "traditional values" and "traditional culture." Secretary of Education under Reagan, drug czar (head of the Office on National Drug Control Policy) under George Bush, Sr., and co-director of Empower America (a think tank that supplies rightwing policy expertise to the Republican party), Bennett has been as shrill and alarmist in his descriptions of inner-city pathologies and the dangers they pose to the suburban middle class as Murray; unlike Murray, though, Bennett enjoyed for some years the "bully pulpit" of high-profile cabinet posts from which to declaim his views. A close friend of Irving Kristol's and his wife Gertrude Himmelfarb, a Ph.D. in philosophy as well as a lawyer, Bennett served as chairman of the National Endowment for the Humanities during Reagan's first term where he distinguished himself by attacking an NEH-funded documentary about Nicaragua as "unabashed socialist-realist propaganda" and denouncing any NEH project with liberal overtones. As secretary of education, he promoted the idea that retreat from time-honored standards was responsible for an alleged decline in American student performance and championed a "back to basics" movement. By the time he was appointed drug czar in late 1988, "Bennett had come to see the nation as engaged in a culture war pitting the liberal elite against the American people. And that war was being fought not just in education but among a broad array of issues facing the nation, including the family, race, and drugs" (Massig 1998, 197). As we shall see, Bennett saw the hollowed-out center of America's large metropolitan areas as a prime symbolic battlefield in this war. His position as "drug czar" gave him an ideal platform from which to preach his view that, as Michael Massig puts it, "the crack and cocaine epidemics were not a public-health crisis but a moral one, traceable back to the counterculture and its nose-thumbing attitude toward authority" (198). Despite mounting evidence to the contrary, Bennett insisted that the drug war could only be won through stricter law enforcement, increased spending on "interdiction" of smuggled drugs, and a policy of "zero tolerance" toward drug use, not through government-funded addiction treatment programs.

Leaving the position of drug czar after a mere nineteen months on the job, Bennett went on to delineate his theories about the country's moral crisis—and in particular about "the American nightmare" of the inner-city drug epidemic—in a series of books written during the 1990s (while at the same time maintaining a lucrative career as public speaker). His 1993 bestseller, *The Index of Leading Cultural Indicators*, is essentially a compendium of data on nineteen social issues, including crime, out-of-wedlock births, drug use, and divorce. All of this data purport to show problems like illegitimacy have risen as a result of increased social spending on the part of government. To deal with our "cultural crisis," Bennett recommends inculcating the values of personal responsibility in our children and (as with Murray et al.) slashing most government spending on poverty relief. His self-aggrandizing memoir of his years serving in various Republican administrations, *The De-Valuing of America* (1992), regaled readers with tales from the frontlines of the culture wars, describing Bennett's visits to public housing projects, crumbling urban schools, and street corners. A typical battle story is the one he tells about "three hours spent with the police in downtown Detroit":

> I thought it important to see what happens when drugs take control of an area, so I had the police take me to a neighborhood where the police said drug abuse involved more than a third of residents. I went to housing projects that had deteriorated badly after becoming havens for crack dealers. We drove around corners and the police captain told me to look at a window to spot a "lookout" before he ducked his head down. We saw crack houses and small groups of young men on corners quickly disperse as we came near them. (Bennett 1992, 105)

The lessons he derives from this tour are characteristically sweeping and demagogic. What he had witnessed, Bennett writes, is "parts of an inner city resembling what the philosopher Thomas Hobbes described as 'the state of nature,' where life is 'solitary, poor, nasty, brutish and short'" (105).

As anyone who has read *Leviathan* knows, Hobbes introduces the concept of the state of nature in order to justify the need for a sovereign who is vested with unlimited and unquestioned power; only if the members of civilized society submit themselves entirely to such absolute power, Hobbes thinks, can the anarchy of the state of nature be avoided. Despite his well-documented hostility to government spending on welfare and social programs, Bennett nevertheless clearly believes that the inner city *qua* state of nature requires a Hobbesian application of authoritarian state power to set it right. Arguing that "the underclass problem is mainly a crime problem," Bennett proposes that what the underclass needs above all is "tougher laws, more cops, more courts, more prosecutors, and more jails and prisons" (193). Violent, inner-city street crime, Bennett came to believe, was the source not just of the misery of the ghetto underclass but of many problems of the surrounding city and of public life in general.

It is not surprising, then, that since the mid-1990s Bennett has devoted much of his attention to the issue of street crime. Together with criminologist John DiIulio, he championed the notion that the root cause of the violent crime and drug abuse that plague our cities is not racial oppression or economic deprivation but rather what they call "moral poverty." By "moral poverty" they mean "the poverty of being without loving, capable, responsible adults who teach the young right from wrong" (Bennett et al. 1996, 13). And, the argument goes, the source of this sort of poverty is not lack of income or jobs but rather "the enfeebled condition—in some places in our society, the near collapse—of our character-forming institutions" such as churches, families, and schools (196). In their book *Body Count: Moral Poverty and How to Win America's War Against Crime and Drugs* (co-authored with John P. Walters, one of Bennett's staffers at the ONDCP and George W. Bush's pick for drug czar), Bennett and DiIulio contend that this moral poverty has transformed many low-income urban neighborhoods into "criminogenic" environments, "places where the social forces that create predatory criminals are far more numerous and stronger than the social forces that create decent, law-abiding citizens" (28). In their view, criminogenic neighborhoods throughout America's cities are breeding "thickening ranks of 'superpredators' . . . radically impulsive, brutally remorseless youngsters, including ever more preteenage boys, who murder, assault, rob, burglarize, deal deadly drugs, join gun-toting gangs, and create serious communal disorders" (27).[6] Throughout the reams of crime statistics and disquistitions on how to interpret them that make up the bulk of *Body Count*, the authors intersperse titillating tale after titillating tale of urban mayhem and ruthless violence perpetrated by their "superpredators." For instance, they tell the story of one Willie Bosket who assaulted a nurse in a state reformatory at age nine, "was shooting and robbing New York subway passengers" by age fifteen, killed two men, and committed twenty-five stabbings before being locked away for life (61–62).

In order to sell such spurious notions as "criminogenic environments" and "superpredators," Bennett and company must first establish a connection between moral poverty and crime. To do this, they rely not on direct observation (i.e., of the process by which such environments "produce" such criminals) but on vague statistical correlations between, for example, increases in the number of single-parent families and rising crime rates. Thus, they try to explain the difference in measured crime rates between whites and African Americans by pointing out that "black and white differences in crime rates have their mirror images in black-white differences in child abuse and neglect, out-of-wedlock births, and other factors which reduce the likelihood that a child will grow up under the guiding, restraining, civilizing influence of decent, nurturing, loving and law-abiding adults" (78). At the same time, the authors attempt to refute the long-noted connection between economic deprivation and crime, as indeed they must if they are to show that flawed moral character and not material want is the main determinant of criminal behavior; while acknowledging that "objective material circumstances do play a role under some conditions," they maintain that "each of many different types of criminal behavior has many possible 'root causes'" (42). But Bennett and company are fudging here and I suspect they know it: when discussing the far more speculative role of "moral poverty" in generating criminal behavior, they conveniently dispense with such qualifying language.

They bolster their empirical arguments with what should be seen as a series of shameless appeals to the "moral common sense" of a media-saturated middle class. Thus, in one striking passage, they directly flatter suburbanite hostility toward the city when they write that "[i]t is true enough that our modern-day 'tangle of pathologies' is concentrated in urban centers and inner cities. That is where the fires burn hottest, where moral poverty is most pronounced, where the pathologies are most obvious, most intense, most intractable" (199). Later, they point directly to the hysterical manifestations of the moral panic over the city as proof that drastic countermeasures must be taken:

> [M]ore and more Americans worry that the social wheels are coming off. The rising body count, the daily atrocity stories, the mounting social science evidence, the horrifying signs of urban decay all around us have seared a deep impression upon the public imagination. The common

citizenry knows that great chunks of America are in the midst of serious moral decline. (200)

Given the weakness of the correlations they cite, what the "common citizenry knows"—thanks largely to the misleading and blood-soaked images of the city circulating through our mainstream media—becomes the ultimate foundation of *Body Count*'s argument.

When Bennett, DiIulio, and Walters turn their attention to the question of how to deal with the growing legions of superpredators allegedly emerging from the inner cities, they opt for predictably authoritarian, strong-arm measures. Essentially what is needed, they argue, is more (and more punitive) law enforcement: "incarceration for violent and repeat criminals, more community-based cops, an end to revolving-door policies, and deference to public safety and victims' rights over prisoners' rights" (136). Moreover, they embrace the idea, first proposed by James Q. Wilson and George Kelling, that the proliferation of minor crimes like graffiti, prostitution, and public drinking in a particular neighborhood serve as an invitation to "incivility, disorder and crime" (72). This theory, often called the "broken window" theory of crime, suggests that the best way to stop outbreaks of serious crime is to consistently prosecute minor ones. The example of this strategy in action that Bennett and company point to most often is that deployed in New York City by Mayor Rudolph Giuliani and his then-police chief William Bratton. Under Bratton's guidance, the New York Police Department "took enforcing the laws against 'minor' crimes and disorders more seriously" and the city enjoyed several years of declining crime rates. In their celebratory discussion of "zero tolerance" approaches to minor crime and quality of life policing, there is hardly a mention of abuse of police power or violation of the civil rights that could result from such policies. According to Bennett and his colleagues, Giuliani-esque anti-crime strategies not only reduce street violence but "can also restore order, civility and beauty to the public square" (16). The question of course is whether the price of such "order, civility and beauty" is deepening racial division, growing economic injustice, and ever more ruthless police-administered oppression.

This was a question that clearly did not occur to the innumerable commentators, pundits, and policy researchers who jumped with Bennett onto the law-and-order bandwagon in the '90s. From wonkish publications like *City Journal* to middle-brow magazines like *Newsweek* and *U.S. News and World Report*, the conventional wisdom shared *Body Count*'s terrified appraisal of juvenile street crime and admiration for no-holds-barred policing. *City Journal*, for instance, published an essay co-written by New York City police chief William Bratton himself in which he congratulates the city's "zero tolerance" scheme for "transforming the subway from a place where young thugs thought they could get away with anything to a place where they felt like they could get away with nothing" (Bratton and Andrews 2000, 75). It also carried a piece by Heather MacDonald arguing that if instead of "stigmatizing the police" Al Sharpton and other critics of NYPD's brutalization of racial minorities "spent half their lung and media power on stigmatizing criminals, and the other half on helping young people compete in the job market, they could transform the city" (MacDonald 2000, 233–34). Columnists and commentators in the mainstream press, meanwhile, fixated on the concept of the savage urban "superpredator." In the pages of *U.S. News and World Report*, columnist John Leo proclaimed that many inner-city communities were "besieged" by lawless youths whose parents refused to control them (Leo 1995, 18). Susan Estrich cautioned readers of her May 9, 1996, *USA Today* column that "the tsunami is coming. . . . [j]uvenile crime is going up and getting worse" (Estrich 1996, 15A). At the same time, prestigious newspapers like the *New York Times* and the *Wall Street Journal* handed over an enormous amount of space on their op-ed pages to promoters of the superpredator scare. John DiIulio's opinion pieces, for instance, appeared thirteen times in the pages of the *Wall Street Journal* between 1994 and 1997. One July 31, 1996, commentary by DiIulio that appeared in the *New York Times* proclaimed that "the nation's juvenile crime problem is grave and growing" and suggested that Americans were right to fear becoming the victims of "youngsters who afterward show us the blank stare of a feral, presocial being" (DiIulio 1996, A15). Such rhetoric was, in turn, replicated by law enforcement officials and local politicians whose endorsement of the "superpredator" theory lent it even greater credibility. Thus, to take just one example, a January 15, 1996, *Newsweek* cover story, "Superpredators Arrive," quoted Chicago-area prosecutor Jack O'Malley bemoaning the fact that "[w]e've become a nation being terrorized by its children" (Annin 1996, 57). The echoes of Bennett and DiIulio in such a statement are impossible to avoid.

As an ideology serving the interests of the right-leaning Clinton-era status quo, the moral poverty/superpredator theory complemented the underclass theory nicely. Just as the concept of the underclass naturalizes worsening inner-city poverty and legitimates public divestment from the urban centers, the idea of moral poverty inexorably producing supercriminals sanctions the law-and-order crackdown on disadvantaged urban communities rendered ungovernable by the destruction of the welfare state. The economic restructuring of the 1980s and '90s—and the ensuing impoverishment of the black and brown urban populations—sparked increasing rage and discontent among those on the receiving end of the devastation. This rage bubbled to the surface on occasions like the so-called Rodney King riots in Los Angeles in 1992, which, as Omi and Winant characterize it, "represented an act of defiance, a somewhat desperate effort to respond to the impoverishment, not only of the ghetto poor but of U.S. society as a whole" (Omi and Winant 1993, 100). The rebelliousness of the socially disadvantaged poses a dilemma for elites: they can respond to it either by providing jobs and aid to the poor (the liberal, New Deal solution) or they can deploy greater levels of police repression (the strategy advocated by William Bennett et al.). Clearly, since 1980 at least, the second type of response has emerged as the preferred one. As Christian Parenti explains, the "emerging anti-crime police state . . . is the form of class control currently preferred by elites because it does not entail the dangerous side-effects of empowerment associated with the co-operative welfare model. The criminal justice crackdown, and its attendant culture of fear, absorbs the dangerous classes without politically or economically empowering them" (Parenti 1999, 241). Images of downtown "criminogenic environments" overrun by "superpredators" and "wilding youth" have helped secure middle-class support for the rising anti-crime police state. In the discourse on the urban underclass, "[c]riminality is spatialized . . . it is identified with certain kinds of social presence in the urban landscape. . . . Urban decline, street crime, and 'signs of disorder'—the sign together with the deeper swell of historical change—are here galvanized into a single malady" (Smith 1998, 3). And during the 1980s and '90s, politicians at all levels of government became expert at brandishing the malady known as the "criminal underclass" to scare the respectable public into line behind their repressive schemes.[7]

Thus, to take an example that will be discussed further below, middle-class fears of an out-of-control city propelled tough-talking former prosecutor Rudy Giuliani into the New York City mayor's office in 1994. Once in power, and informed by the "broken window" theory of crime discussed above, Giuliani instituted a policy of "zero tolerance" toward lifestyle crimes such as panhandling, public drunkenness, and graffiti writing. In practice, "zero tolerance" meant aggressive police harassment of homeless people, an intensified drug war directed at poor black youth, and "the dissolution of existing constraints on police power in the name of 'reversing the decline in public order'" (Smith 1998, 4). By expelling droves of poor and homeless people from New York City proper, the campaign enabled broad cuts in legally mandated city services earmarked for the poor, a political benefit for Giuliani. But such tactics had the added benefit of paving the way for selective gentrification of inner-city neighborhoods by cleansing them of masses of "undesirable" low-rent residents (6–7). It also made it possible to reclaim downtown areas—like New York's newly Disneyfied Times Square—for redevelopment as upscale entertainment centers and festive marketplaces catering to middle-class suburbanites and tourists (and, it goes without saying, excluding less-affluent city residents) (McArdle 2001, 8–9). This trend was not just confined to New York City. Cities from Baltimore to San Diego adopted "zero tolerance" and "anti-panhandler" schemes of their own, often in the service of downtown "tourist" development. So in justifying a crackdown on underclass lawlessness, the discourse on the urban crisis also indirectly served the interests of real estate developers.

The Fruits of "Dependent Individualism":
Blaming Liberalism for the Urban Crisis

If there is a unifying thread running through the right's various inter-pretations of the nation's urban problems, it is the notion that liberal social policies (often labeled simply "sixties liberalism") either directly or indirectly caused the decay, immorality, and violence allegedly con-suming our cities. Smearing the left as somehow responsible for the "mess" in America's cities was, after all, a fairly explicit aim of Murray and Mag-net's diatribes against welfare and Bennett's lament about the leniency of our criminal justice system. Building on and extending the logic of such polemics, policy wonk Fred Siegel in *The Future Once Happened Here* (1997) used the theme of left culpability for urban failures to explain why three of America's most important cities—Washington, D.C., New York, and Los Angeles—have fallen on hard times. A one-time editor at the social democratic organ *Dissent*, Siegel has since become a columnist at the (right-wing, Rupert Murdoch–owned) *New York Post*, a fellow at the center-right, "New Democrat"–affiliated (and grossly misnamed) Pro-gressive Policy Institute, and a senior policy advisor to Rudolph Giu-liani. Unlike many of the commentators whose voices have influenced the debate surrounding the urban crisis, his identification with and pas-sion for cities and urban culture is evident throughout his book; indeed, he tells us that, despite its many travails, Brooklyn remains his lifelong home. Nevertheless, *The Future Once Happened Here* follows Murray, Ben-nett, and others on the right in blaming liberalism for the decline of the city and the public culture it represents.

Rather than focus exclusively on the consequences of misguided federal government programs, Siegel concentrates on the destructive policy choices purportedly made by municipal governments during the 1960s and after. He argues that big-city politics in the '60s came under the influence of a brand of liberalism that "yoked together an antipathy to economic markets and a faith in a free market in morals" (Siegel 1997, x). This liberalism sprayed "economic regulations into every nook and cranny of the economy" while overturning "traditions of social and self-restraint so as to liberate the individual from conventional mores" (x).

In practice, the new liberalism led to such boondoggles as the explosive expansion of New York City's welfare programs during the late '50s and early '60s under Mayors Robert Wagner and John Lindsey and to the subsequent explosion of its welfare population. It created, Siegel writes, welfare mothers like the one who confronted Lindsey at a public meeting:

> "I've got six kids," the mother shouted, "and each one of them has a dif-
> ferent daddy. It's my job to have kids, and your job, Mr. Mayor, to take care
> of them." The mother was a dependent individualist. Not only was she
> entitled to public support, but she was entitled to that support on her own
> terms. (61)

According to Siegel, the dissemination of this attitude of "dependent individualism" marked the end of the city as an arena of minority assimilation and upward mobility. Instead, the growing popularity of this attitude among African Americans in particular encouraged the growth of a self-destructive, unemployable underclass and "in the name of redressing old injustices that treated African-Americans as less than full citizens, it recreated their second-class standing through liberal paternalism" (61). It also allegedly propelled many middle-class New Yorkers to abandon the city. The policy choices that enabled the ascendancy of this nefarious dependent individualism (and created the overly generous poverty programs underwriting it) were in turn driven, Siegel suggests, by politicians eager to appease the urban black communities that had rioted in Watts, Detroit, and elsewhere during the mid to late '60s. As he sees it, our cities continue to live in the shadow of what he, following historian David Sears, calls "the riot ideology," "the assumption that the violence of the sixties riots and their criminal aftermath were both justified and, to a considerable extent, functional in rectifying the sins of racism" (xii). In essence, Siegel is arguing that the jobs programs, generous welfare benefits, and other social services instituted by liberal municipal governments since the '60s are little more than thinly veiled "protection money" distributed to racial extortionists.

Siegel singles out Washington, D.C., as a particularly telling example of the way in which cities have been shaped by "the upheavals of the 1960s" (67) and, symptomatically, identifies an African American politician—former chair of the Student Nonviolent Coordinating Committee (SNCC) turned mayor Marion Barry—as the leading player in "the disaster of D.C." (66). He sees the 1968 riots that followed the assassination of Martin Luther King, Jr. as the turning point in D.C.'s recent history. "Not only did they hasten the exodus of some of the black and remaining white middle class," Siegel writes, "but they showed that violence and even the threat of violence paid" (67). In the wake of the 1968 upheaval, Barry, then running D.C.'s SNCC office, launched a youth program aimed at instilling discipline and self-respect in juvenile delinquents that attracted the secretary of labor (described in the book as "fearing more riots" [69]). Subsequently, Barry's program grew to include job training and even operated several nonprofit businesses, all of which put money in the pockets of Barry's corrupt associates. Siegel goes out of his way to depict Barry as an opportunist deftly exploiting white liberal fears of urban unrest: "By alternating threats and the promise of defusing those threats through payoffs and deal making, he offered liberals a chance to surrender their old color-blind ideals while keeping both a modicum of dignity and their self-image as progressive people" (71). Throughout his rise from the school board to city council to his post as the city's second elected mayor in 1978, Barry continued to alternately bully and cozy up to white liberals in federal government and in D.C.'s local business establishment.

In power, Siegel charges, Barry slashed funding for the police department and stacked its upper echelons with his favorites. "By the early eighties," Siegel says, "thinking he had the police department in his pocket, Mayor Marion Barry was openly buying drugs and sex" (90). Meanwhile, he allegedly turned the public school system into "an adjunct of the race industry" in order to "provide protected employment for the black middle class" (94). In other words, in the name of civil rights for African Americans, Barry "created a mafia-like atmosphere in D.C." (98) and transformed the place into a "Third World City" (109).

As a consequence, Siegel claims, D.C. is "strained by a social and family breakdown so severe that not even the economic boom . . . experienced in the 1980s could stem a rising crime rate and an accompanying suburban exodus by the black middle class" (96).

This is a partial and highly dubious explanation for D.C.'s problems. True, Barry's corruption (coupled with his long tenure in office) doubtless had something to do with the city's decline. But there are other explanatory factors that Siegel either ignores or gives too little consideration: D.C.'s political disenfranchisement; the fact that Congress limits the District's ability to levy taxes; the decades of racist development policies that encouraged white flight while keeping blacks trapped in the city; the design of the city's public transit system to serve suburban commuters and government employees instead of the majority of ordinary black residents; the impact of union-busting on the city's service sector unions—particularly the heavily black janitors' unions—and the subsequent collapse in wages; even deindustrialization (in a city which, admittedly, had little manufacturing to begin with). In passing, Siegel grants that D.C.'s lack of congressional representation is unfair and should be changed (though he says nothing more about it). Yet he mockingly charges that "the District luxuriates in the fantasy of its victimization" (109) and denies that a commuter tax would have any impact on the financial health of the city. Tellingly, he fails to mention any of the other factors. In fact, the structural economic causes of the urban crisis are consistently downplayed throughout the book; instead, he circles back again and again to the moral failings of the black urban leadership who rose to power in the '60s and to the morally problematic social policy they supposedly ushered in. As Siegel sees it, Marion Barry is behind D.C.'s demise; welfare-rights activists and civil libertarians are to blame for the decline of New York City; and the problems of Los Angeles have been exacerbated (and perhaps even caused) by gangster-loving African American politicians like congressional representative Maxine Waters.

According to Siegel, the takeover of our big urban centers by '60s liberals and their terroristic "riot ideology" has led directly to "the moral deregulation of public space" and middle-class revulsion against the city.

Sometime in the 1980s people started to get scared, very scared, of street crime. However, "[w]hat unnerved most city dwellers," he writes, "was not crime per se but, rather, the sense of menace and disorder that pervaded day-to-day life":

> It was the gang of toughs exacting their daily tribute in the coin of humiliation. It was the "street tax" paid to drunk and drug-ridden panhandlers. It was the "squeegee men" shaking down the motorist waiting for a light. It was the threats and hostile gestures of the mentally ill making their homes in the parks. It was the provocation of pushers and prostitutes plying their trade with impunity. It was the trash storms, the swirling masses of garbage left by peddlers and panhandlers, and the open-air drug bazaars on city streets. These were the visible signs of cities out of control; cities, regardless of their economic health, that couldn't protect either their space or their citizens. (169)

He goes on to talk about homeless men kidnapping babies (185) and crack-addicted vagrants terrorizing women in parts of Manhattan's posh Upper West Side (171). This is all presented as the fault of the social movements of the 1960s that "shattered" the moral authority of traditional American institutions (173). In particular, Siegel attacks the ACLU and the civil rights establishment for defending the homeless and drug dealers against arbitrary harassment by police (188). "An unparalleled set of utopian policies," he argues, "produced the dystopia of day-to-day city life" (172).

The Future Once Happened Here—like Bennett's *Body Count*—culminates in an extended ode to Rudolph Giuliani's "accomplishments" in turning New York City around after his election in 1993. Siegel starts by praising Giuliani for his embrace of the "broken window" theory of crime and for his decision to clamp down on petty "lifestyle crimes" like vandalism. He also praises Giuliani for his "workfare" program that forced welfare recipients to work for benefits, often picking up garbage from city parks and sidewalks. "Workfare has made a real difference in cleaning up city parks and highways," he writes, "this is no small matter, as anyone who has walked New York's often trash-ridden streets knows" (227). Given that Siegel was one of Giuliani's key advisors, such cheer-leading is predictable. Not surprisingly, he sets up Giuliani's zero-tolerance crime-fighting strategy as a general model "for redeeming the cities from the damage wrought by the gambles of the 1960s" (241). And, he insists, something like this is already happening: "[b]roadly speaking, city governments are moving from redistribution to economic growth; from social services to private sector jobs; from a belief that poverty causes crime to the reverse; and, in general, from reliance on government to attempts to revive markets" (240). Urban liberalism, Siegel concluded, is dead or at least dying and it is a good thing, too.

The notion that urban liberalism had been a colossal failure be-came an article of faith among up-and-coming politicians in the 1990s. During the decade, a new breed of budget-slashing, police-boosting neo-conservative mayors took office in big cities around the country: John Norquist in Milwaukee, Stephen Goldsmith in Indianapolis, Ed Rendell in Philadelphia, Richard Riordan in Los Angeles, and, of course, Giuli-ani in New York (Frankel 1995; Meyerson 1993; Beauregard 1999). As Robert Beauregard explains, these city-friendly conservatives "discovered a way to combine their moral disapproval of the poor and minorities, on which their initial anti-urbanism was based, and their persistent interest in economic growth with a new appreciation of city life" (Beauregard 1999, 41) And all of them, to one degree or another, shared Siegel's diag-nosis of liberalism's disastrous impact on the cities and espoused crime and welfare policies similar to those implemented by Giuliani.

For instance, in his 1999 book about Indianapolis's experiment with urban conservatism, *The Twenty-First Century City: Resurrecting Urban America*, Stephen Goldsmith argues that America's urban centers are "on the skids" and that "in most cases government itself is the grease that has hastened the pace of decay" (7). For Goldsmith as for Siegel, the begin-ning of the end for America's cities was the War on Poverty and its overly generous urban aid projects. Like most neoconservative urban analysts, he claimed that "urban programs based on the principal of wealth redis-tribution trapped those who did not work in a web of dependency" and "subsidized the breakup of the family" while adding that forced busing "destroyed the fabric of many neighborhoods" (7). To reverse the damage caused by the social policy of the '60s, Goldsmith urged city governments to privatize their municipal services (like wastewater treatment and the management of city jails), restructure their welfare programs so that recipients could be forced into the workforce, invest in vouchers to enable poor children to attend private schools, and, of course, redouble their efforts at fighting crime.

Goldsmith's analysis of America's urban problems was shared by three-term Milwaukee mayor John Norquist, a conservative Democrat who accused cities of adopting a "pity strategy" to extort handouts from the federal government. Norquist wrote a book of his own, *The Wealth of Cities* (1999), in which he denounced government meddling in market-driven urban development and held up the libertarian initiatives he pursued in Milwaukee—such as slashing welfare payments to a bare minimum—as a model for the rest of the country. Goldsmith's and Norquist's '60s-bashing analysis of social conditions in the cities was picked up and replicated by Senators Dan Coats and Spencer Abraham, who in turn wrote an article reciting the standard laundry list of urban problems and arguing that "the liberal love affair with Big Government policies has cost urban areas a great deal" (Coats and Abraham 1998, 36). Moreover, in 1998, Norquist, Goldsmith, and three other conservative big-city mayors joined with the libertarian Cato Institute to issue a new urban manifesto, titled "Markets Not Mandates," that denounced '60s-era urban aid programs, advocated a flat tax, and "called on Washington to adopt a hands-off urban strategy to repair what they consider 30 years of failure" (Borowski 1998, 1). The report's release was greeted with much fanfare and media hype (Borowski 1998; Diaz 1998), and the report itself was sent out to every member of Congress and to President Clinton. The report's triumph underscored just how accepted the right's once-controversial ideas about the urban crisis had become.

The political motivations behind the demagogic attack on the urban failures of the '60s involved more than simply legitimating this or that conservative policy initiative (dismantling the welfare system, expanding the prison system, etc.). As the work of a figure like Siegel makes clear, a central overarching purpose of the discourse on the urban crisis was to shift the blame for post-'60s urban decline onto the left (understood as encompassing all those social movements fighting to expand democracy and social justice, from the civil rights movement to the poor people's movement to the women's movement). Given that the 1960s stand out as perhaps the only era in recent memory in which the American left had a prominent presence in national political debate—so much so that in popular parlance the decade has become synonymous with "radicalism" and "revolution"—linking the movements of the '60s to the imagined chaos of the cities helps to discredit the left as a whole. Indeed, branding the '60s as a period of social breakdown, orgiastic hedonism, and rampant immorality has been central to the rhetorical strategy used by the right to attack progressive ideas since Reagan; in the urban crisis, conservatives discovered a convenient symbol for the social anarchy they imagined was unleashed by the movements associated with the decade. Perversely, the discourse on the urban crisis pins responsibility for the poverty and social disorder of the postindustrial city on the only people who made a conscious, organized effort to stem the rising class polarization, hardening racial division, and deepening inner-city poverty of the '80s and '90s. Even more perversely, it valorizes Republicans and their conservative Democratic allies as the true friends of the underclass, who by slashing aid to cities and "ending welfare as we know it" are paving the way for a triumphant rebirth of the work ethic and an entrepreneurial spirit that will revive our dying metropolitan centers. In the process, it defined (or attempted to define) liberal and left proposals for addressing the misery and want of the capitalist city as beyond the pale, as a priori unworthy of discussion. As *U.S. News and World Report* columnist Michael Barone put it, summing up the ideological consequences he hoped would follow from the Manhattan Institute's repeated assaults on progressive urban policy, "Now that Marx is dead and the criminal underclass has made passé the idealization of the proletariat, we may be ready for the Manhattan Institute's celebration of the bourgeois" (Barone 1994, 26).

Escape from the Metropolis? Urban Center as Parasite, Edge City as Heaven

> The problem with the cities today is that they are parasites. We've got these big parasite cities sucking the lifeblood out of America today. And those cities will have to go off the dole.
>
> —George Gilder, "Tom Peters and George Gilder Debate the Impact of Technology on Location," *Forbes ASAP*, February 27, 1995

Alongside the denunciations of liberalism's damaging impact on cities, alongside the derogatory depictions of the urban minority working class as pathological and of their neighborhoods as so many "criminogenic communities" in need of Giuliani-esque discipline, a significant current of intellectual discourse on the urban crisis in the '80s and '90s painted city life and the big metropolitan center per se as obsolete or beyond repair. Or worse, it represented our cities as, in George Gilder's words, "big parasites." In many ways, this view extrapolated from and complemented the nightmarish cityscapes conjured up by writers like Bennett and Murray. As I have already hinted, it was a view that resonated strongly with broad segments of the suburban middle class. But the roots of such attitudes extend back to the prehistory of suburbia if not beyond. Visionaries and utopians of various political stripes—from anarchists like Kropotkin to American individualists such as Frank Lloyd Wright—have long heralded the passing of the centralized, massified metropolis.

What distinguishes the latest crop of urban doom-sayers from their predecessors is their generally reactionary political bent. Thus, futurist Alvin Toffler, guru of the libertarian right and advisor to former Republican Speaker of the House Newt Gingrich, has argued that since the 1970s, what he calls the "Third Wave" economy—organized around computers, automobiles, and advanced communications technology—is in the process of rendering cities (and governments) obsolete. New "Third Wave" technology, he argues, "alters our spatial experience by dispersing rather than concentrating population" (Toffler 1980, 309) and allows people to "telecommute" to work from their ex-urban and suburban "electronic cottages" rather than make the tedious journey to the city every day (204). He even quotes approvingly the headline of a *Business Week* article that envisions "The Prospect of a Nation with No Important Cities" (309). This stance—this ideology of urban obsolescence—is hardly the exclusive property of wacky "Third Wave" libertarians. It also informed two mainstream, bestselling books that exerted quite a bit of influence over the public discussion of the American city in the '90s: Joel Garreau's *Edge City: Life on the New Frontier* (1991) and Witold Rybczynski's *City Life* (1995).

Washington Post reporter Joel Garreau's *Edge City* is an attempt to discern the outlines of the future shape of American urbanization amidst the implosion of the traditional metropolitan center and the amorphous, cancerlike growth of the suburbs. Noting that suburban office parks and shopping malls like those clustered in Tysons Corner in the Northern Virginia hinterland of Washington, D.C., now house more office space, more retail space, and more jobs than traditional downtowns, Garreau's book examines what, if anything, this new pattern of development can tell us about "what our real values are" (xx). Much of the book consists of evocative economic, sociological, and physical descriptions of places like the Perimeter Center area north of Atlanta, Orange County in Southern California, and North Loop outside of Houston. Garreau paints colorful, detailed portraits of giant malls in New Jersey and suburban Philadelphia, entrepreneurial developers in Texas, and the black middle-class suburbs on the outskirts of Atlanta. Edge cities, Garreau tells us, are cities "because they contain all the functions a city ever has, albeit in a spread-out form that few have recognized for what it is" (4); they are the place "in which the majority of Americans now live, learn, work, shop, play, pray and die" and they will "be the forge of the fabled American way of life well into the twenty-first century" (8). This no doubt represents, as he claims, "profound changes in the ways we live, work and play" (4).

It is clear to Garreau that these changes spell the demise of the traditional metropolis. "An old fashioned downtown . . . is only one way to think of a city. In fact it is only the nineteenth-century version. These sort of cities . . . are proud places," he writes, "[b]ut they are relics of a past time. They are aberrations" (25). Garreau thinks that the black ghetto (and racial segregation more generally) will eventually be abolished by the same relentless process of suburbanization that is laying waste to the traditional downtown. While he admits that a third of all African Americans remain trapped in what he calls "underclass neighborhoods" (150), he enthuses that "the third of black America that is fairly described as suburban middle class is becoming indistinguishable statistically from whites of the same class" (153).

As this upbeat appraisal of Edge City's implications for racial relations indicates, Garreau is hardly a disinterested observer of the changing urban scene: often his descriptions of Edge City read more like pure boosterism than impartial reporting. In one passage after another, he happily attributes profound spiritual meaning to the shining office towers rising up over the ex-urban greenfields next to highway off-ramps: "Edge City represents America striving once again to create a new and better world—lighting out for the Territory, in the words of Huckleberry Finn" (14); it is, he tells us, an extension of "the search for Utopia at the center of the American Dream" (15). And as he sees it, Edge City is the closest thing we have yet seen to the realization of that dream. He points again and again to the fact that Edge Cities, as he defines them, generate most of the wealth and employment in the United States today. He gleefully reports that old established businesses who prefer the status quo stay downtown while "[i]t is the young, fast-growing entrepreneurial start-up—especially in high technology—that is the mark of Edge City" (29). The heroes of his narrative are millionaire developers like Gerald Hines of Houston and Til Hazel of Virginia, people who build fast, on a grand scale, and with minimal oversight by "government bureaucrats." In some respects, in fact, the book can be read as a paean to the virtues of unfettered individualism and the unregulated marketplace; its core agenda is to justify American capitalism as we know it by valorizing the shoddily built, ecologically catastrophic, throw-away landscapes it perpetually produces. For example, in one of his frequent tangents, Garreau ponders the fact that "as we look around us in the late twentieth century, we see that . . . some forms of capitalism seem attractive to a whole lot of people. . . . If industrialism did turn out to be reformable, can we now resolve the contradictions in our new, post-industrial Age world? Can we now turn to reshaping our cities?" (369).

Not only does he dismiss out of hand the idea that white flight or institutional racism have anything to do with the explosion of suburban development that he chronicles (168), but he believes that our "rough and tumble" economic system—which he says "has a stunning track record of transforming illiterate serfs from every mountain and desert on the globe into middle-class suburbanites in three generations or less"—will liberate African Americans by finding a place for them in Edge Cities (155). Indeed, he tells us that "Americans are looking for a new unity in their lives, a way to bring themselves together, to avoid the fragmentation that they perceive all around them, from drugs, to bad schools, to teen pregnancy" (369); significantly, the problems he imagines Americans striving to avoid by decamping for Edge City are precisely those that are often (and wrongly) associated exclusively with cities. Despite the fact that drug abuse and teen pregnancy are also on the rise in suburbia, Garreau insists that Edge City's "superstores" and miles of sidewalkless subdivisions might somehow be an antidote for such ills.

Like Garreau's *Edge City*, Witold Rybczynski's popular history of cities and city life in the United States, *City Life* (1995), adopts a sanguine, "what-me-worry?" outlook on the crisis and prospects of the American metropolis. The book begins by enumerating the many ways in which American cities differ from archetypal European urban centers like Paris: North American cities, Rybczynski confesses, lack the impressive monuments and loveable civic spaces, the public transportation, the vitality, the nightlife, and the sense of personal safety one finds in a city like Paris. "Socially fragmented, recklessly entrepreneurial, relying almost completely on the automobile, and often lacking a defined center, they are without many of the conventional trappings of urbanity that have characterized cities in the past. According to their detractors, they are not real cities at all" (32). The book's animating question thus becomes "Why Aren't Our Cities Like That?"—why aren't Minneapolis, L.A., and Omaha more like Paris?

Rybczynski's answer takes the form of a historical narrative in which he delineates how successive "urban ideals"—some religious in origin, some political, others "technocratic"—have interacted with emerging social and technological forces—industrialization, the invention of the automobile, the rise of the Internet—to create the cities we now inhabit. Much of what he has to say on this score is—for popular history—insightful and lucidly conveyed. However, when he turns his attention to the current urban crisis, Rybczynski begins to exhibit a very Garreau-like willingness to write off the traditional urban center as both obsolete and a font of intractable social ills. He certainly shares the perspective of the dominant discourse on the horrors of the inner city, likening Cabrini-Green to a "war zone" and fixating on "the abandoned cars and broken windows, the battered apartment blocks with walls covered in graffiti and piles of garbage in the corridors" he sees on television coverage of the housing project (166). Indeed, at one point he pays none-too-subtle lip service to the standard right-wing interpretation of "what went wrong" in places like Cabrini-Green; he explains in a footnote that, "[I]n the beginning, public housing projects were a success. Applicants were carefully screened, which ensured a balance between working families and welfare recipients, say, and between two-parent and one-parent families. But by the 1960s, bureaucratic inefficiency and lawsuits launched by the American Civil Liberties Union virtually eliminated the screening process, and public housing became de facto welfare housing, with all the attendant problems such specialization brings" (167).

While he blames (among other things) the ACLU and poor urban planning for the decline of the classic central city, Rybczynski sees suburbanization as an unalloyed manifestation of the popular will. Answering the overarching question of the book, he writes that "the different form of American cities represent[s] a long-standing desire on the part of their inhabitants for a different way of life. Unlike Parisian workers, Americans lived in suburbs by choice and had been doing so for a long time" (174–75). Using Plattsburgh, New York, as a case in point, he goes on to argue that in an era of population dispersal the traditional downtown is essentially dead. "The streets are more or less empty; there is simply none of the bustle or activity normally associated with downtown life," he writes (198). All of that activity and bustle have migrated, he argues, to the local shopping mall. He then launches into a lengthy celebration of malls as the new downtown (in the course of which he gets in yet another dig at ACLU liberals):

> I think that what attracts people to malls is that they are perceived as public spaces where rules of personal conduct are enforced. In other words, they are more like public streets used to be before police indifference and overzealous protectors of individual rights effectively ensured that *any* behavior, no matter how antisocial, is tolerated. This is what malls offer: a reasonable (in most eyes) level of public order; the right not to be subjected to outlandish conduct, not to be assaulted and intimidated by boorish adolescents, noisy drunks and aggressive panhandlers. It does not seem much to ask. (210)

Precisely what Rybczynski finds appealing about malls then is that they approximate what urban centers were like before such spaces became occupied by those unruly Others, by the sort of people who inhabit places like Cabrini-Green, an ethnically and racially heterogeneous underclass seen as incorrigibly "antisocial." Significantly, he yet again criticizes purveyors of civil rights—the defenders of these unruly Others—for allowing urban centers to deteriorate as they have. According to Rybczynski, "[m]ost Americans if given the choice would get out of a big city, not move into one" (222); this, more than any other factor, is why he believes that "[t]he old hierarchy of center and periphery, of downtown and suburb . . . is being replaced by something else—something diffuse, amorphous, and held together . . . by a system of roads and highways and, one could add, by a system of telephone wires, television cables and computer links" (232). For him, as for Garreau, this development should be accepted, even embraced, but certainly not criticized or complicated by political questions. After all, who cares about social justice when you can sip a latte in the well-ordered bliss of the mall food court? Freedom for Garreau and perhaps also for Rybczynski does not, as the old saying goes, breathe "city air" but rather the conditioned and climate-controlled air of the city's sprawling, racially, and economically segregated outgrowth, the 'burbs.

It should be noted that not all conservative commentators endorse the Gilder/Garreau/Toffler thesis that the modern metropolis is nothing more than the leftover wreckage of industrialism. Business writer and libertarian ideologue Joel Kotkin, in his book *The New Geography: How the Digital Revolution Is Reshaping the American Landscape*, agrees with Gilder and Garreau that improved telecommunications and transportation technology "promises to redraw the map of wealth and power away from their traditional abodes, largely the core cities, to a host of newer, previously marginal locations" (Kotkin 2000, 31). Like Garreau and Rybczynski, he thinks that suburbanization was an expression of the will of the masses, of what he calls "the anti-urban impulse" (see his chapter 2), and that the urban centers will never regain their lost stature as engines of commerce and industry (see his chapter 3). Indeed, he argues that the "digital economy" has made possible the proliferation of rural "nerdistans"—communities of high-tech "artisans"—that exist beyond the edges of Edge Cities (38–39). And he contends that the digital revolution "raises the possible specter of permanent geographies of devastation" in the inner-city and the inner-ring suburbs (182). Yet, for all that, Kotkin believes that downtowns around the country are "readjusting themselves to a more modest but sustainable role based on the same economic and cultural niches that have been performed by the core from the beginnings of civilization" (55). Specifically, he suggests that creative industries like the arts, software development, and all branches of the entertainment business continue to reside in and are helping to revitalize the nation's historic downtowns. "Urban space," he writes, "remains virtually unchallenged as an incubator of artfulness" (139). But even as he sounds a note of disagreement with the likes of Toffler and Garreau about the viability of the urban center, Kotkin remains wedded to a sanguine appraisal of capitalism's "free market" as the ultimate arbiter of the fate of geographically bound communities (158–59). And even as he harbors hopes for a revitalization of the urban core, he fails to recognize the central role of government policy (by now, little more than a tool of economic elites) in promoting inner-city poverty and outer-ring affluence.

The Political Repercussions

The political ramifications of the victim-blaming discourse on the city and the urban crisis that rose to prominence during the 1980s and '90s were enormous and, particularly for the urban working class, debilitating. Politicians of the right and center quickly appropriated terms like "underclass" and "superpredator" along with the theories that underwrite them to push for less government support for the urban poor and more money for discipline and punishment. From Ronald Reagan's quips about "welfare queens" driving Cadillacs to George Bush's announcement of a full-scale "war on drugs" to Bill Clinton's promise to "end welfare as we know it," victim-blaming invective directed either implicitly or explicitly against inner-city blacks became a permanent feature of presidential politics. Attacks on the underclass shaped congressional debates and policy discussions dealing with poverty, aid to cities, homelessness, education, crime, drugs, and public health. The specter of rundown metropolitan centers housing bloodthirsty gang-bangers, drug-addled street people, and pregnant welfare moms elected mayors and governors from New York to California. The fear evoked by the postindustrial city's potential violence facilitated the passage of legislation authorizing new prisons, more cops, inner-city youth curfews, and anti–panhandling fines.

At a local level, the discourse on inner-city poverty and disorder helped law-and-order politicians like Rudy Giuliani, John Norquist, and Stephen Goldsmith capture the mayoralties of major cities and generated a "climate of opinion" that enabled them, once in office, to pursue a series of policies that favored suburban commuters and wealthy city dwellers at the expense of the impoverished urban masses. Take, for instance, Rudy Giuliani. As mayor of New York, Giuliani presided over a notoriously heavy-handed police "crack down" on street crime that in practice targeted the homeless and communities of color. Not only did this campaign result in several high-profile incidents of police abuse like the vicious beating of Abner Louima and the killing of Amadou Diallo but, according to a report issued by New York Attorney General Eliot Spitzer, it also involved systematic and unconstitutional racial profiling by the NYPD's Street Crime Unit (Newfield 2002, 82–83). While his zero-tolerance approach to crime was making Times Square safe for suburban tourists, Giuliani was busy slashing more than $6 billion from the public school system's budget and erecting bureaucratic barriers that prevented legions of homeless people from securing spaces in the city's shelters (40, 130). He also created a "workfare" program that forced thousands of welfare recipients to work at low-skill municipal jobs in return for their public assistance checks, eliminating several thousand full-time union jobs in the parks department and at city hospitals as a consequence (Fuentes 1996, 15–16). In short, Giuliani ran New York City in a way calculated to benefit his affluent and corporate backers at the expense of the city's less-fortunate residents.[8] And the endlessly in-voked image of a welfare-addicted, pathological, out-of-control inner-city underclass in need of "tough love" provided just the ideological cover he needed to get away with it.

Of course, the discourse on and panic over the city also had a significant—and, from my perspective, damaging—impact on national urban and social policy. Consider, for example, the role it played in the successful campaigns for the 1994 Crime Control Bill and the 1996 Personal Responsibility and Work Opportunity Act, two of the more reactionary laws passed in the 1990s. In 1993, as debate on the crime bill began, fear of crime was soaring at the same time as violent crime rates were in decline (Perkinson 1994, 12–13). Galvanizing these fears were, among other things, the 1992 riots in Los Angeles, the spread of the so-called crack epidemic, and a highly publicized spate of random attacks by black gangs on European tourists in the Miami area. Having lost the battle for his health-care legislation, and facing the prospects of Republican majorities in the next Congress, Clinton decided to focus his attention on the fight for a new, comprehensive crime bill, one policy area on which he and Congress firmly agreed. After appeasing Democratic liberals by including funding for a few crime-prevention programs like midnight sports leagues and anti-gang grants (both cut from the final package), the bill made it fairly rapidly through both the House and Senate (Lusane 1994, 16). The result was the most draconian and sweeping anti-crime legislation ever passed at the federal level. At a cost of $30.2 billion, the bill funded 100,000 new police, provided $9.7 billion for new prison construction, and authorized $1.2 billion for increased border patrol and Immigration and Naturalization Service policing of illegal immigrants (Perkinson 1994, 13–14; Platt 1995). Moreover, it expanded "federal jurisdiction to 70 crimes and [made] 60 new crimes punishable by death" (Perkinson 1994, 13). It imposed harsh new mandatory minimum sentences (and lengthened existing mandatory minimum sentences) for a whole range of new offenses from selling drugs to a minor (an automatic ten-year jail term) to possession of a firearm during a crime (an additional five years in jail) (Lusane 1994, 17). And, perhaps most notoriously, the bill imposed a "three strikes and you're out" rule, which would put anyone with two prior convictions who is convicted of a violent federal offense in jail for life (18).

Shortly after the passage of the Clinton crime bill, the Republicans under the leadership of soon-to-be appointed Speaker Newt Gingrich regained control of the House for the first time in decades and immediately began agitating for a "final solution" to the problem of the urban underclass, namely an "end to welfare as we know it." President Clinton—who had promised to get tough on welfare mothers during the 1992 campaign—was only too happy to oblige. For close to two years, Congress debated the "welfare problem" and what to do about it. Murray, Bennett, Mead, Gingrich, and their ilk were given regular opportunities by the media to talk about the horrors of the inner city and to point out how Great Society antipoverty programs had destroyed urban minority communities by encouraging "dependency," "deviance," and "pathology." (I explore the contours of this coverage in more detail in the next chapter.) Suffice it to say, the endless flow of right-wing commentary on the urban crisis set the terms by which the landmark "welfare reform" legislation, known as the Personal Responsibility and Work Opportunity Act (PRA), was discussed in the media and in the halls of Congress. Signed by Clinton on August 22, 1996, the PRA was as punitive in its own way as the Crime Bill of two years before. For starters, it abolished Aid to Families with Dependent Children, which provided financial assistance as an entitlement to anyone poor enough to qualify (usually mothers and their dependent children), and replaced it with a block grant to the states (which, unlike AFDC payments, would not increase to keep pace with the poverty rate) (deMause 1996, 28). It limited recipients to a total of five years of aid regardless of their needs or circumstances and limited childless adults to three months of Food Stamps out of any thirty-six-month period. It denied benefits to drug felons and resident noncitizens (illegal or not) (29). And it made it possible for state governments to force recipients, even recipients with very small children, to work at sub–minimum wage jobs in return for their meager benefits (30). Five years later, the human consequences of these "reforms," hardly noticed by the mainstream media, proved to be sobering. "A report by the Urban Institute on the early impacts of welfare reform," Neil deMause notes, "found that up to half of women who've left the rolls report serious problems feeding their families" (17).

Yet, the political functions performed by victim-blaming dogma about the urban crisis and the underclass during the '80s and '90s went beyond merely supplying a patina of intellectual legitimacy for the reign of right-wing mayors and paving the way for welfare reform. The discourse on urban problems—with its nightmarish vision of the inner city and its obsession with the immorality of slum dwellers—proved politically useful for the conservative powers-that-be in other, more profound, and potentially more long-lasting, ways as well.

To begin with, the panic over the urban crisis helped to unify and mobilize various currents of the political right who would otherwise be opposed to each other. The American New Right in the '80s and '90s was an amalgam of disparate movements and ideologies, many of which coexisted uneasily with each other. Christian fundamentalists and capitalist libertarians, for instance, rarely agree about issues like censorship of pornography or government regulation of abortion. Holding together the shaky coalition that is the New Right thus meant identifying issues that solidify rather than strain the coalition. This is where the discourse on the postindustrial city proved so indispensable. Consider the unifying function of right-wing ideas about welfare's role in "creating" the urban underclass. As Ann Withorn has explained, "Almost every right-winger gets deeply satisfying rewards from being against the friendless welfare-state. Racists can tell stories about ne'er-do-well blacks. Libertarians can expose the brutality of a behemoth state. Radical capitalists can show the dire costs of interfering with a free market, whereas Christian moralists can rant passionately about welfare's permissiveness regarding women's promiscuity and family 'breakdown'" (Withorn 1998, 126). Similarly, the different currents of the right each derived benefits from sounding the alarm about inner-city street violence. For capitalists, it justified the creation of a vast system of criminal justice to contain, isolate, and discipline what Marxists call the reserve army of labor (Parenti 1999, chapter 11). For right-wing Christians, it offered proof of the evils of secular values run amok. For white supremacists, inner-city crime provided further evidence of black savagery and impulsiveness, which justifies their preparations for total race war. Moreover, as the examples of the 1994 Crime Bill and the 1996 Personal Responsibility Act attest, the discourse on the urban crisis and the moral panic it produced helped forge a new right-wing consensus on the city's ills that reached beyond the right's traditional constituencies and became the ideological common ground of both major political parties. In other words, it has helped to forge hegemony in the Gramscian sense of creating a platform and political vision uniting heterogeneous political aspirations and identities.

In addition, the new consensus on the urban crisis articulated and systematized aspects of the organic ideology of the suburban middle class, particularly their racialized fears of and resentment toward the urban, minority working class. From his exhaustive study of opinion surveys of suburban voters G. Scott Thomas concludes that "Suburbanites are . . . relatively indifferent to many of America's ills. They believe that the federal government should play a limited role in addressing issues ranging from poverty and illiteracy to homelessness and racial discrimination" (Thomas 1998, 152). For instance, suburbanites were wildly supportive of the 1996 welfare reform bill and significantly more supportive of welfare cuts than urban dwellers (168–69). Moreover, Thomas found that many suburbanites "consider cities to be breeding grounds for criminals, and they worry that their quieter, safer communities might one day be overrun by such brutes" (181). Indeed, one 1996 Knight Ridder poll found that 72 percent of respondents said the danger of being victimized in the largest cities in their state was high and just 6 percent said it was low (while 66 percent said the risk in their own neighborhood was low) (Thomas 1998, 180–81). Other studies have found similar anxieties. For example, 70 percent of respondents to Edward Blakely and Mary Gail Snyder's survey of the homeowner association boards in gated communities indicate that security was "very important" in their decision to live behind a gate (Blakely and Snyder 1999, 126). The right-wing discourse on the urban crisis both justifies suburban anxieties and attitudes toward the city and supplies them with coherence and an intellectual pedigree. And this makes them that much more politically influential.

In addition, at least some of the mainstream intellectual commentary on the postindustrial city ratified the white, suburban middle-class view that our metropolitan centers are now obsolete and that the suburbs owe the cities nothing. Robert Beauregard observes that "[s]uburbanites refer to the decay of the city as the motive for their flight, as the justification for the neglect of the cities, and as the rationale for the spatial and moral distance suburban residents place between themselves and inner-city minorities" (Beauregard 1993, 290). The rosy portraits of Edge Cities and mega-malls one finds in Garreau's work (among others) suggest that new suburban office parks have become the political, economic, and cultural equivalent of the older downtowns, that the suburbs have become insulated from and independent of the cities to which they are attached. This upbeat anti-urbanism resonates with many suburbanites who, surveys find, are convinced that their lives are unaffected by events in the central cities (Thomas 1998, 155). Yet the notion that suburbs have achieved economic independence from their core cities is delusional. A number of studies have consistently found that the economic fortunes of cities and their suburbs remain linked, pointing to positive correlations between city center and suburban growth in incomes, employment, and populations (see *Metro Futures* 1996, 6). Moreover, despite being heralded as the new downtowns, suburban malls lack the diverse populations and vibrant public spaces that characterized traditional metropolitan centers (Sharpe and Wallock 1994, 6). Equating Edge Cities with the traditional centers makes it easier for suburbia and its apologists to overlook those excluded from their verdant bourgeois utopias. And even if it is factually false, celebrating Edge Cities as the new downtowns and heralding the demise of the central city is a politically expedient position for Republican politicians—whose electoral base is in the suburbs—to embrace.

At the same time, the dominant representation of feral cities given over to violence and aberrant, amoral behavior drives a wedge between lower-income suburbanites (often living in decaying inner-ring suburbs) and the urban working class, undercutting the potential for urban/suburban alliances around demands for such common goals as more jobs, a cleaner environment, universal health insurance, affordable housing, higher wages, and better schools. "Scapegoating makes it easier to treat inner-city neighborhoods like outsider cities—separate, unequal and disposable," writes radical economist Holly Sklar. "Scapegoating encourages people to think of 'the poor' as the 'Other America,' Them and not Us. That makes it easier to divide people who should be working together to transform harmful social and economic policies" (Sklar 1995, 70). As we have seen, in the ruling discourse, the city-dwelling, mostly black underclass becomes "a demonized 'Other' which if expunged or contained will eliminate the social ills from which 'we' suffer" (Rothenberg and Heinz 1998, 44). With such an "Other," no commonality, no communication, no shared experience or struggle is desirable or even possible; the only possible relation decent (white, suburban) people can have to such Others is to exclude, control, and confine them.

Yet viewing the urban underclass as completely alien obscures a number of important facts. First of all, it obscures the fact that poverty transcends place and race; many of the poor live outside central cities (in suburbs and rural areas) and poor whites outnumber poor blacks by a ratio of two to one (Jones 1992, 269). In fact, "more poor blacks (11 million) live outside the inner city than in it (6.1 million)" (16). It also obscures the fact that the extreme, persistent poverty of the underclass is merely "a position at the far end of a spectrum of inequality" and that "a focus that lingers solely on ghetto poverty distracts attention from its sources in transformations of the social structure that threaten the well-being of a very large share of Americans" (Katz 1993a, 472). From the point of view of economic interests, the underclass exhibits more similarities with others at the bottom of the United States's income and class hierarchy (both in and out of the city) than they do differences. By treating the city as an alien place inhabited by threatening people "different from you and me," the discourse camouflages those class-based similarities between urban and suburban workers. As Robin Kelley points out, the conception of "class" at work in the discourse on urban decline suggests that "what makes the 'underclass' a class is members' common behavior—not their income, their poverty level, or the kind of work they do. It is a definition of class driven more by moral panic than by systematic analysis" (Kelley 1997, 18). And, it should be added, it is a definition of class that is not likely to form the basis for any kind of broad-based movement for social equality and justice. "The emphasis on . . . anti-poor views works to separate workers from one another by reinforcing the divisive status lines between workers," writes Joe Feagin. "Such views retard joint action by all levels of poor and middle-income workers toward collective ends, particularly toward goals of significant social change" (Feagin 1975, 121).

Perhaps even more importantly, the discourse on the crisis in the inner-city masks the fact that many of the "problems" and "pathologies" treated as characteristic of the underclass pervade the rest of American society too. Thus, the urban poor become scapegoats for broader social trends such as rampant drug abuse, the passing of the male-headed nuclear family, the decline of the Protestant work ethic, and reckless consumerism. Consider drug abuse. Despite the fact that poor, inner-city blacks make up the majority of arrests and convictions for drug offenses (especially for cocaine), the fact is that 75 percent of drug users and 80 percent of all cocaine users are white (Sklar 1995, 126); indeed, studies have found that African-American youth are less likely to use drugs or alcohol than youth from other ethnic groups (128). Or consider the decline of the nuclear family. As Stephanie Coontz shows, in 1992, the United States had four times as many single-parent households as in 1970 and some 30 percent of children were born out-of-wedlock (Coontz 1992, 182). While these trends were more pronounced among the so-called underclass, out-of-wedlock births and single-parent house-holds are on the rise for all races and income groups (not just in the United States but in the developed world as a whole) (Sklar 1995, 90).

Chastising the "underclass" for impulsiveness, irresponsibility, hedonism, violence, drug abuse, and self-indulgence diverts attention from the fact that the middle class is guilty of these same "sins." It makes the white, suburban "Us" appear noble, decent, and pure in contrast to the monstrously pathological "Them." The "othering" rhetoric in which right-wing pundits and their centrist imitators discuss the inner-city poor has had, as Linda Gordon correctly points out, "the further effect of suggesting a fictive unity among the non-'underclass,' among what in the 1990s U.S. is often called the 'mainstream,' as if there were no het-erogeneity, immorality, and irresponsibility among the 'us'" (Gordon 1995, 166). The scapegoating of the city, then, appears to perform for the suburban middle class that venerable operation of creating social cohesion through exclusion: it reinforces social solidarity by directing aggression against the weakest, least liked, and most vulnerable members of society, who are then said to be the cause of all the community's trou-bles and are punished for it (Cohen 1985, 233).

Finally, the discourse on the postindustrial city performs an impor-tant socio-psychological function for the white middle class in that it provides them with a series of code words that permit the expression of deeply felt anti-black and Latino sentiment with little self-consciousness or embarrassment. Since the victories of the civil rights movement, something of a social stigma on overt, naked statements of racist bigotry and white supremacist sentiment has developed in most segments of U.S. society (although the authors of books like *The Bell Curve* have worked assiduously to weaken and reverse it). At the same time, a substantial majority of white Americans exhibit what Robert Entman has called "modern racism," a combination of fear, resentment, and animosity toward blacks, denial that racism is still a problem in the country, and opposition to the political agenda associated with black civil rights leadership (Entman 1992, 342). Unlike the overt, self-conscious racism of the past, modern racism does not see itself as "pro-white" but rather as an objective, "color blind," and "race neutral" way of looking at America's social landscape that reveals blacks to be a source of a disproportionately large number of our social problems. The language deployed in the discourse on the postindustrial city is a fittingly euphemistic vehicle for this kind of modern racism; "color neutral" code words like "underclass," "crack head," "gang member," "superpredator," and especially "urban" stand in for the racial epithets of yesteryear and represent "a repackaging of traditional right-wing prejudices against the poor and Blacks in the language of modern sociology" (Hadjor 1995, 131).

The glowing, boosterish language writers like Garreau and Rybczynski use to discuss suburbia and Edge City similarly serves to euphemize and apologize for the racial apartheid the suburbs have helped to foster. As Sharpe and Wallock have argued, advocates of these "new, suburban cities" "play down suburban parochialism and separatism" by focusing instead on "morphology and aesthetics" (Sharpe and Wallock 1994, 6). In particular, they suppress the realities of white flight and persistent racial discrimination in housing markets. The work of writers like Garreau naturalizes a suburban ideology that, as David Hummon describes it, provides "an acceptable vocabulary of motives for white flight from the interracial city to the confines of suburbia" (Hummon 1990, 108). No doubt the ability of the discourse on the urban crisis to tap into modern racist affect furthers its other ideological functions as well: discrediting the welfare state, legitimating intensified policing of the city, driving a wedge between the urban and suburban proletariat, mobilizing suburban voters against the city, and so on.

Conclusion: Not by Discourse Alone

The discourse on the postindustrial urban crisis, then, has furthered and continues to advance a number of vitally important ideological and political purposes for the powers that be. It proposes "imaginary solutions" to real social contradictions, naturalizes poverty and urban decline, projects the sources of the system's failures onto the system's victims, and makes the denunciation of government aid to struggling cities and their residents sound reasonable, even humane. It unifies white, suburban Middle America against the scapegoat of a monstrous and parasitic inner-city underclass. It renders racist views about the ghetto poor socially acceptable and justifies the imposition of ever-more repressive regimes of policing on urban black and Latino populations. Yet it would be misleading to suggest that the discourse has achieved all this solely by the sheer force of its ideas, theories, and arguments. As we have seen repeatedly throughout this chapter, often those ideas rest upon shoddy, incomplete evidence and indefensible presuppositions.

In large part, what accounts for the popularity and enormous power of the discourse on the postindustrial urban crisis is not so much the quality or persuasiveness of its arguments as the vast resources mobilized to publicize and circulate them. Right-wing think tanks and foundations—backed by the fortunes of billionaire industrialists and leading corporations—have been instrumental in this process (Soley 1992; Stefancic and Delgado 1996; Solomon 1998; Callahan 1999; Lieberman 2000; Alterman 2003). According to one estimate, the top twenty conservative think tanks in America spent more than $1 billion in the 1990s to develop and promote policy ideas (Callahan 1999; Stefancic and Delgado 1996; A Job Is a Right Campaign 1997). At least some of that money went to advocating the authors and views dissected in this chapter. Thus, the right-wing Manhattan Institute raised $125,000 to promote Charles Murray's *Losing Ground* and to pay him a stipend while a grant from the Liberty Fund underwrote a nationwide speaking tour for the book (Lane 1985; Solomon 1998). The Institute also spends $700,000 a year to send 10,000 free copies of its glossy magazine *City Journal*—which regularly features longish pieces by the likes of Murray and Siegel—to journalists, academics, politicians, and other opinion makers (Scott 1997). The Heritage Foundation incubated William Bennett's *Book of Virtues* and later his *Index of Leading Cultural Indicators* (Ridgeway 1997, 14; Stefancic and Delgado 1996, 91). The American Enterprise Institute supported Dinesh D'Souza during the research and writing of *The End of Racism* and spent money to hype it after it was published (Toler 1999, 14). When it comes to conservative ideas about the postindustrial city, at least, there appears to be a strong element of truth to the Marxist dictum that "[m]orality, religion, metaphysics, all the rest of ideology . . . no longer retain the semblance of independence" (Marx and Engels 1978, 47). Without the well-oiled and lavishly bankrolled public relations machinery of corporate-backed, Republican-leaning think tanks, conservative intellectual commentary on the urban crisis would not have become as omnipresent and influential as it was throughout the 1980s and '90s.

However, even the most-well-funded PR machine cannot broadcast ideologically laden discourses, fears, and anxieties throughout society on its own. Conservative authors and pundits did not create a moral panic or set the terms of policy debates by themselves. In order to generate rising waves of hysteria over conditions in the urban core, the interpretations of the city's many troubles generated by the ideologues of the right had to catch on with the mass media. It is via the media, as Stuart Hall and his colleagues pointed out in *Policing the Crisis*, that elite, ideological definitions of social problems are popularized and escalating "spirals of concern" initiated (and sustained). In the chapters that follow, I attempt to show how the right's discourse shaped and circulated through various media representations of the American city. I start by examining news coverage of the postindustrial city and the underclass before moving on to discuss their representation in film and advertising.

CHAPTER 4

Crack Alleys and Killing Zones:
News Coverage of the
Postindustrial City

The media, whose function . . . is to bury and obscure the daily
economic violence of the city, ceaselessly throw up spectres of criminal
underclasses and psychotic stalkers. Sensationalized accounts of killer
youth gangs high on crack and shrilly racist evocations of marauding
Willie Hortons foment the moral panics that reinforce and justify
urban apartheid.

—Mike Davis, *City of Quartz*

The alarmist, pathologizing discourse on contemporary urban reality
promoted by conservative politicians, pundits, and intellectuals—and endorsed by their "centrist" imitators—has not been confined merely to
the sort of policy debates that unfold in magazines of opinion, academic
journals, and the op-ed pages of the *New York Times*. On the contrary, it
has been embraced wholesale by the entire spectrum of the mainstream
news media and informs their coverage of issues from street crime to
homelessness to "welfare dependency." It would be shocking were this
not the case.

Media critics and scholars have long recognized that most journalism relays consistently, and for the most part uncritically, whatever happens to be the hegemonic ideology of the moment. In his classic study
Deciding What's News, sociologist Herbert Gans comments that "with
some oversimplifications, it would be fair to say that the news supports
the social order of public, business and professional, upper-middle-class,
middle-aged, and white male sectors of society. . . . In short, when
all other things are equal, the news pays most attention to and upholds
the actions of elite individuals and elite institutions" (Gans 1979, 61).

Likewise, Noam Chomsky and Edward Herman in their groundbreaking book *Manufacturing Consent* contend that the corporate news media "mobilize support for the special interests that dominate the state and private activity" and "serve the ends of a dominant elite" (Chomsky and Herman 1988, xi, 2).

One needn't look very far for anecdotal confirmation of Chomsky and Herman's thesis. A glance at any mainstream daily newspaper or network television news broadcast reveals clearly enough their basic ideological inclinations. As a rule, official pronouncements by politicians, government officials, established academicians, and captains of industry make up the bulk of the content and most are passed on to consumers without being investigated for accuracy, cogency, or consistency (sometimes, in fact, government or business press releases are transmitted verbatim). Coverage of domestic politics, for the most part, obsessively follows the actions of (mostly high-level) elected officials from the two major parties and when dissidents or grassroots social movements receive coverage they are rarely taken seriously or permitted to expound their positions in any detail. With a few notable exceptions, reporting on international affairs adopts the U.S. State Department (or, worse yet, the Pentagon) line. Economic news deals mostly with the gyrations of the stock market, the rate of inflation, fluctuations in currency exchange rates, and other concerns of affluent investors while labor unions only get mentioned when they go out on strike (if then). Meanwhile, stories that are unflattering to business or reflect badly on ruling elites or might offend advertisers generally get ignored, spiked, or given brief, perfunctory treatment.

Systematic study after systematic study confirms the soundness of these offhand impressions: almost without exception, the mainstream news media showcase the voices and ideas of the wealthy, the educated, and the powerful; support the basic legitimacy of the political status quo; and marginalize political heretics, minorities, and the poor.[1] Thus, a 1994 study by Croteau and Hoynes found that the vast majority of guests who appeared on the ABC News show *Nightline* from 1985 to 1988 were either government officials (33.9 percent) or professionals (39.4 percent). Moreover, they found that the show's guests were 89.7 percent male and 92.1 percent white (Croteau and Hoynes 1994, 72–77). More recently, an analysis of all sources used on network evening news shows in 2001 found that 75 percent of all partisan sources were Republicans, 81 percent of all sources were men, and 92 percent of all U.S. sources were white (Howard 2002, 11). The results, author Ina Howard observes, show that "source selection favored the elite interests that the corporate owners of these shows depend on for advertising revenue, regulatory support and access to information" (11). Thirteen of the twenty most widely syndicated newspaper columnists in the country are conservatives of various stripes who can be counted on to uphold these same "elite interests" (Rowse 2000, 114). Moreover, the evidence indicates that the major 24-hour cable news channels like CNN, FOX, and MSNBC tilt even more heavily to the right than the major newspapers and broadcast network news outfits (Alterman 2003).

Why—despite its commitment to objectivity and its liberal reputation—has the press historically been so identified with and supportive of the political and economic establishment? The most obvious reason is that, as for-profit businesses, media outlets can ill afford to offend their corporate sponsors and owners, a point that Chomsky and Herman, Ben Bagdikian, and others have made repeatedly over the years. Equally important, though, is the fact that, as Michael Schudson among others has noted, "the story of journalism, on a day-to-day basis, is the story of the interaction of reporters and officials" (Schudson 1997, 14). News organizations—especially those operating on tight daily schedules—have a structural need for a reliable flow of stories and information. In order to routinize their work, to render manageable the daunting task of coming up with fresh stories every day, reporters depend heavily on government bureaucracies and other legitimated, socially powerful institutions (universities, think tanks, industry, mainline churches, elite charities, bar associations, chambers of commerce, etc.) as sources of information and commentary—a pattern of dependency that predisposes them to accept official definitions of events and situations. As Stuart Hall and his coauthors point out in *Policing the Crisis*, "[t]he media do not themselves autonomously create news items; rather, they are 'cued in' to specific news topics by regular and reliable institutional sources" (Hall et al. 1978, 57). Journalism's "structured preference" for those in power allows "institutional definers to establish the initial definition or primary interpretation of the topic in question" (57); in fact, the voices of officialdom dominate the news to such a degree that it is fair to claim, as Hall and company do, that one of the central functions of news media is to "translate into a public idiom" official viewpoints (61). And, the authors go on to argue, the official, "primary definition" of a topic, once established, "sets the limit for all subsequent discussion by framing what the problem is" (56). Of course, the media frequently showcase the voices of ordinary citizens alongside the opinions of the powerful. Yet, more often than not, man-on-the-street interviews, soundbites from "average Americans," and other such expressions of the vox populi merely serve to ratify the conventional wisdom as constructed by elite "primary definers."

The media's role in generating the moral panic surrounding "mugging" in Britain in the 1970s illustrates nicely how the symbiotic, almost collusive, relationship between mainstream news organizations and government functionaries structures news coverage of important social issues. In that case, newspapers faithfully reported concerns about "out-of-control" black youth crime voiced by the police, the courts, and politicians and editorialized in favor of heavier sentences or more aggressive policing; the police then used the newspaper accounts as justification for demanding greater powers, the courts pointed to "public outcry" as grounds for handing out longer sentences to juvenile offenders, and politicians seized on the heightened public concern about "mugging" to push for new anti-crime legislation. As such, the newspapers, the courts, politicians, and the police—all of which Hall and company label "agencies of public signification"—"do not simply respond to 'moral panics.' They form part of the circle out of which 'moral panics' develop. It is part of the paradox that they also, advertently and inadvertently, amplify the deviancy they seem so absolutely committed to controlling" (52).

The analysis by Hall and his coauthors of the part played by the news media in initiating and legitimating moral panics can help us make sense of the news media's contribution to the recent public hysteria over the alleged moral decay of America's postindustrial cities. The media's coverage of the city in the '80s and '90s can be fruitfully understood as "translating into a public idiom" the definitions, terms, and ideological assumptions of the evolving elite consensus about the "urban crisis" discussed in the last two chapters. Following a trajectory that parallels the career of the "mugging scare" in Britain during the 1970s, official concern (by politicians, policy experts, and right-wing intellectuals, among others) about the city's seemingly intractable problems initially sensitized the media to the issue; the media's coverage, in turn, helped to popularize (as well as naturalize) the dominant reactionary interpretation of inner-city poverty and crime, stoking the (suburban, middle-class) public's alarm over worsening urban conditions. And this heightened mood of public anxiety gave rise, in a classic case of what Hall and company (following Stanley Cohen) call an escalating "spiral of response," to ever-more frequent, ever-more dire warnings of imminent urban doom from pundits, politicians, and other interested parties (not to mention assorted proposals for draconian security-obsessed solutions to the tribulations of the postindustrial city), all of which have been dutifully reported in the mainstream news. The complex realities of urban life and the larger forces responsible for the city's troubles rarely figure in the self-perpetuating cycle of frightened coverage begetting "get tough" political rhetoric begetting yet more frightened coverage. And the vast social and geographical distance separating the largely suburban, largely middle-class audience for such fare from the communities being singled out as problematic permitted the cycle to continue unquestioned.

The remainder of this chapter documents the way journalistic representations of the American city during the 1980s and '90s echoed and amplified the terrified vision of the urban underclass and rampant street crime championed by law-and-order politicians, right-wing intellectuals, and conservative policy experts. After exploring some reasons for the highly selective nature of the media's coverage of urban reality during this period, I demonstrate—drawing on existing scholarship as well as my own original research on television news treatment of urban issues[2]— that such coverage consistently presented the public with a picture of contemporary urban existence as hopelessly depraved, violent, out of control, and, above all, in need of forceful and punitive discipline. Although some reporting on the city over the past two decades has been motivated by a laudably liberal desire to raise public awareness about urban misery and hopelessness, much of the coverage, intentionally or not, has stigmatized poor neighborhoods and dwelt on the dysfunctions of inner-city communities to the exclusion of other stories about these communities. Moreover, it has relied disproportionately on conservative sources, ideas, and terminology while ignoring the voices of the urban poor and their advocates. In the process, the news media's urban reporting has, often quite explicitly, legitimated precisely the sort of individualistic, moralizing explanations of poverty, racial inequality, and social disorder that are so central to the reigning discourse on the urban crisis.

Missing News: Undercoverage of Urban Social Realities

In order to put the ideological thrust of the news media's coverage of the city and urban life into proper perspective, it is important to underscore the most salient feature of that coverage: its relative infrequency and extremely narrow focus. Even in this era of "urban crisis," mainstream print and broadcast news devote remarkably little attention to the structural socio-economic conditions shaping life in the central cities, to the economic and demographic changes affecting central-city neighborhoods, to deindustrialization, to persistent racism, or to the growing inequality between cities and suburbs; compared to the huge volume of "facts" and "information" the public receives daily about celebrities, mainstream political leaders, consumer trends, and professional athletes, news about the objective social dimensions of the "urban crisis" has been close to nonexistent. And this *despite* the fact that most mainstream print and broadcast media outlets still operate out of central-city headquarters. The only exceptions to this general pattern of neglect tend to be stories that show cities and their poor, minority residents as violating social and moral norms, as pathological, criminal, savage, and strange. As a result, the news media's representations of the American metropolis and its problems tend to focus overwhelmingly on violence or underclass deviance.

The extent of the media's tunnel vision can be gauged by looking at the scant attention most important urban issues receive on nightly network television news broadcasts (which, though waning in popularity, were still among the most influential news outlets in the country in the '80s and '90s). Thanks to the *Vanderbilt Television News Index*, an easily searchable, online catalogue containing detailed abstracts of every network evening news broadcast since 1968, it is relatively easy to identify and track trends in network news coverage of various subjects. If one looks at the number of national network news stories on urban issues listed in the *Vanderbilt Index* from 1989 to 1998—a period of ten years during the heart of the Bush and Clinton administrations—it is clear that such issues rank very low on the networks' list of priorities; indeed, most of the time national television news acts as if the city and its pressing social needs simply don't exist. For instance, a search of all evening news stories run on ABC, CBS, NBC, and CNN for 1998 turned up eight stories on the Department of Housing and Urban Development (the federal agency most responsible for urban policy), five stories specifically on the American inner city, one story on urban unemployment, and no stories at all on sprawl, urban decline, urban crisis, urban policy, deindustrialization, ghettos, or slums. Of the nine stories about poverty in the United States featured on evening news shows in 1998, none dealt exclusively with poverty in cities. And, even though racial segregation in our metropolitan eras remained close to pre–World War II, pre–civil rights movement levels (Massey and Denton 1993), the only stories about racial segregation on the evening news in 1998 were about George Wallace and segregation in the Jim Crow–era south. By contrast, the same year saw the nightly news shows broadcast sixty-eight stories about the anti-impotence drug Viagra (a statistic that indicates with precision which segment of the viewing public network news organizations value most).

Yet as stunning as this neglect of the plight of the cities is, the reasons for it aren't all that difficult to fathom. In his book *Virtuous Reality*, critic Jon Katz argues that "[n]ewspapers and television stations rarely focus on inner-city issues and problems simply because there's no money in it; most people who live in the inner city don't spend enough money to attract advertisers" (Katz 1997, 99). Katz is right. In the current media landscape, where the established media face challenges from both the Internet and cable news channels, competition for sponsors creates increased pressure for news producers to deliver an upscale audience. Thus, as the nation's middle- and upper-class suburbs have grown in size, wealth, and political power, news media of all kinds have tailored their reporting to suit suburban tastes and interests; as one reporter quipped, "marketing [a newspaper] these days means spending more time focusing on the things that concern the people who have all the money and live in the suburbs" (cited in McChesney 1999, 55). Ben Bagdikian has encapsulated the relationship between suburbanization and the transformation of the newspaper business as follows:

> As the country's population grew and new communities arose, the old pattern disappeared. Instead of new papers to meet changing political forces, existing papers pushed beyond their municipal boundaries to the new communities and, increasingly, reached not for all the new citizens but for the more affluent consumers. Soon each metropolitan paper was preempting circulation in thousands of square miles with hundreds of communities and voting districts. . . . [B]ut the papers, and later radio and television stations, could not possibly tell each community what it needed to understand its own problems and needs. (Bagdikian 1997, 176)

This process seems to have accelerated in the 1990s. Nearly every major newspaper in the country now has at least one suburban edition or has added new sections devoted to the news from the hinterlands. Even alternative weeklies, historically committed to a readership of hip, downtown-dwelling twenty-somethings, have modified their content so as to appeal to suburban youth (see Bates 1998).

But beyond working hard to attract up-market suburban consumers, news organizations have diligently attempted to drive away inner-city viewers and readers. Bagdikian, among others, has observed that "[b]roadcasters cannot keep the nonaffluent and elderly from watching or listening to their programs, but they design the content to attract younger, affluent viewers. Newspapers control the readership by not re-porting significantly on the neighborhoods of the low-income and elderly populations and by promoting their circulation in affluent neighbor-hoods with the desired characteristics" (Bagdikian 1997, 199).

The newspaper industry, at least, has been fairly brazen in its efforts to drive away inner-city readers. "There's a dirty little secret in all newspapers," admitted Joseph Lelyveld, one-time executive editor of the *New York Times*. "The advertisers we cater to are not thrilled when you sign up a bunch of readers in some poverty area for home delivery" (Rivers 1996, 197). The Newspaper Association of America, the voice of the nation's newspaper publishers, in 1995 released a report urging papers to cut "fringe circulation" (read here: the low-income, inner-city sub-scribers) and focus on "the good customer who pays on time, preferably in advance and who, in contrast to the 'marginal subscriber' doesn't need to be lured with discounts" (Cranberg 1997, 52). A survey of ninety of the circulation directors at the nation's top hundred papers revealed that most specifically targeted affluent areas while shunning the neighbor-hoods of the urban poor. As Gilbert Cranberg explained, "Some circula-tion directors said they don't deliver to all parts of their cities for safety reasons. A number admitted that, in the inner city, they give fewer dis-counts, demand more payment in advance, and send in sales crews—if at all—only around the first of the month when welfare and Social Security checks are due" (54). A number of papers—including the *Boston Globe* and the *Los Angeles Times*—actually charge a higher newsstand price in the central city than they do in affluent suburban communities ("Globe Newstand Price" 2001; "Los Angeles Times" 2001). One circulation director Cranberg interviewed openly admitted that "[t]he inner city, from an advertiser's standpoint, is undesirable, and for that reason we put our least amount of effort into it" (54). It almost goes without saying that the best strategy for any news organization trying to repulse undesirable inner-city readers is to ignore their lives, struggles, and perspectives as much as possible while playing up their unsavory behavior and moral defects, which is precisely what most newspapers do.

Like newspapers, television news programs have for quite some time now striven to exclude the poor and minorities from their "demo-graphics" while attracting well-to-do suburban viewers. As Hal Him-melstein explains:

> The suburban middle landscape in network news is reflected in news val-ues, dress, and presentational codes. This landscape is presented in news not as a geographical place (the suburb is exceedingly difficult to locate geographically any more, but it is there) but as a state of mind to which an appearance is correlated. Most of the spokespersons, both journalists and sources, seem to come from this place irrespective of their personal life histories or the nature of the story being reported. Their dress and man-nerisms point, above all, to their "belonging." (Himmelstein 1987, 267)

Though written in the mid-'80s, Himmelstein's observation still holds true over two decades later. The main anchors working on the big three networks through 2004—Rather, Brokaw, Jennings—remained prosper-ous, somber, clean-cut, middle-aged, white men. They not only appeared to "belong"—through their speech, looks, and dress—to the suburban middle class but, as we'll see later in this chapter, they often explicitly aligned themselves with it (for example, by using the pronoun "we" when referring to the middle class and "they" when discussing the urban poor).

In fact, it doesn't take much imagination or research acumen for today's broadcast and print journalists to produce news with suburbia or the middle class in mind. Many reside in affluent suburban areas them-selves as do most of the politicians, government officials, and academic experts they rely on for information and sound bites. Even those jour-nalists who still make their homes in the cities earn so much that they literally inhabit a different world from the urban masses. A survey of the home addresses of 3,400 journalists at a cross section of thirteen news organizations conducted by Peter Brown, editor of the Sunday Insight section of the *Orlando Sentinel*, found that journalists are overrepre-sented in elite neighborhoods (that house 26 percent of the nation's population) while they are underrepresented in the less-affluent neigh-borhoods that are home to the plurality of the nation's population. For instance, 29 percent of the *Washington Post*'s staff live in four upscale D.C. suburbs, while only 20 percent of the newspaper's market does (Duin 2000, 2). Perhaps even more striking, of journalists working in medium-sized cities, 42 percent earned $50,000 a year or more (compared to just 18 percent of the general population of those cities). Such statistics suggest that, as Nieman Foundation for Journalism curator Bill Kovach, among others, has argued, "More and more, journalists are part of the elite, socially and economically, of the country" (Duin 2000, 2).

The news media are the public's principal source of daily social, political, and economic information. The facts and ideas they choose to disseminate become the shared context for our political debates, form the basis for our interpretations of social trends, and inform our understanding of public opinion. As such, the media largely sets the agenda for discussion and discourse about a broad range of civic issues; as one critic quipped, "they can't tell us what to think but they can tell us what to think about" (Parenti 1986, 23).[3] The media's relative lack of attention to the social realities and social needs of the cities implies that the problems of our urban centers and of the racial and ethnic "Others" who reside in them are usually not worth attending to and are irrelevant to "ordinary" (read here "white," "suburban," "middle-class") people's lives. It also renders those rare occasions when the urban crisis does receive coverage even more ideologically potent.

Accentuating the Negative

When the mainstream media deign to pay attention to the metropolitan core, they usually restrict their reporting to instances in which cities and city dwellers inconvenience or endanger their suburban middle- and upper-class target audience; that is, they typically only cover the city in connection with street crime (seen as a threat to the safety of average suburbanites) or social welfare spending directed toward destitute urban populations (seen as a financial burden on middle-class families). This selective pursuit of sensational stories about underclass depravity and parasitism (and the concomitant exclusion of almost all other news about cities) always already categorizes the inner city as a place of violence and lawlessness, as the site of "criminal," "dependent," or "pathological" communities. Sometimes this identification takes the form of outright labeling, as in the case of one *New York Times* article on crime in poor areas of New York City that was accompanied by "a map of New York City featuring the black and Latino neighborhoods in question—under the label 'Criminal Communities'" (Muharrar 1998, 15). Typically, the equation of the inner city and "criminality" is not quite so explicit; rather, by repeatedly presenting the metropolitan core as the spatial locus of reported violence and pathology, news organizations subtly "criminalize" the people living there through association.

For instance, one 1987 study encompassing a month of output from Boston's six largest news media (comprising approximately 3,200 stories) found that most of the stories about the city's two predominately black neighborhoods "dealt with crime or violent accidents and, all in all, 85 percent reinforced negative stereotypes of blacks. Blacks were persistently shown as drug pushers and users, as thieves, as troublemakers, and as victims or perpetrators of violence" (Solomon and Lee 1990, 243). Although the study found that news about these neighborhoods "accounted for only 7 percent of the crime news during the thirty-day period, 59 percent of all the news about these two black neighborhoods was about crime" (243). "The tacit message," the study concluded, "is that while all criminals may not be black, most inner-city blacks are criminals" (243).

Research conducted by scholars James Ettema and Limor Peer on newspaper coverage of different sections of Chicago has revealed a similar tendency to criminalize inner-city communities. Ettema and Peer examined all news stories concerning two of the city's neighborhoods— Austin, a poor, mostly black neighborhood on the West Side, and Lincoln Park, a fashionable, affluent, majority white neighborhood located just north of downtown—appearing in the *Chicago Tribune* and the *Chicago Sun-Times* in 1993. Among other things, they found that 111 of the 161 *Tribune* and *Sun-Times* stories about Austin (or 69 percent) were "framed in terms of a social problem" (Ettema and Peer 1996, 839). By contrast, only 34 of the 154 stories about Lincoln Park were framed this way. Moreover, Ettema and Peer found that the newspapers tended to portray Austin almost exclusively as "crime-ridden and drug-infested" (despite the fact that the neighborhood actually had slightly fewer reported criminal offenses [10,370] than Lincoln Park [10,550]). As they explain, "crime . . . not only leads the list of the five most frequently reported problems in Austin; . . . it is the topic of more than half of all problem-oriented stories from that neighborhood" (840). Although crime also leads the list of frequently covered social problems in stories about Lincoln Park, it was the focus of less than a quarter of the problem-oriented stories about that community.[4]

The mainstream media's coverage does more than simply associate particular minority urban neighborhoods with "violence" or "crime," it equates cities and urbanity in general with crime and bloodshed. To cite just one example of this tendency, my analysis of the abstracts collected in the *Vanderbilt Television News Index* found that 70 out of 133 non-sports, non-entertainment stories about Los Angeles broadcast on the nightly network news in 1997 were about crime, illegal drugs, gangs, or violence. That adds up to 52 percent of all hard news specifically about L.A. broadcast on national television that year. While over half of those items concerned the murder of comedian Bill Cosby's son and related events, the rest reported on absolutely stereotypical instances of urban mayhem: a bank robbery that led to a fatal shoot-out (ABC 2/28/97; NBC 2/28/97; CBS 3/2/97; ABC 3/3/97; CBS 3/4/97; ABC 3/5/97); a bust at a ghetto amphetamine lab run by a Mexican drug cartel (CNN 12/5/97); an update on the murder of rap star Notorious B.I.G. (CBS 3/18/97); and a story about homeless men "selling drugs and their bodies" on the city's streets (ABC 5/25/97). Coverage of other cities that same year was similarly marked by a frightened fixation with urban violence: Chicago got national television attention in connection with the killing of an eleven-year-old girl in the Cabrini-Green public housing project (CBS 2/7/97); in New York City, the murder of high school teacher Jonathan Levin by a teenager (CNN 6/3/97; NBC 6/6/97; ABC 6/7/97; CBS 6/7/97; NBC 6/7/97; CNN 6/7/97) and the murder of a man in Central Park by two muggers (CBS 5/24/97; CBS 5/21/97) both received multistory coverage; and five of the sixteen network evening news stories about Detroit in 1997 concerned a single shoot-out that occurred during a bank robbery (ABC 3/11/97; CBS 3/11/97; NBC 3/11/97; CNN 3/11/97; ABC 3/12/97).

In their single-minded obsession with violent criminality, the national nightly news shows follow their local counterparts whose preoccupation with blood and gore, media scholar George Gerbner among others has charged, often preempts "balanced coverage" of urban areas (Gerbner 1996; Sacco 1995). Since 1994, the Rocky Mountain Media Watch has conducted an annual nationwide survey of the content of local television news and every single year they have found a surfeit of crime and violence. For instance, the group's 1997 content analysis of a hundred local newscasts on the night of February 26, 1997, from fifty-five markets in thirty-five states revealed that 33 percent of all local news stories were devoted to crime, making it the most frequently covered news topic (in contrast, only 7.7 percent of the stories were devoted to government, 2.2 percent to elections, and less than 2 percent to such topics as poverty, religion, or the environment) (Klite et al. 1997, 6). Crime was the lead story on 59 percent of the broadcasts and 42 percent of those lead crime stories were about murders (5). Similarly, the group's 1998 survey of 102 local news broadcasts from fifty-two markets on the evening of March 11, 1998, revealed that crime once again dominated the local news, accounting for 29 percent of news airtime, and that, once again, murder was the most frequently covered offense (Klite 1998, 3).

Other, more extensive studies of local television news shows in particular metropolitan areas generally vindicate Rocky Mountain Media Watch's findings. A survey of local television news shows in Chicago found that "eight or nine minutes out of the 14 given to news on an average half-hour broadcast in late 1993 and early 1994 concerned the threat of violence to humans" (Entman 1994, 31). One week-long study of local television news in Los Angeles conducted by Fairness and Accuracy in Reporting found that "crime constitutes anywhere from 23 percent to 54 percent of all news coverage on L.A. stations" (Osborn 1996, 24). A two-month study of local evening news in the Detroit metro area conducted by the *Detroit News* found that 30 percent of local coverage focused on criminal mischief of various sorts (Douglas 1997, 19). Danilo Yanich's research on local television news in the Baltimore and Philadelphia markets found that for both cities crime was the most frequently covered story in 1996, accounting in both cases for roughly a third of all stories covered in the average evening newscast (Yanich 2001, 227). Despite profound differences in the way television stations in these markets presented the geographic distribution of crime in cities and suburbs, "they all conveyed the message that the city was a dangerous and forbidding place" (222).[5]

The local evening news on WSVN, the Fox affiliate in Miami, Florida, stands as a somewhat extreme, though hardly atypical, example of how violence-obsessed local television news has become. According to media critic Larry Platt, a full ten minutes out of the sixteen minutes of "hard news" included in the station's August 17, 1994, broadcast was devoted to crime and other "mean world" stories (Platt 1999, 243). Two studies by University of Miami journalism professor Joseph Angotti demonstrate that the newscast Larry Platt witnessed was no anomaly. Angotti found that in November 1993 roughly half of the average WSVN six o'clock news show dealt with crime or crime-related stories; by May 1994, that percentage had dropped slightly to around 30 percent, still a significant figure (Platt 1999, 243). WSVN's local news is so gruesome, in fact, that in 1994 nine Miami hotels decided to black out all or some of its programming, explaining that tourists "look at Channel 7 (WSVN) and they're afraid to go out on the streets" (243).

Even cases in which mainstream reporting on central cities deviates from its overwhelming focus on street crime and violence, the topics covered seem chosen to cast urban life in the worst possible light. When not depicted as staging grounds for gang warfare and other wanton violence, cities most commonly appeared on television news as backdrops for reports about "welfare dependency" and "the underclass." For instance, in 1995, at the height of the debate over so-called welfare reform, seven of the seventy-four stories about Chicago aired on national television news (or roughly 10 percent) were about welfare (though here again the majority of stories about the city dealt with criminal activity of some kind, including six feature-length pieces about guns and violence in public housing). Other urban stories unrelated to crime that have received significant media coverage in the past few decades include homelessness (which garnered the most media attention in the mid-'80s), and the 1992 L.A. riots and their aftermath. Almost never have the key social, political, and economic factors shaping inner-city poverty, homelessness, and crime been the focus of stories in their own right.

The ideological orientation of the news media, as Ben Bagdikian among others has noted, manifests itself as much in the stories it chooses to cover as in the slant of the coverage itself (Bagdikian 1997, 216–18). The media's fascination with urban savagery and pathology, regardless of the actual content and framing of its coverage of these topics, betrays an investment in the terrified vision of the inner city promoted by conservative pundits like William Bennett and Charles Murray. From the perspective of demagogues like Bennett or Murray, as we have seen, most contemporary urban problems (crime, poverty, homelessness, blight) can be traced to a fearsome minority underclass that is amoral, self-destructive, and prone to lawlessness and drug use. By repeatedly juxtaposing criminality and the city the nightly network news at the very least lends credibility to this view. But this is only half the story. Not merely the focus on crime and "underclass poverty," but the standard images, terminology, concepts, and explanations used in most reporting about the postindustrial city are, I contend, deeply indebted to conservative and racist ideology.

Televising the Lawless Postindustrial City: Framing the "Epidemic of Violence," Explaining "Urban Crime"

In order to underscore the various derogatory, stigmatizing ways journalistic discourse figures and maps the postindustrial metropolis, I want to focus here on what is still the most popular and culturally influential form of such discourse: television news. Despite the rise of cable and "narrow-casting," network television news remains a dominant influence on civic discourse and debate. Until their retirements in 2005, Dan Rather, Tom Brokaw, and Peter Jennings still defined the major political, cultural, and social issues for millions of Americans every evening (on the power of television news, see Hallin 1994). Indeed, the 1997 Roper Starch poll on American attitudes toward various media found that 69 percent of those interviewed got their news from television compared to 37 percent who cited newspapers, 17 percent who cited radio, and a mere 7 percent who cited other people (Davies 1997, 4D). Although the rise of the Internet as a news source has certainly cut into the audience for broadcast journalism, even Internet-savvy young people continue to get much of their information about current events from television; in one 2002 survey, 82 percent of 18- to 24-year-old respondents identified television as their main news source while just 11 percent mentioned the Internet (RoperASW 2002). According to the Pew Center for the People and the Press, 31 percent of Americans regularly watch the network evening news and some 50 percent still tune into the nightly newscasts at least occasionally (Pew Research Center for the People and the Press, 2000). Television news, as Margaret Morse once observed, "performs a cohesive function, linking people together and connecting the isolated and increasingly deinstitutionalized private realm of experience to the public world outside" (Morse 1986, 56); it is televised accounts of significant social and political events, and not the usually much more balanced, informed, and in-depth treatment of the same events provided by newspapers and news magazines, that are talked about around the water cooler at work. Clearly, then, in order to grasp the news media's ideological influence over American's perceptions of cities and urban problems, one has to begin by grappling with television news.

Though the average story on evening television news shows lasts barely two minutes, television news is no mere headline service. As Daniel Hallin points out, the network's nightly newscasts provide "not just information or entertainment, but 'packages for consciousness'— frameworks for interpreting and cues for reacting to social and political reality" (Hallin 1994, 90). Everything from the reporter's narration to the photography to the choice of sound bites and sources contributes to the construction of such interpretive frameworks. In the case of network evening newscasts on the city and its problems, those frames almost without exception map the city as a place of rampant violence and social pathology while offering victim-blaming "moralistic" explanations for urban ills. This can be most clearly demonstrated by analyzing a specific example in detail.

The CBS *Evening News* for September 22, 1995, featured a story on trends in youth crime that typifies the way the networks cover urban realities. It begins, as do most items on regular evening newscasts, with an introduction by the anchor, Dan Rather, shot seated in the studio, directly addressing the camera. Star anchors like Rather dominate the nightly news. Theirs are the most trusted voices in journalism and they are presumed to speak from a position of objective, impassive rationality; their seriousness and perceived passion for the truth endow each newscast with an indispensable "impression of credibility" (Morse 1986, 58–59). As Jimmie Reeves and Richard Campbell observe, they "give both bodily form and personal identity to the ideal of professionalism" (Reeves and Campbell 1989, 27). They also supply the orienting narration through which we as viewers are to make sense of the wealth of heterogeneous information and visuals presented in the average evening newscast.

In this case, Rather's opening immediately creates an edgy apprehensive tone that permeates the remainder of the story:

> A jogger murdered in New York's Central Park, a little girl gunned down in her family's car in L.A. Crimes like these are terrifying partly because they seem to erupt out of nowhere. But crime does not come out of nowhere and some who study it say the worst is yet to come. Correspondent Wyatt Andrews is looking into the wave of the future on tonight's "Eye on America."

Rather's introduction gives the viewer plenty to be scared about—joggers murdered, little girls gunned down, the worst still yet to come—but it also hints, with its mentions of Central Park and L.A., that the proper object of that fear is the inner city. The topic box located over Rather's shoulder during the lead-in—which shows a silhouette of a "big city" skyline with the word "CRIME" in the foreground—visually underscores the association between the city and criminality suggested by Rather's discourse (see Figure 3).

This suggestion is promptly redeemed by grainy, poorly lit footage of what reporter Wyatt Andrews in his voice-over labels "Hispanic gang violence in East L.A." Several studies of television news have found that what viewers remember most about a given story are its visuals. And this footage is nothing if not visually striking, consisting as it does of an extended sequence in which several tee-shirt clad Latino teens beat and then shoot a helpless victim in the middle of a city street while a police car flees off-screen to "call for backup." The footage places the viewer into the privileged position of a voyeur surveying the misfortunes of others, a position that, as Robert Stam has noted of television news in general, "elicits an ambivalent reaction—mingling sincere empathy with mildly sadistic condescension" (Stam 1983, 27). After being subjected to this horrific spectacle, it is difficult not to be persuaded when Andrews's voice-over tells us that the events we've witnessed constitute "a rare and

Figure 3. Dan Rather on youth crime. *CBS Evening News,* September 22, 1995.

degrading snapshot of life in the inner city" that "happens every day" (after which he goes on to warn us that youth crime is on the rise and "by all accounts it won't soon improve"). In television news such faceless voice-over narration lends authority to what reporters say, as Reeves and Campbell put it, by "contributing to the illusion of journalistic distance" and by allowing reporters to pose as recorders or "harbingers" of the facts (Reeves and Campbell 1989, 28). Though this is ostensibly a story about youth crime in general, already Rather's introduction, Andrews's authoritative voice-over, and the footage of the East L.A. gang fight establish the urban core as the source of the coming crime wave.

For those who still haven't gotten the picture, this point is re-affirmed later in the story by having Andrews appear in front of a graffiti-covered alleyway (see Figure 4). As Margaret Morse tells us, "the visual background of the stand-up (for example, the White House, Capital Hill, farm field, or overlook of Jerusalem) is a carefully chosen 'icon,' an image of something 'real,' the significance of which does not depend on any specific event but already exists independently. It functions as a symbol" (Morse 1986, 71). In this story, and in countless others like it, the graffiti-covered wall or alley conjures up the spectacle of street gangs marking out and battling over drug turf; in other words, it becomes an "icon" for the inner city as imagined by the likes of William Bennett, Daniel Patrick Moynihan, and Pat Buchanan.

Having accepted the conservative vision of dysfunctional under-class communities seething with violence, the report then plunges fur-ther into the subject of the impending onslaught of crime. First, we hear from James Fox, a criminologist from Northeastern University, who (according to Andrews's voice-over) thinks that the rising number of children without adult supervision is "a recipe for a coming crime wave" and tells us he's "predicting that by the year 2005 we may very well have a bloodbath." Next, we meet Lorraine Rampersol, a single mom from the Bronx, who talks about how much she fears for the safety of her eleven-year-old daughter. The combined testimony of these two sources—one an academic expert and the other a "decent, upstanding" inner-city res-ident—suggests an apparent social consensus about the existence of an emergent "youth crime problem." This consensus is confirmed for us when Andrews, in a brief "stand-up" appearance before the camera, asks, "So if everybody already knows the new crime wave is coming, everybody from the people in these fearful neighborhoods to a worried federal government, the question is what can be done about it?" Yet it is worth noting that the empirical basis of the consensus Andrews takes for granted is shaky at best. Progressive critics have long claimed that the specter of a rising "youth crime wave" that emerged during the 1990s was a conservative myth designed to win support for more cops and bigger jails at a time when overall crime rates were dropping (see Males 1996, especially chapter 4). In 1995, the year the CBS report ran, urban areas with populations over 1,000,000, while still burdened with more crime than their suburbs, actually experienced a 6 percent drop in reported crime (Cohl 1997, 97). True, murder rates for teens were rising, but murder rates tend to fluctuate wildly from year to year. And in fact, since the mid-'90s, the evidence for such a crime wave together with

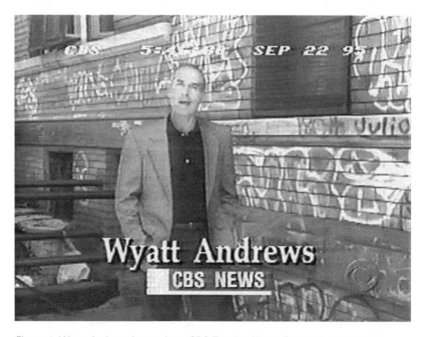

Figure 4. Wyatt Andrews's stand-up. *CBS Evening News,* September 22, 1995.

much of the hype surrounding it have all but disappeared as youth crime rates have plummeted to record lows (Schiraldi 2000; Westphal 1999).

Predictably, the expert strategies for coping with the coming terror trotted out toward the end of the CBS story are in keeping with its general ideological thrust. The first proposal aired comes from criminologist Adam Wallenski who is shown standing on a litter-strewn street declaring that we need "probably 500,000" new police officers at "the very minimum" to respond to the problem. Fox then reappears to argue for more programs to occupy children during their unsupervised after-school hours. Finally, black conservative Shelby Steele is pictured making the case that the focus should be on "fathers who abandon children." Looking at the camera, he solemnly warns, "If you're going to bring children into the world, you've got to raise them. . . . If you don't raise them, the truth of the matter is, there really isn't much anybody else can do." As a representative of what Mike Davis has called the "black-lash" (Davis 1990, 291), he personifies the growing number of reactionary black intellectuals who've built their careers on stigmatizing the "ghetto underclass." His appearance here is doubly important (and perhaps has extra credibility) because he is the one African American expert consulted in the course of the story.

Upon examination, it is clear that each of the experts' proposed solutions is predicated on some problematic and deeply reactionary assumptions. Like Bennett, Siegel, and other advocates for an expanded, more muscular police state, Wallenski assumes that what the unruly postindustrial metropolis needs most is order at all costs; as the savagery of the New York police under the regime of Mayor Giuliani has made clear (Smith 1997), the price African Americans, the homeless, and the poor must pay for the sort of "order" Wallenski favors is high indeed. Both Fox and Steele subscribe to the view—indebted to the theories of Bennett and other right-wing commentators analyzed in the last chapter—that urban crime is the natural result of the "breakdown" of the black family, which in turn has been caused by the irresponsible sexual behavior of poor, young black men and women. Yet, as I've already argued, as an explanation of inner-city crime—and, for that matter, as an explanation of the shifting structure of African American families—this overlooks far too much that is obvious. It overlooks the fact that family structures are changing in virtually every community in America and renders invisible the unemployment, hyper-segregation, and political marginalization that render a life of crime one of the few attractive options for someone growing up in the postindustrial ghetto. Less a serious explanation than a way of creating a convenient group of scapegoats for the economic transformation of the American city and its unsavory social ramifications, the ideas of Fox and Steele have the advantage of being reducible to a succinct set of media-friendly slogans and stereotypes. And by the end of the report on the coming youth crime wave—when Wyatt Andrews asks Lorraine Rampersol, "Is there a way society can go back to the days when parents felt responsibility for the children they have?"—it is their ideas that CBS has openly endorsed.

Obviously, it would be a mistake to draw too many conclusions from a single story on a single nightly newscast. Nevertheless, as I demonstrate below, the ideological subtext and rhetorical tenor of CBS's report is utterly typical of network coverage of the American city in the final two decades of the twentieth century. In what follows, I focus specifically on television's treatment of such topics as the drug war, street crime, welfare reform, urban policy, and white flight, the urban issues discussed most frequently on nightly network news shows. And no matter what the issue, in report after grim report, the networks cast the nation's big cities, and their urban minority neighborhoods in particular, as places to be feared and avoided.

Drug War Zone

The network's vision of inner cities as seething caldrons of crime was perhaps nowhere more evident than in their reporting on what came to be known as the "war on drugs." As Jimmie Reeves and Richard Campbell document in their ground-breaking monograph on television coverage of the cocaine and crack crisis, *Cracked Coverage* (1994), during the Reagan administration (1980–88), the network evening news shows aired some 528 separate items on the subject of cocaine (with the number of stories increasing every year up to 1986, after which coverage tapered off a bit). What their analysis of those reports reveals is the degree to which "journalistic coverage of defining moments in the cocaine narrative corroborated the drug control establishment's self-interested promotion of drug hysteria" (Reeves and Campbell 1994, 103) while at the same time legitimating the New Right's "backlash politics." Above all, Reeves and Campbell found that the discourse of television news was implicated in "converting the war on drugs into a political spectacle that depicted social problems grounded on economic transformations as individual moral or behavioral problems that could be remedied by simply embracing family values, modifying bad habits, policing mean streets, and incarcerating the fiendish 'enemies within'" (3). Early on in the "cocaine narrative," when cocaine was viewed as a status symbol and as a drug of the rich, the affluent, white coke users depicted on television news were repeatedly framed as "redeemable offenders," as unfortunate and weak-willed deviants whose "normalcy" could be restored with the requisite amount of therapy (123–25). As such, the reporting of the cocaine story in the 1970s and early '80s relied less on the police and courts as sources of information than on the voices of drug counselors, treatment program administrators, and therapists (124). The upper-class addicts featured in these stories were treated as morally defective, self-indulgent, and self-destructive, but were rarely pictured as incorrigible or beyond hope; for all their faults, they were presented as members or potential members of mainstream (i.e. "white," "middle-class") society.

All of this changed with the discovery of "crack," a cheap, smokable, and highly addictive form of coke that quickly became popular in the inner-city neighborhoods around the country. In 1985, the symbolic source of cocaine's menace to society shifted from the hot tubs of Hollywood to the mean streets of the ghetto. Typical of the initial explosion of crack stories was the piece filed by NBC's Dennis Murphy on May 23, 1986. Murphy's report, like any number of crack reports that came later, fixated on the threatening, abnormal space of the crack house, "depicted as a terrifying and alien setting; a place where children are held as collateral; 'a modern-day opium den'; 'a filthy room with a steel door and armed guards'" (130). Moreover, the report depicted the crack users themselves as "terrifying" and "alien." As Reeves and Campbell point out, in the late '80s, the frequency of television journalism's coverage of crack took off and the reporting itself increasingly took the side of the police in what one critic described as "the hottest combat-reporting story to come along since the end of the Vietnam war" (134). News crews accompanied SWAT teams on raids of crack dens and into pitched battles with drug dealers in cities like San Francisco, San Diego, New York, Miami, and Camden, New Jersey. In Los Angeles, then–First Lady Nancy Reagan was filmed with Police Chief Daryl Gates surveying the site of an April 9, 1989, ghetto drug bust; glancing at the handcuffed African American suspects lying on the floor of their alleged "rock house," Reagan declared "these people here are beyond the point of teaching and rehabilitating" (136).

Such sentiments, argue Reeves and Campbell, were hardly unusual among the commentators included in network coverage of the crack crisis. For instance, a notable June 21, 1986, NBC report by Jennifer McLogan openly approved of what it called "community action" to "take back the streets" from crack pushers. The piece is interspersed with images of anti-crack demonstrations in the Bronx, Miami, Texas, and Baltimore. As Reeves and Campbell point out, "the report also approves of the religious consecration of expanded police action—a consecration that seems to transform the anti-crack crusade into something of a holy war" (154); significantly, it includes an interview with a "law-and-order" priest from the Bronx—who, viewers are told, has been shot at by "burglars high on crack"—calling for the president to treat the crack situation as a national security issue. McLogan's narration takes for granted the validity of the priest's demands and, as such, is "best thought of in terms of a kind of ventriloquism in that the reporter becomes the mouthpiece for policing forces" (155).

Again and again in the network news organizations' coverage of the crack story, the various crack updates "demonize the threatening inner city while sanctifying threatened Middle America" (159). This demonization of the inner city can be seen clearly in stories like the one aired by ABC on the evening of July 28, 1986. Set in New York City and Miami, the report's rhetoric is, like the rhetoric of so many of these "crisis updates," hyperbolic and profoundly bellicose: one of the Miami scenes features that city's police chief, Clarence Dickson, comparing "packets of crack to bombs in World War II that wiped out whole neighborhoods" (160). Complementing their drug war updates from the "front lines" of the inner city, the networks ran a number of stories on the cancerlike spread of crack to the respectable landscapes of suburbia and small-town USA. By repeatedly pointing to crack as a plague invading affluent white neighborhoods from the outside, "these news stories support a powerful conservative American myth of Middle America being an idealized place of 'community' where human nature is innocent and simple, uncontaminated by the harsh realities of dehumanized, urban America" (160–61).

As narrated by mainstream television news, then, the crack story was one in which "a color coded mob of inner-city criminals threatened the suburbs, small towns, schools, families, status, and authority of (white) Middle America" (136). Ideologically, this way of viewing the "cocaine epidemic" echoed the New Right's scapegoating of the urban poor in general, and inner-city communities of color in particular, for social problems caused by decades of economic and demographic decline and federal divestment. That is, the media's coverage of the "war on drugs" accepted at face value the conservative tendency to treat "people in trouble as people who make trouble." Symptomatic of their ideological convergence with the New Right, Reeves and Campbell argue, was the media's handling of the issue of "crack mothers" and "crack babies." In several stories broadcast in the late '80s, they point out, the monstrous figure of the crack mother and the pitiful bodies of cocaine-damaged infants were held out by television news as "yet another example of the 'poverty of values' crippling America's largely black inner cities" (209). By the early 1990s, the initial surge of crack stories had begun to subside and reporting on the topic became more sober, circumspect, and self-critical.

Society under Siege: Manufacturing an Urban Crime Scare

The television news establishment's "ideological convergence" with right-wing views of urban crime did not, of course, end with the waning of the "crack crisis." If anything, during the '90s, television became more obsessed with inner-city bloodshed and lawlessness and the rhetoric employed by anchors and reporters even more stark and terrifying. So, for instance, Ted Koppel introduced a 1991 ABC story on the random murder of a recently demobilized soldier in Detroit by announcing that "in a lot of American cities, street crime has turned whole cities into war zones" (ABC 3/18/1991). Two years later, CBS anchor Paula Zahn led into a piece about overburdened urban emergency rooms by remarking that "urban violence in this country has grown so severe, some cities resemble urban battle zones every weekend" (CBS 8/29/93). In a 1997 story about a murder in Central Park, correspondent Cynthia Bowers characterized New York as "a city where violence is not unusual" (CBS 5/27/97). And so on. Indeed, though the furor surrounding crack and the drug war did die down by the early '90s, a careful analysis of national television news coverage of the inner city reveals that other figures of urban disrepute—the bloodthirsty gangbanger and the teenage "superpredator," in particular—quickly moved in to take the place of and/or supplement the "crack head" and the "drug dealer."

As a cross section of the seemingly endless flow of inner-city blood and gore the networks dished up for their audiences during the mid-'90s, consider NBC's handling of the urban crime theme. In 1993 and 1994, NBC *Nightly News* aired a series of forty-five stories on ghetto violence and street gangs provocatively titled "Society under Siege." Like the CBS broadcast discussed above, the stories were usually feature length (three to four minutes) and almost all of them centered around lurid footage of gang warfare and of African American and Latino victims and perpetrators. One story in the series began with shots of six or seven women described as members of "a Hispanic girl gang" pummeling another woman in a gang initiation ceremony (NBC 4/6/93); another opened with a montage of bloodied black bodies on stretchers and under plastic tarps (NBC 3/8/94). Quite a few "Society under Siege" stories also made liberal use of "raid footage" in which a hand-held camera accompanies police during a "forced entry" into a drug house or gang lair. Such footage, as Reeves and Campbell correctly observe, "represents nothing less than the convergence of the reportorial outlook with the policing point of view" (Reeves and Campbell 1994, 135). To appear on camera, in such footage, is to be immediately accused (and found guilty) of criminal misbehavior. When suitably terrifying visuals were unavailable, NBC made up for this lack by attempting to draw viewers in with harrowing descriptions of urban violence and its aftermath. Often these descriptions emphasized the random, indiscriminate nature of violence in the central city. Thus, in a report on murders among the youth of Washington D.C., it was implied that because the "epidemic of violence" is so severe "children are planning their own funerals" (NBC 11/1/93). And a 1994 story on the outbreak of an apparent gang war in Chicago lamented that "many victims are unsuspecting youngsters on gang turf" (NBC 8/15/94).

Fittingly, the rhetoric used by Brokaw and the correspondents throughout the "Society under Siege" series bordered on the hysterical; the network's representatives consistently adopted that "demanding voice of alarm" which Jimmie Reeves and Richard Campbell have called "the campaigning voice," a style of address in which a reporter "drops any pretense of being a disinterested reporter" and instead expresses "moral disgust" and "righteous exhortation" (Reeves and Campbell 1994, 176). For instance, Brokaw began one report with the lead-in, "we go to Ft. Worth Texas now, a place where street violence is out of control" (NBC 3/8/94). His opening monologue to a report on the shooting of a seven-year old in Chicago's Cabrini-Green housing project included the observation that for the project's residents "home is a war zone, life is under siege" (NBC 10/19/92). Moreover, when the roots of what Brokaw repeatedly characterized as "an epidemic of violence" were examined, which wasn't often, the explanations offered invariably traced the violence to broken families and "fatherless" inner-city youth. Thus, in one

1993 broadcast, Brokaw could assert without qualification that "a big problem is the growing number of kids growing up on the streets, even kids with parents and homes. Too many parents simply can't cope" (NBC 11/5/93).

Like the CBS broadcast on the coming youth crime wave and the many crack narratives examined by Reeves and Campbell, the stories in NBC's "Society under Siege" series relied almost exclusively on police, "crime-fighting" politicians, and criminologists for commentary and analysis. Indeed, often the perspective of the reports and of the "law-and-order" advocates they frequently consulted seemed to merge, so that "like a ventriloquist's dummy," the series voiced "police objectives as dire objective necessities or public mandates" (Reeves and Campbell 1994, 175) Hence, the remedies to the epidemic that received consideration in the "Society under Siege" series were invariably of the "tough," force-based variety. For example, the story about the seven-year old killed at Cabrini-Green detailed Mayor Richard Daley's plan to install metal de-tectors and one-way turnstiles at the entrances of all of Chicago's public housing projects while at the same time ordering police to search all units for illegal guns (see Figure 5). Although the piece did include a brief comment from a resident opposed to the plan, correspondent Mike Boettcher concluded his discussion of Daley's proposal by noting approv-ingly that, "Action was demanded and action was delivered" (NBC 10/19/92). The piece on Ft. Worth's gang problem celebrated the "un-usual steps" the police have taken "to try to cool things down" (NBC 3/8/94). These steps included a campaign to harass and arrest suspected gang members that included systematically stopping cars in so-called gang-occupied neighborhoods for even the most minor traffic viola-tions. To an impartial observer, such draconian remedies might raise questions about the alleged gang members' constitutional protection against "unreasonable search and seizure," but the reporter's attitude in this story was openly congratulatory. Even more sobering, the 1994 story on the broken gang truce in Chicago concluded with reporter Dawn Fri-tangelo enthusiastically describing the city's decision to station several dozen more officers in "gang turf" as "an unprecedented show of force

that will try to rival a heavy gang arsenal that is turning a Chicago summer into a season of rage" (8/15/94); the notion that such a "show of
force" could lead to more and more severe violence for the neighborhoods in question apparently didn't occur to her.

NBC's approach to covering urban crime is unfortunately all too
common on commercial television news. During the period from 1992
to 1994, while NBC was raising the alarm over the cities' "epidemic of
violence," ABC's and CBS's national nightly news programs carried hundreds of stories on gangs, drugs, and murder in America's inner cities
identical in content, tone, and political slant to those run on "Society
under Siege." For instance, in 1994, ABC weighed in with a sensational
story about a shoot-out in the police headquarters of Washington, D.C.
(ABC 11/23/94) and aired an in-depth feature about "the epidemic of
murder by children," which focused on an eleven-year-old Chicago boy
from the projects who was executed by fellow gang members (ABC

Figure 5. Mayor Daley gets tough on crime in the projects. *NBC Nightly News,*
October 19, 1992.

9/4/94). In the same year, CBS did a segment on a Philadelphia teen who died because 911 operators failed to dispatch police to a nasty street fight (CBS 11/24/94) and carried a piece about a knife-wielding homeless man living in Washington, D.C.'s Lafayette Park (CBS 12/12/94). It also aired a gut-wrenching story about a boy living in a New Orleans public housing project who sent President Clinton a hand-written letter begging him to "stop the killing in the city" only days before being murdered (CBS 7/18/94). No matter what channel they were watching, then, television news viewers in the '90s were told that society was besieged by an epidemic of violence issuing from the inner cities (see Figure 6).

Predictably, even coverage of relatively innocuous urban crimes like "graffiti vandalism" was infused by the networks with a sense of extreme foreboding. For instance, Brian Williams introduced an NBC report on Philadelphia's anti-graffiti program by announcing that graffiti writing "has been a signature of urban blight for decades" (NBC 8/4/93). Peter Jennings framed a story on rival "tagging crews" (graffiti-writing gangs) in Southern California by declaring that "police in L.A. are confronting an ugly and violent new form of vandalism" (ABC 12/18/92) (see Figure 7). These reports, like television stories on other urban crimes, repeatedly endorsed "tough" responses to even these artistic manifestations of urban lawlessness. As part of their May 24, 1994, newscast, CBS aired a long and strikingly sympathetic story on a proposal by St. Louis alderman Freeman Bosley to hold public floggings of graffiti writers (see Figure 8). "Some lawmakers believe the way to beat crime is to beat criminals," explained anchor Connie Chung in her lead-in. "They say Singapore has the right idea." The report proceeded to give Bosley a platform from which to explain why such harsh measures are needed to counter what correspondent Scott Pelley labeled "the city's urban scrawl"; only one of the quoted sources included in the report was critical of Bosley's proposal (and even that source expressed support for the spirit of his plan). Thus, even in cases of petty crime, television news worked to foment hysteria and at least implicitly supported forceful repression of inner-city residents (especially ghetto youth) as a catchall solution to the perceived problem of growing social disorder.

Shadowy Figures: Covering the Homeless, the Underclass, and Welfare Reform

Stories about street crime weren't the only instances in which television coverage of the postindustrial city during the '80s and '90s was guided by a fixation on urban pathology and conservative blame-the-victim ideology. The networks' reporting on homelessness, destitute urban neighborhoods, poverty, public housing, and welfare reform also tended to emphasize the deviance, dangers, and moral deficits of inner-city communities in tones as shrill and alarmist as the one adopted by Dan Rather in the report on youth crime discussed above. As critic Caryl Rivers observes, mainstream reporting on the poor and welfare since Reagan has fallen "neatly into the snare of the dual mythology that the poor are evil and that all individuals can transcend their circumstances, no matter how difficult" (Rivers 1996, 191).

Figure 6. Dan Rather talks about the epidemic of crime in Chicago. *CBS Evening News,* October 21, 1992.

Figure 7. The "graffiti problem," according to ABC News. *ABC World News Tonight,* December 18, 1992.

Figure 8. Alderman Bosley advocating the flogging of graffiti writers in St. Louis. *CBS Evening News,* May 24, 1994.

Consider, for instance, the way television news has reported on the pressing social issue of homelessness, a phenomenon typically (though probably improperly) equated with the big city. In his comprehensive analysis of the 246 television news items on the topic broadcast by the major networks between 1981 and 1988, Jimmie Reeves found some intriguing parallels (as well as some striking differences) between the network news organizations' "homeless narrative" and their coverage of crack during the same period. According to Reeves, in the early 1980s, television reporting on the homeless was, unlike reporting on the "drug crisis," focused on, and in some cases guided by, homeless activists highly critical of Reaganism and Reagan-era social and economic policy. Yet by the end of the Reagan administration, "the homeless had been redefined in the network news as 'a danger to themselves and others'— as a policing problem, a personal problem, or a problem for private volunteer organizations—but not an economic problem" (Reeves 1999, 60). Central to this process, Reeves maintains, was the networks' treatment in 1987 and 1988 of the controversy surrounding Joyce Brown, a homeless woman living in an affluent New York City neighborhood who was taken off the streets against her will and committed to a psychiatric hospital. In the three network news packages devoted to the Joyce Brown story, she and the homeless in general are marked off as "people whose suffering results from personal deficiencies associated with chemical dependency and/or madness" (49). Later, *60 Minutes* did a follow-up piece that rescued Brown from the charge of madness—in part by giving her air time in which to press her claim that she is "a professional homeless person"—but reinforced the dominant meaning of homelessness by presenting her story as an exception to the rule.

Insung Whang and Eungjun Min's analysis of television news discourse about the homeless also identifies a pronounced tendency in the network's coverage to both pathologize and demonize homelessness. Television news, they argue, has taught us to see homelessness as "a national emergency," one which is often figured as a "serious threat to our well being" (Whang and Min 1999b, 95). Thus, for instance, a December 21, 1993, ABC *World News Tonight* report tells of a Portland resident calling 911 after finding a homeless man digging through his trash and details the complaints of a Seattle suburbanite about her church's practice of providing shelter for the homeless (ABC 12/21/93). As Whang and Min point out in their close reading of a 1991 CBS "Eye on America" story on public antagonism toward the homeless in Santa Monica, television news shows convey the sense of difference and threat attached to the homeless by means of both visual and verbal signs. In an early sequence of that report, Whang and Min note, correspondent Bob Faw is given "optimum camera framing" while homeless people appear in a series of medium- to long-range shots taken from a high angle; the camera, in other words, literally looks down upon the homeless. This, Whang and Min speculate, "may signify the superior (higher) position of the reporter and the viewer as the representative of 'normal' America, in contrast to the inferior (lower) position of the homeless people" (100). Moreover, Faw's lead-in to the report explicitly articulates a "middle class" (and implicitly suburban) perspective on homelessness when he observes that "[o]ne reason homelessness is such a big problem is because so many people are shouting, 'Don't put the homeless in middle-class America's back yard.'" Following the introduction, footage of an "anti-homeless" rally in Santa Monica further showcases this complaint. A placard is shown "reading 'Bums' with a line drawn diagonally across it and 'Make Santa Monica Safe.'" Speakers at the rally refer to themselves as "middle class," "citizens," or as a "community" while the homeless are labeled "bums." Moreover, the rally speakers who appear on screen (Dorothy Fitzpatrick and Robert Stranieri) are "verbally or visually 'nominated' [i.e., identified by name] . . . while the homeless are not" (100). Later in the report, so-called homeless advocates, though not the homeless themselves, are allowed to respond to the concerns raised by the rally speakers. Yet, revealingly, the advocates "are mostly seen busy defending themselves against the middle class worry about what the homeless might be able to do" (103). And the homeless themselves are never allowed to speak.

As with television's coverage of urban crime, then, the network's coverage of homelessness privileges the voices of an alarmed middle class over the voices of the people with a direct stake in the issue. In their analysis of the fifty-four "magazine" or feature stories on homelessness broadcast on network evening news between 1985 and 1994, Whang and Min found this "marginalization" of the homeless perspective to be a fairly consistent pattern. As they explain, in these stories, the homeless rarely speak on camera and "no homeless people, even those allowed to speak, have been nominated either visually or verbally" (Whang and Min 1999a, 127–28). Perhaps even more important, when network news stories examine the causes of homelessness, they typically adopted an attitude that "exclusively identifies the homeless as the problem itself" (121). And, it almost goes without saying, the homeless problem is frequently identified on television news shows as a "downtown" or "urban" issue (by filming the homeless in vacant city lots, sleeping in city parks, or living in urban alleyways), while the society that is victimized is almost always projected as white, middle-class, and suburban.

Like homelessness, poverty, the underclass, and "welfare" also figure heavily as topics in television news reporting on the postindustrial city. In his article "Television, Black Americans, and the American Dream" (1989), Herman Gray offers an analysis of the representations of (urban) black life in the 1985 CBS special report, *The Crisis in Black America: The Vanishing Family*, which exposes precisely the sort of ideology that I have found continues to inform the media's fear-generating depictions of the underclass. Typically, Gray notes, "the black underclass appears as a menace and a source of social disorganization in news accounts of black urban crime, gang violence, drug use, teen pregnancy, riots, homelessness, and general aimlessness. In news accounts, poor blacks (and Hispanics) signify a social menace that must be contained" (378). In the case of the CBS special report, the very title—containing the terms "vanishing family" and "crisis"—suggests "an abnormal condition that must be recognized and addressed" (379), even though the decline of the two-parent family as a secular trend is hardly exclusive to African-American communities. The report's projection of "abnormality" onto the urban black life, Gray contends, is further framed by its visual rhetoric. Shots of "welfare lines," "couples arguing," "the police," and "housing projects" permeate the report and tie the specific theme of the "vanishing black family" to a broader (and deeply racist) discourse about American race relations. As he notes, "These images . . . draw on and evoke images of crime, drugs, riots, menace, and social problems. The people and communities who appear in these representations are labeled as problematic and undesirable" (380). The visual imagery's construction of urban black communities as deviant and criminal is complemented by the theme of the moral irresponsibility of the underclass that is developed through interviews with "immature, selfish, irresponsible" young men who've fathered children out of wedlock (381). Moralistic explanations for the problems of the underclass also receive the imprimatur of the report's host, Bill Moyers, and are endorsed by a number of "black adults of the community who claim that the problems facing the community stem from poor motivation, unclear and unsound values, and a lack of personal discipline" (382). Taken together, the visual footage, the interviews with black youth, the voice-over discourse of the report's host, and the views articulated by selected "community elders" all work to displace social explanations for the travails of urban black communities.

Television journalism's interest in the subject of inner-city poverty, welfare, and the underclass peaked most recently during the national debate over so-called welfare reform that preoccupied Congress and the White House during much of the Clinton era. In 1994, overhauling the welfare system, which had long been a priority for the Clinton administration, topped the agenda of the newly elected Republican majority in the House of Representatives and was considered particularly important by newly appointed Speaker of the House Newt Gingrich. In the first months of the 1994 congressional session, both Democrats and Republicans floated proposals for "ending welfare as we know it"—all of which included provisions eliminating the Food Stamp and Aid to Families with Dependent Children programs, requiring "work" in return for assistance, instituting limits on the lifetime duration of aid for any individual, and imposing penalties on recipients for having additional children.

A search of the abstracts for national evening news broadcasts in the mid-1990s catalogued in the *Vanderbilt Television News Index* reveals a huge spike in television attention to welfare that coincides perfectly with the major parties' push to eliminate aid to the poor: in 1993, the three major networks and CNN aired a mere 25 stories about welfare and welfare reform; in 1994, the number of stories on the topic had jumped to 75; in 1995, the first full year of the new Republican Congress, the number of items broadcast about welfare soared to 148; in 1996, the number of items the networks and CNN devoted to the issue fell slightly to 114; in 1997, the year after Clinton signed the Republicans' welfare-reform bill, the number of stories on welfare aired on national television news shows had fallen again, to 53. At the height of the welfare-reform debate, the networks zealously reported every new development in the unfolding saga, covering speeches in Congress, televising press conferences, reporting on the various provisions of rival reform bills, interviewing a veritable army of "poverty experts," conducting and announcing the results of dozens of opinion polls on the issue. Even more important, they used the story as a pretext to descend on public housing projects, medical clinics, and welfare offices in order to examine, and pass moral judgment on, the lives, families, and behavior of the black and Latino urban poor. Like the Moyers special report analyzed by Gray, most such reporting cast the poor of all races as behaving and thinking differently from "normal" (that is, white, middle-class) Americans, usually as irresponsible and undisciplined, and occasionally as a menace to polite society. But more than that, like television coverage of crime and homelessness, such reporting actively stigmatized the inner-city neighborhoods and communities it mapped, and in so doing helped to perpetuate and naturalize the worst middle-class prejudices against the city.

The standard ideological framing of the urban underclass and the ghetto in television news reports on "welfare reform" can perhaps be made transparent by closely scrutinizing a few symptomatic examples. Take for instance two CBS *Evening News* feature stories that aired on successive evenings in February 1994 as part of a week-long series on the topic.

The first of these reports, broadcast on February 8, focused on unwed fathers; this choice of focus is somewhat unique—most coverage of welfare and urban poverty dealt overwhelmingly with unwed mothers and their children—but the ideological framing of its subject is typical of the networks' coverage as a whole. The story begins, as usual, with an introduction from anchor Dan Rather. "Welfare reform—" intones Rather, "It helped get President Clinton elected in '92 and will get other candidates elected in the months ahead. But why?" His explanation: "American taxpayers are spending billions of dollars to support children they don't even know. In many cases they are children created by fathers they don't even know." Already in Rather's opening remarks, one can sense a certain animus against welfare and its recipients, an animus that is thoroughly taken for granted; by emphasizing that American taxpayers "don't even know" the children they are supporting, Rather insinuates that such support is somehow illegitimate, that these unknown children have no reasonable claim to the taxpayer's sympathy and aid (all this despite the fact that many more tax dollars regularly go to defense contractors and government officials who taxpayers also "don't know"). The grounds for Rather's (and, it is suggested, the American public's) antagonism toward these children quickly becomes apparent in the opening sequence of the report itself.

Narrated by veteran correspondent Bob McNamara, the story opens with a shot of two men silhouetted against a gritty, downscale city street. "They are there everyday" McNamara's voice-over begins, "outside Chicago's big housing projects, shadowy figures who gather on street corners and stand in doorways, hang out near the playground and sometimes push baby strollers." Meanwhile, the image track illustrates McNamara's ominous narration: we are treated first to a shot of four black men in stocking caps sitting on the stoop of a severe, institutional brick building; this is followed by a shot of black men standing in shadows, a shot—partially obscured by steam rising from the gutter—of a group of men on a street corner, a glimpse of three black men standing in the doorway of a housing project, a shot taken through chain link fencing of some men milling around an outdoor basketball court, and, finally, a quick take of a black man pushing a baby stroller past a desolate vacant lot (see Figure 9). The use of shadow, steam, and backlighting render the men pictured in these images both anonymous and vaguely threatening; they appear quite literally as McNamara's "shadowy fig-ures." The fact that this opening montage is made up mostly of long shots of these men and that they are shown clustered in groups (in which they often turn away from the camera) only heightens the impression that they are potentially hostile and involved in furtive, illicit activities. "They" McNamara continues, "are unwed fathers, the flip side to an unsettling American dilemma." By the end of its first twenty seconds, the report has thoroughly "othered" and "pathologized" its ostensive sub-jects, the "unwed fathers" of children being supported by AFDC. These men, only one of whom is allowed to speak on camera, are represented as thoroughly shiftless and irresponsible.

After his lead-in, McNamara, shown standing in the doorway of one of the public housing complexes, notes that while the majority of the legal residents of Chicago's public housing are women and their chil-dren, "some fathers don't go far, staying on in the projects, living with women, fathering children," a line that hints that these men are breed-ing with uncivilized and reckless abandon. Yet, McNamara continues later in the report, "many of the women who live here say they are better off without a man in their lives." In support of this claim, we are introduced to Latisha Lehman, an overweight, white, twenty-seven-year-old unwed mother of three (multiracial) children who, she tells us, all have different fathers. Lehman is, in the context of the report, a stand-in and icon for all welfare mothers; with the exception of her skin color, she certainly fits the established stereotypes: she's overweight, has a brood of wild, disobedient, multiracial kids, lives in a messy apartment, and appears to spend most of her time sitting in front of the television. "The men in her life have not been dependable," McNamara's voice-over asserts, and then we hear Lehman complain that she has only a single, blurry picture of one of the fathers of her children. Later in the inter-view she tells McNamara, "I think if you look out the window you'll see gang members out there and drug dealers out there." The camera fol-lows her instructions, training its gaze out her window onto a group of three black males hanging out on the sidewalk below. The men who fathered her children are absent, this visual implies, because they spend their time on the streets.

Just as significant as this report's vision of a ghetto populated by shiftless black men, unwed welfare moms, and fatherless children is the way it makes sense of this imagined state of affairs. The lone "expert" McNamara consults to explicate the phenomena of "unwed fathers" is Chicago Housing Authority director Vincent Lane. "We've got to find a way to not let the children suffer," he explains. "We didn't set standards. We didn't hold people accountable for their actions. And we should have. And now we're thirty years later trying to figure out how we undo that." Lane, McNamara quips in the voice-over, "has harsh words for some fathers." Lane then continues with his lament: "There's a lot of men out there who believe it is not their responsibility to take care of the children, it is only their responsibility to bring them into the world." He goes on to explain that the mothers, too, have to realize that "there is no free lunch."

Figure 9. Shadowy figures in the city. *CBS Evening News,* February 8, 1994.

This diatribe is utterly consonant with the main motifs of conservative ideological discourse on the urban crisis, the "break-up" of the family, and welfare: the problems of the inner-city poor are not caused by racism or an unjust economic system or a failure of democracy but by a chronic lack of "standards" and a failure of personal "accountability"; welfare mothers are looking for a "free lunch" while the men who father their children could not care less about their offspring and so on. Like Shelby Steele in the report on youth crime analyzed earlier, Lane is an educated black man in a position of power, and that gives his views extra credibility, as does the fact that what he has to say is never "balanced" with an opposing view. Moreover, Bob McNamara's concluding remarks seem to reiterate Lane's position. Over a series of shots of people looking out of windows and doorways set in the carceral-looking facades of a Chicago housing project, with a siren (that has been added during the editing process) blaring ominously in the background, McNamara tells us, "It is a system that started with the best intentions and has become for many a prison. Where people can see a better life but can't become part of it. Where their children too often learn how to give up instead of how to get out." These comments neatly summarize the reactionary "common sense" about public housing and the entire welfare system—that these things were started with the "best intentions" but now "imprison" the poor and foster in them a debilitating dependency—which has guided the story from the beginning.

The "Eye on America" report CBS ran the following evening, February 9, 1994, hews even more closely to the conservative line on the underclass than the one on unwed fathers. Once again, Rather sets the scene by indicating that the quandary at the heart of the welfare-reform debate is whether taxpayers should be paying "billions of dollars that support unwed mothers and their out-of-wedlock children." The story proper, again narrated by Bob McNamara, opens by introducing us to a seventeen-year-old Latina woman from Dallas, the mother of a newborn, who is described as "single and scared" and "dependent on public assistance." It then cuts to a clip of a speech by former vice president Dan Quayle in which he declares, "Bearing babies irresponsibly is simply wrong. I know it is not fashionable to talk about moral values. But we need to do it." This soundbite is followed by a shot of President Clinton saying, "We cannot renew our country when more than one half of children are born into families where there has been no marriage."

Having created through the juxtaposition of these two statements at least the illusion of complete bi-partisan agreement about the evils of "unwed motherhood," the report proceeds to provide a platform for Charles Murray's mean-spirited neo-Malthusian critique of AFDC. Murray, McNamara tells us in the voice-over, has made "a sociological splash" with his theory that welfare leads to unwed motherhood and the growth of the underclass. "I use the word 'epidemic' just as I use the word 'illegitimate' to try to make a point," Murray tells the camera. "These are not neutral behaviors." If the epidemic of unwed births continues to spread unchecked, he cautions, "we will have white urban neighborhoods that look and feel like black urban neighborhoods." Thus, even without the standard visuals of gangbangers hanging out on street corners or menacing-looking public housing complexes, this report, through Murray's calculatedly provocative speculation, manages to invoke the terrifying threat of a feral urban core. McNamara "balances" Murray's attack on public assistance by pointing out that while the "boom in births to single women has some people calling for an end to welfare and a return to the days when unwed motherhood was a source of shame, behind all those theories are real people whose problems don't lend themselves to easy solutions." He then visits a group of black women enrolled at a Dallas high school for pregnant teens who complain tearfully that they "need" their benefits. Yet immediately after this sequence, the report allows Charles Murray to have what in effect is the "last word." "The woman has a choice not to get pregnant," Murray says as if in reply to the tearful faces the viewer has just seen. "We used to do it that way in the United States. There's no reason we can't do it again." McNamara's wrap-up coveys what can only be interpreted as a kind of tentative approval of this point of view. "The world may never be the way it used to be," McNamara says over black-and-white stock footage of a 1950s church wedding, "but for some, there is a new longing for that old simplicity, when a family began with a husband and wife instead of a mother and child." While this conclusion presents itself as an impartial *commentary* on the nostalgia for the mythic nuclear family of days gone by—such is the thrust of the remark that "there is a new longing for that old simplicity"—the structure of the report itself, and particularly the forum it provides for Murray's views, serves to perpetuate and reproduce that nostalgia.

These two CBS pieces exemplify the way the standard treatment of the inner city and the underclass in network coverage of the welfare-reform story relied on and reproduced the right-wing discourse on the urban crisis. To begin with, these reports—like most network television news stories on these subjects—portray poverty and "the breakdown of the family" almost exclusively as urban, minority problems. Take, for instance, the way these issues are dealt with in the piece on "unwed fathers." By focusing exclusively on those "shadowy figures" who haunt the playgrounds of the postindustrial ghetto and allegedly father children irresponsibly, it presents its viewers with a grossly distorted interpretation of the nature of "fatherlessness" in American society. Single-parent families are on the rise in suburbia as well as in the urban core; in white, wealthy communities as well as in black and Latino ghettos (Coontz 1992, 182). Like the Moyer report on the African American family analyzed by Herman Gray, then, this CBS story treats as a proof of the ghetto's "abnormality" what is, in fact, a fairly broad, societywide trend.

Moreover, most network reporting on welfare and poverty in the '80s and '90s consistently put a black or, less frequently, Latino face on the poor. Thus, if one looks at the February 8 "unwed fathers" story, the vast majority of the poverty stricken who appear on screen at some point in the piece are identifiably black or Latino (and this despite the fact that three of the four poor people interviewed in any depth are white); and all the poor people pictured in the February 9 story on "unwed moms" were either black or Latino. As Martin Gilens shows in his book *Why Americans Hate Welfare*, the image of the poor in the news media has been "racialized" in misleading, even dishonest, ways since the late 1960s. Gilens found that the 3,387 stories aired by ABC, NBC, and CBS on the topic of poverty between 1969 and 1992 "substantially exaggerate the extent to which blacks compose the poor" (Gilens 1999, 131). In the years between 1988 and 1992, for example, more than 60 percent of the poor people pictured on network news broadcasts were black. And despite the fact that a mere 6 percent of Americans living below the poverty line are blacks who reside in urban ghettos, the ghetto is the preferred setting for just about every television news story having anything to do with poverty or welfare (132).[6]

To cite just one of the many examples that emerged from my research, NBC correspondent Mary Alice Williams begins her August 27, 1993, story on welfare dependency with a montage showing the dilapidated houses of Camden, New Jersey, and a group of black and Latino kids playing on a cluttered porch. "When they talk about the permanent underclass," Williams notes, "they are talking about places like Camden, New Jersey." Similarly, a January 31, 1995, CBS piece on how Michigan's draconian welfare-reform program is forcing women to work for public assistance checks included a gratuitous shot of some shoddily dressed African Americans ambling down a grungy Detroit street bristling with signage for bars and billboards advertising the lottery. Welfare, poverty, the underclass—all become metonymically linked in such pieces to urban space and city life. The ideological effect of this linkage, of the disproportionate attention given to the ghetto underclass by the media in their reporting on poverty, is to encourage the viewing audience to see the poor in general as "different" and "undeserving." By making economic deprivation seem to be the exclusive condition of strange urban Others, the media, as Robert Beauregard puts it, "exacerbates moral indifference" toward poverty and the effects of urban decline (Beauregard 1993, 311).

Even more nefarious, network coverage of welfare and the underclass during the Reagan era and after regularly granted anti-welfare, anti-urban, underclass-bashing academics, policy analysts, and government officials access to the airwaves while marginalizing the voices of welfare recipients and their allies in government and the academy. In the CBS stories discussed above, Charles Murray and Vincent Lane get to expound their stigmatizing theories about welfare causing "illegitimacy" and complain about the moral defects of the underclass for what, in the context of two- to three- minute stories, seems like an eternity. Perhaps even more significant, they are allowed to condemn and chastise the urban poor without direct contradiction from equally "authoritative" sources opposed to their punitive policy prescriptions. This is a recurrent pattern in the television news construction of the "welfare-reform" narrative. The typical network "welfare-reform story" of the 1993–97 period almost always included some footage of a politician or high-ranking government official attacking welfare and/or the underclass as undermining social order and as a source of creeping moral rot. So, for instance, a November 16, 1994, CBS story on welfare reform included a remarkable soundbite from Newt Gingrich in which he declares that anti-poverty programs "ruin the poor. They create a culture of poverty and a culture of violence which is destructive of this civilization." In another CBS story broadcast on June 15 of the same year, Gingrich claims, "The person who stays at home and gets a government check without working is literally morally broken down."

While most of the official sources consulted in television news stories on welfare and the underclass weren't quite so strident, some have come close. For instance, one January 29, 1995, CBS story includes a quip from governor of Florida Clay Shaw declaring that "[t]o give a 13-year-old child cash to raise a child is federally funded child abuse." President Clinton, in an interview with Tom Brokaw that was broadcast on the December 3, 1995, NBC evening news, states that Charles Murray's analysis of what's wrong with welfare is "essentially right" and claims that "once a really poor woman has a child out-of-wedlock it almost always locks her and that child into a cycle of poverty which then spins out of control further." Even the minor government officials interviewed for the network's welfare-reform coverage adhered to the anti-welfare, underclass-bashing consensus. Thus, Patrick Murphy, child advocate for Cook County (i.e., greater Chicago) appears on a December 7, 1994, NBC newscast to claim, "If someone says welfare doesn't lead to teenage pregnancy, to abuse and neglect and delinquency, I don't think they've been hanging around the courts." More often than not, perspectives like Murphy's were presented without rebuttal and only rarely were they qualified or interrogated by the correspondents' narration.

Indeed, when not giving conservative-to-centrist government officials or politicians airtime in which to denounce the immorality of the ghetto-dwelling poor, network coverage of the welfare-reform story showcased the views of a tiny group of right-wing intellectuals and pundits. From 1994 through 1997, Charles Murray appeared as a source on the nightly network news eleven times and Heritage Foundation "poverty expert" Robert Rector appeared ten times; by contrast, the chief liberal defender of AFDC, Marian Wright Edelman of the Children's Defense Fund, appeared only eight times over the same span of time (and most of those appearances were associated with a single event, the Children Defense Fund's 1996 Stand for Children rally in Washington, D.C.). Rector's statement in a February 2, 1995, CBS story on teen pregnancy is, I would contend, fairly representative of the sort of expert opinion on welfare and the urban underclass that made it into television news stories about the welfare debate. "The federal government should never have been in the business of saying to a 16-year old girl, or a 19-year old, have a child out-of-wedlock and we'll send you a check in the mail," Rector argued. "Everyone realizes that's a disaster."

Given the sources television journalists relied on to make sense of the welfare-reform narrative, it is hardly startling that many of their stories accepted as a matter of consensus the idea that the problems of the urban poor stem either from welfare or from their own "inborn" deviance, immorality, and irresponsibility. But these reports often did more than simply provide a platform for the stigmatizing views of their predominantly right-wing guests; the correspondents and anchors themselves appeared to share, or at least to entertain, the right's demeaning picture of the urban poor. Thus, their commentary and voice-overs repeatedly and approvingly invoked the American public's presumed disapproval of supposedly lazy, promiscuous "unwed mothers." Rather's setups for the reports discussed above are prime examples of this. So, too, is the way Tom Brokaw introduced a December 12, 1994, story on

Republican welfare-reform proposals by pointing out that such proposals "take direct aim at what most Americans agree is an overwhelming social problem: young unwed mothers and their children." Occasionally, the correspondents for such stories went beyond simply relaying America's supposed condemnation of the ghetto underclass and adopted a morally censorious position of their own. For instance, in her February 2, 1995, story on teen pregnancy, reporter Linda Douglas could barely contain her disapproval of one Latina teen, Nyl Medina, surviving on welfare with her infant daughter. At one point in the report, Douglas, with a stern look on her face, comments that "Nyl Medina says sometimes trouble just happens and when it does she has no problem asking the taxpayers to help bail her out. . . . Nyl feels that having children is her right. She hopes to support herself someday but she expects the government to be there if she can't." The rhetoric here clearly conveys a certain impatience with and skepticism toward Medina's point of view. To note that Medina "has no trouble asking the taxpayers to help bail her out" makes her out to be a reckless, irresponsible freeloader; to emphasize that Medina "feels" (as opposed to reasons, argues, claims, or asserts) "that having children is her right" is to raise doubts about that right. Similar outbursts of journalistic outrage over the dependence or irresponsibility of the inner-city poor are scattered throughout network coverage of the welfare-reform debate.

Finally, the everyday lives of the urban poor—and their alleged "deviance," "irresponsibility," and "dependency"—are represented in reporting on the welfare-reform debate with only token reference to the broader social, political, and economic contexts in which they are embedded. Though, as Peter Parisi puts it, "the very nature of journalism seems opposed to portrayals of the 'big picture' " (Parisi 1998, 187), mainstream journalism's rigid refusal to attend to the structural causes of postindustrial urban poverty leads to coverage that can only confirm the right's discourse on the urban crisis. Parisi's complaint that *Washington Post* reporter Leon Dash's Pulitzer Prize–winning articles on a "typical" underclass Washington, D.C., family never portray "[t]he full community dynamics of poor neighborhoods, . . . yet the narrow situation the series examines is termed 'an urban crisis'" (199) applies equally well to the even less-nuanced coverage of such families by network television news. In television's framing of the urban poor's woes during the years of the welfare-reform debate, there's very little mention of inner-city unemployment, white flight, red-lining, racial segregation, or inner-city deindustrialization; nor is there much discussion of families struggling to survive in the ghetto who don't fit the behavioral profile of the so-called underclass. Indeed, the only background or contextual information ever presented as part of such stories is the history of public assistance to the poor, a history which is inevitably presented as a record of failure and plans gone awry. It is as if the journalists covering welfare reform believed—à la Murray—that public aid to the poor is itself a main cause of inner-city destitution.

The postindustrial metropolis that emerges from network television coverage of welfare, like the one constructed by network crime reporting, is thus an utterly amoral place whose residents are caught in a "tangle of pathology" and a "culture of dependency." And as was the case with those city residents unfortunate enough to appear in television news coverage of homelessness and crack, the people who live in the urban neighborhoods on display in television journalism's welfare reform narrative are repeatedly classified not as people *in* trouble but as people who *cause* trouble (indeed, as people who *are* trouble) (Reeves and Campbell 1994, 73).

Rationalizing White Flight and "Benign Neglect"

While the American city most often figures in television news as a setting for stories about street crime or sensationalized investigations into the sordid world of scapegoated, stigmatized, social outsiders like "the homeless" or "the underclass," it does from time to time receive attention as a subject in its own right. In these extremely rare instances, the reporting often focuses narrowly on one and only one facet of contemporary urban conditions: the strained relationship between the white middle class and the metropolis. Indeed, it is arguable that a majority of the nightly network news stories aired in the last two decades that addressed themselves explicitly to urban issues concerned either the urban-dwelling middle class's abandonment of inner-city neighborhoods or the suburban-dwelling middle class's detachment from and indifference toward the city. Moreover, with very few exceptions, such stories justified and rationalized this detached indifference.

For reasons alluded to earlier, the fact that television adopts this particular perspective is hardly surprising. The middle and upper class fleeing to, thinking of fleeing to, or already ensconced in suburbia are, after all, the desirable demographic the network news shows promise to deliver to their advertisers. Their paranoid attitude toward urban life—shaped by a succession of moral panics over the city—must be validated, their media-generated prejudices against the horrors of the postindustrial ghetto flattered, their avoidance of public space made to appear sane and sensible. Thus, in the few stories network reporters filed on urban policy and the city per se during the 1990s, they perversely adopted the perspective of a white middle class that has left or is on the verge of leaving what is seen as a dying metropolitan civilization (and this despite the fact that each of the three big network news operations remains based in our largest metropolis, New York).

As a case in point, consider the piece that NBC aired on March 17, 1992, in the midst of that year's hotly contested presidential campaign. Set in Chicago and reported by Bob Kur, the story contrasted the feelings of two professional families, one white and living in the suburbs, the other black and living in the city, about the upcoming election and analyzed the reasons for the relative invisibility of urban issues in the campaign. We are initially introduced to the urban black family consisting of Al Orendorf, his wife, and his two-year-old son. Orendorf poses a severe critique of the presidential candidates' neglect of the metropolis: "The idea of by-passing and giving short shrift to the problems of major metropolitan areas is never right and can never be right." This statement is immediately followed by an interview with Bob and Diane Getke, the suburban white family. "The suburbs seem to be more self-sufficient," Bob Getke explains. "The city doesn't. So, yeah, we owe them something but I'm not going to go out on a limb and pay extra for it." The reasons politicians court the favor of the suburban plurality, Diane Getke adds, is that "people in the suburbs do vote." The candid confrontation of the growing imbalance in political power between America's cities and suburbs one finds in these opening segments is, of course, totally out of character for NBC or, for that matter, either of the other big broadcast giants; it is, as such, extremely refreshing.

However, rather than attempt to investigate and adjudicate the rival perspectives presented at the outset, in the succeeding segment the report and Bob Kur side summarily with the suburban viewpoint. Illustrated by what we can now recognize as a thoroughly formulaic montage meant to represent the foreboding American cityscape—including, among other things, a sidewalk view of a downtown street teeming with a shabby, ethnically heterogeneous crowd and an almost perfunctory shot of a burned-out building isolated against a field of vacant lots—Kur spins a narrative that is essentially an alibi for suburbanite indifference to the proverbial dependent, disadvantaged inner-city Other. "It is not that candidates stay away from the city," Kur says in his voice-over, "[i]t's just that it's no longer a priority to visit run-down housing projects and problem-plagued streets that often provided emotional backdrops for Democratic presidential campaigns." Facing the camera, standing somewhere in Chicago's central business district, Kur continues, "It seems candidates have picked up on a feeling that's hard to miss when you speak to suburban voters. It's a feeling that's been described as 'compassion fatigue.' After years of pouring money into cities, suburbanites haven't seen enough improvement to justify more big spending." As Myron Orfield among others has shown, the idea that the suburbs are or have been "pouring money" into the cities is largely untrue, an ideological myth (Orfield 1997, 7); that Kur accepts this notion at face value indicates clearly enough where his real sympathies lie. So does his rhetorical posture: when he talks about how big spending on the cities lacks justification, he doesn't present the proposition merely as what suburbanites think but rather reports it as if it were a matter of consensus, a proven and incontrovertible fact. His wrapup proceeds to endorse what is in essence Joel Garreau's specious theory that the suburbs have attained something like functional independence from their urban cores. "Commuters once had more of a connection to the cities but now when they get home to the suburbs there's little reason to leave. So called Edge Cities have sprung up providing enough of everything," Kur enthuses. In confirmation of this point, we once again hear from Bob Getke who talks about the "sad story about the city" he sees in the media and about how he feels "it no longer pertains" to him. The piece then concludes with a shot of a train pulling out of the Chicago railyards accompanied by Kur's narration: "In 1992, the campaign train is headed for stops in Edge City and the suburbs and the candidates are all aboard." Any viewer accepting the terms of this report would be compelled to conclude that this state of affairs, the politician's flight to the suburbs, was not only reasonable but inevitable.

As Robert Beauregard astutely observes, media discourse on urban decline largely "functions ideologically to legitimate urban decline" (Beauregard 1993, 306). The main thrust of this discourse, he contends, has been to explain why "cities must be left to decline, the middle class must move to the suburbs, minorities are confined to inner-city neighborhoods and funds must be spent on redevelopment" (307). In other words, the discourse presents capitalist urbanization's pattern of "uneven development"—and the socio-economic divisions separating cities and suburbs—as the product of impersonal, intractable, quasi-natural forces. One practical implication of this stance, as Beauregard rightly points out, is to "absolve individuals, businesses, and governments of the collective responsibilities associated with decline" (312). As a consequence, "collective opposition to the forces of decay is undermined"; the immiseration of the cities and the rise of the suburbs, the media's discourse insinuates, can't be challenged, only "adapted to" (317). And this seems to be precisely the message of Kur's report. His concluding remarks, in particular, appear to be little more than an apology for what he calls "compassion fatigue," a sense on the part of the affluent that the needy have been asking for too much for too long.

The depressing thing is that Kur's stance in this report seems fairly representative of television coverage of the urban policy debate that briefly became the touchstone of the 1992 presidential campaign in the immediate aftermath of the L.A. riots. The way NBC introduced a May 16, 1992, feature story about a Washington, D.C., rally demanding more federal aid for cities is emblematic. "They are places millions of Americans call home," intoned reporter Henry Champ over a montage showing big-city skylines and crowded streets. "They are places millions of Americans have fled from to seek a better life in the suburbs. They are our cities and they are in trouble." The story went on to mention the marchers' demand for an infusion of $35 billion in additional federal money to help rebuild the cities. Yet, it wrapped up by pointing out that President Bush favors targeted "tax cuts" and "enterprise zones" over more direct aid to cities and skeptically observed that "few politicians in the '90s support more federal programs." A July 12, 1992, CBS campaign story analyzed the "plight of the inner city . . . that takes the form of homelessness, poverty, unemployment, drugs, crime and violence" and quoted then-governor of New York Mario Cuomo warning of an impending social disaster in urban America. The visuals for the package reinforced Cuomo's message, showing typical scenes of urban squalor (see Figure 10) and desperation (see Figure 11). Yet, the report quickly segued to the observation that a candidate for president "cannot focus on inner cities alone if he expects to develop the kind of broad voter base needed to win an election" and concluded that "whoever wins this election, the problems of the cities will be waiting for them." An April 3, 1992, ABC story on "what the candidates are not saying about the cities" struck a similarly despairing note, holding up New York City—site of the 1992 Democratic National Convention—as an example of the urban crisis at its worse. "Like many American cities, New York City often seems on the edge of implosion," explained correspondent Jim Wooten, "a great melting pot, melting down to a formless heap of crime and poverty." Accompanying this jarring description was a typically grim montage of burned-out buildings, garbage-filled lots, and homeless people sleeping on park benches (see Figure 12). After outlining the extremely vague plans for addressing the urban crisis proffered by candidates Bill Clinton and Gerry Brown, Wooten proclaimed that "urban policy is no longer the campaign centerpiece it once was for the Demo-crats" because "this year for the first time most of the voters are in the suburbs."

Indeed, whenever network television news shows covered urban problems and the various candidates' urban policy positions during the '92 campaign, they did so from an explicitly middle-class (and suburban) point of view, and the candidates' willful neglect of the urban crisis was repeatedly legitimated by reference to the wishes of the suburban or middle-class majority. Sometimes in such reporting, as in the March 17 NBC feature discussed above, the middle-class or suburban view was "balanced" by including an urban perspective (albeit one which was often marginalized). More often, though, the middle-class view of the cities' woes was the only one presented. So, for instance, a May 30, 1992, NBC story on policies designed to address big city social problems inter-viewed a group of white, middle-class residents in rural Decatur, Illinois, about the L.A. riots and what should be done to prevent further urban

Figure 10. New York City squalor. *CBS Evening News,* July 12, 1992.

disturbances. "I'm afraid we haven't seen the last of it," said a woman working at a daycare center. "Don't give anybody anything for nothing," protested one elderly gentleman at a coffee shop, "Make 'em work for what they get." According to correspondent Mike Boettcher, none of the people he interviewed "was keen to spend middle America's tax dollars to rebuild and reinvigorate the nation's inner cities." And since Boettcher didn't bother to include the perspectives of those who might be "keen" to reinvigorate the inner cities in his story (the urban poor, civil rights leaders, big-city politicians) the effect was to justify as "common sense" a callous disregard of the fate of the cities.

Although stories about urban policy received unusually intense coverage during the '92 campaign, the networks did air other stories in the '90s that dealt with urban policy issues. Not surprisingly, those stories also tended to justify public indifference to the fate of big metropolitan centers while celebrating suburbia as a refuge from their burgeoning problems. For instance, a September 20, 1991, feature on "Edge

Figure 11. Urban desperation. *CBS Evening News,* July 12, 1992.

Cities" aired by CBS described the built-up Washington, D.C., satellite Reston, Virginia, and other such built-up suburbs as "a new world," "a gleaming suburb," and "an emerald city" (see Figure 13). The report asserted that "six out of ten Americans" now live and work around such places and talked glowingly of how they were the home of a host of "hi-tech," computer-dependent, "information age" jobs. The report also included a short interview with Joel Garreau who—in keeping with the analysis he laid out in his influential book—asserted that Edge City "is not racist but it is classist." Correspondent Wyatt Andrew's voice-over narration ratified Garreau's position, asserting boldly that the shiny office parks of suburbs like Reston "may be the most colorblind places in America." This sanguine appraisal was balanced by a brief comment from Howard University professor Ron Walters, who said that "what we've created ironically is a modern form of apartheid." Despite Walters's brief sour note, the report concluded by proposing Edge City as a

Figure 12. "A great melting pot, melting down to a formless heap of crime and poverty." *ABC Nightly News,* April 3, 1992.

kind of postindustrial utopia that "represents an America that has the power to build itself anywhere and choose what it wants to be," essentially echoing Garreau's bestselling panegyric to the wonders of the newly built-up suburban periphery.

Later in 1991, NBC ran its own feature story (12/25/91) on what it termed "the new frontier" of Edge City, which focused on Tyson's Corner, another satellite community outside Washington, D.C. While the report noted that city dwellers might see the office parks and gargantuan shopping malls of Tyson's Corner as "sterile, tacky, and uninviting" it went on to air a collection of upbeat soundbites by residents talking about how "friendly" and "convenient" Edge City is compared to the urban core. "Everything you need is nearby"enthused one woman talking about her suburban community. The story also made the point that Edge Cities "are not only changing where we live but how we vote" and discussed the declining political influence of big cities in presidential

Figure 13. Reston, Virginia, a "gleaming suburb" of Washington, D.C. *CBS Evening News,* September 20, 1991.

campaigns. Curiously, though, the report ended on an ambivalent note: over shots of crowded highway on-ramps and glistening suburban office towers, the voice-over narration concluded that "more and more Americans call Edge City home, quite possibly at the expense of a sense of community or soul." Here appended to an otherwise upbeat story as something of an afterthought, such doubts about the virtues of suburban living were notably absent from most coverage at the height of the panic over the urban crisis.

While most network reporting in the '90s was content to let viewers draw their own (obvious) conclusions from stories about the safety and convenience of suburban life, some went so far as to explicitly justify population flight from the mean streets of the urban centers to the happy, middle-class world of Edge City. For example, ABC ran a feature on middle-class flight from the cities on April 30, 1994, that treated the phenomenon as the tragic but unavoidable result of families doing "what is best" for their children. After presenting statistics on the massive middle-class exodus from Washington, D.C., since 1960 and somewhat dismissively surveying a proposal by the National Conference of Black Mayors detailing a variety of ways cities can retain or lure back middle-class families, the report focuses on Sharon Crosley, a white woman (with a two-year-old daughter) leaving her racially integrated Washington, D.C., neighborhood for suburbia because she's concerned about safety and about the quality of urban schools. "We've had some purse snatchings and car break-ins and house break-ins," she says in a matter-of-fact tone. "It's everywhere but it's a little bit closer than I'd like it to be."

The view that moving to the urban periphery is the only thinkable solution to the crisis in the inner cities was also brought to the foreground in a February 4, 1993, ABC story on "relocating the disadvantaged." Calling public housing in Chicago "the worst in the country, riddled with drugs, gangs and frightening violence," the reporter, Carole Simpson, poses the question, "What happens when you give those people [living in public housing] a chance to move on?" The case studies of welfare moms and their kids who've relocated to the suburbs that she covers in the subsequent report point to a sanguine answer: their lives improve dramatically for the better. While the idea of integrating the suburbs advanced in this story is, from any perspective concerned about social justice, an immensely appealing one, it nonetheless has the draw-back of further legitimating the notion that the cities are beyond redemption.

The overarching thrust of network television news reporting on urban policy debates during the Bush and Clinton years thus extended and confirmed the disheartening narrative about the central cities woven into the network's coverage of street crime, homelessness, and welfare. The moral of that narrative was unequivocal: with the exception of the gentrified downtowns with their middle-class tourist attractions, tele-vision news argued, the nation's cities are social disaster areas to be shunned, cordoned off, and abandoned; or, as NBC correspondent Bob Herbert put it in a 1993 story examining President Clinton's half-hearted attempts at urban policy, "for many Americans the cities are terrific places to visit but God help you if you live there" (NBC 4/30/93).

Into the Echo Chamber: From the News Media to Other Arenas of Media Culture

Informed by an ideologically conservative discourse on urban crisis and decline, compelled by bottom-line pressures to cater to suburban middle- and upper-middle-class audiences, the news media since the early 1980s consistently provided the American public with an apprehen-sive and stigmatizing vision of the postindustrial city and its poorest res-idents. The sensational images and alarmist rhetoric generated by this coverage, in turn, was appropriated by other branches of the media and cultural industries as raw material for further representations of the urban world. As Cameron McCarthy et al. point out, the news media's endlessly recycled pictures of inner-city dysfunction and mayhem, of bestial black and brown criminals, became the "reality code" for the rest of the culture and the source of a new "common sense" about urban real-ity (McCarthy et al. 1997, 282). Thus, "signifiers of the inner city as the harbinger of violence, danger and chaos loop into the mass media and the suburbs and Hollywood and back again" (279).

The Hollywood film industry was especially zealous in its treatment of the inner city as just such a "harbinger of violence, danger and chaos." Nor is this surprising. As Todd Gitlin has observed, film (and television) producers and executives get their ideas about public opinion and popular feeling from the "standardized channels of executive culture," channels made up of national newspapers (the *New York Times*, the *Washington Post*, the *Los Angeles Times*), national magazines *(Time, Newsweek)*, and network television news (Gitlin 1983, 203–5). If Hollywood film often reflects some sort of broader cultural or ideological *Zeitgeist*, as sometimes has been argued, it is the *Zeitgeist* according to Dan Rather, Tom Brokaw, and their (establishment) sources, a cultural mood filtered through the political angle of vision particular to the mainstream, national news media. Predictably, as network news organizations and leading newspapers fanned the flames of the panic over the urban crisis, countless Hollywood movies followed their lead in framing the nation's cities quite literally as places of terror. It is to an analysis of those films that I now turn.

CHAPTER 5

The Cinema of Suburban Paranoia

The imagined landscape of the city has become, inescapably, a
cinematic landscape.

—James Donald, *Imagining the Modern City*

In Hollywood film the city has long functioned to focus psychic
processes of paranoia, hysteria and repression.

—Liam Kennedy, *Race and Urban Space in Contemporary
American Culture*

Consider the following scene from director David Fincher's hugely successful and critically acclaimed 1995 thriller *Seven*.[1] It is nighttime and
it's pouring rain. It is almost impenetrably dark. We see a seedy boule-
vard that looks vaguely like it belongs on the Lower East Side of Manhattan (see Figure 14). Detective William Sommerset (played by Morgan
Freeman)—a dour, weary-looking old man wearing a trench coat and
fedora—is shown dashing from the door of his apartment building, past
a couple of grubby homeless men sharing a bottle, to hail a cab. He sighs
upon entering the vehicle and gazes out onto the street with a look of
utter exhaustion as the cab moves slowly into traffic. Through the back-
seat window we catch a passing glimpse—from Sommerset's point of
view—of uniformed cops dressed in clear plastic rain gear bending over
what appears to be a corpse sprawled out on a glistening, crowded sidewalk. We hear a siren. On the opposite side of the cab, a police cruiser pulls
into view, its lights flashing. "Where you going?" asks the driver, glancing into the rearview mirror. "Far away from here," responds Sommerset still staring out the window. The camera then lingers for two or three
seconds more on his furrowed, bone-tired face before cutting away.

This particular sequence isn't especially central to the action of the
film that follows Sommerset and his inexperienced new partner from

"upstate," Detective David Mills (Brad Pitt), as they track the perpetrator of a series of demented, biblically inspired murders through a murky, rain-soaked metropolis. In terms of the plot, the scene serves merely to convey the character of Sommerset from his apartment, where he restlessly ponders the exotic details of the slayings, to the library where he does the research that eventually leads him to the murderer, Jonathan Doe (Kevin Spacey). Nor is the scene—drawing as it does on the well-worn conventions of film noir (tired, trench coat–clad detective, slick streets, looming darkness, bleak tone etc.)—especially innovative aesthetically. However, it *is* emblematic of the way *Seven* constructs its "big city" setting as an oppressive space of gloom and ambient violence, a locus of quotidian horror, the kind of place any sane person would want to stay "far away from."

Since the early '80s, Hollywood has produced a spate of enormously popular movies that share *Seven*'s nightmarish vision of the American urban scene. Dark, comic book–inspired films such as *Batman* (1989),

Figure 14. Detective William Sommerset's view from the cab in *Seven*.

Darkman (1990), and *The Crow* (1994), along with their respective sequels, cast their imagined cities as breeding grounds for criminality, bloodshed, and moral chaos that can only be tamed by merciless superhero vigilantes. A cycle of ghetto crime dramas such as *Colors* (1988), *New Jack City* (1991), *Menace II Society* (1993), *Trespass* (1992), and *Sugar Hill* (1993) depict the inner city as little more than a battleground for warring youth gangs; action thrillers like the *Dirty Harry* and *Death Wish* series, Steven Segal's many movies and their low-budget imitators like *Street Justice* (1989) all present a similar and similarly chilling picture of our metropolitan centers wracked by murder and mayhem. Meanwhile, America's suburban schools are pictured as veritable combat zones in movies like *The Substitute* (1996), *187* (1997), and *Dangerous Minds* (1996). And current cinematic science fiction can envision only two possible futures for the American metropolis: either its current trajectory of decline and dilapidation is extrapolated into the near future, as in *Escape from L.A.* (1996) and *Johnny Mnemonic* (1995), or, more usually, it is subjected to the kind of spectacular annihilation witnessed in *Independence Day* (1996), *Volcano* (1997), *Deep Impact* (1998), *Armageddon* (1998), and *Godzilla* (1998).[2] As Douglas Muzzio notes, the dominant cinematic images of U.S. cities in the 1980s and 1990s "have been grim, almost irrespective of genre, location and director" (Muzzio 1996, 196). This is not to say there weren't other, more sanguine representations of urban life in Hollywood film during this period. Movies like *Sleepless in Seattle* (1993), *You've Got Mail* (1998), *It Could Happen to You* (1994) and *Desperately Seeking Susan* (1985) imagined New York City as a magical place of adventure, self-discovery, and romance. Yet, these upbeat urban stories were exceptions to the gloomy, blood-drenched vision of the city that was the norm on the big screen.

Of course, edgy, apprehensive portrayals of city life are hardly unique in the history of Hollywood film. The mean streets and cutthroat mob underworld of '30s' gangster films like *Little Caesar* (1930) or *Public Enemy* (1931) were hardly a good advertisement for the pleasures of urbanity. Nor, for that matter, was the horrified, expressionist vision of urban existence that pervades classic film noir. The noir pictures of the

1940s and '50s—films like *Scarlet Street* (1946), *The Woman in the Window* (1945), *The Big Sleep* (1946), and *Kiss Me Deadly* (1955)—notoriously depicted the city as "a shadow realm of crime and dislocation in which benighted individuals do battle with implacable threats and temptations" (Krutnik 1997, 83). But the menacing cities on display in mainstream movies during the '80s and '90s articulated a shrill anti-urbanism unprecedented in the most pessimistic of the classic noirs and unusual even in the long annals of Hollywood's distrust of the city. So, for instance, *The Crow* (1994) presents us with a hyperbolically degenerate Detroit ruled by a sinister mastermind who sleeps with his half-sister, grills the gouged-out eyeballs of his victims, and every Halloween has his lecherous, drug-addicted henchmen set fire to the city for the sheer joy of it. Similarly, *Batman*'s Gotham City is a sunless, brooding playground for muggers and super-criminals that one character frankly admits is unfit for habitation by "decent people." The barbarous urban wasteland of *Escape from L.A.* is presided over by (pseudo-revolutionary) gangs, con men, and psychotics. And in *The Devil's Advocate* (1997), Satan is a Park Avenue lawyer and New York is crawling with his demonic minions. According to Hollywood, it seems, cities haven't merely fallen on hard times, they've been condemned to the fires of eternal damnation.

It is worth asking why such hysterically terrified representations apparently resonated so well with the movie-going public of the past two decades. What meanings do they convey? What exactly is at stake ideologically in these images? How do they, to use a phrase of Douglas Kellner's, "transcode political discourses and in turn mobilize sentiment, affection, perception and assent toward specific political positions" (Kellner 1995, 60)? What anxieties, what fears are being allegorized in these dark visions?

These questions take on added weight if we bear in mind the enormous cultural and ideological power of Hollywood's considerable output. Though not the "total environment" that television is for most Americans, film nevertheless plays an important cultural role as an interpreter of social experience and a promoter of values. As Graeme Turner has argued:

[i]t is now more or less accepted that film's function in our culture goes beyond that of being, simply, an exhibited aesthetic object. . . . Popular films have a life beyond their theater runs or reruns on television; stars, genres, key movies become part of our personal culture, our identity. Film is a social practice for its makers and its audience; in its narratives and meanings we can locate evidence of the ways in which our culture makes sense of itself. (Turner 1988, xiv–xv)

That Hollywood film exerts a profound ideological, moral, and psychological influence on its audiences is in fact recognized by the leaders of the industry. Thus, former head of Columbia Studios David Puttnam once candidly admitted that "Whether we like it or not filmmakers are in the propaganda business . . . film sets the social agenda—more so, in my view, than television. Attitudes are altered by film, particularly kids' attitudes" (Puttnam 1986, 45). And while it would be a mistake to treat mainstream films as automatically "reflecting" or "mirroring" the prevailing values and hegemonic ideology of a given historical moment, it can't be denied that they frequently do assume, reproduce, and lend credibility to concepts and myths drawn from dominant ideological discourses.[3] This "propaganda" function is clearly in evidence in the movies employing "the city as nightmare" trope dissected below.

In this chapter I argue that the dominant images of American cities and urban space circulating through Hollywood film in the 1980s and '90s derived their shared fantasy about contemporary urban reality largely from the conservative interpretation of street crime, gangs, and the "underclass" that became so prominent in news reporting and public discourse during this period. Along with welfare-bashing politicians and "if it bleeds it leads" journalism, these representations catered to and amplified the panic of a mostly suburbanized, mostly white middle class over the mayhem supposedly raging in America's largely black and Latino central cities. Like the moralistic interpretation of ghetto poverty offered by Myron Magnet and William Bennett or the coverage of the "crack epidemic" on network news shows, they mystified the source and nature of the real social and economic problems faced by our major cities even as they selectively exaggerated their severity. And, like the shrill rhetoric spouted by the conservative demagogues of the era, Hollywood's framing of the social and economic troubles of our metropolitan areas during the Reagan, Bush, and Clinton years offered a series of ideological justifications for the punitive attitude toward the ghetto poor and the urban working class that prevailed under those administrations.

This chapter demonstrates the extent to which Hollywood has perpetuated reactionary mystifications of urban woes by surveying a broad range of films produced during the 1980s and '90s. To begin with, I examine the tendency of mainstream movies to imagine the city—and particularly the distressed urban core—as a racialized zone of unfettered criminality and social pathology. I also briefly consider the appropriation and exploitation of this vision of urban space in African American–directed "ghetto-centric" gangster films like *New Jack City* and *Menace II Society*. I go on to argue that the conservative politics of Hollywood's conception of inner-city ills is thrown into high relief by a group of films—*Judgment Night* (1993), *Falling Down* (1993), *Grand Canyon* (1991)—each of which center around the story of middle-class white men who find themselves lost in the wilderness/jungle of the postindustrial metropolis and are forced to fight their way out. Next I show how a number of popular films of the '90s postulate urban violence and criminality as a threat to an embattled and besieged middle-class family. Finally, the chapter concludes by examining the now-common cinematic trope of the city as the embodiment of an absolute, often supernatural evil—as Babylon, Sodom and Gomorrah, or even Hell itself—deployed in David Fincher's hit thriller *Seven*.

The City as Police Problem

Since at least the early '70s, Hollywood films have tended to define the ever-more socially heterogeneous American city as a police problem, an unruly place overrun by dangerous, amoral, usually minority undesirables from whom the rest of society must be vigilantly protected. In many of these films, the old racist, imperialist image of the anonymous mass of natives against whom "is always counterposed the isolated white figure" (Hall 1995, 21) gets resurrected and set in a modern metropolitan context. Such movies depict the (usually black and brown) residents of the city as self-destructive and "out of control," as not merely people in trouble but "people who make trouble." The result, in film after film, is "a pervasive sense that life in the urban center is a self-made hell" (McCarthy et al. 1997, 285). Rarely is this characterization of the "urban crisis" put on screen without an accompanying plea for brutally repressive state action as a response.

A perfect example of this tendency is John Carpenter's dystopian thriller *Escape from New York* (1981), in which the island of Manhattan has become a giant prison governed by its own depraved inmates. Its residents live in squalor, dress in outrageous, tattered punk attire, and hoot and scream wildly at the gladiatorial contests staged for them by the settlement's overlord, the Duke. The film's city is, as Douglas Kellner and Michael Ryan correctly observe, "a conservative nightmare of minorities and criminals run rampant" (Kellner and Ryan 1990, 258). Indeed, all the urban specters that haunt the middle-class imagination are there: the homeless psychotics, the punk rock hooligans, the gangbangers, the angry mobs. The narrative leaves little doubt about how best to restore order to this mutinous assemblage. Forced against his will to descend into the city in order to rescue the president of the United States, who has fallen into the clutches of Manhattan's gangs, a Rambo-esque martial arts expert named Snake (Kurt Russell) shoots first and asks questions later. Snake is conservative ideology's archetypical strong individual; a former military hero and renegade who has nothing but disdain for both the government he is helping and the dehumanized low-lifes he has to kill to complete his mission. Throughout, the film asks us to identify with Snake's point of view, and from his perspective New York appears mainly as a collection of assaults to be repelled and pitfalls to be avoided.[4] One could hardly ask for a better metaphoric rendering of the conservative interpretation of America's central cities.

A more recent example of Hollywood's definition of the city as a space of violent criminality is the 1990 sci-fi action picture *Predator 2*, which also takes as its narrative premise the conservative fantasy of a "fallen city" run by hoodlums. As Christopher Sharrett explains, the film dramatizes:

> the true conscience of the commercial industry in conflating the blood-thirsty, unstoppable alien invader (whose head armor resembles dread-locks) with Jamaican, Colombian and other Third World "drug posses" whose chaotic gun battle with police opens the film and sets its tone. The Predator is an Other as comprehensive as Coppola's Dracula, with a different focus. Los Angeles, the postmodern hellscape besieged by crime (not grounded in the social), the Babel whose conscientious and multi-ethnic law enforcement apparatus must do battle with bureaucracy and entertainment media, incarnates a scapegoat in the predator, who not incidentally is viewed by the bemused Third Worlders as a deity and whose predatory tactics mimic their own. (Sharrett 1993b, 108–9)

The chaos and savagery that neo-imperialist fictions like *Rambo II* (1985) or *Clear and Present Danger* (1994) impute to Vietnam or Colombia has here invaded the imperial homeland. Indeed, there's virtually no difference between the film's black and Latino villains and, say, the swarthy enemies that populate the *Rambo* cycle; the threat to American civilization posed by the foreign armies and the domestic underclass, it is intimated, is identical. The fact that the original *Predator* (1987) was set in the battle-torn jungles of Central America only strengthens the parallel *Predator 2* tries to draw between the ghettos of L.A. and the hostile Third World imagined by apologists for the New World Order. The idea that the ghetto constitutes a "combat zone" as perilous and volatile as any in Southeast Asia is a point that is made often and bluntly in the course of the story. For instance, the television reporter (Morton Downey Jr.) whose alarmed voice-over accompanies *Predator 2*'s frenetic opening gun battle, concludes his report by observing, "It's a fucking war down here." The detective leading the campaign against the Jamaican and Colombian drug dealers (played by Danny Glover) echoes the reporter's view, telling a new member of his team that "metro command is a war zone."

Characterizing the city as an unruly Third World "battlefield" naturally invites no-holds-barred military intervention (at least according to the twisted "logic" of the new American imperialism of the 1980s and '90s). After all, if the city, or—more specifically—the ghetto, is as treacherous and uncivilized as Vietnam, Iraq, or Central America, if it is a place of "guerrilla combat" and "unconventional warfare" populated with devious, bloodthirsty natives, then almost any atrocity committed against its inhabitants can be justified. The trope of the inner city as war-torn jungle forms a significant common thread running through Hollywood's treatment of the subject over the past two decades or so. As Scott Forsyth has argued, in the openly Reagan-esque action thrillers of the 1980s and early '90s "the black and increasingly Hispanic masses . . . are the exact equivalent to the exotic masses of the third world; repeatedly, the ghetto is labeled a jungle" (Forsyth 1992, 280–81).

Take, for instance, Dennis Hopper's *Colors* (1988), which depicts the black and Latino neighborhoods of South Central Los Angeles as a staging ground for perpetual combat between feuding youth gangs. Although the film's claim to fame is the "realism" of its representations of L.A.'s notorious youth gangs, the real heroes (and narrative focus) of the story are the police, particularly a likeable old veteran of the LAPD's special anti-gang task force named Bob Hodges (Robert Duvall). Endlessly patrolling the ethnically balkanized communities of South Central, Hodges and his tough, trigger-happy partner Danny McGavine (Sean Penn) unsuccessfully try to head off an escalating war between the Crips and the Bloods. The African American and Latino neighborhoods that Hodges and McGavine patrol are depicted exclusively as graffiti-covered alleys overflowing with junk, settings for drive-by shootings, abandoned buildings or crumbling houses that have been transformed into gang hangouts, and street corner drug markets. Every youth the pair encounters is either a member of a gang (as signified by their "colors," sartorial badges of gang membership) or wants to be one. In more than one scene, several of these teens drink beer and smoke pot to the point of near collapse. Meanwhile, most of the adults Hodges and McGavine encounter in such communities are either the broken, disheartened parents of the victims of street violence or anti-gang activists whose efforts to steer community youth away from gang activity are depicted as utterly ineffectual. The viciousness and pathology of the inner city is further reinforced by its contrast with the warm, safe, comfortable domesticity enjoyed by "normal people" like Hodges and his wife (which we are invited to witness when they entertain McGavine and his girlfriend in their suburban home).

In the final analysis, the central message of the movie is one of hopelessness. The residents of the inner city, the film suggests, are powerless to change the endless cycle of violence and victimization in which they find themselves caught. This is made clear by the scene in which a gang from a small Latino neighborhood attacks the headquarters of a ruthless group of Crips. After the Latino gang has blown up and machine-gunned several Crips, one of their leaders—Loony Tunes—faces down the remaining Crip: both are armed with machine guns and both have an opportunity to turn away and save themselves; instead they simultaneously shoot each other to pieces (in slow motion, of course). This senseless mutual slaughter stands as a fitting symbol of the incorrigible "self-destructiveness" that the film—in an obvious echo of the right's discourse on the problem of the underclass—repeatedly attributes to inner-city youth. The police, we learn, are also relatively powerless to change the tragic dynamics of the ghetto: they might be able to save a few kids from getting involved in crime and drug abuse but they can do little to stop the majority of inhabitants of the ghetto from inevitably annihilating each other.

Yet even as it acknowledges the limits of the LAPD's power to address the problems of the postindustrial ghetto, the film seems to endorse police measures like the anti-gang task force as better than nothing. Indeed, it heroizes the character of Detective Hodges. He is gentle, sensitive, and tolerant; he relates to and is respected by most of South Central Los Angeles's gangs; he does them favors and they do him favors in return; he is intent on preventing the children of the communities he patrols from imitating the "creeps" who belong to gangs. By having Hodges senselessly murdered by a PCP-crazed gangbanger,

Colors, unwittingly or not, turns him into a martyr for the cause of the (nearly all-white) police force who appear to be the only institution working for peace in the midst of the South Central's bloody killing fields. And this, Ed Guerrero has pointed out, ultimately amounts to "a cop's view of the 'hood'" (Guerrero 1993, 185).

The View from the 'Hood?
The City in Ghetto-centric Action Films
In contrast to the alarmist law-and-order message of films like *Predator 2* and *Colors*, one might expect African American–directed films dealing with the same central city terrain to articulate something like a critical, anti-racist alternative to the mainstream perspective. But, in fact, such are the constraints of the for-profit film industry that the "new wave" of commercially viable black filmmakers like John Singleton, Mario Van Peebles, and the Hughes brothers have found it difficult to break entirely with the hegemonic Hollywood definition of the inner city as a lawless killing zone. To be sure, the work of these filmmakers often tries to contextualize ghetto poverty and street crime in a way that appropriately lays blame for the growing urban crisis on official government policy, institutional racism, and the deindustrialization of the cities. Yet just as often these efforts at critical recontextualization of the standard stereotyped image of the inner city fail, allowing spectators to read the new wave of ghetto-centric movies as so many vindications of conservative discourse on the urban crisis. As Liam Kennedy observes, in such films "efforts to critique racism are blurred by spectacular displays of black-on-black violence and other forms of autodestruction" (Kennedy 2000, 117).

Van Peebles's *New Jack City* illustrates this tendency nicely. The film begins with a long aerial shot of downtown Manhattan accompanied by rap music by Queen Latifah and snatches of radio news items on various hot social issues of the day. The information conveyed by the news blurbs is of the sort that's absolutely necessary for any critical understanding of the urban crisis: we hear statistics about the high rate of black unemployment, discussions of the growing gap between the rich and poor in Reagan's America, and a factoid about the rising black murder rate. The film then goes on to tell the fairly predictable saga of the rise and fall of drug lord Nino Brown (Wesley Snipes) and his ruthless Cash Money Brothers crime syndicate. A mise-en-scène foregrounding the trappings of hip-hop culture—from a rap music club that doubles as the syndicate's headquarters to the omnipresent gold chains on Nino's henchmen—and an "inside look" at the manufacture and distribution of crack are the only things that distinguish New Jack City from any number of other formulaic gangster films. Throughout, the social context for the rise of black gangsterism that was briefly invoked at the film's outset all but disappears. It resurfaces briefly in the concluding trial scene, when Nino points to the oppression and denied opportunities of his ghetto childhood as a rationale for his criminality, but his flippant attitude cues the audience not to take this explanation seriously. Further compromising the film's critical force is the fact that Van Peebles seems to support a retributive, "take no prisoners" approach to the Ninos of the world. Ed Guerrero comments that "[t]he biracial cops (Ice-T and Judd Nelson) of New Jack City are depicted as the violent, institutionally sanctioned, extralegal solution to the black community's drug and crime ills" (Guerrero 1993, 187). And, one might add, their rough, vigilante justice is the only viable solution even entertained in the movie.

The films of other widely acclaimed black directors go beyond the token dissent from the conservative stigmatization of the city we see in Mario Van Peebles's neo-Blaxsploitation vehicle. John Singleton's Boyz in the Hood (1991), a coming-of-age story set in a black neighborhood in South Central Los Angeles, offers an unapologetically oppositional, black-identified interpretation of the inner-city's problems. Its adolescent protagonist, Tre Styles (Cuba Gooding, Jr.), struggles through one "rite of passage" after another in a quest to avoid getting caught up in gang violence or assassinated by vicious cops and survive long enough to attend college in Atlanta. Tre fortunately has the guidance of a loving but somewhat authoritarian father, Furious Styles (Laurence Fishburne) to help him negotiate this treacherous journey. His two good friends, half-brothers Ricky (Morris Chestnut) and Doughboy (rap star Ice Cube), are not as fortunate: their fathers are absent from their lives and by the conclusion of the story both have met violent ends.

In its sympathetic attention to the myriad forms of oppression endured by those forced to live in the ghetto, *Boyz* couldn't be more different from a movie like *New Jack City*. It is, as Paula Massood has argued, a film focused intently on "the power relations inherent in space and geography" (Massood 1996, 90). As she notes, the film's mise-en-scène is filled with signs—from "Stop" and "One Way" signs to yellow police tape around a murder scene—which signify the various obstacles that work to isolate the residents of the 'hood from the rest of society. In addition, the LAPD is everywhere, a ubiquity signaled by "a proliferation of aural and visual signs . . . most notably through the repeated searchlights and off-screen sounds of police surveillance helicopters" (90). The police themselves are repeatedly shown to be predatory and sadistic in their relations with community members. In one pivotal scene, for instance, Tre is arbitrarily stopped by a pair of cops, one of whom roughs him up and thrusts a gun in his face just to scare him. By drawing attention to the constraints imposed by the ghetto on his characters' movements and life opportunities, Singleton attempts to expose the social conditions and economic realities driving the urban crisis that are effaced in the standard Hollywood treatments of the subject. That this is part of Singleton's agenda is underscored by a didactic speech about crack, liquor stores, and the Asian American–led gentrification of black neighborhoods that Furious delivers to his son in one scene. Speaking from a position recognizable as "black nationalist," he condemns the incursion of Asian stores into South Central on the grounds that their presence diverts capital and consumer dollars that should be going to struggling black-owned businesses. It is the sort of radical, "community control" position on the ghetto economy once espoused by the Black Panthers.

Be that as it may, some critics have, rightly in my view, taken even the critical politics of a film like *Boyz in the Hood* to task for accepting too readily an essentially conservative definition of contemporary black urban experience. In their article "Danger in the Safety Zone: Notes on Race, Resentment, and the Discourse of Crime, Violence, and Suburban Security," Cameron McCarthy, Alice Rodriguez, and their colleagues contend that "the images of the inner city produced by the current new wave black cinema corroborate rather than critique mainstream mass media" (McCarthy et al. 1997, 282). They note that Singleton's *Boyz* and the Hughes brothers' *Menace II Society* echo the themes of television news and play to the prejudices of the suburban middle-class spectators by constructing the inner city as "a harbinger of violence, danger and chaos" (279). The "realism" of *Boyz* and other ghetto-centric action films, they argue, is in fact predicated on a mainstream "reality code" defined by a conservative preoccupation with inner-city violence, sexual license, and drug use. As a consequence, "[t]he gangster film has become paradigmatic for black filmic production coming out of Hollywood" (283), so much so that even a talented auteur like Spike Lee has felt compelled to try his hand at the genre (in *Clockers*).[5] Furthermore, McCarthy and his co-authors point out that in the work of black directors like Singleton and the Hughes brothers, the problems of the black community are all too often laid at the feet of single mothers who, it is implied, "cannot properly raise their sons" (286). This too seems to corroborate the conservative discourse on the inner city and the underclass. Though a generation of commercially successful African American filmmakers in the '90s critically interrogated certain elements of Hollywood's mythology about contemporary urban existence, that mythology was powerful enough that their portrayals of the inner city all too often "transformed it into a space marked by a stylized nihilism" (Massood 2003, 152), an embodiment of white fears about reckless, antisocial ghetto youth.

Not Safe for Normal (White, Middle-Class) People

The demonization of urban life in mainstream '80s and '90s film is even more evident in a set of films—among them *After Hours* (1985), *Something Wild* (1986), *Bonfire of the Vanities* (1990), *Bad Influence* (1991), and *Judgment Night* (1993)—that critic Barry Keith Grant has dubbed the "yuppie horror film" (Grant 1996).[6] According to Grant, the yuppie horror film "addresses the anxieties of an affluent culture in an era of prolonged recession" (4). The typical yuppie horror film pits a young, usually male, professional against a monstrous doppelgänger (or a monstrous situation) that disrupts their anal-retentive predilection for self-mastery as well as their comfortable lifestyles. In keeping with the generic conventions of the horror film, it often thrusts its protagonists into a "terrible place," which in the case of the yuppie horror film is almost always some desperately impoverished slum or ghetto. Thus, to cite just three examples, *Trespass* traps its white middle-class main characters in an abandoned East St. Louis factory where they are forced to do battle with an Uzi-wielding black gang, *Bonfire of the Vanities*'s rich anti-hero, Sherman McCoy, gets into trouble when he takes a wrong turn in the Bronx, and *After Hours* chronicles the misadventures of a white-collar professional named Paul who gets stranded in the strange, bohemian world of Soho. As Grant argues, "These scenes of crossing over into the nether world of urban decay 'exude the Manichean, middle-class para- noia that once you leave bourgeois life, you're immediately prey to crime, madness, squalor and poverty'" (5). In constructing their "nether worlds," most yuppie horror films—regardless of their ostensive politi- cal commitments—deploy the conservative myths and ideologically over- determined images that are so central to the hegemonic discourse on urban life. Consider the following examples of the (sub)genre that diverge dramatically in their overt politics while sharing a profoundly conserva- tive conception of the postindustrial city and its problems: *Judgment Night*, a formulaic "road movie" about a group of middle-class suburban- ites being chased through the mean streets of Chicago; *Grand Canyon*, a liberal social message film about the fractiousness and social divisions that shape life in contemporary Los Angeles; and *Falling Down*, a film about an "angry white male" who lashes out at his multicultural urban environment.

Judgment Night's themes, settings, and choice of cast make it an almost perfect (and perfectly formulaic) example of Grant's "yuppie hor- ror" genre. Premised on a crudely drawn binary opposition between the safe comforts of suburbia and the mortal dangers of the inner city, it tells the story of a group of suburban men driving to a boxing match who take a wrong turn into a "bad neighborhood" on Chicago's South Side, wit- ness a murder, and spend the rest of the film running from the drug deal- ers who are responsible for the killing. The persecuted suburbanites rep- resent a cross-section of middle-class manhood: Frank (Emilio Estevez), the responsible, level-headed leader of the group, has a baby and a wife who doesn't approve of his wild friends; John (Stephen Dorff), Frank's troubled, slightly rebellious brother; Ray (Jeremy Piven), a fast-talking salesman; and Mike (Cuba Gooding, Jr.), a macho African American womanizer. Soon after the group takes to the road in a state-of-the-art RV—which is obviously meant as a metaphor for and constant reminder of the luxurious suburban neighborhood that Frank and the others call home—a traffic jam forces them to take a detour. Once they turn off the highway (in an area of Chicago that the knowledgeable viewer immediately recognizes as somewhere near the notorious "vertical slums" of the Robert Taylor Homes), they enter into a truly nightmarish urban landscape of dimly lit streets, vacant lots littered with blowing paper, and loitering bums. As they are driving along, someone dashes into the path of the RV; after stopping the vehicle, the group finds an injured man on the road and, when they take him on board, discovers that he has been shot. Shortly after, the drug dealers who shot him, led by a sneering hood named Fallon (Denis Leary), crash their car into the RV, kill the injured man, and then decide to eliminate the witnesses as well, setting off the chase that takes up the remainder of the film.

It is typical of the "yuppie horror" genre that the battle of wits that ensues between Fallon's gang and the frightened suburbanites is presented as a test of the group's collective manhood. In an early scene, Mike asks Frank if "married life" is making him "soft"; in the rest of the film the anxiety expressed in that question—anxiety about the potentially "emasculating" effects of suburban domesticity, affluence, and a life of comfort—is dramatized and, in the end, assuaged. The urban landscape Frank and his friends stumble into is a lawless environment, a "Wild West," in which only the "strongest" and most "masculine" will survive. Fallon alludes to this fact when, while hunting through a rail yard for Frank and company, he tauntingly refers to them as "ladies" and asks, "what do ya think of the neighborhood?" The conceit of making the inner city into a breeding ground for a particularly aggressive, pathological form of hyper-masculinity echoes the fables that conservatives like Charles Murray and William Bennett spent decades spinning about underclass neighborhoods and urban "superpredators." Indeed, the standard, demonized image of the inner city and its inhabitants forms the template for the film's vision of Chicago's near South Side. For instance, in the rail yard, Frank and his friends meet a band of homeless men (one of whom babbles incoherently through most of the sequence) who greedily take their money in return for not revealing their whereabouts to Fallon. Next, to the sound of rap music, they wander into a foreboding housing project composed of brick tenement buildings illuminated by low-key, infernal sulfurous lighting (see Figure 15). They go into one of the buildings and roam through the halls desperately banging on doors, begging for help, but no one responds to their pleas. Eventually they find a couple of women who grudgingly agree to let them use their phone. Meanwhile, the housing project's resident gang tells Fallon and his crew how to find Frank's group in return for a roll of bloodstained hundred dollar bills. With the exception of the two women who let Frank and his pals use their phone, then, the denizens of the inner city

Figure 15. In *Judgment Night,* Frank and his friends race through the inner city.

are presented as morally on par with the ruthless Fallon and his gang. As Ray exclaims at one point, "This is hell."

Naturally, Frank and his friends don't survive their trip through the urban netherworld unscathed. The first to go, predictably, is Ray, the slick dealmaker. He gets caught by Fallon on the roof of one of the tenements and tries unsuccessfully to sweet talk his way out of the inevitable. "You're the kind of milk-fed fucker I hate," Fallon tells him before tossing him off the roof. While the death of the effete Ray seems almost preordained according to the gendered logic of the narrative, tough guys Mike and John also find themselves injured and incapacitated in the lead-up to the final showdown in an empty downtown marketplace. The sole remaining healthy member of the group, Frank, is thus left to fight it out with Fallon alone. The climactic hand-to-hand battle turns out to be pretty standard action-movie fare: Frank nearly succumbs but at the last minute, after Fallon threatens to hurt his family, he summons up the strength to shove Fallon to his death. In the end, the police and the paramedics arrive, Mike and John are wheeled off to a waiting ambulance, and a cop tells Frank, "Your wife's outside." At the most obvious level of interpretation, Frank's triumph signals a victory of "normal" middle-class suburban manhood over the deviant, violent manhood associated with the inner city. But beyond that, it implies that the middle-class nuclear family, far from rendering Frank "soft," is what gives him the strength to defeat Fallon. It is hard not to see such an ending as vindicating the conservative "family values" preached by the likes of Dan Quayle and Charles Murray. If *Judgment Night* has a coherent politics, it surely centers on its valorization of the suburban domesticity over and against the deviance and wildness of urban life.

As one would expect from the man who created *The Big Chill*, the definitive Hollywood post-mortem on the cultural and political upheavals of the sixties, the main ideological thrust of director Lawrence Kasdan's *Grand Canyon* is considerably more "liberal" than *Judgment Night*'s celebration of vigilantism in the service of the middle-class family. The film chronicles a few months in the lives of a cross-section of Los Angeles residents coping with a variety of existential crises (most of which are precipitated by the pressures of urban life). As in *After Hours* and *Judgment Night*, the story's main animating crisis occurs when a middle-class white man, in this case an immigration lawyer named Mack (Kevin Kline), takes a wrong turn and ends up in the heart of the ghetto. Soon after he is passed by a car blasting rap music and loaded with hostile-looking young black men, Mack's car breaks down. A short while later, the same group spots him stranded and circles back around to harass him. The gun-wielding leader of the gang is about to force him out of the car when Simon (Danny Glover), a black tow-truck driver, arrives on the scene to defuse the situation. The whole episode is, as Lisa Benton has observed, "the quintessential white, middle-class urban nightmare" and "reveals Los Angeles as a landscape of tension and conflict, of emerging language and custom barriers, of contests over space and 'turf rights'" (Benton 1995, 156). But unlike most yuppie horror flicks, in which the sanctioned response of the white middle-class protagonist to the threat posed by the city is always some Rambo-esque flurry of violence, *Grand Canyon* holds out hope that the city's divisions can be bridged and conflicts healed. Thus, Mack eventually seeks out Simon to thank him for saving his life and the two strike up a (somewhat awkward) friendship. Mack manages to find an apartment for Simon's sister, allowing her to move out of her dicey, crime-ridden neighborhood, and even arranges a date between Simon and a secretary who works in his building that sparks the beginning of a relationship. By the end of film the two men and their families take a joint vacation to the Grand Canyon. The final shot pictures the two families on the edge of the Grand Canyon, black and white, affluent and working class, united in their awe of nature's wonders, a fitting symbol of *Grand Canyon*'s personalized, therapeutic approach to social conflict and polarization. All the divided metropolis needs to escape its problems, this ending suggests, is more goodwill, personal warmth, and "camaraderie" among its residents.

Interestingly, though, *Grand Canyon*'s patina of liberalism does not prevent the film from taking at face value what is an essentially conservative understanding of the urban crisis. The South Central neighborhood where Simon's sister and her children live, in particular, is envisioned as a veritable "landscape of violence." As Simon's sister and her daughter walk home one day, they pass a woman scrubbing bloodstains off the sidewalk. On another occasion, a salesman who sells life insurance policies that cover funeral expenses for children shows up at her door. And, in an especially terrifying scene, the family's house is riddled with bullets during a late night drive-by shooting. Nor are the dangers of urbanity confined exclusively to South Central. A demented, disheveled assailant shoots Mack's movie-producer friend Davis (Steve Martin) in the thigh outside a swank restaurant in order to steal his watch. Mack's wife Claire repeatedly encounters a sullen, muttering homeless man camped out in the alleyway behind an upscale shopping street (see Figure 16).

Inevitably, as in the television news stories discussed in chapter 4, the film interprets the city's dangers as emanating from the underclass. It is an underclass that *Grand Canyon* candidly admits is the product of the widening gap between the affluent and the rest of society, between the white suburbs and the racially heterogeneous city. As the character of Davis explains: "There is an ever-widening gulf between people who have stuff and people who don't have shit. It's like a big hole in the ground— like the Grand Canyon—what comes out of this hole is an eruption of rage, and rage creates violence, and violence is real." Despite this shocking admission, the film makes no moral or political judgment about, and assigns no social agent responsibility for, the widening gulf itself. The city's social tensions and the explosive conflicts such tensions create are presented simply as evidence that things are, as Mack puts it, mysteriously "going to shit." In this way, the film can allow its white upper-middle-class characters to lament the urban crisis without registering their own complicity in its creation. At most, they feel terror and confusion mingled with a vague, inchoate sense of guilt, as when Claire declares, "The world doesn't make sense to me. Babies lying in the streets, people who sleep in boxes. People are ready to shoot you if you look at them and we are getting used to it. The world is so nuts. It makes me wonder about the choices we made." Despite its liberal leanings, in the end *Grand Canyon* elaborates no critique of the structural forces driving the urban decline it laments.

The frequency with which the yuppie horror film's nightmare world adopts the guise of "bad neighborhoods" in the inner city suggests a return of the repressed: it is a coded acknowledgment that the lavish upper-middle-class lifestyle depends (to some degree, at any rate) on the very economy responsible for immiserating those neighborhoods and exploiting the black and Latino working people who reside there. The accidental voyages into those areas that the white middle-class protagonists in *Judgment Night* and *Grand Canyon* undertake allow them to face down the specter of the monstrous underclass nemesis. The conservative politics of *Judgment Night* requires that this meeting end in a fight to the death from which the middle-class subject necessarily emerges victorious; in the case of *Grand Canyon*, the encounter gives rise to therapeutic soul searching and individual good deeds that nonetheless pose no challenge to the prevailing arrangement of political and social power. Yet despite the surface political differences between the two films, their rhetorical construction of the inner-city menace is similarly alarmist and similarly indebted to the right's interpretation of the urban crisis.

Figure 16. Claire crosses paths with a deranged homeless man in *Grand Canyon*.

Though differing from the standard "yuppie horror film" in some key respects, the controversial hit movie *Falling Down* (1993) shares with *After Hours* and *Judgment Night* the organizing story-arc of a white man's embattled odyssey through a multicultural urban wilderness. Dubbed by one reviewer "a *Taxi Driver* for the '90s," it tells the story of a day in the life of Bill Foster (known in the film as D-Fens for his personalized license plate), a divorced, laid-off defense worker played by Michael Douglas, whose rage and frustration with everyday life in Los Angeles finally boils over in the form of a cross-town rampage that puts him into conflict with a Korean shop owner, a Latino gang, a neo-Nazi, and a pushy panhandler, among others. As Carol Clover describes the plot, "like Odysseus, [D-Fens] is heading home, except that instead of Scylla and Charybdis there are Chicano gangs and homeless people, and instead of Penelope waiting patiently in Ithaca there is a former wife with a restraining order in Venice Beach" (Clover 1993, 6).

At its most obvious, *Falling Down* dramatizes the much-publicized crisis of white male authority that pundits in the '90s alleged had been precipitated both by the forces of "political correctness" (i.e., feminism and identity politics) and by changing demographics that were gradually rendering white men a minority in many areas of the country. D-Fens is, as critic Jude Davies asserts, "a specific type, the Average White Male facing a crisis of power at a particular moment in U.S. history" (Davies 1995, 216). Indeed, *Falling Down*'s notoriety in the spring of 1993 helped launch a thousand polemics about the plight of "angry white men." *Newsweek*'s March 29 cover story titled "White Male Paranoia" used the film as a touchstone for a discussion of the question of whether these discontented white men are "victims of multiculturalism or . . . just bad sports" (Gates 1993, 48). As the article explained, "'Falling Down', whether it's really a message movie or just a cop film with trendy trimmings, pushes white men's buttons. The annoyances and menaces that drive D-Fens bonkers . . . are a cross-section of white-guy grievances" (48).

What the film leaves maddeningly unclear is whether such grievances are actually being endorsed or, as Davies would have it, "ironized" (215). The fact that D-Fens ends the film, as he himself puts it, in the position of "the bad guy," and is gunned down in the closing scene ostensibly gestures toward a condemnation of his actions. Yet, as Liam Kennedy has argued, "in its depiction of ethnic and racial stereotypes the film sends out very mixed, confused messages about the hysterical white male subject it constructs at its center" (Kennedy 1996, 92). Moreover, the film participates in Hollywood's ongoing backlash against feminism by presenting D-Fens's problems as caused at least in part by his neurotic ex-wife's assertion of control over the family home and their daughter, Adele (Mahoney 1997; Clover 1993).

Falling Down's vision of Los Angeles territorializes the objects of D-Fens's animus, an animus that by its very intensity manages to outshine and perhaps even negate the film's political ambivalence. Throughout, Los Angeles is presented, in the words of critic Peter Rainer, as a smog-choked "melting pot nightmare" (Rainer 1993, F7). The film opens with the scene of the nerdish D-Fens—decked out in a buzz cut, blindingly white shirt and tie, and black-rimmed plastic glasses—trapped in a gridlocked L.A. traffic jam, one that a quick pan indicates is as multiracial and cacophonous as the city itself. As repeated intercutting between the tense, sweating face of D-Fens and the stalled traffic around him underscores, he is a time bomb with a perilously short fuse. Soon enough he leaps out of his car and clambers up the highway embankment, telling an irate driver behind him that he is "going home." Thus begins his journey by foot across most of downtown L.A. to Venice Beach, where he hopes to be reunited with his daughter and estranged wife in time to celebrate his daughter's birthday.

One thing that becomes apparent in the course of his journey is that D-Fens "has no sense of ownership or rootedness; the space of the city has been taken over by racial and/or sexual 'others'" (Mahoney 1997, 174). Everywhere he turns, he encounters (spatial as well as social) barriers and exclusive enclaves standing in his way. At one point, he stumbles onto the graffiti-marked turf of a Latino gang who demand a toll (see Figure 17). Later, he is forced to walk through a public park crowded with homeless people (see Figure 18). It is worth quoting Liam Kennedy's description of this scene in full:

The camera surveys these people and foregrounds excessive images of poverty: there is an emaciated white man holding a sign which reads "We are dying of AIDS please help us!"; there is a black man in a wheelchair holding a sign reading "Homeless Vet Needs Food Money"; there are two young black men with a trolley full of empty cans, being arrested by the police—and the background is filled with predominantly African-American and Latino people. (Kennedy 1996, 95)

As he traverses the park, D-Fens is accosted by an annoying panhandler (munching happily on a sandwich) who badgers him until he turns over his briefcase and then complains when it contains nothing but a bag lunch. As Kennedy points out, this entire scene constitutes "an obscene depiction of collective 'underclass' existence, with these people represented as degenerative signifiers of social immiseration and victimization" (Kennedy 1996, 95). In what one guesses is a half-hearted effort at "even-handedness," *Falling Down* implies that the rich are as much to

Figure 17. D-Fens on gang turf in *Falling Down*.

blame for D-Fens's alienation from the urban landscape as the abject poor: "D-Fens breaches two high walls in the course of his long walk home," Clover notes, one surrounding a country club and the other surrounding a plastic surgeon's mansion (Clover 1993, 9). D-Fens's "homelessness" and complete alienation is further underscored by the fact that his ex-wife replies to his telephone call announcing his impending return by telling him "this is not your home anymore" and by asking the police for protection.

D-Fens responds to the annoyances and obstacles the city places in his way with escalating violence. He smashes up the store of a Korean shopkeeper who refuses to give him change and charges exorbitant prices for sodas. He uses a baseball bat to repel the Latino gang members who accost him and later shoots one of them in the leg after they try unsuccessfully to gun him down. He murders a neo-Nazi storekeeper who mistakes him for some sort of kindred spirit. Finally, he chases his ex-wife and daughter out onto a pier and traps them there (with the intention,

Figure 18. Homeless people in the park in *Falling Down*.

the viewer supposes, of killing them both). There he is cornered by the aging white male cop, Prendergast, who has been tracking him for much of the movie and who kills D-Fens when the latter challenges him to "draw."

Yet, as I have already implied, it would be a mistake to read *Falling Down* as a critique of the white male anger simply because D-Fens dies in the end. First of all, by pointedly contrasting D-Fens to the character of the viciously racist, homophobic Nazi storekeeper, the film shows him in at least a partially sympathetic light. Moreover, as Kennedy has argued, "even as the film parodies the tale of regeneration through violence in the narrative of D-Fens, it reproduces it more soberly in the narrative of his double within the film, the white policeman Prendergast" (Kennedy 1996, 98). Prendergast begins the story as an ineffectual detective, a henpecked husband, and a general object of ridicule on the police force who regains his authority (both on the job and in the home) precisely by hunting down and killing D-Fens. While the film ostensibly repudiates D-Fens's vigilantism, it clearly approves Prendergast's legally sanctioned (liberal-minded) violence and, as such, "ensures the reproduction of white masculine authority in a new register" (99). And even the repudiation of D-Fens's violence is lukewarm at best. The harassment he endures at the hands of the Latino gang and in the person of the homeless man at least appear to excuse his rough reactions. Indeed, his actions all respond in one way or another to irritations of urban living that, as in the opening traffic jam, he can no longer shut out. As in *Batman* or *Predator 2*, the city in *Falling Down*, to quote Peter Rainer, is "made to stand in for all that [is] rotting and malevolent in society" (Rainer 1993, F7); it is an equation that, circulating widely throughout contemporary popular culture, goes a long way toward legitimating the white male rage that D-Fens embodies. As McCarthy and his coauthors put it, in the film "the discourse of crime, violence and suburban security has come . . . to justify suburban revenge and resentment. We now have a white man [D-Fens] who enters the 'hood to settle moral scores with anything and anyone that moves" (McCarthy et al. 1997, 284).

Demonizing the Urban Public Realm

As with the park scene in *Falling Down*, Hollywood over the past two decades has typically projected urban public amenities like parks and playgrounds as dangerous, dirty, and in ruins, as symptomatic of the blight of the contemporary American city as a whole. In particular, the spaces defined by public schools and public transit—arguably two of the signature achievements of American urban civilization—have been singled out for unflattering treatment. In mainstream film of the Reagan era and after, big city schools are uniformly lousy and the subways are all stalked by muggers.

Exemplary of this trend is the grim portrayal of urban schools in the 1996 movie *Dangerous Minds*, the story of a white ex-Marine turned teacher-in-training named LouAnne Johnson (Michelle Pfeiffer), who is doing her student teaching in an inner-city high school. Hired as an English teacher in a program for students who are considered "unteachable," Johnson is immediately confronted with an out-of-control classroom full of black and Latino youth who blast loud music, rap, dance, shout, and generally disregard her authority. As presented by the film, these are kids who, to quote Henry Giroux, "have brought the 'worst' aspects of their culture into the classroom" (Giroux 1997, 47). As Giroux explains, the initial scenes of Johnson and her class "work powerfully in associating black and Hispanic kids with the culture of criminality and danger. They also make clear that whiteness as a racial identity is both vulnerable and under siege, as well as the only hope these kids have for moving beyond the context and character of their racial identities" (47). Taking a page from the standard ghetto action-picture, *Dangerous Minds* underscores the (minority) violence that haunts Johnson's school both by means of the graffiti that appears to cover its every available surface (which functions here, as in other media texts, as a generic signifier of gang activity) and by means of the ubiquitous rap soundtrack featuring hard-core gangster rapper Coolio among others.

Johnson eventually wins the respect of her class and manages to inculcate them with a love of (white) poetry, but only after she impresses the students with her old Marine uniform and demonstrates her knowledge of karate moves. As Giroux explains, "[t]hrough her assumption that fear and danger are the only emotions the kids recognize as important, LouAnne crosses a racial divide by rooting her sense of authority in a reactionary notion of discipline" (48). Significantly, Johnson's struggle to uplift her underclass charges is opposed every step of the way by the school's black principal, Mr. Grandey (Courtney Vance), a rigid and unfeeling bureaucrat. In the end, *Dangerous Minds* "reinforces the highly racialized . . . mainstream assumption that chaos reigns in inner-city public schools and that white teachers alone are capable of bringing order, decency, and hope to those on the margins of society" (49).

Dangerous Minds's basic formula of a tough white teacher acting as savior to otherwise hopeless underclass kids is taken to absurd extremes in another 1996 release, *The Substitute*. In *The Substitute* it is not an ex-Marine turned student teacher but, even more implausibly, an unemployed mercenary named Shale (Tom Berenger) masquerading as a substitute teacher who brings order to a stereotypical inner-city high school. As in *Dangerous Minds*, the film's high school is dominated by (in this case, largely Latino) gangs who intimidate and terrorize the teachers, among them Shale's girlfriend Jane (Diane Verona), all to the accompaniment of a hard-core rap soundtrack. Shale gets drawn into this toxic environment when Jane is attacked "by a six-foot-six Seminole" in what he suspects is a hit orchestrated by her student Juan Lacas (Marc Anthony), leader of the bluntly named Kings of Destruction gang. No sooner has Shale infiltrated the school posing as Jane's substitute than he is breaking his students' fingers and twisting their arms in an effort to subdue his unruly classroom. "I'm in charge of this class," he announces after he has sent a couple of disobedient teens to the nurse's office, "I'm the warrior chief. I'm the merciless god of anything that stirs in my universe. Fuck with me and you will suffer my wrath." Again echoing *Dangerous Minds*, Shale's strong-arm classroom reforms—depicted in the film as being unequivocally successful—are thwarted by an African American principal, Claude Rolle (Ernie Hudson), who Shale eventually discovers is running a massive cocaine ring out of the school's basement with the Kings of Destruction's cooperation. This premise is so outrageous that one almost hesitates to draw attention to its obvious racism. Yet, Rolle's depiction as a slick personification of evil is only slightly more hyperbolic than the generally negative portrayal of most of the nonwhite students and teachers in the film. In the end, Shale and his band of mercenary buddies "clean up" the school in a pitched battle with Rolle's hired guns. Again, as so often in Hollywood films of the '80s and '90s, the answer to the inner city's problems proposed by *The Substitute* is an orgy of violence directed at people of color.

The treatment of the crisis in urban public education in both *The Substitute* and *Dangerous Minds* harkens back to an earlier film, *Lean on Me* (1988), based on the life story of black New Jersey high school principal Joe Clark. In early 1988, Clark—whose habit of carrying around a baseball bat as he patrolled the halls and screaming at students through a bullhorn earned him the nickname "Crazy Joe"—burst into the limelight when he summarily expelled sixty-six of his students without due process. The action provoked a confrontation with the school board; the board's disapproval of his methods was further exacerbated by Clark's characterization of the dismissed students as "hoodlums, thugs, and pathological deviants." His severe brand of discipline did, however, endear him to prominent conservatives. As *Time* magazine reported shortly after Clark's run-in with the school board, "President Reagan has commended Clark as an exemplar of the tough leadership needed in urban schools. In the wake of the school board battle, U.S. Secretary of Education William Bennett telephoned to urge Clarke to 'hang in there'" (Bowen 1988, 53). Clarke was even offered a post as a White House policy adviser (which he turned down).

Lean on Me celebrates Clark (played by Morgan Freeman) and his strong-arm methods in a morality tale as didactic and reactionary as a parable from Bennett's own *Book of Virtues*. From the opening sequence on, we are given an impression of Clark as a stern, stubborn, but energetic teacher who is willing to buck convention to help his students reach their potential. East Side High circa 1982, the school Clark takes over, is constructed as a place as wild and disorderly as he is strong-willed.

We're introduced to it by means of a chilling montage encapsulating what is supposed to be the beginning of a typical class day. It begins with a shot of a brawl in the main hallway, cuts to two large black students hurling a sink through a bathroom window, then to kids playing with a terrified white teacher's tie, and is followed by a shot of a white woman accosted by four black women in a bathroom who rip off her shirt and bra. This is followed by shots of a student making a drug deal on the school steps with what looks like a teacher, a student selling pills in the cafeteria, a teenage boy checking his revolver, and a skirmish between some students that results in the beating of a teacher. The montage ends with a young kid being locked into his locker.

Shortly after taking charge, Clark, using his trademark tactics, trans-forms this mayhem and squalor into the picture of cleanliness and order. The delinquents and drug dealers are banished, the graffiti cleaned up, the kids develop an eagerness to learn, and a collection of former trou-blemakers learns to proudly sing an *a cappella*, "soulified" version of the school song on demand. The last third of the film centers, therefore, not on Clark's struggles with his students—they have by that point willingly submitted to and even learned to love his tough authority—but on his clashes with a sleazy white mayor, an opportunistic black school board member, and a racist fire chief. This, of course, bestows on Clark's author-itarianism the status of "rebellion" against a corrupt status quo; indeed, from the moment we first see Clark as a young teacher in the 1960s wear-ing an Afro and dashiki, the film makes an effort to associate Clark, how-ever tenuously, with the tradition of radical black nationalism. The film's Reagan-esque message of "discipline" and "no excuses for failure" is thus all the more nefarious because it is packaged (especially in the final scene of students cheering Clark and singing the new *a cappella*, Eastside anthem) as an organic and triumphant expression of black pride.

If *Dangerous Minds*, *The Substitute*, and *Lean on Me* all endorse force and strict discipline as answers to the problems of urban public educa-tion, the bleak 1997 release *187* suggests that those problems are at bot-tom intractable and that city schools are beyond rescuing. The film tells the story of a dedicated high school science teacher, Trevor Garfield

(Samuel Jackson), who struggles to cope with his anxieties and manage an unruly urban classroom after being viciously stabbed by a student. The film opens, appropriately enough, with a nightmare sequence—shot in a gloomy, diffuse blue light—in which Trevor relives the circumstances that lead up to his stabbing: teaching physics in a Brooklyn high school to a group of boisterous, mostly minority students, he discovers that one of his students has scrawled the numbers "187"—the police code for homicide—on one of the textbooks. Shortly after, we see Trevor being stalked down the school hallway by a tough-looking black kid wearing a stocking cap who sneaks up behind him and sticks a home-made "shiv" in his back. Trevor awakens, sweating, from his nightmare not in New York but in sun-baked Los Angeles where he has taken a job as a substitute teacher (and where, we soon learn, the school system is even more vile).

The inner-city school to which he is assigned overflows with all the stock horrors: thuggish looking minority teens (some of whom he spots spray painting graffiti on the school basketball court); a nasty Latino gang that appears to run the place; a teacher who—for self-protection—keeps a handgun in his desk; and a by-the-book principal who cares more about students filing lawsuits against the school district than about the safety of his teachers (see Figure 19). Trevor, committed pedagogue that he is, tries to make the best of it, succeeds in "reaching" a promising young Latina student named Rita, and engages a fair number of his other students. Nevertheless, from his confrontation with the resident troublemakers on his first day of class onward, Trevor seethes with frustration and barely contained rage. When the one friend he makes on the faculty, a pretty white computer teacher named Ellen (Kelly Rowan), tells him that gang leader Benny Chicon (Lobo Sebastian) has been terrorizing her because she testified against him in a school disciplinary hearing, the audience is prepared for Trevor to take matters into his own hands. Benny soon goes missing and we naturally suspect that Trevor had something to do with it. Benny's gang, it turns out, has similar suspicions, and under the new leadership of Cesar Sanchez (Clifton Gonzalez Gonzalez), a truly loathsome character who in one scene beats his own mother, they trash Trevor's lab, destroying the desks, spray painting obscenities on the walls, tearing apart books, even impaling the class's pet rat with scalpels. Later, when Cesar kills Ellen's dog, Jack, Trevor retaliates by drugging him and cutting off his "trigger" finger. Cesar and his gang naturally come gunning for him shortly thereafter (having painted the fatal number "187" all over his garage as a portent of things to come).

Given the basic narrative pattern of the teacher-as-savior genre, one would expect a happy, uplifting resolution to this conflict, one in which Trevor's actions are shown to be necessary and heroic, the gang is vanquished, and the school is restored to a state of prelapsarian tranquillity. But it is here that *187* diverges sharply from the generic mold established by films like *Dangerous Minds* and *Lean on Me*. First of all, Ellen begins to suspect Trevor of killing Benny and distances herself from him as a result. Meanwhile his "special project," Rita, decides she doesn't want to graduate. Then the principal, fearing a potential sexual

Figure 19. Trevor's new school in *187*.

harassment lawsuit, fires Trevor after finding out about his private meetings with Rita. Moreover, if killing Benny and slicing off Cesar's finger are not proof enough, Trevor's actions at the end of the film confirm that he is dangerously unbalanced, perhaps even insane.

After Cesar and his henchmen break into Trevor's house, Cesar, reenacting a scene from *The Deerhunter*, forces Trevor to play Russian roulette, which he does willingly. Trevor proclaims that he is "crazy" and acts it; when Cesar hesitates to take his turn, Trevor grabs the gun and shoots himself in the head (after which, Cesar, not wanting to be beaten at the game, also shoots himself in the head). Thus, *187* can be read as something of an immanent critique of the conventions of the teacher-as-savior genre. The intolerable situation—and the sense of frustration and hopelessness—that in *Lean on Me* or *The Substitute* finds its antidote in order imposed by a judicious use of force here triumphs in the end. The teacher does not conquer but instead is conquered by the horrible conditions in inner-city schools. Even vigilante violence makes no difference. This despairing message is made explicit by the closing scene in which shots of Ellen clearing out her desk and throwing away her teaching credentials are intercut with Rita reading a heartfelt eulogy for Trevor at the graduation ceremony. "You can push a good teacher too far," Rita says tearfully. "Teachers don't get no respect." The film closes with a text informing the audience that "[o]ne in nine teachers have been attacked at school. Ninety-five percent of those attacks were committed by students. A teacher wrote this movie."

Where *Dangerous Minds* and *Lean on Me* at least held out the possibility that city school systems (and by implication the cities that operate them) could be renewed by getting tough on troublemakers, *187* can be read as arguing that the only sensible course of action is a wholesale evacuation of and retreat from public schools and from the degenerate metropolitan culture they represent. Such a view would no doubt resonate with the growing sector of both the urban and the suburban middle class who are placing their children into private schools at record rates and are clamoring for government-funded vouchers to help pay for it. As Henry Giroux comments, the film "capitalizes on the popular conception . . . that public education is not safe for white, middle-class children, that racial violence is rampant in the public schools, that minority students have turned classroom discipline into a joke, that administrators are paralyzed by insensitive bureaucracies, and the only thing that teachers and students share is the desire to survive the day" (Giroux 1999, 49).

Like its portrayal of urban schools, the film industry's view of public mass transit—that other iconic fixture of the modern metropolis—has been uniformly bleak. For those who ride public transit in the movies, bloodshed, gun fights, hijackings, and catastrophic accidents are apparently par for the course. Thus, *The Warriors* (1979) features a series of gang battles on the trains between the Bronx and Coney Island. *Blue Steel* (1990) climaxes with a chilling gunfight on a New York subway platform. The 1994 blockbuster *Speed* features a Los Angeles city bus wired with a bomb rigged to explode if it slows down and culminates in scenes of hand-to-hand combat aboard a runaway train. *Die Hard: With a Vengeance* has a group of demonic criminals blow up a New York subway to create a diversion for a robbery. The awful *Money Train* (1995) follows two disgruntled New York Transit cops as they round up the veritable army of criminals who appear to populate the subways and dream up ways to rob the "money train" (the train that collects all the cash from the transit system's daily operations). This latter film, it should be noted, was blamed for a group of "copycat" arsons in which one New York Transit police officer was killed. But *Money Train* is hardly the most disturbing story about public transportation created by the celluloid dream factory; that distinction is properly reserved for the chilling 1997 horror flick *Mimic*.

In some ways, *Mimic* is little more than an updated version of the Frankenstein story (or, better, of the '50s horror classic *Them*): in order to stop a deadly outbreak of a cockroach-borne illness that's killing off the children of New York, entomologist Dr. Susan Tyler (Mira Sorvino) releases a species of insect genetically engineered to kill roaches, the "Judas" bug, into the city's subway system; the Judas bugs wipe out the roaches but, true to their name, turn on their creators. We soon learn that the Judas bugs have metamorphosed from the tiny, innocuous creatures Tyler created into six-foot tall man-eating predators who can disguise themselves as humans. It turns out they have set up an enormous colony in the dark, dank bowels of the New York subway system and the colony's "warrior" bugs are busy picking off priests, street kids, and sweet little retarded boys. Unlike the creature in the original Frankenstein story, the monsters here are irreducibly "Other" and thoroughly demonized; from their unintelligible language of clicks to their grotesque cockroach-like appearance and their frenzied, mechanical method of dismembering their victims, the Judas bugs are presented as abnormal in a way that bolsters rather than challenges hegemonic conceptions of normalcy. In this, *Mimic* participates in what Christopher Sharrett has identified as the neo-conservative "cooption of the horror film's radicalism" (Sharrett 1993b, 100).

What is especially interesting here is how the film maps the repellent Otherness of the Judas bugs onto the subway system itself.[7] One way that it does this is by representing the subways quite literally as the murderous insects' hunting ground. Thus, in one terrifying scene, we see two kids scavenging through the system's service tunnels savagely butchered, and, in another, Dr. Tyler is snatched off a subway platform by a flying Judas bug. Another way *Mimic* projects the monstrousness of the bugs onto the subway system is by establishing the tunnels themselves as a realm of near total darkness. Most of the underground action takes place in murky abandoned tunnels and closed stations; even the active platforms are equipped with dim, flickering lights. The tunnels are marked off as alien territory in other ways as well: the passages leading to the heart of the colony are pictured not only as choked with garbage but as covered with the bugs' excrement and offal (the scatological symbolism serving to underscore just how abhorrent and deserving of annihilation the bugs really are). There's even a room stacked from floor to ceiling with sticky Geiger-esque "egg pods." By the end of the film Dr. Tyler finds herself, her husband, and a few other hearty souls being hunted by the Judas bugs through this dark maze as it dawns on her that the insects are planning to colonize the rest of the country. Luckily, the world is saved when her husband chances upon the colony's central nest in some sort of giant furnace room and blows it up. The underworld threat is vanquished but an unrelieved sense of foreboding—fostered by the moaning music of the sound track and the dour expressions on the actors' faces—lingers on even after Tyler and her husband are reunited at the end.

Together, images like those in *Mimic* or *Money Train* reinforce the undeserved bad reputation public transit has gotten in the suburban-riented news media. And beyond that, they help fuel a general suspicion of public places that is snuffing out what remains of urban civic culture. In light of such depictions, it is understandable that at least a few managers of urban public transportation systems have begun to fight back: New York Transit Authority chief Alan Kiepper has frequently denied filmmakers' requests to use the city's subways as showcases for violent chase scenes and has refused to let them paint graffiti on his meticulously clean fleet of cars (Pierce 1994, 5). Unfortunately, such small gestures can do very little indeed to dispel the myths that *Mimic* and films like it help to perpetuate.

Under Siege: The Threat to the (Suburban) Middle-Class Family

If Hollywood over the past few decades of conservative ascendancy has increasingly framed the big city as hostile territory, it has also tended to present the sparkling clean, well-lit world of the suburban middle-class family as "under siege" from a range of sexual, criminal, and moral threats that are typically urban in origin. Alan Nadel has noted that the "house-at-risk motif" was "common to many films of Reagan's America" (Nadel 1997,195) and, I might add, remained popular in the Bush and Clinton eras as well. For instance, *Home Alone* (1990) centers on a little boy defending his well-appointed home from a pair of inept burglars; *Unlawful Entry* (1992) tells the story of a middle-class couple terrorized by a working-class police officer after he investigates a break-in at their suburban residence; *Pacific Heights* (1990) is about a demented tenant who ruins a yuppie pair's turn-of-the-century house and nearly ruins their lives; and *The Hand That Rocks the Cradle* (1992) shows us an affluent family menaced by their live-in nanny.

Perhaps no film exemplifies the siege narratives of the 1980s and 1990s as well as Adrian Lyne's 1987 thriller *Fatal Attraction*. This story of a single professional woman, Alex (Glenn Close), who seduces and then persecutes a married man, Dan Gallagher (Michael Douglas), has been correctly diagnosed by most critics as an assault on feminism and a naked celebration of "family values" (Faludi 1991, 112–23; Nadel 1997, 184–90). Spurned by Dan after their one-night stand, Alex kidnaps his daughter and eventually invades his home with a butcher knife. In a frenzied final confrontation, Dan and his wife are forced to kill the interloper in order to save their own lives. The obvious, anti-feminist message of all this is that independent career women and casual sex are potentially lethal, especially to families. Significantly, the threat personified by Alex issues from outside the stereotyped setting of middle-class existence: she lives in a trendy downtown loft apartment surrounded by art and the haunting sounds of Puccini's *Madame Butterfly*, a milieu that is almost the diametric opposite of the cozy, suburban one Dan and his family are in the process of settling into. The film thus implies a moral equivalence between the "feminist" woman and the downtown vice that the news media of the 1980s and '90s warned was "spreading" to nice middle-class neighborhoods.

Interestingly, the excessive brutality that *Fatal Attraction* authorizes Dan and his wife to use in defense of their home—which results in Alex being beaten, drowned in their bathtub, and then shot—parallels the sort of spectacular violence movies like *Judgment Night* or *New Jack City* recommend as a solution to the problem of ghetto crime. As Nadel has pointed out, although most "siege" films—like *Fatal Attraction, Pacific Heights*, and *Unlawful Entry*—"reject the specifics of the black menace to the neighborhood, they evoke the narrative of the black menace as the context in which white psychopaths are supposed to be striking and shocking anomalies" (Nadel 1997, 197). Indeed, given a social context in which the news media and the political establishment consistently fixate on inner-city crime, the siege narrative's focus on what Nadel terms the "pathology of the perverse stranger" can't help but activate the specter of an out-of-control underclass for most audiences. That this is so can be seen even more clearly in two popular siege narratives, *Eye for an Eye* and *Ransom*, both released in 1996.

Eye for an Eye dramatizes the imagined danger to middle-class security posed by the pathologically depraved Other in terms even more heavy-handed than *Fatal Attraction* and associates this threat even more closely with the city. It tells the story of Karen McCann (Sally Field), a busy professional with a loving husband (Ed Harris), two beautiful daughters, and a palatial home in the suburbs (an early establishing shot of which, as in many a conservative siege narrative, singles it out as a privileged, almost sacred site of warmth and familial harmony).[8] This domestic idyll is soon shattered when a psychotic delivery man brutally rapes and then kills the older daughter on the living room floor as Karen, stuck downtown in a traffic jam, listens helplessly to her screams on a cellular phone. As Detective Sgt. Denillio (Joe Montegna) tries to track down the murderer, the McCanns attempt to cope with this horrible violation by installing a security system and joining a support group for people who've lost loved ones to violence. Denillio eventually discovers and arrests the killer, Robert Doob (Kiefer Sutherland), a smirking, sleazy career-felon who, Karen tells her husband, "has been in and out of jail his entire life." He is so evil that at one point in the film he gratuitously pours hot coffee on a stray dog (see Figure 20). Yet, because—in an obvious reference to the O. J. Simpson trial—the L.A. County prosecutors failed to share DNA evidence with the defense, Doob goes free.

Beside herself, Karen becomes obsessed with Doob and begins spying on him, eventually following him to the seedy, downtown flophouse where he lives. Doob's neighborhood—L.A.'s notorious Skid Row area—is pictured as the grotesque antithesis of Karen's tranquil, bucolic suburb. While Karen's neighborhood is preternaturally quiet, Doob's is rocked by the sounds of rap music, yelling, traffic noise, and Mexican pop tunes. The McCann house stands alone amidst a picturesque lush green landscape; in contrast, the rundown hotel Doob calls home is surrounded by streets full of bumper-to-bumper traffic and sidewalks teeming with raucous multiethnic, multiracial crowds. The people milling around in these crowds—many of whom are drinking beer or stronger liquor from bottles in brown paper bags—look uniformly disheveled and sullen; at least one, a large African American woman in a ragged house-dress, is a raving lunatic who berates passers-by in every scene in which she appears. Doob's association with this milieu naturalizes his violence and psychosis as a normal feature of the inner city, as the "law" of the "urban jungle." In *Eye for an Eye*, as in countless other movies like it, threats to middle- and upper-middle-class safety and comfort arise al-most exclusively from the urban poor and environments like Doob's grungy neighborhood.

Eye for an Eye leaves little doubt about the best method of counter-acting the urban Other's brutal disruption of suburban domestic bliss. When Doob discovers Karen has been trailing him he begins harassing her surviving daughter and this spurs Karen to seek out members of a support group who may be taking justice into their own hands. At their urging, she practices shooting at a firing range. Eventually they obtain a

Figure 20. Doob pours coffee on a stray dog in *Eye for an Eye*.

gun for her and draw up plans for a "hit" on Doob. Karen appears to agonize over the deed and calls the vigilante group to back out after being tipped off about an undercover FBI investigation into their activities. But this is just a ruse to trick the authorities and she subsequently lures Doob into her home, where—according to Hollywood's version of the law—killing intruders is always justified. "This is personal!" she screams before pumping four slugs into the attacking Doob. Detective Denillio, who arrives on the scene later to investigate, correctly suspects that the shooting was a set-up, but ultimately signals his approval by telling another police officer that "it looks like a clear-cut case of self-defense" (as does Karen's husband, who reluctantly takes her hand when he arrives back at the house). As with conservative crime dramas since *Dirty Harry* and *Death Wish*, *Eye for an Eye* endorses violence and vigilantism as the only solution to crime and blames the "liberal" judicial system for failing to lock up the "scumbags."

In Ron Howard's blockbuster *Ransom*, which pulled in box office revenues in excess of $125 million in 1996, it is not an upper-middle-class family but an extremely wealthy one that finds itself "under siege" by hostile Others; however, the framing of and final solution to the problem is nearly identical to that proposed by *Eye for an Eye*. At the beginning of the film, we're introduced to self-made millionaire Tom Mullen (Mel Gibson) who is enjoying what appears to be an ideal life: he owns a successful airline and has a penthouse apartment overlooking Central Park, a gorgeous wife, and an intelligent son. He even stars in his own television advertisements. All that changes when kidnappers seize his son, Sean, one day when he and Tom are out playing in the park (another not-so-subtle attempt to brand urban public space as unsafe). The FBI is called in and head agent Lonnie Hawkins counsels a terrified Tom to comply with the kidnappers' demands. There's immediate tension between Tom and Lonnie, in part because the FBI had spent the previous three years investigating Tom for possibly giving a bribe to the head of one of the unions at his airline. Meanwhile, the kidnappers—a gnarly looking collection of petty criminals who are working for a crooked cop named Jimmy Shaker (Gary Sinise)—keep Sean locked up in a squalid basement apartment somewhere in the "bad part" of Brooklyn. The first time Tom attempts to pay the $2 million ransom he follows the kidnappers' orders meticulously, but just as he is about to hand over the money he realizes the kidnappers have no intention of handing over the boy.

At this point, Tom decides to get tough with his son's abductors. He goes on television to offer a $2 million reward for the kidnappers' capture. Just as Tom had hoped, this stratagem subverts Shaker's plans and sows discord in his gang. As a result, Shaker ultimately kills off his partners and poses as Sean's liberator in order to claim the bounty himself. There are at least three things worthy of note about the way *Ransom* stages the standard family-under-siege narrative. First, there is the characterization of the kidnappers themselves, a group which is a veritable typology of urban criminality (but which is cast as all white). Shaker is not only shrewd and backstabbing but is driven by a palpable and all-consuming class hatred. Maris (Lili Taylor), Shaker's second-in-command, is utterly callous, insists on keeping Sean tied up, refuses to feed him, and comes close to killing him a couple of times. Clark (Liev Schreiber) and Chubby (Donnie Wahlberg) are archetypal stocking-cap-wearing small-time hoods but at least Chubby has a soft spot in his heart for the boy. The group's computer whiz, who's responsible for throwing the FBI off the kidnappers' trail, is perpetually drunk. And as Krin Gabbard points out, "the kidnappers regularly adopt speech patterns and a metalanguage associated with African Americans" (Gabbard 2001, 19), suggesting a connection to the ghetto underclass and its "tangle of pathology." There's not a sympathetic character in the bunch and Shaker and Maris in particular are framed as richly deserving of their respective violent ends.

Second, the film is obsessed with the contrast between Shaker's run-down lower-class world and Tom's luxurious one, repeatedly juxtaposing the Mullens' affluent apartment with the kidnapper's basement lair. The contrast is remarked on by Shaker when he compares Tom's house in the sky to that of the elite Eloi in H. G. Wells's *Time Machine* and again as he admires the Mullen place when he shows up there to pick up the reward check.

In the end, though, the spatial contrast between Tom's penthouse and Shaker's basement becomes a metaphor not just for the class differences between the millionaire and the crooked cop but for the moral differences between them as well. Though Tom as a representative of his class is not without flaws (it turns out Tom did pay off the unions, just as the FBI suspected), the moral and psychological shortcomings of the rich are excused in light of the atrocities perpetrated by creatures of the street like Shaker and his gang. Tom, after all, loves his wife and child; Shaker, on the other hand, shoots his own lover in order to get his hands on the reward money. Finally, in siding with and ultimately rewarding Tom's "no compromise" approach to Shaker's domestic terrorism over the FBI's ineffectual strategy of appeasement, *Ransom* like *Eye for an Eye* can be read as an argument for the fascistic approach to crime control advocated by William Bennett and Rudy Giuliani, for retribution and repression rather than prevention, rehabilitation, and social justice.

Despite the absence of minority villains, *Eye for an Eye* and *Ransom* are fairly open about their politics and about the (racist, anti-urban) fears they aim to conjure up. Both in their idealized, sentimental conception of the normal, white nuclear family and in the way that they locate the source of the threat to this family in a stereotypically slum-like space, these films openly echo the conservative discourse on the underclass with its construction of the inner city as an uncivilized space responsible for dissolving the bonds of family and community. That there is, to use Stuart Hall's term, a certain *inferential racism* to such constructions, no matter what color skin the menacing urban Other in these films happens to have, almost goes without saying (Hall 1995).

"A deadly sin on every street corner": Evil and Urbanity in *Seven*

The association between cities and metaphysical evil has grown so strong in popular consciousness since the early 1980s that a number of successful Hollywood films have taken up the trope of the damned or hellish city as their central theme and narrative pretext. I'm thinking here of what could be called "urban gothic" films like *Batman* (1989), *The Crow*

(1994), or the Hughes brothers' *From Hell* (2001) that picture the city as a brooding, Stygian world haunted by "creatures of the night." Rendering the imagined menace of the urban center visually as a *shimmering darkness*, these films break with the codes of cinematic "realism" in order to give full expression to the most hysterical fantasies about the horror of contemporary city life. Indeed, the fact that these representations of the city are openly fantastic, cartoonish, even surreal makes them uniquely suited as vehicles for the rising middle-class moral panic over urban conditions. Following critic Robin Wood's remarks on the social meaning of horror films, I'd like to argue that it is precisely the "fantastic" nature of films like *The Crow* or *Batman*—indeed, of any film that purports to be simple entertainment, pure spectacle, or mere illusion— that allows them to give voice to fears and anxieties habitually repressed or disavowed by viewers in their more rational moments. As Wood puts it, in the unreal world of the horror film, "the censor (in both the common and the Freudian sense) is lulled to sleep and relaxes vigilance" (Wood 1985, 203). The "urban gothic" movies of the '80s and '90s, I want to suggest, articulated in a coded way the creeping, semi-conscious, media-generated paranoia about urban disorder that increasingly troubled the affluent comfort of the suburban middle-class. There's arguably no better example of this than David Fincher's *Seven.*[9]

As the sequence cited at the beginning of the chapter indicates, the makers of *Seven* represent its unidentified, New York–style urban setting as a thoroughly noxious, menacing place, an allegorical Hell as full of suffering and anguish as the *Inferno* of Dante on which it appears to have been modeled. This contributes to the film an oppressively despairing, apocalyptic mood. But the function of the urban environment in *Seven* goes beyond providing a suitably expressive backdrop for the film's bleak story. In the course of the film, the city's nastiness and immorality—and the sense of defeated resignation it imposes on its residents—emerges as an explicit and recurring theme. In *Seven*, as Amy Taubin has argued, "cities are cesspools of contagion, spreading sin faster than TB" (Taubin 1996, 23). And no one, whether innocent or not, escapes the city's contaminating influence. In fact, the "moral breakdown" that characterizes

Seven's metropolis provides the motivation for the actions of more than one of the main characters.

The first hint the viewer is given of the malevolence of the film's city occurs immediately before the opening credits. After meeting Mills at the scene of a routine domestic shooting, Sommerset lounges in his apartment reading. As he lies there on his bed, the sounds of distant shouting, of tires squealing, of a dog barking, and finally of a car alarm blaring invade his bedroom. Even before the first of Jonathan Doe's grotesque murders is discovered, these noises—which Sommerset habitually drowns out using a metronome—signal the relentless brutality of the surrounding milieu. Equally important, the fact that similar sounds of distress penetrate the space of Sommerset's bedroom again in later scenes underscores just how inescapable and quotidian such ambient violence actually is (which is precisely the point of the casually displayed corpse in the scene with the cab driver described at the start of this chapter). Such sounds—together with the jarring, post-punk theme song by Nine-Inch Nails—define our initial image of the cinematic city and continue to inflect our experience of it throughout the film.

That experience is even more heavily colored by the graphic and incomprehensibly sadistic violence that drives the plot. Thus, following the opening credits, Sommerset and Mills are called in to inspect the bloated, discolored remains of Doe's first victim, an incredibly obese man who has been forced to literally eat himself to death (that is, until his stomach bursts). This begins their futile race to track down the killer before he claims yet another victim. Each clue they uncover, each step they take, only leads them belatedly to the scene of another of Doe's series of meticulously planned, artistically carried-out slayings. There appears to be a definite ethico-religious logic to Doe's killings, each of which dispatches an individual who epitomizes one of the deadly sins using a symbolically "appropriate," Dante-esque method of punishment: a greedy uptown lawyer bleeds to death after being made to slice out a pound of his own flesh; a prostitute is killed with a razor-tipped dildo that Doe makes one of her hapless clients use on her; a vain fashion model has her nose sliced off ("to spite her face," as Sommerset notes), and so on. Doe's murders are, as Sommerset correctly discerns, a form of "preaching" and the film's big mystery is whether he'll get a chance to finish his sermon.

Interestingly, Doe's savagery is rarely represented directly on the screen; the sort of dramatically choreographed action that is so omnipresent in slasher films and standard *policiers* is—with the exception of a single chase scene—virtually absent here. Rather than give us gun play and acrobatic fight scenes, from the opening shot to the last, the film confronts us with the gruesome "physical evidence" of mind-boggling acts of violence slowly and gradually revealed. Not only does this create tension and uneasiness, it compels the viewer to linger over the gore. Much of the terrifying visual impact of *Seven* relies on the vividly depicted and often hideously mutilated bodies, and pieces of bodies, Doe leaves behind. These grisly tableaus owe much of their distinctive look to visceral "body horror" of genre films like *Hellraiser* as well as, perhaps, to the necrophilic aesthetic of avant-garde photographer David Watkins. The camera records each hideous wound and disfiguration with unflinching, pornographic, almost clinical accuracy. Among other things, we see the dissected and reassembled body of the fat man, an amputated hand, and the skeletal, barely alive body of a man covered with oozing bedsores. One could argue that the real suspense in the film has more to do with the anticipation of the inevitable spectacle of horror that awaits the investigators at each new crime scene than it does with actually locating the killer. And this, in turn, endows the city—which is presented above all else as a collection or network of crime scenes—with a pronounced sense of foreboding.

Meanwhile, the built environment projected by the film as the showcase for all this butchery radiates a definite aura of decay and despair. *Seven*'s metropolis appears to be in an advanced state of decrepitude. Its buildings are filthy, weathered, crumbling, and moldy, their walls full of cracks and holes, their paint peeling and stained, their floors creaking. The fat man's house, to cite a memorable example, has windows so heavily streaked with dirt they barely admit light. The apartment building where the detectives find the man murdered for personifying "sloth" has hallways and stairwells covered with litter and slick from rain that has seeped in through fissures in the roof. Piles of overflowing black plastic garbage bags, disintegrating cardboard boxes, and abandoned pieces of furniture crowd the streets. Graffiti is present in nearly every outdoor shot; even the lampposts appear to have been "tagged." Even those buildings that don't appear to be decomposing—like the police station or the lawyer's office or the library where Sommerset hunts for clues—look old and exhausted, their paint fading and their decor and fixtures dated.

Nicholas Christopher argues that the city in classic film noir and in more recent noir revivals is frequently constructed as a nightmarish labyrinth, one which perpetually threatens to enmesh, engulf, and over-whelm the hero (Christopher 1997, 16–17). This is certainly true of *Seven*, in which Mills and Sommerset confront a metropolis that is not only in the process of collapsing in on itself but is punctuated by spaces that are maze-like, disordered, and disorienting in the extreme (see Figure 21). Thus, after the pair discover Doe's apartment, he leads them on a con-fusing chase through several floors and rooms of the building, over a roof top, through what looks like an abandoned ballroom, across a busy thoroughfare, and into an alleyway where Doe knocks Mills uncon-scious. It is, as Amy Taubin has observed, "a chase scene so dark that we can't tell one good guy from another, let alone good from bad" (Taubin, 1996, 24). The layout of Doe's apartment, which the partners search shortly after the failed chase, likewise proves difficult to negotiate. The place is a maze of clothes racks, bookshelves, cabinets, rooms, and hall-ways connected in one instance by what seems to be a secret (or at least carefully obscured) doorway. Even more disturbing, every single win-dow in the apartment is covered and the walls appear to be painted pitch black. Small wonder, then, that it takes Mills what seems like an eternity to track down the phone when it starts ringing in the middle of the detectives' search of the premises. The omnipresent clutter—the piles of garbage, the paper strewn everywhere—render the film's disordered spaces even more chaotic. And the multiplicity of labyrinthine spaces adds to the perceived hostility of the setting by holding out the possibility of unforeseen pitfalls and dangers hidden in their shadowy recesses.

Other elements of the mise-en-scène, most notably the lighting, also strengthen the impression of *Seven*'s city as unwelcoming and perilous terrain. Noir-inspired lighting plays a key role in defining the film's tone.[10] Night shots are bathed in blackness and even in daytime shots the lighting is murky and muted.[11] Direct sunlight is virtually absent. Hard back- and side-lighting is used frequently to create ominous silhouettes and shadows. Crime scenes in particular are typically darker than the rest of the film and depend on low-key lighting and available sources of illumination like floor lamps, neon signage, and flashlights. Moreover, what light is allowed to enter a scene often enters at odd angles and in the form of jagged slices, odd patches, and narrow beams. Even the darkest of the classic noirs—films like *T-Men* (1947) or *Touch of Evil* (1958)—were never quite this dark. So, for instance, when Mills and Sommerset examine the body of Doe's first victim, it is in a room so dimly lit that the only details of the scene we can really make out are those illuminated by the thin beams of their flashlights. The movie's color palette—which runs from black to an infinite variety of browns and grays to putrid

Figure 21. A dark, rainy alley in *Seven*.

greens with blood and wounds rendered in a deep, inky crimson—highlights the sinister associations of the lighting scheme. In the brothel where the prostitute is found murdered, a red neon light provides her room with suitably infernal illumination. Similarly, in Doe's apartment a bright red neon cross and an assortment of dim lamps provide most of the light. The apprehensive atmosphere created by this use of light and color is rendered gloomier by the fact that the unidentified metropolis is deluged by what seems like perpetual rainfall. As in film noir, the darkness and the inclement weather echo and indeed become an "objective correlative" of the metropolis's climate of moral decline.

Seven's grim urban wasteland exerts a profound, tangible pressure on the psyches of the main characters. And no one exhibits the strain of life in the metropolis as clearly as Detective William Sommerset. Kevin McNamara writes that the detective in film noir, from Philip Marlowe to *Blade Runner*'s Rick Deckard, is "a man who has seen everything but is powerless to change much of anything" (McNamara 1996, 177). Sommerset certainly fits this description. As the archetypal cynical, world-weary yet all-knowing career cop, he possesses a vast store of accumulated knowledge about the moral depravity of the streets, which he is perpetually trying to share with his naive young partner (and, through him, with the audience). It is significant, then, that one of first things we learn about him is that he has decided to quit the police force and retire to the country. Throughout the film, Sommerset wants nothing more than to escape the city: when Mills's wife, Tracy (Gwyneth Paltrow), asks him over dinner, "how long have you lived here?" his only rejoinder is "too long." His running commentary makes it clear that he regards the film's shadowy metropolis as incomprehensibly vicious. Thus, when his captain attempts to dissuade him from retiring, Sommerset tells him a story about a man who just the night before was randomly attacked while walking his dog and stabbed in both eyes, concluding that "I don't understand this place anymore." As he sees it, the apathy and callousness of "this place" gives the Jonathan Does of the world freedom to operate. "In any major city," he explains to Mills as they discuss the case, "minding your own business is a science. The first thing they teach women in rape prevention is to yell fire. Nobody answers to 'help.'"

Sommerset is not the only character in the film who finds the city unbearable. Tracy too views her surroundings as loathsome. Early in the film she complains to David about the excessive traffic noise outside their apartment, commenting that "I thought we moved here to get away from tractor pulls." Later this annoyance with city life turns to open repugnance. At one point she arranges to get together with Sommerset behind David's back because he is the only person in town she knows and she needs desperately to talk. When they meet, Tracy, who was a fifth-grade teacher when she lived "upstate," describes how she has looked for work in the local school system but discovered that "the conditions are just horrible." Then, revealing that she is pregnant and having second thoughts about carrying the pregnancy to term, she tearfully confesses that "I hate this city." The tortured, helpless expression on her face speaks volumes about her feelings toward her new home.

Jonathan Doe, we discover, basically shares Tracy and Sommerset's perspective on urban existence. We are hardly surprised to learn, therefore, that the two thousand handwritten notebooks the detectives find in his apartment include page after page of misanthropic diatribe in which the city figures prominently (an allusion, perhaps, to Dostoyevski's *Notes from Underground*). "On the subway today a man came up to me to start a conversation," Sommerset reads out loud from one of Doe's journals. "He made small talk, this lonely man, talking about the weather and other things. I tried to be pleasant and accommodating but my head began to hurt from his banality. I almost didn't notice it had happened but I suddenly threw up all over him. He was not pleased. And I couldn't stop laughing." Doe's solution to the horror around him is an apocalyptic one. In keeping with millenarian Christian fantasy, he believes that only total violence can redeem a fallen, godless social world.[12] Fittingly, he sees himself as a sort of avenging angel, insisting that "I did not choose. I was chosen." He had to resort to such extreme measures, Doe tells Sommerset and Mills, because "wanting people to listen you can't just tap them on the shoulder anymore, you have to hit them with a sledge hammer." After he has turned himself in to the police and is guiding Sommerset and Mills to the alleged location of his latest victims, Doe justifies his deeds by pointing to the pathologies and moral failings of the city. "Don't ask me to pity them. We see a deadly sin on every street corner, in every home and we tolerate it," explains Doe. "We tolerate it because it's common, it's trivial. We tolerate it morning, noon and night." His victims, he argues, are as deserving of punishment (and as undeserving of sympathy) as "the thousands who died at Sodom and Gomorrah."

The film itself stakes out a profoundly ambiguous stance toward Doe's murders and toward his justification for them. What Doe does is clearly monstrous, but the depiction of the metropolis as a vast den of iniquity implies that at least some of his violence is an appropriate reaction to the monstrousness of his social environment. His first few victims are, after all, hateful, immoral people with whom the audience feels absolutely no connection. Indeed, with the exception of the pathetic Tracy, none of the denizens of *Seven*'s city—Sommerset and Mills included—come off as even remotely sympathetic. However revolted we are by Doe's brutality, the film more or less demands that the audience adopt a position from which the regeneration of the world through some sort of cleansing conflagration or orgy of bloodshed perversely makes sense.

Of the major characters, only Mills with his boundless enthusiasm and bravado seems totally oblivious to the malevolence of his surroundings. Impulsive, not very bright, emotional to a fault, and basically optimistic, he is the diametric opposite of Sommerset's stoic reserve and cynical realism; next to Sommerset, he appears as a regular country yokel. His ignorance of the pitfalls and depravity of the big city and his lack of self-control appear fated to get him into trouble from the start. Thus, it seems perfectly fitting that he and Tracy have been tricked into renting an apartment next to a noisy subway line. Nor is it accidental that Mills's explosive temper threatens to compromise the Doe investigation on more than one occasion: first, when he almost refuses to give Sommerset the money to obtain an FBI computer list of people reading about deadly sins and then again when he kicks in the door to Doe's apartment without a warrant, potentially tainting the evidence inside. Moreover, without the aid of his knowing, street-smart partner, Mills's investigation of Doe's murders would go nowhere. It is Sommerset, after all, who spots all the important clues, who figures out Doe's *modus operandi*, and who leads the pair to the suspect's lair. Given his persistent disregard for Sommerset's warnings about the treacherous nature of *Seven*'s metropolis, it is entirely predictable that Mills becomes the film's most abject victim.

Seven's ending essentially vindicates the despairing outlook already manifest in Doe and Sommerset's view of urban life (while at the same time repudiating Mills's strutting confidence and macho posturing). Throughout the film, Doe remains in charge and in control, dictating the action and easily eluding his pursuers even after they have tracked him to his apartment. When Doe allows himself to be taken into custody, it is only so he can complete his "masterpiece" (by revealing that he has killed Tracy out of envy, thereby provoking Mills to "become wrath" and execute him). That Doe successfully carries his plan to its bloody conclusion confirms what we already know: that the guardians of public order are helpless to contain the elemental forces of violence and barbarity being bred at the heart of the metropolis. The fact that he manages to destroy Mills's life in the process symbolizes the fate in store for those who underestimate the power of those forces. Despite a tacked-on voice-over by Sommerset avowing that the world is "worth fighting for,"[13] and despite an indication that he might not leave the police force after all, the film's conclusion leaves us emotionally exactly where we began: with a gloomy, unrelieved sense of foreboding about the threat posed by the city. No other outcome is even imaginable. In a sense, the fatalistic ending was already implied by the visual and thematic emphasis given to the urban setting. As Christopher has pointed out, in classic film noir, "the labyrinth . . . the city-as-world is made to appear implacable and unassailable, and the hero puny and vulnerable" (Christopher 1997, 32). Naturally, this way of framing the confrontation between the individual and the environment bodes ill for the individual. In this respect *Seven* once again pushes the basic noir formula to its logical limit: the looming omnipresence of the film's latter-day Sodom and Gomorrah from the very first frame suggests that all the protagonists' efforts will be losing ones and that the protagonists themselves will come to bad ends.

Seven's portrayal of the city as a blighted, decaying zone of unfettered criminality and vice, as a place where one finds "a deadly sin on every street corner," more or less directly transcodes the reactionary view of urban problems promoted by the mainstream news media and the conservative punditocracy. Like countless other Hollywood films that have come out since the early 1980s, it validates middle-class suburbia's revulsion for a (mostly poor, mostly of color) urban core understood as *essentially* unruly and beyond hope. As Homi Bhabha points out, "the conservative suburban attitude is founded on the fear of difference; and a narrow-minded appeal to cultural homogeneity. It is a kind of national paranoia that draws the boundary between what is acceptable and what is unacceptable ever more tightly around the norm of the 'known' . . ." (Bhabha 1997, 299). A number of different currents of ideologically motivated anxiety feed the "national paranoia" Bhabha refers to here. Concern about the economic decline of America's metropolitan regions (along with concomitant concerns about national decline), racialized fear of street crime, anxiety about the "breakdown" of the family and civilized morality in the ghetto, apprehension about the threat to social order posed by "inner-city" drugs like crack, skepticism about government's capacity to address urban problems—all figure prominently in the conservative discourse that *Seven* and other contemporary cinematic representations of urban life confirm and circulate.

To begin with, the dilapidated structures and litter-filled alleys we see in *Seven*—and, even more hyperbolically, in the post-apocalyptic L.A. of films like *Escape from L.A.* and *Blade Runner*—give visual form to the suspicion that our central cities are now economically obsolete. In the conservative suburban imagination, the nation's downtowns and the neighborhoods that surround the downtowns are not merely struggling but already in ruins, reduced to vast dumping grounds for marginal populations of various sorts. As explained in chapter 3, this image of post-industrial urban failure performs some important ideological functions for the middle class, most notably by providing them with a justification for distancing themselves from urban minorities and inner-city neighborhoods. Moreover, by "siting" economic and social decline in central cities, the dominant, right-wing interpretation of urban reality obscures both the deeper causes of such decline and its real scope (since the forces

of economic decline and deindustrialization are now doing to our suburbs, especially our older, inner-ring suburbs, exactly what they did to
the central cities). *Seven's* city functions as a symbol of decline not
merely because it is falling apart and overflowing with garbage, but also
because it appears quite literally to be stuck at an earlier moment in the
history of urban development. Most of the film's interiors appear to date
from the 1940s or before (as, for that matter, do most of Sommerset's and
Mills's suits). This anachronism is obviously meant to evoke the dark
universe of classic film noir. But it is also, I think, a reflection of the discourse that treats central cities and the lifestyles associated with them
as hopelessly out of date and on the verge of extinction. In this age
of mega-malls, Wal-Mart, and "telecommuters," the official voices of
mainstream America—writers like journalist Joel Garreau or conservative pundit George Gilder—often charge that cities are doomed because
they have failed to evolve to keep up with the sweeping changes wrought
by information-age capitalism; as Garreau claims in *Edge City,* classic central cities like Manhattan and San Francisco "are relics of a time past.
They are aberrations" (Garreau 1991, 25). By envisioning its metropolis
as a relic from the 1940s, *Seven* makes a similar accusation.

Of the popular fears surrounding the contemporary American city
that are tapped into by *Seven,* the fear of urban crime articulated by the
film perhaps resonates most powerfully with middle-class suburbanites.
I have already detailed how paranoia about street crime has spurred the
growth of the private security industry, the rapid spread of gated communities from Los Angeles to New York, and rising public support for
punitive crime-fighting legislation. Crime hysteria has also played and
continues to play a major role in the ongoing out-migration of middle-
class families fleeing urban neighborhoods for the greener pastures of
suburbia. For instance, a 1993 *Chicago Tribune* series on the motives of
people leaving Chicago for the suburbs found that fear of urban crime
was more of a motivating factor for most migrants than any positive feature of their new homes. As one person interviewed for the report put it,
"We became worn out by the traffic, parking hassles, noise, crime, lack
of being able to feel safe, etc. We did not feel the City of Chicago was a

good place to start a family" (Reardon 1993, 10). Sentiments like these are clearly and approvingly echoed in *Seven* and in films like it. When Sommerset talks longingly about retiring to the country or when Tracy worries out loud about raising a child in the city, they are speaking from the ideological position of all those families who have fled or dream about fleeing the city for the perceived safety and comfort of the suburbs.

Moreover, a movie like *Seven* takes the gory, blood-drenched image of urban life painted by law-and-order politicians and local television news shows at face value—and then renders it even bloodier. The film indulges right-wing fantasies about the violence of the city to the point where violence becomes the city's sole distinctive feature. In this, *Seven* follows a well-established Hollywood trend. The identification of the American metropolis with violence in films like *Trespass*, *Predator 2*, *Menace II Society*, or *New Jack City* is so complete that, as Jerry Herron has argued, "a city without violence would be irrelevant because it would appear unreal to the majority of contemporary Americans" (Herron 1993, 186).

But *Seven* doesn't just exaggerate the extent of urban violence. It also decontextualizes (and thereby mystifies) it. In the film, as in reactionary discourse on crime in general, violent criminality is seen as the result of individual psychological aberrations or personal moral failing rather than as the product of systemic social and economic forces. Though Doe's misguided vigilantism is provoked by the wickedness around him, the fact that he is independently wealthy, white, and totally psychotic renders any sociological understanding of his bizarre killings moot. And the other murders we learn about—the man who is shot by his wife, the corpse Sommerset sees from the cab, the man who is attacked while walking his dog—appear inexplicable and unmotivated if not outright random. But we know, as a matter of fact, that criminal behavior is rarely truly random and that poverty and joblessness are at the very least contributing factors to most sorts of street crime. As noted in chapter 1, rates of crime, and particularly rates of violent crime, are generally higher in poor neighborhoods than in middle-class and wealthy ones,[14] and residents of economically distressed inner-city black and Latino neighborhoods are much more likely to become victims of crime than other city-dwellers.[15] In other words, the assaults and muggings that so terrify suburbia—the quotidian street crime that *Seven* makes such a point of showing us—are properly seen as stemming directly from the deepening poverty and contracting opportunity structure that has accompanied the deindustrialization of our nation's inner-city communities of color. Yet *Seven*, like most films that deal with the subject, conspicuously avoids confronting the underlying dynamics of the urban violence and criminality it is so preoccupied with depicting. As framed by the film's narrative, the imputed barbarism of the city is utterly unrelated to entrenched racial oppression or a dysfunctional economy; rather, it is a manifestation of pure evil. This moralistic view of crime jives perfectly with the perspective championed by conservatives like Charles Murray and William Bennett, which in a not-so-subtly racist way insists that the social problems of America's minority communities are caused by their own moral failings and not by institutional racism of the larger society or the inherent contradictions of capitalist development.

It is noteworthy that in *Seven* the perpetrators of violence are all, as far as we know, white, and that the main representative of law and order, Sommerset, is black. This appears to break with the standard right-wing narrative in which heroic white cops defend the white, suburban public against the implicitly black violence of the city. However, I would argue that the film's pointed and excessive association of bloodshed with the big city—which in the current universe of political discourse has become synonymous with the deviant racial "Other"—subtly *codes* its violence as black (or, better, reinforces stereotypes about criminality and violence that are often applied exclusively to inner-city people of color). The rundown tenements and the garbage-choked streets one sees throughout the film likewise can be read as connoting "the ghetto" or ghetto-like conditions even in the absence of African American "bad guys." And the sheer pervasiveness of cops and crime scenes in the film is bound to conjure up images of rampant black lawlessness to the suburban viewer weaned on *Cops* and television coverage of the "crack crisis." In this way, hysterical white fear of black street crime perhaps receives in the film a kind of displaced, deracialized expression that avoids opening up questions about the systemic causes of the very real violence tearing apart poor, urban, minority neighborhoods.[16]

But more than anything else, it is the fatalism one finds in *Seven* and other recent Hollywood attempts to deal with American urban reality that dovetails with the most reactionary sentiments of the suburban middle class and articulates the worst aspects of the hegemonic discourse on the urban crisis. As I argued in chapter 1, the epochal migration of the American population away from the central cities to the suburban fringe has been above all a flight from communal, public life to the comforts of a privatized existence centered around the single family home, the automobile, and the TV set. As William Schneider notes, "Suburbanization means the privatization of American life and culture. To move to the suburbs is to express a preference for the private over the public" (Schneider 1992, 37). In the political realm, this fondness for the private becomes skepticism about how much municipal government can do to address nagging social ills like crime, poverty, and illicit drug use. "A major reason people move out to the suburbs is simply to buy their own government," explains Schneider. "These people resent it when politicians take their money and use it to solve other people's problems, especially when they don't believe that government can actually solve those problems" (37). The image of the city as beyond redemption, as hopelessly dysfunctional, justifies the generally individualistic, antisocial bent of suburban politics. Thus, when *Seven* portrays the city as locked in a downward spiral of decay and shows the police as hopelessly ineffectual, it vindicates the suburbanite's hostility to "government spending" and "money for cities." Likewise, Sommerset's longing for retirement (which, remember, he intends to spend in the country) echoes the increasingly respectable middle-class desire to simply abandon (politically, materially, and culturally) those left behind by suburbanization. Along the same lines, the celebration of apocalyptic vigilantism in *Batman* and *The Crow*, and the fantasy image of a feral metropolis safely cordoned off from the rest of America that one sees on display in *Escape from New York* and its sequel, each express in their own way a deep sense of hopelessness about the future of the city.

Conclusion

The alarmist images of and rhetoric about cities on display in so many Hollywood films of the 1980s and '90s replicated and amplified the fear and loathing of all things urban so adroitly exploited (and encouraged) by the forces of the political right. Sometimes, as in *Predator 2* or *Falling Down* or *The Substitute*, such films are nakedly racist in their terrified depictions of vice-ridden black and brown inner cities. More often than not, though, as in *Eye for an Eye* and *Ransom*, they give white, middle-class fears of the urban underclass a coded, disguised form of expression. As we have seen, even ostensibly liberal films like *Grand Canyon* and movies made by the "new wave" of black filmmakers find it difficult to free themselves from the terms of the conservative discourse on the urban crisis.

Nowhere in the Hollywood cinema of the past two decades are reactionary nightmares about the postindustrial city more in evidence than in the proliferation of "urban gothic" thrillers such as *Seven*. Like the malevolent urban environment in *Batman*, *The Crow*, and other movies of its ilk, the dark, decaying, crime-ridden metropolis constructed by Fincher's film reflects the terrified perspective of people who over the past few decades have done their utmost to "get far away from" the city and the collective responsibilities and human solidarities upon which the city is based. *Seven*'s vision of its metropolis confirms the middle-class suspicion that our cities are overrun by violence, morally degenerate, economically moribund, and essentially beyond repair. When Sommerset gives his junior partner a photocopied version of a diagram of Dante's *Inferno* to aid him in the investigation of the Doe killings, the gesture makes explicit what is clear throughout the film and is axiomatic for many of its suburban middle-class viewers: the city is Hell. This bleak vision—which dovetails so perfectly with right-wing discourse on social problems and which so thoroughly mystifies the problems facing America's metropolitan areas—wasn't just confined to films and television news reports. As the next chapter demonstrates, it even seeped into the eye-catching imagery and thirty-second narratives of advertising.

CHAPTER 6

Wouldn't You Rather Be at Home?
Marketing Middle-Class Agoraphobia

Fear is the raw material that sustains the flourishing industries
of private security and social control, and it's in steady supply . . .
[A]ll of us—some more, some less—are turning into guards and
prisoners: guards keeping an eye on whoever's nearby and
prisoners of fear.

—Eduardo Galeano, *Upside Down: A Primer for the Looking-
Glass World*

Home computer giant Packard Bell's breakthrough 1996 national advertising campaign spoke volumes about the cultural pervasiveness of the
moral panic over the city in late twentieth-century America. Handled by
M&C Saatchi at an estimated cost of $20 million, this was Packard Bell's
first concerted effort to "build its brand" and establish an identity in the
minds of consumers around the country—and it certainly did. The ensuing campaign produced one of the most memorable and visually striking
TV spots of the 1990s. The ad, "Home," opens with images of a postindustrial rabble, most dressed in rags, some clutching torches, all looking depressed and beaten down, trudging through mud, debris, and
what looks like pools of oil toward a foreboding, gloomy, *Batman*-esque
metropolis looming in the distance. The sky is black. Smog and smoke
rise past the city's neo-Gothic skyscrapers (see Figure 22). Next we're
shown a dingy library patrolled by jackbooted guards with the word
"Quiet" scrawled across their faces and a dour group of people shuffling
along in huge, slow-moving lines inside an ominous-looking bank. The
gargoyles in front of the library come to life and howl. A woman standing in line inside the bank grows old and withered before our very eyes
while the people standing in line out front get drenched by a sudden
downpour. All of this is set to dirge-like music and the ominous sounds

of thunder and rain. In short, the opening half of this mini-narrative presents us with a vision of contemporary urban landscape as a veritable hell, as a kind of post-modern Inferno. Indeed, in the library scene, the creators of the ad carefully include—as a hermeneutic clue for the college-educated among the viewers—a child with his head buried in an ancient, leather-bound copy of *Paradise Lost*. The viewer is then transported up past the somber facades, gargoyles, and jagged towers of the city, out of the rain, out across a sunny, green suburban landscape, past a picket fence and into a bright yellow house (see Figure 23). The camera finally comes to a halt with a shot of a Packard Bell computer perched on a desk in front of a cozy chair. "Now you can do it all from home," a warm, authoritative voice tells us, "with the world's number-one selling home computer." The ad ends with the voice-over intoning the tag line, "Wouldn't you rather be at home?"

This ad transparently seeks to exploit the middle-class target audience's dread of the blighted, inhospitable inner city and appeals to an

Figure 22. Packard Bell's dystopian, postindustrial metropolis.

idealized image of the home and family as a haven in a heartless world. As Bob Garfield puts it in his *Advertising Age* review, the "stunningly directed," "[v]isually spellbinding" spot "defines a grotesque 'out there' from which anybody would want to seek refuge at home—if not actually to withdraw from life, at least to do errands" (Garfield 1996, 61). Like the urban gothic movies it so clearly borrows from, the ad constructs its metropolis as an inexplicably frightening, supernaturally nightmarish— not to mention technologically backward and unbelievably dilapidated— place. And, remarkably, it does so without once depicting anything remotely resembling a criminal or a violent act. Rather, the horror of the place is conveyed entirely through its bleak atmosphere, despairing inhabitants, and neo-expressionist architecture. That is, the ad articulates suburban fears about urban evil at a purely connotative, symbolic level. There's no need to actually show predatory criminals and vicious street crimes; the cold darkness and dense gloom of the city contrasted with the relative warmth and sunny lightness of the suburban house

Figure 23. Packard Bell's vision of suburban bliss.

already sets up a moral opposition between the two spaces that is diffi-cult to miss. And this rigid binary in turn lends credibility to the ad's central message: that the only true path to happiness is to withdraw into the home, an escape made possible by modern information technology like the Packard Bell computer.

Packard Bell is hardly alone in crafting promotional messages that seek to capitalize on the middle class's rising fear of a dangerous, men-acing, markedly urban "outside" world. Since the late 1980s, advertising campaigns for all sorts of commodities (everything from sport utility vehicles to cell phones) and concepts (safe driving habits, crime preven-tion, etc.) have made frequent use of anti-urban sentiments. Moreover, in ads of all sorts, one increasingly sees the thoroughly "privatized," family-and-home-centered existence associated with suburbia both cel-ebrated and presented as under perpetual attack from assorted external, predatory "threats."

Of course, manipulation of consumer fears has long been a staple of mass market advertising. In his classic study of advertising and the genesis of consumer consciousness in the 1920s, *Captains of Consciousness*, Stuart Ewen remarks that the ads of the period presented the consumer with a world "in which fear justifiably reigned" (Ewen 1976, 97). He notes, for example, that ads used anxiety about intruders "tampering at the door" to sell Yale locks ("Yale banishes fear from your home!"), un-easiness about "ashtray breath" to sell mouthwash, apprehension about "underarm offense" to sell deodorants and so on. Ad men of the era lauded the use of such terroristic tactics as nothing less than heroic: "We've a better world with a bit of the proper kind of Fear in advertis-ing" (99). In these ads "there was one bastion of security, one area in which people were held together—the industrial corporation" (99). Only the corporation and its cornucopia of consumer goods, these parables proposed, could quell fears about the stalking mugger and banish para-noia about bad breath. And though there is a world of difference be-tween fear of urban crime and self-consciousness about body odor, the point is that the ad men of the 1920s were willing to tap into any anxi-ety (nervousness about becoming a "failure" in business, xenophobia, paranoia about being socially ostracized, etc.) strong enough to short-circuit critical judgment and motivate a sale.

The basic logic of fear-based marketing hasn't changed much since the 1920s. What has changed, perhaps, is that in the 1980s and '90s, advertising returned to elemental appeals to fear that had fallen out of fashion during the intervening decades. There is an inherent danger for any advertiser in tapping into consumer fears: the terror evoked by a fear-driven ad is just as likely to scare the viewer off as to trigger an impulse purchase. That may be why, historically, appeals to fear have been used in moderation by all but the most daring, revolutionary advertisers. In the post-Reagan era, that reluctance disappeared.

The anxieties activated by the fear-driven ads of the '80s and '90s seem especially suited to our suburbanized epoch: dread of bums and "street crazies," of ominous black or immigrant neighborhoods, of predatory criminals prowling the streets and public spaces, of savage outsiders from feral cities invading the peaceful sanctuary of the suburban domicile. Scattered testimony from ad industry insiders confirms that appeals to middle-class agoraphobia have become increasingly crucial to advertising's arsenal of marketing gimmicks. Thus, Renee White Fraser, president of the ad agency Fraser/Young in Santa Monica, claims that advertising took a fearful turn in the 1990s largely because "[i]n the boomers' mind, there is a pervasive sense of doom. There is still a concern that bad things can happen" (Woodyard 1997, 1B). Nor was Fraser the only ad executive to see things this way. According to marketing consultant Wendy Liebmann, "The sense of life is very fragile today. Americans have a sense the country is in better shape, (yet) there is an underpinning of insecurity" (1B). Renowned trend spotter Faith Popcorn, author of *The Popcorn Report* and head of futurist marketing firm BrainReserve, in the early 1990s coined the term "cocooning" to describe the middle class's renewed dedication to and withdrawal into a home-centered lifestyle. By the end of the century, she was arguing that nervousness and uncertainty about public order was compelling most of the population "to curl up and hide in armored cocoons," so much so, she claimed, that 90 percent of consumer products by the year 2010 would be home-delivered (Moore 1999, 46). One can easily envision the type of ads designed to appeal to Popcorn's nation of frightened, armored homebodies; no doubt, they would look and feel something like the spot for Packard Bell analyzed above. And even if this dystopian scenario fails to materialize, there is no denying that, as Chris Woodyard puts it, "mainstream marketers pitching everything from autos to floor wax are using security and safety to sell products" (Woodyard 1997, 1B).

That this should be the case is hardly surprising. Given the degree to which anxieties about the perils of public space and about the savage urban Other have permeated political and cultural discourse since the early 1980s, it is only logical that advertising and advertisers would pick up on and appeal to such sentiments. As Roland Marchand and other historians of advertising have observed, advertisers have always been particularly attuned to changing styles, habits, behaviors, and trends; they are cultural bellwethers, always the first to notice and publicize emerging fads, fashions, and shifts in public opinion (Marchand 1985). Ads don't impose alien ideas and values on society, as the vulgar critique might have it; rather they reflect and often amplify ideas and passions that are "in the air" (to the degree, of course, that those ideas and passions can be harnessed to the task of moving merchandise). Promotional discourse, as Barthes has argued of *myth* more generally, is essentially a second-order sign system, parasitic upon other, first-order systems of signification for its very existence (Barthes 1972). "Advertising," Sut Jhally reminds us, "does not work by creating values and attitudes out of nothing but by drawing upon and rechanneling concerns that the target audience (and the culture) already shares. As one advertising executive put it: 'Advertising doesn't always mirror how people are acting but how they're dreaming. In a sense what we're doing is wrapping up your emotions and selling them back to you'"(Jhally 1995, 80).

This process of packaging and recycling popular sentiments is, as Robert Goldman has argued, "never ideologically impartial" (Goldman 1992, 85). "When ads reframe and position our meaningful relations and discourses to accommodate the meaning of their corporate interests," Goldman explains, "then, advertising intervenes as a potent political institution in mediating meanings of freedom, individuality, work and leisure, community and family life" (85). Though advertisers themselves may not intend for their ads to have ideological import, the very fact of selecting which values, images, and concerns to link to a particular product, service, or corporation makes what they do inherently ideological. Moreover, since in late capitalist society we find ourselves literally inundated by advertising and promotional appeals, the ideological messages promulgated by the advertising industry are likely to exert a certain degree of influence over popular mentalities and perceptions of the world. What Roland Marchand has said of the ads of the 1920s is no doubt true of advertising as a whole: "by disseminating certain incessantly repeated and largely uncontradicted visual clichés and moral parables, the ads were likely to shape or reinforce the same popular attitudes they sought to reflect" (Marchand 1985, xx). By using anticrime hysteria, anxiety about the urban Other, and a general mood of agoraphobia to manipulate middle-class audiences, the discourse of advertising arguably did as much as Hollywood film and television news to popularize such attitudes.

In what follows, I examine the ways in which particular ads and advertising campaigns "wrapped up and sold" anti-urban fears to an already jittery middle class. I start my analysis with a blatant case of fear-based marketing—the massive advertising effort on the part of home alarm and security companies—and move on to discuss appeals to fear of the city in ads for automobiles and an assortment of anti-crime and anti-drug public service announcements.

"The Protection Your Home and Family Deserve": The Rhetoric of Security Ads

As measured by opinion polls at least, public concern about urban crime and violence, and about the threat such lawlessness poses to the safety of the middle-class family, grew to epidemic proportions in the 1980s and '90s. One industry that moved aggressively to capitalize on this paranoia about urban mayhem was the home security business. Spending on home protection systems grew by more than 10 percent a year throughout the 1990s (Magner 1996, 3C). Indeed, the amount spent on professionally installed security systems climbed from $10 billion in 1995 to $13.2 billion in 1997 (Kushner 2000, G1). According to one estimate, by 1996 one in five American households owned some sort of home security system (Magner 1996, 3C). Spending on personal security devices—from hand-held personal alarms, to pepper spray, to firearms—has also risen dramatically. Mace defense spray sales at one company, MI Inc., shot from $960,000 in 1988 to $9.6 million five years later (Zbar 1994, 19). These exploding sales trends were being driven, in part, by advertising campaigns that skillfully exploited, amplified, and underscored media-generated middle-class anxieties about being encircled by random violence and social pathology.

Take, for instance, Radio Shack's $6 million, month-long 1994 campaign for its extensive line of home security products (Zbar 1994, 18). A creepy TV spot created by Lord Dentsu & Partners for the campaign ushers viewers through the darkened, blue-tinted interior of a spacious, well-appointed two-story home. As the camera—following the trajectory of a would-be robber—moves from room to room, the voice-over narration talks about all the valuables in the house; eventually, this nocturnal journey comes to an end with a shot of a baby sleeping peacefully in a crib. The commercial then flashes a graphic announcing that Radio Shack, The National Crime Prevention Council, and The National Sheriffs Association are "United Against Crime." Like so much advertising for home security, and in common with suburban vigilante films like *Eye for an Eye*, this ad forces the spectator to imagine a nameless, faceless intruder invading his or her domestic space and doing horrible things to his or her loved ones. It is designed to instill in the viewer a general sense of unease and insecurity, a pronounced apprehension about the alleged vulnerability of the home and the family. It is worth noting that this particular ad was not promoting any specific product. Rather, during the month this spot was running, Radio Shack circulated newspaper ads and circulars promoting specific products that boasted the tagline "If security is the question, we've got the answer" (Zbar 1994, 18). Thus, the television ad raised general "free floating" anxieties for which the print ads supplied specific commercial remedies.

The fear-mongering on display in the Radio Shack spot is fairly common in home security advertising. For instance, in September 1999, Brink's Home Security launched a $20 million direct response TV campaign managed by Deutsch (Goetzl 1999, 8). One of the commercials created for the campaign centered on an image of a sleeping toddler and instructed viewers to think about how special their children look asleep. Then it asked viewers in somber tones to imagine a burglar looking at their children, something, the commercial acknowledged, "that no one wants to think about." The spot ended with the slogan "Your World Made Safer" and a toll-free number viewers could call for more information about Brink's products.

Some home security ads consciously try to avoid conjuring up the disturbing picture of burglars staring at sleeping kids. After all, as noted above, fear could just as easily paralyze a potential buyer as motivate a purchase. Thus, leading home security firm ADT in 1997 aired a comparatively up-beat television commercial showing beaming home owners standing in front of their large, upscale, suburban houses holding signs bearing slogans such as "No Longer Alone" and "Safe at Last." Yet, even this commercial couldn't avoid referencing the idea of the family encircled by outside dangers; one of the signs shown in the spot read "370 days since the last break-in."

The most striking feature of all these ads is the degree to which they openly depend on this image of the white, economically secure nuclear family, sequestered in its comfortable, detached (and, we are lead to assume, suburban) home, besieged by forces from the "outside." Unlike the Packard Bell commercial, none of these spots confront the viewer with scenes of urban decomposition or decay; nevertheless, the very idea that the middle-class home and family must be segregated, for their own protection, from the rest of the world dovetails perfectly with the anti-urbanism of the suburban moral panic. The ads position the viewer as the potential guardian of a vulnerable and deeply sentimentalized domestic space, a space projected as innocent, loving, free of conflict, and brimming over with warmth. Shielding the family from the dangers of society at large has always been defined in American gender ideology as the duty of the husband and father, the "man of the family" (whose "home is his castle"). As such, it could be said that these ads position the viewer as a sort of idealized, paternalistic suburban male authority figure, along the lines of the larger-than-life, know-it-all Dads of *Leave It to Beaver* and *Father Knows Best*. All of this can be seen clearly by looking at some of the ideologically heavy-handed brochures and direct mail literature distributed by the nation's leading home security firms.

Consider the pamphlet for Radionics 6112 Residential Security Systems, an alarm system offered through Sears. It features a cover photograph of a box containing assorted souvenirs, a ticket from the 1939 World's Fair, a black-and-white snapshot of an adolescent boy, a toy frog, wooden building blocks, and marbles, all of which are clearly meant as mementos of a 1930s boyhood (see Figure 24). In the lower left corner of the picture, we see an adult male hand placing one of the marbles into the outstretched hand of a child. The headline running over the picture reads, "When their future is in your hands." "Protect all that's most precious to you," the message continues along the top of the inside pages; beneath this, on the first inside page, there is a saccharine, soft-focus photo of a young red-headed girl reading a picture book to her assembled collection of teddy bears. On the facing page, in the upper right-hand corner, is a picture of several objects jumbled together: a string of antique pearls, a silver spoon, and two framed black-and-white photographs, one of which shows—what else?—a father and child. The brochure's copy goes on to explain that "when you're making a decision about the best way to protect your home and family, you want time-proven reliability."

This ad is symptomatic of the kind of nostalgic appeal to "family" and "family values" that has been fairly popular in advertising since the 1970s. Robert Goldman has argued that "advertisers' exhortation and cheerleading on behalf of 'the classical family of Western nostalgia' . . . was organized to combat a perceived crisis of legitimacy and to boost sales by tapping into shared (and manufactured) ideals of what family life ought to be like" (Goldman 1992, 87). As his analysis of the narrative of the family in McDonalds advertisements shows, ads picturing families

Figure 24. Radionics advertisement.

both "offer justification and support for the sanctity of family life" (100) and disseminate "an image of a congenial family in which intimacy and personal fulfillment are achieved through the consumption of commodities" (104). The standard depiction of family life in mass advertising emphasizes its essential privacy, its role as retreat and enclave. As Goldman puts it, countless ads "portray the family as a private, protected site of affective individualism" (102).

Goldman's observations apply remarkably well to the Radionics pamphlet and other home security ads. The representation of a treasured "family heirloom"—a marble—being passed from father to child that graces the cover evokes the family as a site of intimacy and intense affective relationships. So do the framed family pictures and the soft focus photograph of the girl with her teddy bears in the inner pages. At the same time, the conscious reliance on nostalgia—the visual emphasis on all those mementos of bygone days—"substitutes the solace of quieter, simpler times for a present that is represented as a time of social and cultural crises and disintegrating community relations" (Goldman and Papson 1996, 115). Despite the reassurance offered by the pamphlet's nostalgic mood, the warning to "protect all that's most precious to you" suggests that the idyllic family life being depicted here is in jeopardy. It is not clear—aside from passing references to burglary and fire in the pamphlet copy—exactly who or what threatens the family's charmed circle. It is clear, however, that the addressee of the warning, the person in charge of security, is none other than dear old Dad. This is signaled, above all, by the fact that the adult hand on the front cover is male but also by the photo in the "memory box" of a little boy (who presumably has grown up to be the man handing off the marble).

The interpellation of the reader as a protective father/husband charged with overseeing the safety of his wife and kids is just as pronounced in the literature for other home security systems. For example, a brochure for Ameritech's SecurityLink residential security services features a picture of a woman sitting on a couch reading a book to a little girl clutching a teddy bear juxtaposed with an outside view of a large, modern house. The tagline—"the protection your home and family deserve"—inscribed above these images unambiguously speaks to the husband and father who presumably stands outside and watches over the depicted domestic scene. Likewise, the pamphlet for ADT's "state of the art anti-theft system" asks "Why should you protect your home with the power of ADT?" and answers its own rhetorical question by including on the cover pictures of an infant gazing directly into the camera and a woman asleep in bed (see Figure 25). Honeywell's 1998 security system brochure at least depicts the usually absent father protector. "Home. It's a place where you should always feel safe, secure, and comfortable," declare the pamphlet. "And you can trust Honeywell to help protect the people and things you value most." At the bottom of the page is a photo of a child (as always, with the ubiquitous teddy bear) being tucked in by her mother while Dad hovers (protectively) over both. As with most home security advertising, this brochure leaves the precise nature of the threat to the home's security unspecified and its tone is mild and reassuring. The 1993 pamphlet for Brink's Home Security is, by contrast, positively alarmist. The headline on its plain white cover states "Dear Brink's Home Security . . . our Brink's system saved us from a disaster." Inside, beneath a picture of a mother and daughter, is printed the following testimonial: "My three children were home alone when a man kept going from our front door to back door and pounding. Then he started kicking in our back door. One of my children ran and hit the Brink's panic button and the man ran away. It terrifies me to think what might have happened if it had not been for our Brink's alarm system." Here the specter of the frenzied outsider is blatantly mobilized to frighten up sales. An accompanying piece of Brink's literature instructing potential customers on how to secure their homes actually features a bull's-eye target superimposed on a single family home (see Figure 26).

Not surprisingly, the demonized figure of the urban street criminal has been used to market other, more personal "security devices" as well. A 1994 Violence Policy Center study revealed that during the '80s and '90s the firearms industry responded to a downturn in sales to white

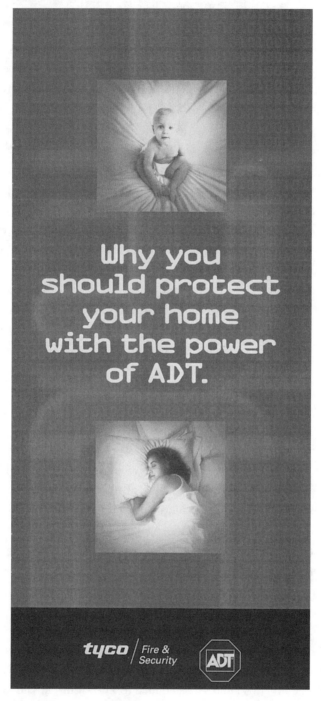

Figure 25. ADT advertisement.

men by aggressively targeting women as an emerging niche market for handguns (Glick 1994). The ad campaigns concocted for the industry's new line of women's handguns centered on fear of rape and in particular rape at the hands of predatory strangers:

> The primary marketing tactic is . . . fear. The pitch to women is simple: You're a woman. Some stranger is going to try and rape you. You'd better buy a handgun. People buy handguns out of fear and stranger rape—it is theorized—is what women fear most. As a result, the gun lobby has been relentless in its use of fear of rape to promote handguns as self-defense weapons. (Glick 1994, 1)

Thus, in 1989 Smith & Wesson introduced its Ladysmith handgun for women (complete with baby blue grip) by means of ads with terrifying slogans like "Things that go 'bump' in the night aren't always your imagination." Another gun maker, Colt, ran ads in the *Ladies Home Journal* that showed a mother tucking her daughter into bed and advised, "for protecting yourself and your loved one, we recommend a dependable Colt semiautomatic pistol" (3). At the same time, the National Rifle Association ran full-page ads in newspapers that warned female readers "[h]e's followed you for two weeks. He'll rape you in two minutes"; further down the page the now-terrified reader was instructed that she had the option of buying a compact, easy-to-use handgun for self-defense (Brady 2001). Nor were the NRA's efforts to foment fears about personal security aimed only at women. One 1987 NRA ad pictured a man in a business suit being beaten by two thugs on a city sidewalk. The headline that filled the top of the page asked "Why can't a policeman be there when you need him?" and the caption to the picture explained that "in major U.S. cities, police response time to a crime in progress can range from 6 minutes to over an hour" (Surette 1998, 215). The last line at the bottom of the ad exhorted readers to "defend your right to defend yourself." And, the disturbing picture and alarmist copy implied that readers should be especially conscientious about defending themselves against the menace of the city.

Figure 26. Brink's Home Security pamphlet.

Afraid at the Wheel

It was utterly predictable that advertising for handguns or home security systems would embrace scare tactics. After all, protecting houses and the people in them from burglars and other unwanted intruders is the very point of these products. What's surprising is the degree to which the sort of fear appeals one sees in the Brink's and Radio Shack ads are being used to sell products with less obvious, less "organic" links to security concerns. Take, for instance, cars. Automobile manufacturers—who for decades have marketed cars as a source of fun and youthfulness or as symbols of technological progress and modernity—have increasingly turned to the promise of "safety," "security," and protection for the imperiled "family" as selling points.

Consider the late 1990s campaign for GM's Buick LeSabre. One widely aired TV spot for the vehicle depicts a father steering it through treacherous traffic, dodging on-coming cars, while his wife and daughter sleep undisturbed in their seats. As Buick's Mark Rollinson commented, "The message comes through: 'I'm responsible for my family'" (cited in Woodyard 1997, 2B). This message is reinforced again and again in print ads for the car. A full-page ad that ran in the March 2, 1998, *Newsweek* features a sepia-toned picture of a father and his ten-year-old daughter walking down a sidewalk holding hands while gazing lovingly into each others eyes. In large red letters across the top of the page are written the words "Status Report." The text at the lower left-hand corner of the page explains that "[f]or you the most important status reports don't happen at the office. Because your family is top priority, LeSabre has an impressive list of safety and security features." To the left of the text is a small picture of a red LeSabre underneath which is written the tagline "LeSabre by Buick, Peace of Mind." Another LeSabre ad that ran in *Newsweek* a year earlier was even more explicit in its appeal to middle-class anxieties about threats to the family. It pictures a white, middle-class nuclear family—a father, mother, boy, and girl—sitting together on the steps of a sun-drenched wooden porch. The mother is reading a book to her son while the father and daughter exchange smiles. Over the picture is a caption that reads "LeSabre. The Family's Safely Home . . . " Further down the page is text describing the car's dual air bags and anti-lock brakes along with the perfunctory picture of the car and the "Peace of Mind" slogan. Yet another print ad for the car, a two-page spread that ran in the April 21, 1997, issue of *Newsweek*, shows an older, white, well-to-do couple lounging in their enormous living room with a verdant suburban landscape visible behind them through the oversized windows (see Figure 27). The LeSabre's "arsenal of safety features will give you a sense of inner peace," the copy promises, "Make you feel almost invulnerable." Like the TV spot, these print ads invite the viewer to identify with the position of a protective father, a patriarch whose family relies on him to keep the dangers of the outside world at bay. In the print ads, the threats to the family are only hinted at and never identified with any precision. Yet by asking us to buy into the proposition that LeSabre will deliver our families "safely home," give us "peace of mind" and "make you feel almost invulnerable," they suggest that world beyond the domestic sphere—the public realm—is at least potentially hostile.

Figure 27. LeSabre boasts about its "arsenal of safety features."

While the ultimate source of the outside threat to the embattled middle-class family in the LeSabre ads is never really specified, other automobile ads suggest unequivocally that the proper object of the addressee's fears is the city. In fact, in the past few years it seems as if there's been a minor explosion in ads that depict the city as violent, scary, grim, and noxious while offering the cars being advertised as tools for surviving, and perhaps mastering, a lethal urban milieu.[1] An animated ad for the Chevy S-10 truck that aired in 1997 can serve as an illustration. The commercial—painted in "cartoon expressionist" style, using a palette of black, white, and blue—begins with a truck careening out of a tunnel, past the gargoyle-covered facades of some tall buildings and down an urban street shrouded in fog (see Figure 28). Accompanied by foreboding organ music, a winged gargoyle perched on the roof of one the passing buildings comes to life, swoops down toward the road, and pursues the truck, which turns down a litter-filled alley, knocks over a

Figure 28. A creepy urban street in an animated television commercial for Chevy's S-10.

garbage can, and makes a hairpin turn. Next we see the truck, still being chased by the gargoyle, rushing past a long chainlink fence topped by razor wire. The vehicle bounces off a decrepit brick wall (which the gargoyle promptly crashes into, shattering into several pieces) before skidding to a halt in the parking lot of a grim-looking institutional building. The camera then pulls back to show film footage of a young, hip-looking guy holding a piece of paper on which this final scene of the car and the building is painted. Behind him is the Chevy S-10 parked in the lot in front of the building. "Meet Chris Wirth," the voice-over narrator tells us, "Knows Good. Knows Evil. Knows the value of a good partner. Chevy S-10. Like a Rock." Obviously, this spot is meant to be taken as a piece of dark cartoonish fantasy; after all, it draws attention to its own unreality by foregrounding the animator who drew the ghouls and shadowy tunnels the Chevy had to navigate. Nevertheless, the menacing cityscape depicted here suggests that the evil mentioned in the voice-over is a uniquely (though perhaps not exclusively) urban phenomenon, a notion that a certain segment of suburbia seems to accept wholeheartedly. And it goes on to promote the truck by imagining it as a powerful force of good, à la the comic book superhero, capable of conquering the sinister city.

A certain anti-urban mood also figures as a sub-theme—albeit, a subtle one—in the much larger class of automobile ads that depict the car as a means of breaking free from a boring or oppressive daily life. Automobile makers have always marketed their vehicles as a means of transcending restrictive material and social surroundings. Mike Budd, Steve Craig, and Clay Steinman observe that, as it is represented in most car commercials, "the automobile . . . gives us *freedom*, provides *command* and *control* over our environment, whether that environment is a natural landscape, city or suburbs, or other people" (Budd et al. 1999, 87). In a number of ads, this freedom and control take the form of an auto-aided flight from the urban core into nature or wilderness of some sort: verdant fields, rugged mountains, lush forests, majestic mesas, etc. An ad for Jeep that ran in the April 3, 2000, issue of *Sports Illustrated* exemplifies this convention (see Figure 29). The picture that takes up the bulk of the page shows the skyline of a decent-sized downtown as seen through a

JEEP WRANGLER

Take your body where your mind has already wandered. Out there. Where water doesn't come in coolers. The air is free from the ring of phones. And the only meeting you have is a one-on-one with a 12-pound trout. In Jeep Wrangler, you have the freedom. The kind  of freedom afforded by legendary off-road prowess. Like shift-on-the-fly 4-wheel drive and Quadra-Coil™ suspension. But Jeep freedom is a state of mind as much as it is state-of-the-art engineering.

In Wrangler, you connect with something individual. Yet, at the same time, something bigger. You join a membership of owners that covers the globe.

Expand the scope of your wanderings. Visit our Web site at www.jeep.com or call 1-800-925-JEEP.

Jeep

THERE'S ONLY ONE

Figure 29. Jeep's fantasy of escape from the city.

generic office window. In the distance, beyond the high-rise office towers, rises a snow-capped mountain range. The occupant of the office
appears to have doodled the crude likeness of a Jeep in marker on the
windowpane so that it appears (from our vantage point) as if the Jeep is
actually ascending the slope of one of the mountains. "Take your body
where your mind has already wandered," reads the copy. "Out there.
Where water doesn't come in coolers. The air is free from the ring of
phones. And only the only meeting you have is a one-on-one with a 12-
pound trout." Jeep thus explicitly promises the reader escape from the
annoyances and artificiality of office work as well as from the constrain-
ing "downtown" provenance of the office worker. Similarly, an 1998 ad
for the Hyundai '98 Tiburon FX that ran in *Rolling Stone* tells readers to
"hit it . . . and leave worry in the dust" while showing a shiny red car
speeding along a tree-lined highway with a downtown full of office towers receding behind it in the distance. "Escape," says the copy, "just make
sure you're back by Monday" (see Figure 30).

While ads like the ones for Jeep or Hyundai urge us to imagine a
rather fanciful, lighthearted escape from an urban scene portrayed as
merely hum-drum, an ad for the 1998 Isuzu Rodeo that ran in the October 1997 *Car and Driver* plays to more serious anti-urban impulses. Its
silvery black and white image pictures a sleek-looking Isuzu SUV rushing away from a shadowy modernist metropolis composed entirely of
stark, block-shaped, gridded buildings (see Figure 31). "You would not
be very human if you did not mostly prefer to be not-here, not-now," the
ad's text tells us; "Elsewhere wants you." Where the Jeep ad simply
appealed to the professional paper-shuffler's understandable desire to get
outside and away from the rat race, this ad constructs—à la Packard
Bell—a grim urban realm that any normal person, anyone who is even a
tiny bit "human," would seek to escape.

Clean Up Your Community . . . Using Johnson Wax

It is one thing to use agoraphobic fantasies to pitch trucks and anti-theft
alarms, but marketers have also tapped into public anxieties about street
crime and urban social chaos in even more unusual ways.

For instance, a 1997 Sunday newspaper insert put out by Johnson Wax promoted a nationwide "Clean Up Crime in Your Community" program with coupons for Windex and other cleaning products. The piece urged readers to join with their neighbors on a particular evening to talk about crime-fighting strategies. A vague analogy between cleaning windows and bathroom tiles and "cleaning up the streets" in

Figure 30. Hyundai leaves the city "in the dust."

this case constitutes the only connection between the nation's obsessive concern with public order and Johnson Wax's apparently unrelated products.

Even more bizarre, though, is the series of alarmist driving safety ads and pamphlets developed by Shell Oil in conjunction with the National Crime Prevention Council and the National Safety Council. One of the ads in this series published in the February 17, 1999, *New York Times* pictures a young woman driving alone at night, glancing anxiously into

WE are Specialized Worldwide Builders of Adventure Machines, meaning our expertise is in building rugged sport utility vehicles.

IT is the completely reinvented Isuzu Rodeo, with a sleeker tighter design and more horsepower (205), to urge you not to dream idly of elsewhere but to drive there without delay.

Elsewhere wants you.

800 726 2700 / www.isuzu.com

The new 1998 Rodeo.

ISUZU
Go farther.

Figure 31. Isuzu mostly prefers "not-here, not-now" to the contemporary metropolis.

her rearview mirror. Through the rear window one sees the headlights of a truck that is tailgating her. The headline reads "Predator" and beneath that is a smaller subhead that says "How to avoid being the prey." The copy below that is truly disconcerting. "You're being followed," it states ominously; "Even after you turn, he's close behind. You're frightened. What do you do? Don't go home. You don't want to lead him to your loved ones. Instead, drive to a well-lighted place where there are lots of people. A store, service station, hospital or police station. Once there, make a scene. Lean on the horn. Draw attention." The text goes on to suggest how readers can pick up a copy of Shell's free pamphlet, *Alone behind the Wheel*, which contains more advice on staying safe when driving alone (see Figure 32). Shell's corporate logo and the tagline "Count on Shell" are printed in the lower right-hand corner of the ad.

The scenario sketched out in this ad—of a perfect stranger stalking some unfortunate driver like a predator following its prey—is improbable. So-called random crimes of the type imagined here are infrequent to the point of statistical insignificance. But the central point of this ad and the accompanying pamphlet is not to provide accurate information about the real risks faced by drivers. Rather both advertisement and pamphlet aim to give voice to and validate empirically baseless middle-class anxieties about ruthless carjackers haunting urban streets and predatory criminals lurking around parking garages. Thus, *Alone behind the Wheel* tells readers that "parking garages can be dangerous places, especially at night. If you have a choice between the elevator and the stairs, take the elevator. It's quicker and you're less likely to come in contact with someone loitering there." And, even more ominously, it advises "if you are confronted by a robber or carjacker, don't resist. . . . Remember, possessions can be replaced. Your life can't be" (7). The other pamphlets in Shell's "safe driving" series—with titles like *Driving Dangers* and *Crash Course*—seem similarly designed to fan fears about the terrors of the road. Why would Shell go to such lengths to invoke middle-class nightmares about the menace of city spaces? As with the Packard Bell commercial I considered earlier, the Shell ad provokes alarm in order to

Figure 32. Shell Oil evokes the threat of random violence on the road as part of its "Count on Shell" campaign.

position the Shell brand as a source of comfort and reassurance in a hazardous and uncertain world: in other words, "Count on Shell."

The National Crime Prevention Council, the Ad Council, and Anti-Crime Public Service Announcements: Agoraphobia as Public Service

A number of the ads discussed so far mention an organization called the National Crime Prevention Council (NCPC). Sponsored by a consortium of national, state, and local crime prevention groups, the NCPC is the force behind the National Citizens' Crime Prevention Campaign, an ad-driven "anti-crime" public education effort that features McGruff the Crime Dog. Though posturing as an independent, nonprofit public interest organization, the NCPC has strong ties to the home security industry, an industry that naturally has a material interest in promoting both fear of crime and the industry's various privatized solutions to the perceived problem. In 1994, for instance, ADT Security Systems, Inc., helped the campaign pay for Crime Prevention Month kits that were passed out to school children as well as the general public, and Radio Shack distributed four million "United against Crime" brochures that were developed in consultation with the NCPC. In 1999, ADT and the NCPC co-sponsored an extensive and widely reported national survey of people's attitudes about "three key crime prevention areas: personal and home security, safety of children and neighborhood and community prevention efforts" (ADT, 1999) and have since promised to make the survey an annual event. These links to the alarm and security business perhaps help to explain the content of the NCPC's omnipresent anti-crime public service announcements (or PSAs), which, as we shall see, invariably complement and reinforce the agoraphobic thrust of the security companies' own commercials.

FCC-licensed broadcasters are obligated to set aside time for public service messages and, indeed, according to one mid-1980s estimate, broadcasters donate nearly 3 percent of all airtime for this purpose. In addition, magazines and newspapers also donate millions of dollars worth of free space for PSAs every year. While many PSAs are local (and usually produced by state and local government or local civic organizations), most nationally seen PSAs are the creation of the Advertising Council, a corporate-backed nonprofit that according to one estimate is the second largest advertiser in the world (Parenti 1986, 72). Founded in 1942 by a coterie of leading advertising industry executives to counteract "the public's increasingly negative attitude toward advertising" (Peck 1983, 45), the Council enlists volunteer ad agencies to produce campaigns promoting individual action and philanthropy as the solution to national problems. Its best-known campaigns include the famous series of fire safety ads featuring Smokey the Bear and its anti-littering TV commercials featuring a weeping "Indian Chief." Since the 1980s, though, it has turned its considerable resources disproportionately to the task of "fighting crime." In the 1990s, in fact, the NCPC was the Ad Council's top client. As such, their slickly produced anti-crime PSAs—most notably the McGruff TV spots urging kids to "Take a Bite Out of Crime" and more recent ads aimed at curbing teen gun violence—tended to dominate spending on public service advertising. In 1994 alone, their ads won $92 million worth of donated space and time on television and radio and in the print media, making it the second largest campaign in Ad Council history (National Crime Prevention Council, 1995).

As the Ad Council's many critics have pointed out, the Council's campaigns studiously avoid issues that could be construed as controversial or politically divisive. Hence, their PSAs typically reinforce "existing conceptions of acceptable civic activity" and "contribute to the general stock of cultural symbolism" (Peck 1983, 44). Moreover, the central ideology that permeates the Ad Council's commercials has been described as the belief that "private interests can invariably meet the demands of the public interest" (44), that individual initiative and good sense can ameliorate even the worst social maladies. It is easy to see why the Ad Council during the 1990s became so preoccupied with the problem of (what was often explicitly identified as distinctly urban) crime, social disorder, and violence. Not only did the inner-city "crime problem" remain near the top on the national political agenda for much of the decade, but popular, individualized solutions to the "problem" were readily available in the form of alarm systems and handheld mace dispensers, solutions peddled by home security firms (ADT, Brink's Home Security, Radio Shack) who invest in multi-million-dollar ad campaigns. By taking on the scourge of street crime, the Ad Council could thus both respond to an officially recognized social ill *and*, as an added side-benefit, drum up business for some of the advertising industry's biggest customers.

So, how did the Ad Council and the NCPC approach the issue of urban crime? Two TV spots starring President Bill Clinton aimed at halting "youth violence" broadcast in 1994 are representative of the Ad Council's treatment of the subject (Clinton Stands Up, 1994, 4). Produced by Saatchi & Saatchi, one of the spots focuses on 14-year-old Alicia Brown, a Washington, D.C., girl who has already witnessed six of her friends murdered in her short life. The other confronts the viewer with a montage of gritty, black-and-white images of generically menacing, inner-city "mean streets": there's a shot of two teenage boys—one of whom boasts the standard signifier of "gang affiliation," a baseball cap worn backwards—handling a handgun in a parking lot; there's an image of young black child looking out from behind a carceral-looking iron gate; there is a shot of a playground surrounded by yellow police tape that bears the words "Crime Scene Do Not Cross." Both spots imagine the inner city, according to the reactionary formulae we have seen so often in this book, as a sort of "purgatory of lost souls"; in this case, the ads identify those lost souls as (black) children, who, the ads tacitly assert, have been so degraded and brutalized by their ghetto environment that violence has become second nature for them. The innocence and natural goodness of children remains a central myth of middle-class culture and the spots' focus on children being shot and witnessing murders naturally appears calculated to provoke middle-class outrage as well as to "moralize" the entire subject of urban crime. Clinton's appearance in both these spots trades on his much-publicized "law-and-order" posture (remember, 1994 was the year his draconian crime bill became law) as well as his equally well-known "stern," paternalistic attitude toward the urban poor to further intensify the moral disdain directed against the inner city. Directly facing the camera, he beseeches the viewer to

"Give our children back their childhood." Insofar as either spot proposes a concrete strategy of stopping youth violence, it is implied that ending the horrors they describe depends above all on the moral resolve of communities, neighborhoods, and individuals. In other words, it is as if Clinton is chastising the urban poor for failing to keep order in their own neighborhoods.

Clinton's berating of poor, urban, minority communities for failing to take "individual responsibility" for social maladies like youth violence draws on and extends the conservative, victim-blaming discourse on the inner city. And, it should be mentioned, such browbeating is hardly confined to ads featuring the president. Moral condemnation of underclass misbehavior and Bennett-esque injunctions to decency and virtue are ubiquitous in the Ad Council and NCPC's ads. Thus, a 15-second TV spot entitled "Enough Is Enough" opens with a shot of a stack of tabloid newspapers (themselves signifiers of sleazy, cynical metropolitan culture) topped by a paper bearing the screaming, 72-point headline "Toddler Slain in Cross Fire" along with a picture of a smiling African American girl. The announcer's voice-over tells us that "Every day ten children are killed by gunfire" and, while we watch a hand place a telephone on top of the papers and begin to dial, declares that "It's time we said enough is enough. Find out what you can do." The spot ends by flashing a 1-800 number as the announcer's voice-over says "Not one more lost life. Not one more grieving family. Not one more." Like many of the Ad Council's crime-fighting ads, this PSA really does little more than reiterate the call for viewers and readers to "do something" about the chillingly evoked specter of gun violence against children without specifying what (although presumably people who call the 800 number will receive some useful crime-fighting tips). Stopping the slaughter of America's children, it is implied, is really a matter of individual initiative.

Though "Enough Is Enough" merely hints at the putative big-city origins of the youth violence problem, other ads in the same campaign are more explicit about the essential urbanity of the violence they are intended to combat. A prime example is the Ad Council's harrowing TV commercial, "Rosana." The PSA opens with a teenage black girl sitting on the stoop of a typical tenement-style apartment building. "I would like all my friends to be there," she says dreamily, a smile on her face, "I want my mother to be there." The camera slowly moves in for a close-up. "My hair's gonna be done so beautiful. A lot of music. A nice blue dress. I want to be beautiful for every single person there." And then, her smile disappears. "If I get shot," she says soberly, "I want to have a nice funeral." The spot then ends with the same "Not One More" tagline and 800 number as the 15-second spot discussed above.

Both of these spots depict inner-city (minority) youth as essentially an endangered species, prey to ubiquitous and random violence. And while it is true that the numbers of black, urban youth killed by gunfire rose to unprecedented levels in the 1990s, the emphasis on youth violence here, as in the media more generally, obscures the fact that during the same period people in their early twenties were more likely to be killed by guns than teenagers (Males 1996, 108) and that the vast majority of youth, urban or otherwise, lead lives untouched by crime or violence. Perhaps more important, the single-minded obsession with inner-city youth violence obscures both the parallels between youth and adult violence and their common social etiology, especially the fact that both are strongly correlated with poverty. As Mike Males explains, "There is no discernible difference between adolescents and the adults of the age groups who are raising them. Teenagers do not respond to poverty more or less violently than do grownups; teenagers just experience more poverty. Once the poverty factor is removed, 'teen violence' disappears, and with it all the agonized why-why-why saturating the media and political landscape (usually fanned by experts who should know better) whenever the cameras roll to another teen murder scene" (108). These spots are not so much an effort at spotlighting a significant social ill as they are an exercise in scapegoating and sensationalism. On the one hand, by promoting essentially a "personal solution" to the thousands of youth killed by guns each year (i.e. "call a 1-800 number to find out how you can help"), by treating these killings as a problem that can be ameliorated through individual volunteerism rather than collective social action, they allow the roots of urban youth violence in entrenched patterns of social disadvantage to remain, as Mike Males puts it in his analysis of right-wing theorizing about juvenile crime more generally, "unexamined and unexplained" (128). On the other hand, they make it appear that every young person living in the ghetto is, like the fictional Rosana, planning his or her own funeral, that every inner-city child is marked for death, that our urban neighborhoods are little more than killing fields, images that occupy a central place in the conservative, law-and-order imagination.

Indeed, though the Ad Council purports to combat stereotyping of inner-city youth, and in fact has printed a number of anti-crime posters showing "street kids" who helped "clean up parks" or "start a neighbor-hood watch," its PSAs often actively construct the inner city and its spaces in terms drawn directly from the right's discourse of panic and pathology: as treacherous, shadowy, labyrinthine, full of lurking dangers, and, above all, to be avoided. This comes through most clearly in an animated crime-fighting PSA featuring McGruff the Crime Dog entitled "Scruff's Adventures II." The spot opens with McGruff telling the audience that his nephew Scruff is "about to run into trouble again"; Scruff then proceeds to stumble into various sorts of criminal "trouble." About halfway through the PSA, we see Scruff, dressed in what can only be called "typical hip-hop attire," urging his friends Leander and Inez to take a "short cut" through a narrow, shadowy, litter-clogged alley-way. "Not down there, square," Leander replies. "I don't think it's safe," says Inez. "C'mon the coast is clear," says Scruff who then walks into the darkened passage. There, surrounded by garbage cans and confining brick walls, he confronts a gang of three bullies. "Well, well," says one of the bullies, a hulking, heavy-set white teen wearing a backward baseball cap, "Hello, dog face. Come to give us your sneakers?" This little scene combines the shop-worn image of the dark, dank alley with a tired cliché about urban teen violence—that ghetto kids battle, sometimes to the death, over sneakers—to create a cautionary tale about what can happen to kids who wander into the wrong places. True, Scruff is coded through his clothes and speech as black and his attackers are depicted as white. Yet it is likely that this inversion of the standard racial coding of the gang threat is a bit of politically correct cover for a "plot line" that recapitulates in synoptic form all those scapegoating narratives about the pervasiveness (and senselessness) of black street crime circulating through popular culture, television news, and Hollywood film.

The Ad Council's anxiety about the menace of urban streets is more succinctly summed up by one of its anti-drug ads that ran in *Time* magazine in 2000 and 2001 (see Figure 33). In the foreground, a young African American boy riding his bike glances over his shoulder; in the out-of-focus background, the blurry multistory facades of a city street hover ominously. The headline declares "At 4:00 my kid will be at _____" and the copy in the corner of the ad explains that "if you can't fill in the blank, you need to start asking. . . . It's not pestering. It's parenting." Both the image and the accompanying text suggest in no uncertain terms that kids who venture unmonitored out into urban space run the risk being ensnared by a host of "dangers" (drugs, crime, perhaps even abduction) that vigilant parents should guard against. In post-Reagan America, agoraphobia can be tapped to sell just about anything, including evidently "good parenting."

One can only speculate as to the long-term cultural effects of fear-based advertising such as the examples discussed in this chapter. Such ads no doubt inflate the perceived menace of the nation's metropolitan centers in the minds of at least some of their viewers. Ads depend on implicit social assumptions to communicate their messages; by communicating those messages they tend to reinforce and replicate the social assumptions that render those messages intelligible. For this reason, Leiss, Klein, and Jhally (1997) have argued, advertising must be recognized as "an integral part of modern culture": "its creations appropriate and transform a vast range of symbols and ideas; its unsurpassed communicative powers recycle cultural models and references back through the networks of social interactions" (5). If this is true, then it would be difficult to imagine the fear-driven marketing I have been discussing here *not* helping to disseminate and legitimize the media-generated moral panic over the postindustrial city on which it is at least partially based.

Figure 33. The Ad Council's scare tactics in action.

CONCLUSION

Awakening from Urban Nightmares

The discourse [on urban decline] smothers the actual causes of our
discontent. It stifles awareness of how cities might be different. As
a result, we are unable to imagine cities where shared prosperity,
democratic engagement, and social tolerance are norms and not
exceptions.

—Robert Beauregard, *Voices of Decline*

Political subversion presupposes cognitive subversion,
a conversion of the vision of the world.

—Pierre Bourdieu, *Language and Symbolic Power*

If the argument in this book has done nothing else, it has demonstrated
that the dominant representations of the American city circulating through
media and public discourse in the 1980s and 1990s framed the poverty-
stricken centers of our urban areas in ways that obscured "the actual
causes of our discontent" (Beauregard 1993, 324), and in the process
shifted blame for the deplorable conditions in our metropolitan centers
onto those suffering under them. It has critiqued the conservative ideological premises and flawed theoretical concepts on which those representations rested. It has drawn attention to the way such representations
pandered to and exacerbated middle-class, largely suburban concerns about
the danger and immorality of the inner city and the so-called underclass.
Even more important, the analysis delineated here has shown that the
scary picture of the urban life created by mainstream politicians, intellectuals, and the media ultimately served the interests of the ruling class,
the only people who actually profited from social polarization and the
immiseration of the metropolitan core. In short, this book has interrogated the panic over the city that has agitated America from the Reagan
era onward in an effort to understand how it was produced and how it

worked to the benefit of the powerful and to the disadvantage of the oppressed.

As the preceding chapters illustrate, conservatives in recent years have seized control of the public conversation on urban issues, dictating its terms, deciding its focus, drowning out most other competing voices, stoking fear every step of the way. Ideologues like Charles Murray and William Bennett succeeded in popularizing divisive, stigmatizing notions like the "underclass" and "moral poverty"; their mystifications of the damage wrought by economic and demographic polarization on our cities became accepted as "common sense" in the media and across the political spectrum. Indeed, their perspective became so firmly entrenched during the closing decades of the twentieth century that even fair-minded, well-intentioned commentators often used discussions of urban reality as an occasion to chastise ghetto-dwelling "welfare moms" for their moral laxity or to wax indignant about "the epidemic of violence" supposedly plaguing big-city streets. Ancient, long-discredited ideas about poverty stemming from "bad values" and criminality resulting from "character defects" came into vogue once more. The view that our metropolitan centers had been ruined by the excesses of "'60s liberalism" or rendered obsolete by the Internet became intellectually respectable. Even commentators who were not vehemently anti-urban in their outlook decried the "barbarism" and "nihilism" they saw lurking in the ghettos and barrios of cities like New York, Los Angeles, and Detroit.

The mainstream corporate media, as we've seen, played a vital role in the dissemination of the right's alarmist, mean-spirited interpretation of the postindustrial city's troubles. Conservative intellectuals were showcased prominently in coverage of urban issues, their books were enthusiastically reviewed by major news outlets, and their opinions set the agenda for most reporting on the welfare system, urban policy, street crime, and homelessness. The right's views on cities also oozed into the broader media culture. Visions of the American cityscape as a lethal and noxious space cropped up over and over in Hollywood blockbusters. Films like *The Crow*, *Seven*, and *Mimic* inflated the menace of the city as narrated by mainstream news and political discourse into spectacles of pure horror. Meanwhile, movies like *Judgment Night, Falling Down,* and *Eye for an Eye* pitted white middle-class protagonists against inner-city villains portrayed as bloodthirsty, brutal, and culturally alien. Advertisements for cars and home security systems as well as anti–drug abuse campaigns all referenced the city as nightmare.

The media's ubiquitous images of urban mayhem (along with the dark fears they aroused) were skillfully harnessed by reactionary politicians to further their agenda of strengthening the punitive, policing powers of the state while scaling back its (liberal, ameliorative) role as a provider of aid to cities and relief to the poor. Thanks in large part to their relentless promotion by well-heeled think tanks and their endless iteration in the press, conservative interpretations of the city's social and economic troubles thoroughly saturated political debate at every level of government. Not coincidentally, they were also enormously effective in dictating urban policy (with dreadful consequences for those directly affected by the new policy initiatives). From "zero tolerance" policing schemes to welfare cutbacks to the slashing of federal spending on urban public housing, the right's plan for the cities and the urban poor largely triumphed in the post-Reagan era. As with the British mugging scare analyzed by Stuart Hall and his colleagues in *Policing the Crisis,* in the United States the media-fed moral panic over the imagined violence and immorality of the postindustrial urban core functioned "as a mechanism for the construction of an authoritarian consensus" (Hall et al. 1978, viii), one which continues to inflect popular and elite attitudes toward our metropolitan centers today.

It would be easy to conclude here on a mournful and pessimistic note. Yet, it is important to recognize that throughout the Reagan, Bush, and Clinton years there were—in the media as well as in politics—scattered signs of dissent from the reigning "authoritarian consensus" on the tribulations of the American city; from time to time, politically progressive readings of the urban crisis did surface in the flow of media representations to challenge right-wing shibboleths about the "underclass" and to refute reactionary arguments for the need to discipline the profligate cities. Poor people's groups like Up and Out of Poverty and Alliance of Community Organizations for Reform Now (ACORN) occasionally got their messages into the mainstream press. Residents of public housing projects got together to publish their own newspapers— like Chicago's *Residents' Journal*—critiquing the attack on the welfare state and public housing. Journalists like Alex Kotlowitz and social scientists like Douglas Massey, Nancy Denton, and Mike Davis drew attention to the daunting economic, social, and cultural barriers confining large segments of the black and Latino poor in America's worst urban ghettos (see Kotlowitz 1991; Massey and Denton 1993; Davis 1993; and Davis 1998). The left press—especially socialist magazines like *In These Times*, *Monthly Review*, *Z Magazine*, and *Dissent*—consistently challenged the right's misguided theories about urban crime and poverty, confronted them with hard facts, and proposed rational, economic, and sociologically grounded analysis of urban conditions in their place. Amy Goodman and Juan Gonzales of the syndicated radio show *Democracy Now!* contributed hard-hitting investigative journalism that told stories about welfare reform, the "prison industrial complex," public housing, police brutality, and the conservative assault on civil rights that diverged sharply from the conventional wisdom of the mainstream press. Meanwhile, architectural critic James Kunstler attacked the government policies and planning philosophy driving the spread of suburban sprawl and the annihilation of vibrant urban neighborhoods (Kunstler 1993).

Each of these attempts at wresting the definition of the American city's problems away from the likes of Murray, Bennett, and the Manhattan Institute have, from time to time, succeeded in shifting the debate, if only momentarily; but arguably none of these reframings of the postindustrial city's many troubles received as much public exposure as those constructed by two of the leading "maverick" filmmakers of the post-Reagan years, Spike Lee and Michael Moore.

Alternative Readings of the Urban Crisis: Lee's *Clockers* and Moore's *Bowling for Columbine*

Consider, first, Spike Lee's *Clockers*, an inner-city crime film that appropriates and, as Paula Massood puts it, "deconstructs and problematizes" the ideological assumptions of the ghettocentric gangster genre associ-ated with films like *New Jack City* and *Menace II Society* (Massood 2003, 189). Based on a novel by Richard Price, Lee's film stands out from ear-lier "hood" films by virtue of its refreshingly unformulaic treatment of urban violence, its sympathetic portrayal of ghetto residents trying to lead decent lives in horrible surroundings, and its trenchant critique of police racism. Even more distinctive, perhaps, is Lee's nuanced, three-dimensional portrait of the young black drug dealers, or "clockers," who are the main protagonists of the film's narrative.

Set in the fictional Nelson Mandela housing projects somewhere in Brooklyn, *Clockers* tells the story of Strike (Mekhi Phifer), a small-time crack dealer, who becomes the focus of an investigation into the murder of another clocker lead by white homicide detective Rocco Klein (Har-vey Keitel). Despite the fact that Strike's morally upstanding family-man brother, Victor (Isaiah Washington), confesses to the crime, Rocco—

Figure 34. Dead bodies sprawled on the street in the opening credit sequence of *Clockers*.

who suspects Victor is covering for his sibling—pressures Strike to admit to the killing. The detective relents only after Strike's paranoid boss, Rodney Little (Delroy Lindo), attempts to have his underling killed (tragically enmeshing one of Strike's young protégés, Tyrone (Peewee Love), in the violence as a consequence). In the end, Rocco accepts Victor's claim that he killed in self-defense and saves Strike from Rodney's wrath by putting him on a train out of town.

While *Clockers*'s plot exhibits vague similarities to other "hood" films, Lee's treatment of ghetto violence does not. Unlike other ghetto-centric films that revel in the fast-paced spectacle of drive-by shootings and gang warfare, this film depicts violence using what Leonard Quart calls a "contemplative and restrained rather than action-oriented style" (Quart 1996, 11). The film opens, for instance, with a somber montage of "police photographs" showing close-ups of black bodies riddled with bullet holes and headlines from tabloid papers announcing horrific inner-city killings (see Figure 34). Later, rather than showing us the actual murder that leads Rocco to initiate his investigation, Lee shows us a band of white detectives examining the victim's blood-drenched corpse while engaging in callously racist banter. Even the one full-blown action sequence in the film—which involves Strike being beaten by a neighborhood cop, spitting up blood with every blow he absorbs—seems designed more to disgust than to titillate. As Liam Kennedy contends, Lee's approach to violence in the film pointedly challenges "the casual reification of morbidity surrounding postindustrial ghetto life" typical of mainstream media representations (Kennedy 2000, 159).

Clockers's depiction of the community that inhabits the looming towers of the Nelson Mandela housing project also breaks with standard media images. A number of the project's residents— Strike's hardworking brother Victor, a single mother trying to steer her young son away from street life, a tough black cop who tries to protect neighborhood kids from the drug trade, etc.—embody "decent values" and try to live moral lives despite the frustrations and sense of entrapment that come with living in the ghetto. With the exception of a few crack whores who hover around the project's courtyard drug market, virtually none of the inhabitants of the Mandela houses fit the underclass stereotype. More-over, throughout the film Lee carefully charts the many obstacles that stymie the residents' quest for a better life, from the presence of crimi-nal gangs (like Strike's) to the degrading, low-paid jobs that are the only legal employment available to strivers (like Victor).

Perhaps even more important, *Clockers* draws attention to the way the vicious racism of the borough's virtually all-white police force con-tributes to the oppressive atmosphere of the projects. Rocco and his white partner refer derisively to all black people as "yos," "niggers," or "Nubians." The local drug enforcement squad swoops in on Strike and his crew whenever they please, subjecting them to humiliating public strip searches and verbal abuse while demanding protection money. Lee's depiction of the cops and their relationship to the black characters in the film is clearly meant as a critique, among other things, of Giuliani's noto-rious crime-fighting policies. Indeed, at one point when the drug squad is frisking Strike, one officer remarks that they can shake down petty drug dealers with impunity now because Dinkins is out and Giuliani is in charge.

As unconventional as anything else in the film is Lee's characteri-zation of Strike (see Figure 35). Strike is in many ways the antithesis of the ruthless, macho, posturing gangsters that populate most ghettocen-tric films. As Paula Massood explains, "Strike is relatively soft—he drinks a Yoo Hoo–like soft drink called Moo Moo rather than the ubiquitous 'forties' malt liquor, he collects and plays with model trains, and he's often emasculated in the face of authority" (Massood 2003, 191). More-over, he is incapable of violence, unable to carry out a "hit" when Rod-ney orders him to, and unable to fight back when attacked by a cop who wants to force him to leave New York. He even suffers from a bleeding ulcer, caused by the stress of the clocker lifestyle. While Lee makes it clear that many of Strike's problems are self-incurred, he refrains from turn-ing him into a monster. Indeed, the director humanizes Strike by having him befriend Tyrone, by showing his fascination with model trains, and by showing his efforts to raise bail money for his brother Victor.

With its critical identification with its drug-dealer protagonist, its critique of police callousness toward the black population, and its nuanced portrayal of the frustrations of inner-city life, *Clockers* can be read as a progressive response to films like *Colors, Menace II Society,* and *New Jack City.* Rather than relying on hackneyed images of underclass degeneracy and gang-related bloodshed, Lee's film confronts us with the dismal social forces that crush dreams of upward social mobility and lead so many inner-city youth like Spike into the drug economy.

Like Spike Lee, Michael Moore is a polemical, left-leaning filmmaker—and a surprisingly successful one at that. As Christopher Sharrett and William Luhr point out, "[h]e stands virtually alone, not as a filmmaker who interrogates social and corporate power, but as one able to place such films into the multiplexes of America" (Sharrett and Luhr 2003, 36). His darkly humorous documentary about the impact of deindustrialization on his hometown of Flint, Michigan, *Roger and Me* (1989), and his short-lived television series about corporate malfeasance, *TV Nation* (1994), established Moore's reputation as a confrontational

Figure 35. Strike against the backdrop of the Nelson Mandela housing projects in *Clockers*.

interviewer with a goofy, populist persona and a knack for making progressive social criticism entertaining (Mattson 2003). In *Bowling for Columbine* (2002), which won an Oscar for best documentary and garnered top prizes at Cannes, he trains his attention on America's culture of guns and violence. Like his other films, *Bowling* is a loosely structured "essay" that is full of autobiographical digressions—what Stuart Klawans calls "narrative egomania" (Klawans 2002, 32)—and pop cultural references; and like *Roger and Me* in particular, *Bowling* inverts traditional documentary form by making powerful celebrities and corporate representatives (rather than the disenfranchised) the main target of Moore's interrogations (Orwell 1994/95, 17). Along the way, the film mounts an amusing critique of the media-generated myths about inner-city violence that have permeated the culture over the past few decades.

The overarching theme of the film is Moore's attempt to make sense of the 1999 shootings at Columbine High School in the Denver, Colorado, suburb of Littleton. Rejecting the standard explanation that the two young shooters responsible for the killings were amoral "monsters," Moore seeks to explain such murderous outbursts by tracing them not just to the easy availability of guns in the United States but to America's history of militarism and its stingy welfare state. It is, as Sharrett and Luhr complain, a rather "haphazardly assembled" and contradictory—albeit richly suggestive—analysis of the American problem of violence (Sharrett and Luhr 2003, 38).

Within the context of this larger exposition Moore raises pointed questions about the way the media stigmatizes and scapegoats those at the bottom of the social hierarchy and creates a climate of fear that leads the public to arm themselves for protection. Thus, at one point in the film, the director strolls with Barry Glassner, author of *The Culture of Fear,* through South Central L.A. and remarks that the image we have of the neighborhood from the news media is that it is home to "dangerous black guys." Yet, as the two walk unmolested around the intersection that was the scene of some of the worst fighting of the L.A. riots of 1992, Glassner notes that "the odds something is going to happen to you are very, very slight." After Glassner explains that they are probably at greater risk from the polluted air they are breathing than they are from random street crime, Moore ambles off to try to convince a police officer and a passing TV camera crew to do something about the smog. Intercut with the L.A. footage is an interview with Flint, Michigan, prosecutor Arthur Busch who explains that "in suburbia . . . there's some notion that there's going to be an invading horde coming from the city or from someplace unknown to savage their suburban community." Later, Moore interviews Dick Herlin, former producer of *Cops* and executive producer of *Wildest Police Videos* and questions why his shows relentlessly "demonize black and Hispanic people." When Herlin responds that he is not sure how to make corporate or upper-class misbehavior into reality TV, Moore pitches an idea for a series called "Corporate Cops," a show that would feature corrupt bosses being shaken down like street hoodlums.

Taken together, these bits add up to an unprecedented effort to use the resources of a major Hollywood studio to debunk, rather than advance, the right's discourse on the city. To be sure, Moore's film has its flaws. It is odd that in a documentary ostensibly about America's gun culture he spends so little time talking about the greater-than-average rate of gun violence in our inner cities. He could have perhaps done more to show how street violence in places like South Central is related to the limited economic opportunity available to ghetto youth, to the underground drug economy, to the brutality of the police, and to the structures of racial oppression. But for a film with such a large audience—reflected in its record take at the box office—*Bowling for Columbine*, with its attack on standard alarmist representations of the city, is fairly remarkable.

Oppositional films like *Clockers* and *Bowling for Columbine* remind us, then, that there are other ways to imagine the problems facing the postindustrial city, that the right's decontextualized images of underclass depravity and viciousness were not the only representations possible. They remind us, in other words, that the popularity of the "city as nightmare" trope and the triumph of the moral panic it helped to generate were hardly total or inevitable. Yet to overemphasize the importance of

Moore's and Lee's films risks creating a false sense of balance. Films like *Bowling for Columbine* are rare exceptions to the grim depictions of inner-city mayhem and pathology that have ruled the multiplexes for the past quarter century. Detailed exposés of capital's role in the urban crisis published in the lightly read pages of *In These Times* or *Dissent* pale in cultural impact next to reports on underclass deviance appearing in the *New York Times* or on *CBS Evening News*. For every sympathetic, humanizing portrayal of the urban working and lower class that appeared in the news, on television, or on film during the '80s and '90s, there were a thousand more that painted them out to be little more than pathological criminals living in neighborhoods of hellish squalor and brutality. Chas Critcher has noted that "[t]he development of a closed discourse in the media is a hallmark—now, a constitutive element—of a moral panic. At the point where there is only one way of 'speaking about' an issue, when other ways of speaking are excluded, then we have the discursive precondition for the emergence of a moral panic" (Critcher 2003, 174). While voices critical of the right's discourse on the cities occasionally broke the media sound barrier in the post-Reagan era, for the most part they were marginalized, and only one way of speaking about urban issues, Murray's and Gingrich's way, prevailed.

Awakening from Our Urban Nightmares

Representation—the way we imagine and picture or speak about our shared reality—matters. As Wolfgang Natter and John Paul Jones III observe, "the representation of social life (in, e.g., film, television, political discourse, cartography, and the media) and social life as 'lived' are dialectically interwoven. The conditions of material life are shaped *through* their representation as certainly as representations are shaped by material life" (Natter and Jones 1993, 155). Such representations never simply reflect—isomorphically or even approximately—the contours of a stable, self-contained reality. Rather, as Stuart Hall insists, the very concept of representation "implies the active work of selecting and presenting, of structuring and shaping: not merely transmitting the already-existing meaning but the more active labor of *making things mean*"

(Hall 1982, 64). The representations we construct of the city, its residents, and its problems help determine their social meaning and guide our collective, political actions toward them. As Maria Balshaw and Liam Kennedy correctly observe, they "promote and maintain (but also challenge and question) common notions of urban existence" (Kennedy and Balshaw 2000, 4). The panicked response of mainstream politicians and suburbanites to the social and economic polarization of America's metropolitan areas was in no way an automatic by-product of the dour political economic and demographic trends detailed in chapter 1; rather, it was a response to the right's hegemonic, widely circulated interpretation of those trends. The middle-class perception that places like Detroit and Philadelphia were spiraling downward toward some sort of apocalyptic end was not a spontaneous or natural reflection of "the situation on the ground"; it was the effect of endlessly repeated images that linked urban space to spectacular violence, bloodshed, and horror. Likewise, the worsening economic insecurity endured by the nation's urban working class in the years since Reagan's first election was not predestined; it was facilitated in no small part by policy decisions dictated by the conservatives' victim-blaming theories, by their particularly mean-spirited, moralistic way of *making meaning* of the inner city's woes.

Things could have turned out differently. The public could have greeted the economic distress of the central cities with empathy, solidarity, and compassion rather than fear and revulsion. White, blue-collar suburbanites stuck in declining inner-ring suburbs could've joined forces with central-city communities of color to demand regional tax sharing, more rapid cleanup of industrial brownfields, universal healthcare, more equitable funding of schools, more money for public transit, more public-sector jobs, less-severe (and less-racist) policing of the urban poor, and so on. Enlightened suburban feminists could have rallied to the side of predominantly urban welfare-rights coalitions in their struggle for a less-degrading, more generous welfare system, for better pay for female workers, and for government-subsidized, government-licensed childcare. Just about everyone but the very rich could have joined together to demand a more progressive income tax and other measures to reverse the dramatic polarization of wealth and incomes that wreaked such havoc on working-class urban neighborhoods.[1]

But of course this didn't happen. Instead, an increasingly nervous middle class became fixated on the pathological behavior, violence, and immorality they believed had taken over the urban core, and that fixation more or less guaranteed that none of the coalitions I have just imagined had much chance to materialize. Again and again the suburban middle class chose racial and spatial fears over solidarity and social justice; again and again they allowed themselves to be carried away by the moral panic that divided them from urban workers and led them to support repressive solutions to underclass violence and disorder. Not that any of this is especially surprising; the representations of the urban crisis and the underclass embraced by the media, the academy, and the politicians rendered less-apprehensive, less-authoritarian approaches to the postindustrial city's problems basically unthinkable.

Yet, despite the distressing story set forth in this book, the roads not taken remain open, at least for the time being. It is easy enough to identify the basic building blocks of a movement that could fight for economic justice for the residents of the postindustrial slums and oppose the regressive policies that have contributed to the dramatic social polarization of our metropolitan regions. Poor people and low-wage workers would form the center of such a movement as would community organizations and people of color involved in the struggle against racism in its many forms. All of these groups would benefit directly from reinvestment in urban areas and nonstigmatizing, nonrepressive remedies for our most pressing urban problems. To that core, one could add labor unions, which desperately need to reach out to central-city black and Latino workers if they are to rebound from their current appallingly low membership numbers, and environmentalists, who realize we must put a halt to suburban sprawl and invest heavily in public transit if we are ever to have truly "sustainable" cities. Even more important, a progressive coalition dedicated to fighting the urban crisis would have to encompass the residents of older, inner-ring suburbs. Like residents of the inner city, people who live in such declining areas have a direct material interest in seeing to it that wealthy outer-suburbanites contribute to the general good of the metro region; and, like those trapped in our decaying central cities, inner-suburb dwellers have an interest in actually reducing the number of people in poverty (as opposed to merely ghettoizing, excluding, and imprisoning them). Bring these forces together around a comprehensive program for reviving and democratizing our cities and who knows what could be accomplished. In fact, here and there, in places like Portland, Oregon, or Minneapolis–St. Paul, Minnesota, coalitions have been mildly successful at mobilizing multicultural urban/suburban coalitions in favor of a forward-looking urban agenda that includes measures like urban growth limits, municipal "living wage" laws, and regional tax-revenue sharing (see Orfield 1997).

Nevertheless, bridging the distances separating welfare recipients from union members, ghetto residents from inner-ring suburbanites, and African American community organizers from affluent white progressives will necessarily involve more than simply spelling out a pie-in-the-sky political platform, pointing out common interests, and then hoping against hope that everyone comes together. It will require tireless organizing and alliance building. It will involve setbacks and mistakes. And, as my argument in this book strongly implies, it will require a concerted effort to combat the reigning discourse on the urban crisis, to debunk its terms and ideological presuppositions, and to defuse the moral panic it has helped to generate.

This, in turn, will mean that those committed to fighting urban inequalities will have to pay closer attention to cultural representations of the postindustrial city and their ideological ramifications. They will have to conscientiously challenge and critique the distorted, stigmatizing pictures of the urban underclass and the inner city produced by Hollywood, television, and the Heritage Institute and respond effectively to middle-class paranoias (and here, perhaps, they can take their cue from films like *Clockers* and *Bowling for Columbine*). They will have to strive to give voice to the destitute and marginalized (in the cities as well as the inner suburbs) whose views are so often missing from public political debates and the mainstream media. And they will have to devise and popularize nonstigmatizing vocabularies in which to talk about poverty, urban disorder, and crime; vocabularies that underscore the relationship between conditions in the inner city and the destructive, antisocial logic of the capitalist system. As activist-scholar Matthew Ruben has suggestively argued, "the reintegration of class into the language of urban representation" could perhaps "serve as a countervailing force to isolation and division" (Ruben 2001, 463). In short, those campaigning to transform our cities into centers of democracy and prosperity will have to become self-consciously involved in the struggle for cultural hegemony, "for political and moral leadership" over vast segments of an increasingly polarized and geographically fragmented society. Antonio Gramsci, author of the theory of hegemony, argued that political and social groups can only establish such leadership by "bringing about not only a unison of economic and political aims, but also intellectual and moral unity, posing all the questions around which the struggle rages not on a corporate but on a 'universal' plane" (Gramsci 1971, 181–82). This is precisely what the intellectual champions of the right have been doing for the past few decades with such disturbing results: orchestrating hegemony by defining the very questions "around which the struggle rages" and crafting the very language through which social reality is understood and debated.

As this book has made clear, the alarmist discourse on the moral decline, violence, and disorder of the postindustrial metropolis was absolutely instrumental to the right's political success during the 1980s and '90s. Unless we as a society awaken from the ideologically laden nightmares that this discourse has conjured up for us, addressing the real needs of contemporary American cities will be next to impossible. As Bourdieu (1991) reminds us, any effort at subverting our unjust political and social order presupposes "cognitive subversion, a conversion of the vision of the world." Radically transforming the way we represent and think about our cities and their problems would be a good start.

Acknowledgments

This book would have been impossible without the support, encouragement, inspiration, and constructive criticism of countless teachers, friends, and colleagues. First, I would like to thank the Program in Comparative Studies in Discourse and Society at the University of Minnesota, where this project was first conceived, for being such a strange and wonderful incubator of intellectual experimentation and interdisciplinary inquiry. I owe a special debt of gratitude to Roger Miller, who advised the dissertation on which this book is based, for his warmth, enthusiasm, and sage advice every step of the way. More than anyone else, he is the person who got me interested in cultural representations of the city; the entire book (or, at least, the good bits) bears the imprint of his influence as a teacher and a scholar. Thanks too to John Archer for his prompt, helpful answers to my queries about everything from revising chapters to locating a particular SUV ad. I'm grateful to Jack Zipes for insisting that I turn the dissertation into a book and for guiding me through the early stages of the process. I also thank John Mowitt, Bruce Lincoln, Gary Thomas, Richard Leppert, Prabhakara Jha, George Lipsitz, and all the other faculty and students associated with CSDS who taught me so much about the media, politics, critical theory, and contemporary American culture. I also express my appreciation to the staff of the Vanderbilt TV News Archive for help during my two research trips there.

The faculty and administrators at North Central College have made the three years that I have been at that school the most productive of my academic career. The former chair of my department, Roger Smitter, and my division chair, Sara Eaton, did everything in their power to give me the time and resources I needed to finish the book. The Faculty Development Committee awarded me a summer research grant that allowed me to make a follow-up visit to the Vanderbilt Archive. Dean Devados Pandian granted me a one-term leave from teaching, which enabled me to complete a second round of research and writing on the manuscript. My colleagues at North Central (especially Sophie Hand, Ann Keating, Lisa Long, Anna Leahy, Jennifer Jackson, Lou Corsino, Mara Berkland, Richard Paine, Wioleta Polinska, and Debbie Rindge) welcomed me into a vibrant intellectual community that supports unconventional, interdisciplinary research and teaching. I'm grateful to them all.

Many other friends and colleagues sustained me during the writing of this book; unfortunately, space does not permit me to acknowledge them all. I particularly thank Andrew Kincaid, Benet Haller, Bruce Campbell, Cara Letofsky, Carrie Rentschler, Clay Steinman, Craig Wilkins, Ed Wells, Elizabeth Walden, Erik Jensen, Ian Lipsky, Jack Stuart, Jeanne Freiburg, Joe Peschek, Jonathan Sterne, Larry Shillock, Lisa Woolley, Lynne Woehrle, Michelle Lekas, Michelle Stewart, Ole Gram, Peter McAuley, and Rebecca Hill.

I owe an even greater debt to my family. My father, Joseph Macek, taught me critical thinking and the pleasure of argument. My mother, Ellen Macek, passed on to me her passion for history and reading. (She also took time off from her own research to proofread several chapters at the eleventh hour.) Both gave me their unconditional love, something that I have really only begun to appreciate now that I have kids of my own. My wife's parents, Gerry and Bill Leder, were unflagging in their support throughout the protracted writing process and graciously allowed me to live in their home while I conducted the early research for this project. I'm grateful to my children, Aleeza and Sebastian, for bringing so much laughter, joy, and frenetic energy into my life. I'm even more grateful to my partner, Jackie Leder, who supported me emotionally, morally, and, sometimes, financially while I wrote the dissertation and then had to endure the whole ordeal again as I struggled to turn the dissertation into a book. She was always willing to listen to me ramble on about my topic and to take on extra childcare duties so I could write. And despite her busy schedule as a public defender, she somehow found time to proofread the entire text. Twice.

My editor, Doug Armato, deserves special thanks for his patient guidance and for helping me sort through a number of vexing questions about how to revise the original manuscript. I thank the entire production team at the University of Minnesota Press for making the experience of publishing the book so surprisingly pleasant, and I acknowledge the two anonymous readers who reviewed the manuscript for the Press and thank them for their thoughtful, and often extremely helpful, suggestions.

Finally, I thank the many progressive and radical political organizations I have worked with and for over the years, especially Progressive Minnesota, the Independent Progressive Politics Network, Graduate Students Against Militarism, the Graduate Student Organizing Committee, Mayday Books (in Minneapolis, Minnesota), Meeting the Challenge, the Green Party, the Union for Democratic Communications, Chicago Media Action, Free Press, Du Page Against War Now, and the Du Page Peace Through Justice Coalition. The radically democratic, egalitarian politics these groups champion is the only real antidote to the problems plaguing our cities (and our world) and informs my analysis in this book from start to finish.

Selected National Television News Stories about the Urban Crisis, 1989–97

Date	Network	Topic (News Series)
06/08/97	CNN	New York City teacher shot
06/07/97	ABC	New York City teacher shot
06/07/97	NBC	New York City teacher shot
06/07/97	CNN	New York City teacher shot
06/07/97	CBS	New York City teacher shot
06/06/97	NBC	New York City teacher shot
06/03/97	CNN	New York City teacher shot
05/27/97	CBS	Central Park murder update
05/24/97	CBS	murder in Central Park
05/21/97	CBS	murder in Central Park
03/18/97	CBS	murder of Notorious B.I.G.
03/12/97	ABC	bank shoot-out—Detroit
03/11/97	ABC	bank shoot-out—Detroit
03/11/97	CBS	bank shoot-out—Detroit
03/11/97	NBC	bank shoot-out—Detroit
03/11/97	CNN	bank shoot-out—Detroit
02/07/97	CBS	Cabrini-Green shooting
05/20/96	CBS	welfare reform debate
05/04/96	CNN	Clinton on single mothers
01/11/96	CBS	fear of crime/Polec murders

12/03/95	NBC	Clinton on poor moms, welfare
10/17/95	CBS	gang violence
09/22/95	CBS	crime in the inner city ("Eye on America")
09/21/95	ABC	wrong-turn murders
05/16/95	NBC	welfare reform ("Critical Choices")
03/21/95	NBC	comments on welfare reform (Bill Moyers)
02/21/95	NBC	graffiti shootings
02/02/95	CBS	unwed mothers and teen pregnancies
01/31/95	CBS	welfare reform—state level
01/29/95	CBS	welfare reform
01/14/95	NBC	debate over *Bell Curve*
12/12/94	CBS	homeless man with knife—D.C.
12/07/94	NBC	welfare moms/the underclass
12/07/94	ABC	Murray on welfare mothers
11/24/94	CBS	Philadelphia teen dies in street battle
11/23/94	ABC	shoot-out in D.C. bank
11/23/94	ABC	shooting at D.C. police HQ
11/16/94	CBS	welfare reform and culture of poverty
11/01/94	NBC	welfare cheating in California
10/19/94	CBS	*Bell Curve* ("Eye on America")
10/23/94	ABC	public school dress codes and gangs
09/04/94	ABC	epidemic of child murders
09/04/94	NBC	juvenile murders blamed on welfare
08/15/94	NBC	Chicago gangs ("Society under Siege")
07/18/94	CBS	New Orleans boy killed in projects
06/15/94	CBS	welfare reform debate
05/24/94	CBS	flogging graffiti writers
04/30/94	ABC	flight from crime—D.C.
04/06/94	ABC	welfare ("America Up Close")
03/08/94	NBC	Ft. Worth, TX, gangs ("Society under Siege")
02/18/94	NBC	neglected children

02/09/94	CBS	unwed mothers ("Eye on America")
02/08/94	CBS	unwed fathers ("Eye on America")
12/21/93	ABC	complaints about the homeless
12/03/93	NBC	families in crisis
12/02/93	NBC	families in crisis
12/01/93	NBC	families in crisis
11/30/93	NBC	families in crisis
11/29/93	NBC	families in crisis
11/05/93	NBC	kids on streets ("Society under Siege")
11/01/93	NBC	D.C. under siege ("Society under Siege")
10/30/93	CBS	Hartford, CT, gang violence
10/27/93	CBS	gang violence in Portland, OR
10/14/93	NBC	society under siege
10/07/93	ABC	street gangs ("American Agenda")
08/29/93	CBS	urban emergency rooms
08/27/93	NBC	the underclass/welfare dependency
08/24/93	CBS	welfare reform ("Eye on America")
07/29/93	NBC	welfare dependency
07/24/93	NBC	urban violence in Denver, CO
07/21/93	NBC	San Diego, CA, gangs
07/20/93	CBS	street gangs ("Eye on America")
04/30/93	NBC	Clinton's urban policy
04/06/93	NBC	Los Angeles girl gangs ("Society under Siege")
04/01/93	NBC	Atlanta, GA, drive-by shooting
02/04/93	ABC	relocating the disadvantaged to suburbs
01/31/93	CBS	gang violence in Los Angeles
12/18/92	ABC	Los Angeles graffiti
10/19/92	NBC	Cabrini-Green killing ("Society under Siege")
10/15/92	ABC	Cabrini-Green killing of 7-year-old
06/19/92	CBS	Las Vegas, NV, slums
05/30/92	NBC	rural views of city problems
05/16/92	NBC	march for aid to cities

05/09/92	NBC	Los Angeles riots
05/08/92	NBC	Los Angeles riots
05/07/92	NBC	Los Angeles riots
05/07/92	CBS	Los Angeles riots
05/07/92	ABC	Los Angeles riots
05/06/92	NBC	Los Angeles riots
05/06/92	CBS	Los Angeles riots
05/06/92	ABC	Los Angeles riots
05/05/92	NBC	Los Angeles riots
05/05/92	CBS	Los Angeles riots
05/05/92	ABC	Los Angeles riots
05/04/92	NBC	Los Angeles riots
05/04/92	CBS	Los Angeles riots
05/04/92	ABC	Los Angeles riots
05/03/92	NBC	Los Angeles riots
05/03/92	CBS	Los Angeles riots
05/03/92	ABC	Los Angeles riots
05/02/92	NBC	Los Angeles riots
05/02/92	CBS	Los Angeles riots
05/02/92	ABC	Los Angeles riots
05/01/92	NBC	Los Angeles riots
05/01/92	CBS	Los Angeles riots
05/01/92	ABC	Los Angeles riots
04/30/92	NBC	Los Angeles riots
04/30/92	CBS	Los Angeles riots
04/30/92	ABC	Los Angeles riots
04/12/92	CBS	Mario Cuomo on the urban crisis
04/03/92	ABC	urban issues in presidential race
03/20/92	NBC	single black mothers
03/17/92	NBC	city and suburbs in the 1992 campaign
03/16/92	NBC	families in crisis ("Brokaw Report")
12/26/91	CBS	gang violence ("Eye on America")
12/25/91	NBC	Edge City: Tyson's Corner
11/22/91	CBS	Washington, D.C., urban violence

11/01/91	ABC	children of poverty revisited
09/24/91	ABC	crack in Chicago
09/20/91	CBS	Edge Cities
06/19/91	ABC	the shortened childhood of poverty
06/12/91	CBS	Dallas, TX, curfew
03/18/91	ABC	Gulf War vet shot in Detroit, MI
03/11/91	NBC	Los Angeles gang shooting
07/30/90	NBC	murder epidemic
06/15/90	NBC	drugs and street crime
04/14/90	ABC	Los Angeles gangs and colors
02/20/90	ABC	girl gangs
02/19/90	ABC	girls in gangs
02/07/90	NBC	inner-city gangs ("Commentary")
12/15/89	CBS	drugs ("One Nation under Siege")
06/27/89	NBC	kids of Camden, NJ/public schools
06/26/89	NBC	kids of Camden, NJ/teen pregnancy
01/16/89	ABC	Charles Murray on War on Poverty

Notes

1. The Origins of the Crisis

1. For an opposing view, one that argues that federal policy was not an enormously important factor in postwar suburbanization and central-city decline, see Beauregard 2001.

2. Though the ultimate cause of this restructuring is still debated, a strong case can be made that it was part of a more or less conscious response to a "crisis of over-accumulation" in the early '70s. Relocating manufacturing plants to less-developed countries in order to take advantage of their cheap, non-unionized labor, for instance, was clearly part of an effort to expand flagging profit margins at the expense of American workers. See Harvey 1989, especially chapter 9.

3. The economic decline of the central city has not been confined only to manufacturing. Since the 1970s, cities have also lost quite a few corporate offices along with the tax revenues and white collar jobs they generated. For instance, New York City in 1965 was home to the headquarters of roughly all Fortune 500 companies; by 1998, that number had shrunk to forty-six (Hayward 1998, 18).

4. See, for example, Mike Davis's discussion of the collapse of "the unionized branch-plant economy" in the black and Latino communities of South Central L.A. (Davis 1990, 304–7). See also Thomas Sugrue's penetrating analysis of the deindustrialization of Detroit and its aftermath (Sugrue 1996, chapters 5 and 6).

2. Inventing the Savage Urban Other

1. For a discussion of the nineteenth-century perception of Paris as disorderly and dangerous, see Harvey 1985, 168–87; for Berlin, see Fritzsche 1996.

2. Once in office, Nixon sponsored legislation that created "no-knock warrants" allowing cops to kick in doors without warning, gave secret grand juries expanded power, and created a special police force (the 300-person Office of Drug Abuse Law Enforcement) accountable only to the White House, which he put to work hunting down street-level drug dealers in a few big cities (see Parenti 1999, 9–18).

3. It must be stated, however, that the facts certainly did not support Moynihan's sensational claim that "the family structure of lower-class Negroes . . . is approaching complete breakdown" (Rainwater and Yancey 1967, 51).

4. See, for instance, Carol Stack's nuanced ethnography of survival strategies in the black ghetto, *All Our Kin* (1974).

3. Catastrophe Is Now

1. It should be noted that the book's claim that measured IQ determines "life chances" and income levels is also open to challenge. Even if one accepts that IQ scores accurately measure cognitive ability, re-analysis of Murray and Herrnstein's data shows that family income, parents' education, and parents' occupational status play as large a role in determining a person's occupation and income as IQ (Korenman and Winship 2000).

2. This is a position that apparently resonated with at least one very important right-wing politician: President George W. Bush, who often cites Olasky as an influence and frequently used the Olasky-coined phrase "compassionate conservatism" to describe his philosophy on social policy during the 2000 presidential campaign. Bush's plans to funnel federal monies to faith-based charities who work with the poor were inspired directly by Olasky's work (see Hart 2000).

3. Much of what she has to say about these individuals is pure character assassination. For instance, she includes a gratuitous and withering observation about how Havelock Ellis was unable to consummate his "affair" with Olive Schreiner because "such sexual impulses as Ellis had were aroused by the sight of women urinating" (199). Smears like this one appear to be a forte of Thatcherite intellectuals. Himmelfarb admirer and fellow Brit Paul Johnson's *Intellectuals* (1990) is essentially a compendium of unflattering gossip about every left-wing intellectual from Rousseau to Sartre.

4. This explanation gained favor with other conservative ideologues during the '90s. Thus, in his best-selling attack on liberalism, *Slouching towards Gomorrah*, former Supreme Court nominee and right-wing pundit Robert Bork claims that the rise in illegitimacy and crime rates since the 1960s have their root in the cultural changes identified with that era. "[R]ising crime, illegitimacy and student rebellion had a common cause," he argues. "While middle-class student radicals turned to dreams of revolution and the destruction of institutions, some of the lower classes turned to crime" (Bork 1996, 155). Similarly, Heather Mac-Donald charges that the failure of elite opinion "to render judgment on self-destructive behavior is part of a moral climate that has done real and lasting harm to the poor" (MacDonald 2000, 42).

5. This nostalgia is explicit in the work of communitarian conservatives like Alan Ehrenhalt. His panegyric to 1950s Chicago, *The Lost City* (1995), hailed the city for its superior "moral culture," strong families, and exemplary communities while excusing its racial segregation and notorious political corruption (Ehrenhalt 1995).

6. The irony here is that the real "criminogenic environment," the milieu best suited to producing hardened career criminals, is not the inner city but the prison, the very place Bennett wants to consign ghetto youth for even the most trifling infractions. See Foucault's comments about the prison's role in producing the delinquent in *Discipline and Punish* (1979, 277–82).

7. The notion of the "superpredator," though not as widely circulated as the more-encompassing concept of the underclass, was nevertheless very popular with the new generation of law-and-order mayors who were elected in the '90s. For instance, Stephen Goldsmith, Republican mayor of Indianapolis, referred to "the complete amorality of the young adult, street tough 'super-predators' " in making his case for mandatory minimum sentences for juveniles and more intensive policing of inner-city neighborhoods (Goldsmith 1999, 146).

8. A similar charge could be leveled at the other right-wing "super-mayors" of the '90s. See, for instance, Michael Grunwald's exposé of Stephen Goldsmith's tenure as mayor of Indianapolis, a reign that proved to be a boon for private companies and a disaster for the poor, public schools, and drug addicts, among others (Grunwald 1998).

4. Crack Alleys and Killing Zones

1. See, for example, Sparrow 1999; Bennett 1983; Barnouw 1997; Bettig and Hall 2003; McChesney 1999; Rowse 2000; and Lieberman 2000. See also

Edward Herman's sharply worded defense of this view of the news media as agents of propaganda against some standard criticisms in Herman 1999.

2. Unless otherwise noted, the data presented in this chapter about the numbers and types of stories aired by the networks is derived from the *Vanderbilt Television News Index*, an online database that contains detailed abstracts of every prime-time network television news broadcast since 1968. In 1996 and again in 2003, I made research trips to the Vanderbilt Television News Archive during which I reviewed videotapes of some 275 separate stories that I identified as particularly germane to the topic of the contemporary American urban crisis. With the exception of television news stories described in the secondary literature discussed here, descriptions of and quotes from individual television news items included in this chapter are based on my notes from those trips.

3. For a more detailed account of the media's "agenda setting" function, see Rogers, Hart, and Dearing 1997 and Iyengar and Simon 1997.

4. Ettema and Peer do note that a majority of the stories about Austin contain some "good news" about the community's efforts to respond to its problems (Ettema and Peer 1996, 842). Nevertheless, one has to wonder whether the perfunctory mention of "community response" to the neighborhood's problems can counteract the impression that it is an essentially dangerous place.

5. While newspapers tend to be less obsessed with urban criminality than their broadcast counterparts, street crime remains a staple of their daily reporting. According to Barry Glassner, "in the early to mid-1990s, 20 to 30 percent of news items in city newspapers concerned crime" (Glassner 1999, 29).

6. A follow-up study by Rosalee Clawson and Rakuya Trice analyzing the photographs that accompanied stories on poverty in five U.S. news magazines from 1993 to 1998 found that blacks were similarly "over-represented" in the magazines' pictures of the poor (Clawson and Trice 2000). Perhaps even more significant in the context of this book, they also discovered that the magazines constructed poverty as "almost completely an urban problem" and that "[n]inety-six percent of the poor were shown in urban areas" (58).

5. The Cinema of Suburban Paranoia

1. *Seven* grossed over $100 million in 1995 in the U.S. market alone, making it one of the top ten domestic money-makers that year. (http://www.boxofficereport.com/ybon/1995.shtml [accessed November 27, 2005]).

2. In his brilliant *Ecology of Fear*, Mike Davis notes that the destruction of Los Angeles has been such a popular theme in recent cinema that "[t]he entire

world seems to be rooting for Los Angeles to slide into the Pacific or be swallowed by the San Andreas fault" (Davis 1998, 276–77).

3. Whether or not the process by which films assume elements of the dominant ideology should be described as a process of "reflection" is open to debate. To talk about a film "reflecting" the dominant ideology assumes that a) that ideology is a closed, preconstituted system of ideas, meanings, etc. and b) that this preconstituted system of meanings is imported into the film untransformed. Neither proposition stands up to scrutiny: first because the dominant ideology is always evolving and in flux; and second, because a film's "operationalization" of ideological concepts always changes, deepens, and expands their meanings. It would therefore perhaps be better to speak of film as helping to define the dominant ideology rather than as merely reflecting it.

4. This becomes even clearer in the *Escape from New York* video game based on the film. In the video game, literally every street, every alleyway, and every subway car harbors potential attackers that the player/Snake must destroy; indeed, in the game's rendition of the film's carceral New York, there are no safe spaces at all.

5. As I point out in the conclusion to this book, Lee's film uses the conventions of the ghetto-centric gangster film in a way that breaks politically with the genre's acceptance of key aspects of the right's pathologizing discourse on the underclass. In this respect, *Clockers* is the exception that proves the rule.

6. Technically speaking, Grant's designation is something of a misnomer because the protagonists of many of these films, while they ostensibly share the lifestyle, mentality, and values typically associated with yuppies, live in the suburbs—making them *young suburban professionals* as opposed to *young urban professionals*.

7. As Andrew Ross remarks, the subways and sewers of New York and other metropolitan centers have often been linked to "the alien presence of immigrant populations busily breeding mutant Americans" and, as he points out, "the rich zoological life of the underworld has continued to be a source of representation for threats to the urban racial order" (Ross 1994, 135–36).

8. Alan Nadel has argued that "the establishing shot is the representation of the Establishment, in that it presents the unchallenged assumptions necessary to allow the scene to unfold. It frames the framing of the subsequent shots by delimiting the imaginary space in which they are situated" (Nadel 1997, 143). In the case of *Eye for an Eye*, the reverential establishing shot of the McCanns'

giant upper-middle-class house doesn't merely specify the imagined space of the house as the site of much of the film's action but also posits the house and the lifestyle that centers around it as essentially good and decent.

9. This section of the chapter draws on my article on *Seven* and fear of the city in contemporary Hollywood film (Macek 1999).

10. For more on the expressionistic use of light and shadow to develop distinctively bleak urban settings in classic film noir see Ford 1994, Christopher 1997, and Krutnik 1997. It is important to point out that the sort of lighting and black and white color palette one sees in *Seven* is not exclusively associated with film noir. This particular style owes as much to directors who've come to film from working in advertising (and, in Fincher's case, music videos) as it does to noir.

11. Fincher's desire to foreground darkness in the film led him to employ the rarely-used silver retention method of processing that, as Amy Taubin explains, "produces more luminosity in the light and more density in the darks" but is also extremely expensive (Taubin 1996, 24). The process is so costly and time-consuming, in fact, that only a few hundred of the prints of *Seven* in circulation are silver retention.

12. In this respect, at least, Doe's solution to urban problems resembles Travis Bickel's famously violent, apocalyptic response to the mean streets of New York in Scorsese's *Taxi Driver.* For more on the apocalyptic "redemption" of the city in *Taxi Driver* (1976) see Sharrett 1993a.

13. According to Richard Dyer, whose excellent monograph on *Seven* appeared at roughly the same time as my *College Literature* article on the film, this tacked-on and utterly unpersuasive voice-over was "a cap desired by the studio, intended to give some crumb of Hollywoodian comfort in a film so extraordinarily un-American in its pessimism" (Dyer 1999, 77). I have been unable to confirm this claim but the voice-over at the end is so incongruous with the bleak spirit of the movie that it would be surprising if it were not the result of some sort of studio tampering.

14. Lauren Krivo and Ruth Peterson have recently conducted research confirming that "extremely disadvantaged communities have higher levels of crime than less disadvantaged areas, and that this pattern holds for both black and white communities" (Krivo and Peterson 1996, 640).

15. For further discussion of the social factors driving high levels of black street crime, see Hacker 1992, 179–98.

16. In this respect, the film bears some resemblance to *Batman*, which, as

Andrew Ross has argued, depends heavily on a veiled racial subtext to construct its vision of a crime-threatened Gotham City (Ross 1990).

6. Wouldn't You Rather Be at Home?

1. There are, of course, exceptions to this trend. For instance, there are any number of ads for sleek-looking luxury cars that show them hurtling through the city loaded with beautiful, well-dressed occupants before pulling up to fancy restaurants or hip urban nightspots. And, as one anonymous reviewer of this chapter pointed out, Volkswagen a few years ago ran a television spot that showed a couple driving down rainy New Orleans streets as the people outside do things in time to the beat of their windshield wipers. The city in such ads is still imagined as exotic or strange but in these commercials the exoticism of urban life is seen not as threatening but as enticing.

Conclusion

1. For a lucid statement of just such a progressive urban policy agenda, see Rogers and Luria 1999.

Bibliography

A Job Is a Right Campaign. 1997. *The Feeding Trough: The Bradley Foundation, the Bell Curve & the Real Story Behind Wisconsin's National Model of Welfare Reform.* Milwaukee: A Job Is a Right Campaign.

Adams, John, Barbara Van Drasek, and Laura Lambert. 1995. *The Path of Urban Decline.* Minneapolis: Center for Urban and Regional Affairs.

ADT News Press Release. 1999. "Are Kids Safe?" National Survey Reveals Increased Fear for Kids. October 26.

Albelda, Randy, and Ann Withorn, eds. 2002. *Lost Ground: Welfare Reform, Poverty and Beyond.* Cambridge, MA: South End Press.

Alterman, Eric. 1999. *Sound and Fury: The Making of the Punditocracy.* Ithaca, NY: Cornell University Press.

———. 2003. *What Liberal Media? The Truth About Bias and the News.* New York: Basic Books.

Annin, Peter. 1996. "Superpredators" Arrive. *Newsweek.* January 22, 57.

Archer, John. 2004. Suburban Planning, in *Encyclopedia of Twentieth-Century Architecture,* ed. R. Stephen Sennott, 3: 1270–73. Chicago: Fitzroy Dearborn.

Ashkins, Cindy D., and Joseph F. Sheley. 1981. Crime, Crime News and Crime Views. *Public Opinion Quarterly* 45: 492–506.

Ashton, Patrick J. 1984. Urbanization and the Dynamics of Suburban Development under Capitalism. In *Marxism and the Metropolis,* ed. William Tabb and Larry Sawers. New York: Oxford University Press.

Attinger, Joelle. 1990. The Decline of New York. *Time.* September 17, 36–44.

Auletta, Ken. 1982. *The Underclass*. New York: Random House.

Austin, Joe. 2002. *Taking the Train: How Graffiti Art Became an Urban Crisis in New York City*. New York: Columbia University Press.

Bagdikian, Ben H. 1997. *The Media Monopoly*, 5th ed. Boston: Beacon Press.

Banfield, Edward C. 1968. *The Unheavenly City*. Boston: Little, Brown and Company.

Barnouw, Erik, ed. 1997. *Conglomerates and the Media*. New York: New Press.

Barone, Michael. 1994. Seeking Civility in America's Cities. *U.S. News and World Report*. April 4, 26.

———. 2001. Changing Minds. *U.S. News and World Report*. July 30, 25.

Barthes, Roland. 1972. *Mythologies*. Translated by Annette Lavers. New York: Hill and Wang.

Bates, Eric. 1998. Chaining the Alternatives. *The Nation*, June 28, 11–18.

Baughman, James L. 1992. *The Republic of Mass Culture: Journalism, Filmmaking, and Broadcasting in America since 1941*. Baltimore: The Johns Hopkins University Press.

Beauregard, Robert. 1993. *Voices of Decline: The Postwar Fate of U.S. Cities*. Oxford: Blackwell.

———. 1996. Why Passion for the City Has Been Lost. *Journal of Urban Affairs* 18, no 3: 217–31.

———. 1999. The Politics of Urbanism: Mike Davis and the Neo-Conservatives. *Capitalism, Nature, Socialism* 10(3), no. 39 (September): 40–45.

———. 2001. Federal Policy and Postwar Housing Decline: A Case of Government Complicity? *Housing Policy Debate* 12, no. 1: 129–51.

Beckett, Katherine. 1997. *Making Crime Pay*. Oxford: Oxford University Press.

Bellah, Robert, Richard Madsen, William Sullivan, Ann Swidler, and Steve Tipton. 1985. *Habits of the Heart: Individualism and Commitment in American Life*. Berkeley and Los Angeles: University of California Press.

Bennett, Lance. 1983. *News: The Politics of Illusion*. New York: Longman.

Bennett, William. 1992. *The De-Valuing of America*. New York: Simon and Schuster.

———. 1993. *The Index of Leading Cultural Indicators*. New York: Broadway Books.

———, John DiIulio, and John Walters. 1996. *Body Count: Moral Poverty and How to Win America's War Against Crime and Drugs*. New York: Simon and Schuster.

Benton, Lisa. 1995. Will the Reel/Real Los Angeles Please Stand Up? *Urban Geography* 16, no. 2: 144–64.

Best, Joel. 1999. *Random Violence: How We Talk About New Crime and New Victims*. Berkeley and Los Angeles: University of California Press.

Bettig, Ronald V., and Jeanne Lynn Hall. 2003. *Big Media, Big Money: Cultural Texts and Political Economics*. New York: Rowman and Littlefield.

Bhabha, Homi. 1997. Bombs Away in Front-line Suburbia. In *Visions of Suburbia*, ed. Roger Silverstone, 298–303. London: Routledge.

Blakely, Edward, and Mary Gail Snyder. 1997. Divided We Fall: Gated and Walled Communities in the United States. In *Architecture of Fear.*, ed. Nan Ellin, 85–100. New York: Princeton Architectural Press.

———. 1999. *Fortress America: Gated Communities in the United States*. Washington, DC: Brookings Institution Press.

Blankenhorn, David. 1995. *Fatherless America: Confronting Our Most Urgent Social Problem*. New York: Harper Collins.

Booth, Charles. 1888. Conditions and Occupations of the People in East London and Hackney, 1887. *Journal of the Royal Statistical Society* 51: 326–91.

Bork, Robert H. 1996. *Slouching Towards Gomorrah: Modern Liberalism and American Decline*. New York: Regan Books.

Borowski, Greg. 1998. Mayors Call for New Urban Strategy. *Milwaukee Journal Sentinel*, November 17, 1.

Bourdieu, Pierre. 1989. Social Space and Symbolic Power. *Sociological Theory* 7, no. 1: 14–25.

———. 1991. *Language and Symbolic Power*. Cambridge, MA: Harvard University Press.

Bowen, Ezra. 1988. Getting Tough. *Time*. February 1, 53–58.

Boyer, Christine. 1987. *Dreaming the Rational City*. Cambridge, MA: MIT Press.

Boyer, Paul. 1978. *Urban Masses and the Moral Order in America, 1820–1920*. Cambridge, MA: Harvard University Press.

Brady, Sarah. 2001. Marketing Handguns to Women: Fair Advertising or Exploitation? *The Brady Center*. http://www.gunlawsuits.org/features/articles/markettowomen.php

Bratton, William J., and William Andrews. 2000. What We've Learned About Policing. In *The Millennial City: A New Urban Paradigm for 21st-Century America*, ed. Myron Magnet. Chicago: Ivan Dee.

Budd, Mike, Steve Craig, and Clay Steinman. 1999. *Consuming Environments: Television and Commerical Culture*. New Brunswick, NJ: Rutgers University Press.

Bullard, Robert D., and Glenn S. Johnson, eds. 1997. *Just Transportation: Dismantling Race and Class Barriers to Mobility*. Stony Creek, CT: New Society Publishers.

Buying a Movement: Right Wing Foundations and American Politics. 1996. Washington DC: People for the American Way.

Callahan, David. 1999. $1 Billion for Conservative Ideas. *The Nation*. April 26, 21–23.

Chadwick, Edwin. 1842. *Report . . . on an Inquiry into the Sanitary Conditions of the Laboring Populations of Great Britain*. London: W. Clowes.

———. 1874. *Transactions of the Sanitary Institute of Great Britain*. London.

Chomsky, Noam, and Edward Herman. 1988. *Manufacturing Consent*. New York: Pantheon.

Christopher, Nicholas. 1997. *Somewhere in the Night: Film Noir and the American City*. New York: The Free Press.

Clarke, John. 1991. *New Times and Old Enemies: Essays on Cultural Studies and America*. London: Harper Collins Academic.

Clawson, Rosalee A., and Rakuya Trice. 2000. Poverty As We Know It: Media Portrayals of the Poor. *Public Opinion Quarterly* 64, no. 1: 53–64.

Clay, Phillip L. 1992. The (Un)Housed City: Racial Patterns of Segregation, Housing Quality and Affordability. In *The Metropolis in Black and White: Place, Power and Polarization*, ed. George C. Galster and Edward W. Hill, 93–107. New Brunswick, NJ: The Center for Urban Policy Research.

Clinton Stands Up for Kids. 1994. *Advertising Age*. March 21, 4.

Cloud, Dana. 1998. The Rhetoric of "Family Values": Scapegoating, Utopia, and the Privatization of Social Responsibility. *Western Journal of Communication* 62, no. 4 (Fall): 387–419.

Clover, Carol. 1993. White Noise. *Sight and Sound*. May, 6–9.

Coats, Dan, and Spencer Abraham. 1998. Liberalism's Mean Streets. *Policy Review*, no. 90 (July): 36–40.

Cohen, Stanley. 1972. *Folk Devils and Moral Panics: The Creation of the Mods and Rockers*. Oxford: Martin Robertson.

———. 1985. *Visions of Control: Crime, Punishment and Classification*. Oxford: Blackwell.

Cohl, H. Aaron. 1997. *Are We Scaring Ourselves to Death?* New York: St. Martin's Griffin.

Collins, Chuck, Chris Hartman, and Holly Sklar. 1999. *Divided Decade: Economic Disparity at the Century's Turn*. Boston: United for a Fair Economy.

Collins, Chuck, and Felice Yeskel. 2000. *Economic Apartheid in America*. New York: The New Press.

Coontz, Stephanie. 1992. *The Way We Never Were: American Families and the Nostalgia Trap*. New York: Basic Books.

Corwin, Miles. 1993. Guns for Hire. *Los Angeles Times Magazine*. 28 November, 24–26.

Cranberg, Gilbert. 1997. Trimming the Fringe: How Newspapers Shun Low-Income Readers. *Columbia Journalism Review* (March/April): 52–54.

Critcher, Chas. 2003. *Moral Panics and the Media*. Buckingham and Philadelphia: Open University Press.

Croteau, David, and William Hoynes. 1994. *By Invitation Only: How the Media Limit Political Debate*. Monroe, ME: Common Courage Press.

D'Souza, Dinesh. 1991. *Illiberal Education: The Politics of Race and Sex on Campus*. New York: The Free Press.

———. 1995. *The End of Racism*. New York: The Free Press.

Danielson, Michael. 1976. *The Politics of Exclusion*. New York: Columbia University Press.

Davies, Jonathan. 1997. Few Using Internet as News Source. *Denver Rocky Mountain News*, June 21, 4D.

Davies, Jude. 1995. Gender, Ethnicity and Cultural Crisis in *Falling Down* and *Ground Hog Day*. *Screen* 36, no. 3 (Autumn): 214–32.

Davis, Mike. 1990. *City of Quartz*. New York: Vintage.

———. 1993. The Strange Death of Liberal Los Angeles. *Z Magazine*, November, 49–53.

———. 1998. *Ecology of Fear: Los Angeles and the Imagination of Disaster*. New York: Henry Holt and Company.

DeMause, Neil. 1996. Mean, Base, Down Right Lowdown. *Z Magazine*, October, 28–31.

———. 2000. Turning the Tables: Welfare Reform Faces a Time Limit of Its Own. *In These Times*, June 12, 16–18.

Diamond, Sara. 1995. *Roads to Dominion: Right-Wing Movements and Political Power in the United States*. New York: Guilford Press.

Diaz, Kevin. 1998. Mayor's Report Calls for Reduced Federal Aid, More Marketplace Reliance. *The Star Tribune*, November 17, 3B.

Dicter, Midge. 1992. How the Rioters Won. *Commentary* 94, no. 1 (July): 17–22.

DiIulio, John. 1996. Stop Crime Where It Starts. *New York Times*, July 31, A15.

Donald, James. 1999. *Imagining the Modern City*. Minneapolis: University of Minnesota Press.

Douglas, Susan. 1997. Body-Bag Journalism. *The Progressive*. April, 19.

Dreier, Peter, John Mollenkopf, and Todd Swanstrom. 2001. *Place Matters: Metropolitics for the Twenty-First Century*. Lawrence: University of Kansas Press.

Duin, Julia. 2000. Editor's Study Finds Elitist "Gap" between Journalists, Readers. *The Washington Times*, March 29, 2.

Dyer, Richard. 1999. *Seven (BFI Modern Classics)*. London: British Film Institute.

Eagleton, Terry. 1991. *Ideology: An Introduction*. New York: Verso Books.

Edsall, Thomas, and Mary Edsall. 1992. *Chain Reaction: The Impact of Race, Rights, and Taxes on American Politics*. New York: W. W. Norton.

Ehrenhalt, Alan. 1995. *The Lost City: The Forgotten Virtues of Community in America*. New York: Basic Books.

Ehrenreich, Barbara. 1990. *Fear of Falling: The Inner Life of the Middle Class*. New York: Harper Collins.

———, and Deirdre English. 1973. *Complaints and Disorders*. New York: The Feminist Press.

Entman, Robert. 1994. African-Americans According to TV News. *The Media Studies Journal* (Summer): 29–38.

Epstein, Helen. 2003. The New Ghetto Miasma. *New York Times Magazine*, October 12, 75–108.

Estrich, Susan. 1996. Immunize Kids Against Life of Crime. *USA Today*, May 9, 15A.

Ettema, James, and Limor Peer. 1996. Good News from a Bad Neighborhood: Toward an Alternative to the Discourse of Urban Pathology. *Journalism and Mass Communication Quarterly* 73, no. 4: 835–56.

Ewen, Stuart. 1976. *Captains of Consciousness*. New York: McGraw-Hill Book Company.

Faludi, Susan. 1991. *Backlash: The Undeclared War against American Women*. New York: Crown.

FBI Crime Data. 2002. *The State of the Cities Data Systems* (website). Sponsored by the U.S. Department of Housing and Urban Development. Available at http://socds.huduser.org/FBI/FBI_home.htm. Accessed July 23, 2002.

Feagin, Joe R. 1975. *Subordinating the Poor: Welfare and American Beliefs*. Englewood Cliffs, NJ: Prentice-Hall.

———, and Harlan Hahn. 1973. *Ghetto Revolts: The Politics of Violence in American Cities*. New York: Macmillan.

Finney, John. 1968. Nixon and Reagan Ask War On Crime. *New York Times,* August 1, 1.

Fishman, Robert. 1987. *Bourgeois Utopias: The Rise and Fall of Utopia.* New York: Basic Books.

———. 1990. Megalopolis Unbound. *Wilson Quarterly* (Winter): 25–48.

Ford, Larry. 1994. Sunshine and Shadow: Lighting and Color in the Depiction of Cities on Film. In *Place, Power, Situation, and Spectacle: A Geography of Film,* ed. Stuart Aitken and Leo Zonn, 199–236. Lanham, MD: Rowman and Littlefield.

Forsyth, Scott. 1992. Hollywood's War on the World: The New World Order as Movie. In *Socialist Register 1992,* ed. Ralph Miliband and Leo Pantich, 270–85. London: The Merlin Press.

Foucault, Michel. 1979. *Discipline and Punish: The Birth of the Prison.* New York: Vintage Books.

Fox, Kenneth. 1985. *Metropolitan America: Urban Life and Urban Policy in the United States, 1940–1980.* New Brunswick, NJ: Rutgers University Press.

Frank, Tom. 2000. *One Market under God: Extreme Capitalism, Market Populism, and the End of Economic Democracy.* New York: Doubleday.

Frankel, Bruce. 1995. No More Business as Usual for Many Cities. *USA Today.* February 16, 6A.

Franklin, Ben A. 1968. Agnew Deplores Disorder in U.S. *New York Times,* September 29, 74.

Franklin, Raymond S. 1991. *Shadows of Race and Class.* Minneapolis: University of Minnesota Press.

Fraser, Nancy. 1995. Clintonism, Welfare, and the Antisocial Wage: The Emergence of a Neo-Liberal Political Imaginary. In *Marxism in the Postmodern Age,* ed. Antonio Callari, Stephen Cullenberg, and Carole Biewener. New York: Guilford Press.

Fraser, Steven, ed. 1995. *The Bell Curve Wars.* New York: Basic Books.

Fredrickson, George. 1995. Demonizing the American Dilemma. *The New York Review of Books* 42, no. 16, 10–16.

Frey, William H. 2001. *Melting Pot Suburbs? A Census 2000 Study of Suburban Diversity.* Washington, DC: The Brookings Institution.

———, and Alan Berube. 2002. *A Decade of Mixed Blessings: Urban and Suburban Poverty in Census 2000.* Washington DC: The Brookings Institution.

Fritzsche, Peter. 1996. *Reading Berlin 1900.* Cambridge, MA: Harvard University Press.

Fuentes, Annette. 1996. Slaves of New York. *In These Times*. December 22, 14–17.

Gabbard, Krin. 2001. "Someone Is Going to Pay": Resurgent Masculinity in *Ransom*. In *Masculinity: Bodies, Movies, Culture*, ed. Peter Lehman. New York: Routledge.

Gans, Herbert. 1979. *Deciding What's News: A Study of CBS Evening News, NBC Nightly News, Newsweek, and Time*. New York: Pantheon.

———. 1988. *Middle American Individualism*. New York: Oxford University Press.

———. 1995. *The War against the Poor: The Underclass and Anti-Poverty Policy*. New York: Basic Books.

Garfield, Bob. 1996. Packard Bell Builds Home into Refuge. *Advertising Age*. November 11, 61.

Garland, David. 2001. *The Culture of Control: Crime and Social Order in Contemporary Society*. Chicago: University of Chicago Press.

Garreau, Joel. 1991. *Edge City: Life on the New Frontier*. New York: Doubleday.

Gates, David. 1993. White Male Paranoia. *Newsweek*. March 29, 48–53.

Gerbner, George. 1995. Television Violence: The Power and the Peril. In *Gender, Race, and Class in Media: A Text-Reader*, ed. Gail Dines and Jean M. Humez, 547–57. Thousand Oaks, CA: Sage Publications.

———. 1996. TV Violence and What to Do About It. *Nieman Reports* (Fall): 10–12.

Giddens, Anthony. 1979. *Central Problems in Social Theory*. Berkeley and Los Angeles: University of California Press.

Gilder, George. 1995. Tom Peters and George Gilder Debate the Impact of Technology on Location. *Forbes ASAP*, February 27, 56–61.

Gilens, Martin. 1999. *Why Americans Hate Welfare: Race, Media, and the Politics of Antipoverty Policy*. Chicago: University of Chicago Press.

Giroux, Henry. 1997. Race, Pedagogy, and Whiteness in *Dangerous Minds*. *Cineaste* 22, no. 4: 46–49.

———. 1999. Substituting Prisons for Schools. *Z Magazine*, April, 46–49.

———, and Susan Searls. 1996. Race Talk and *The Bell Curve* Debate: The Crisis of Democratic Vision. *Cultural Critique* (Fall): 5–26.

Gitlin, Todd. 1983. *Inside Prime Time*. New York: Pantheon.

Glassner, Barry. 1999. *The Culture of Fear*. New York: Basic Books.

Glick, Susan. 1994. *Female Persuasion: How the Firearms Industry Markets to Women and the Reality of Women and Guns*. Washington, DC: The Violence Policy Center.

Globe Newstand Price Halved for Commuters. 2001. *The Boston Globe*, May 5, C1.

Goetzl, David. 1999. Brink's Breaks a $20 Mil Direct-Response Campaign. *Advertising Age*, September 13, 8.

Goldman, Robert. 1992. *Reading Ads Socially*. New York: Routledge.

———, and Stephen Papson. 1996. *Sign Wars: The Cluttered Landscape of Advertising*. New York: Guilford Press.

Goldsmith, Stephen. 1996. May We Fit All on Front Page? *Pittsburgh Post-Gazette*, October 27, E1.

———. 1999. *The Twenty-First Century City: Resurrecting Urban America*. Lanham, MD: Rowman and Littlefield.

Goldsmith, William, and Edward J. Blakely. 1992. *Separate Societies: Poverty and Inequality in U.S. Cities*. Philadelphia: Temple University Press.

Gordon, David M. 1984. Capitalist Development and the History of American Cities. In *Marxism and the Metropolis*, ed. William Tabb and Larry Sawers, 21–53. New York: Oxford University Press.

Gordon, Linda. 1995. The "Underclass" and the U.S. Welfare State. *Socialist Register 1995*, ed. Leo Pantich. London: The Merlin Press.

Gottdiener, Mark. 1986. Recapturing the Center: A Semiotic Analysis of Shopping Malls. In *The City and the Sign: An Introduction to Urban Semiotics*, ed. Mark Gottdiener and Alexandros Logopoulos. New York: Columbia University Press.

Gould, Stephen Jay. 1981. *The Mismeasure of Man*. New York: W. W. Norton.

Gramsci, Antonio. 1971. *Selections from the Prison Notebooks*, ed. Quintin Hoare and Geoffrey Nowell Smith. New York: International Publishers.

Grant, Barry Keith. 1996. Rich and Strange: The Yuppie Horror Film. *Journal of Film and Video* 48, no. 1-2 (Spring/Summer): 4–16.

Gray, Herman. 1989. Television, Black Americans, and the American Dream. *Critical Studies in Mass Communication* 6, no. 4 (December): 223–43.

Greenberg, Stanley R. 1995. *Middle-Class Dreams: The Politics and Power of the New American Majority*. New York: Times Books.

Greinacher, Udo. 1995. The New Reality: Media Technology and Urban Fortress. *Journal of Architectural Education* 48, no. 3: 176–184.

Grunwald, Michael. 1998. The Myth of the Supermayor. *American Prospect*, no. 40 (September/October): 20–27.

Guerrero, Ed. 1993. *Framing Blackness: The African American Image in Film*. Philadelphia: Temple University Press.

Guinther, John. 1996. *Direction of Cities*. New York: Viking.

Hacker, Andrew. 1992. *Two Nations: Black and White, Separate, Hostile and Unequal*. New York: Ballantine.

Hadden, Jeffrey K., and Josef Barton. 1973. An Image That Will Not Die: Thoughts on the History of Anti-Urban Ideology. In *The Urbanization of the Suburbs*, ed. Louis Masotti and Jeffery Hadden, 79–116. Beverly Hills, CA: Sage Publications.

Hadjor, Kofi Buenor. 1995. *Another America: The Politics of Race and Blame*. Boston: South End Press.

Hall, Peter. 1988. *Cities of Tomorrow*. London: Basil Blackwell.

Hall, Stuart. 1982. The Rediscovery of "Ideology": Return of the Repressed in Media Studies. In *Culture, Society, and the Media* , ed. Michael Gurevitch, Tony Bennett, James Curran, and Janet Woollacott, 56–90. London: Routledge.

———. 1995. The Whites of Their Eyes: Racist Ideologies and the Media. In *Gender, Race, and Class: A Text-Reader*, ed. Gail Dines and Jean M. Humez, 18–22. Thousand Oaks, CA: Sage Publications.

———, Chas Critcher, Tony Jefferson, John Clarke, and Brian Roberts. 1978. *Policing the Crisis: Mugging, the State, and Law and Order.* New York: Holmes and Meier.

Hallin, Daniel C. 1994. *We Keep America On Top of the World: Television Journalism and the Public Sphere*. London: Routledge.

Hannigan, John. 1998. *Fantasy City: Pleasure and Profit in the Postmodern Metropolis*. London: Routledge.

Harrington, Michael. 1962. *The Other America: Poverty in the United States*. New York: Macmillan.

———. 1984. *The New American Poverty*. New York: Penguin Books.

Harris, Fred R. 1998. The Kerner Report Thirty Years Later. In *Locked in the Poorhouse: Cities, Race, and Poverty in the United States*, ed. Fred R. Harris and Lynn A. Curtis, 7–19. Lanham, MD: Rowman and Littlefield.

Hart, Patricia Kilday. 2000. Conservative. Compassionate? *Texas Monthly*. July, 99.

Harvey, David. 1985. *Consciousness and the Urban Experience*. Baltimore: The Johns Hopkins University Press.

———. 1989. *The Condition of Postmodernity*. Cambridge: Basil Blackwell.

———. 1997. The Environment of Justice. In *The Urbanization of Injustice*, ed. Andy Merrifield and Erik Swyngedouw. New York: New York University Press.

Hayward, Steven. 1998. Broken Cities: Liberalism's Urban Legacy. *Policy Review* March/April, 12–23.

Hebdige, Dick. 1979. *Subculture: The Meaning of Style*. London: Methuen.

Heinz, Andreas, and Julia Rothenberg. 1998. Meddling with Monkey Metaphors—Capitalism and the Threat of Impulsive Desires. *Social Justice 25*, no 2: 44–64.

Henwood, Doug. 1994. *The State of the U.S.A. Atlas*. New York: Simon and Schuster.

Herman, Edward. 1998. The Propaganda Model Revisited. In *Capitalism and the Information Age*, ed. Robert McChesney, Ellen Meiksins Wood, and John Bellamy Foster. New York: Monthly Review Press.

Herron, Jerry. 1993. *Afterculture: Detroit and the Humiliation of History*. Detroit: Wayne State University Press.

Herszehnhorn, David M. 2001. Rich States, Poor Cities and Mighty Suburbs. *New York Times*, August 19, 39.

Himmelfarb, Gertrude. 1983. *The Idea of Poverty*. New York: Alfred Knopf.

———. 1992. *Poverty and Compassion: The Moral Imagination of the Late Victorians*. New York: Vintage Books.

———. 1994. *The De-moralization of Society*. New York: Vintage Books.

Himmelstein, Hal. 1987. Television News and Television Documentary. In *Television: The Critical View*, ed. Horace Newcomb. New York: Oxford University Press.

Horne, Gerald. 1995. *Fire This Time: The Watts Uprising and the 1960s*. Charlottesville: University of Virginia Press.

Houseman, Gerald. 1982. *City of the Right: Urban Applications of American Conservative Thought*. Westport, CT: Greenwood Press.

Howard, Ina. 2002. Power Sources. *Extra!* May/June, 11–14.

Hoyt, Charles S. 1877. The Causes of Pauperism. *Tenth Annual Report of the State Board of Charities, New York*.

Hummon, David. 1990. *Commonplaces: Community Ideology and Identity in American Culture*. New York: State University of New York Press.

Hymowitz, Kay. 2000. The Teen Mommy Track. In *The Millennial City: A New Urban Paradigm for 21ˢᵗ-Century America*, ed. Myron Magnet, 236–46. Chicago: Ivan Dee.

Iyengar, Shanto, and Adam Simon. 1997. News Coverage of the Gulf Crisis and Public Opinion: A Study of Agenda Setting, Priming, and Framing. In *Do the Media Govern? Politicians, Voters, and Reporters in America*, ed. Shanto Iyengar and Richard Reeves, 248–57. Thousand Oaks, CA: Sage Publications.

Jackson, Jannine, and Jim Naureckas. 1994. Crime Contradictions. *Extra!* May/June, 10–13.

Jackson, Kenneth T. 1985. *Crabgrass Frontier: The Suburbanization of the United States.* New York: Oxford University Press.

Jackson, Peter. 1989. *Maps of Meaning.* London: Unwin Hyman.

Jargowsky, Paul A. 1996. *Poverty and Place: Ghettos, Barrios, and the American City.* New York: Russell Sage Foundation.

———. 1998. Urban Poverty, Race, and the Inner City: The Bitter Fruit of Thirty Years of Neglect. In *Locked in the Poorhouse: Cities, Race, and Poverty in the United States,* ed. Fred R. Harris and Lynn A. Curtis, 79–94. Lanham, MD: Rowman and Littlefield.

Jewell, K. Sue. 1993. *From Mammy to Miss America and Beyond: Cultural Images and the Shaping of U.S. Social Policy.* New York: Routledge.

Jhally, Sut. 1995. Image-Based Culture: Advertising and Popular Culture. In *Gender, Race, and Class in Media: A Text-Reader,* ed. Gail Dines and Jean M. Humez, 77–87. Thousand Oaks, CA: Sage Publications.

Johnson, Paul. *Intellectuals.* New York: Perennial, 1990.

Jones, Gareth Stedman. 1971. *Outcast London: A Study in the Relationship between the Classes in Victorian Society.* New York: Pantheon.

Jones, Jacqueline. 1992. *The Dispossessed: America's Underclasses from the Civil War to the Present.* New York: Basic Books.

———. 1994. American Others. *In These Times,* February 7, 14–17.

———. 1995. Back to the Future with *The Bell Curve:* Jim Crow, Slavery, and G. In *The Bell Curve Wars,* ed. Steven Fraser, 80–93. New York: Basic Books.

Judd, Dennis R. 1995. The Rise of the New Walled Cities. In *Spatial Practices,* ed. Helen Liggett and David Perry, 144–66. Thousand Oaks, CA: Sage Publications.

———, and Todd Swanstrom. 1994. *City Politics: Private Power and Public Policy.* New York: Harper Collins.

Kambler, Michael. 1994. New York's Mayoral Campaign. *Z Magazine,* December, 43–45.

Karp, Stan, Robert Lowe, Barbara Miner, and Bob Peterson. 1997. *Funding for Justice: Money, Equity, and the Future of Public Education.* Milwaukee: Rethinking Schools, Ltd.

Kasarda, John D. 1985. Urban Change and Minority Opportunities. In *The New Urban Reality,* ed. Paul E. Peterson, 33–68. Washington, DC: Brookings Institution Press.

———. 1995. Industrial Restructuring and the Changing Location of Jobs. In *State of the Union: America in the 1990s*. Vol. 1, ed. Reynolds Farley. New York: Russell Sage Foundation.

Katz, Jon. 1997. *Virtuous Reality*. New York: Random House.

Katz, Michael. 1989. *The Undeserving Poor: From the War on Poverty to the War on Welfare*. New York: Pantheon.

———. 1993a. Reframing the "Underclass" Debate. In *The "Underclass" Debate: Views from History*, ed. Michael Katz, 440–77. Princeton, NJ: Princeton University Press.

———. 1993b. The Urban "Underclass" as a Metaphor of Social Transformation. In *The "Underclass" Debate: Views from History*, ed. Michael Katz, 3–23. Princeton, NJ: Princeton University Press.

Kaus, Mickey. 1992. *The End of Equality*. New York: Basic Books.

Kay, Holtz Jane. 1997. *Asphalt Nation: How the Automobile Took Over America and How We Can Take It Back*. New York: Crown.

Kelley, Robin D. G. 1997. *Yo' Mama's Disfunktional!* Boston: Beacon Press.

Kellner, Douglas. 1995. *Media Culture*. London: Routledge.

———, and Michael Ryan. 1990. *Camera Politica: The Politics and Ideology of Contemporary Hollywood Film*. Bloomington and Indianapolis: Indiana University Press.

Kennedy, Liam. 1996. Alien Nation: White Male Paranoia and Imperial Culture in the United States. *Journal of American Studies* 30, no. 1: 87–100.

———. 2000. *Race and Urban Space in Contemporary American Culture*. Edinburgh: Edinburgh University Press.

———, and Maria Balshaw. 2000. Introduction: Urban Space and Representation. In *Urban Space and Representation*, ed. Maria Balshaw and Liam Kennedy, 1–21. London: Pluto Press.

Kenworthy, E.W. 1968. Nixon Is Found Hard to Fathom on Basis of Public Statements. *New York Times*, October 26, 21.

Kershaw, Sarah. 2002. The New Front in the Battle against TB. *New York Times*, May 20, B1.

Kirp, David L., John Dwyer, and Larry Rosenthal. 1995. *Our Town: Race, Housing, and the Soul of Suburbia*. New Brunswick, NJ: Rutgers University Press.

Klawans, Stuart. 2002. Moore's Dystopia. *Film Comment*. November/December, 32–35.

Klein, Joe. 1996. The True Disadvantage. *The New Republic*, October 28, 32–36.

Klite, Paul. 1998. *Not in the Public Interest: Executive Summary*. Denver: Rocky Mountain Media Watch.

————, Robert Bardwell, and Jason Salzman. 1997. *Baaad News: Local TV News in America 2/26/97*. Denver: Rocky Mountain Media Watch.

Knox, Paul. 1993. Capital, Material Culture, and Socio-Spatial Differentiation. In *The Restless Urban Landscape*, ed. Paul Knox, 1–34. Englewood Cliffs, NJ: Prentice Hall.

Korenman, Sanders D., and Christopher Winship. 2000. A Reanalysis of *The Bell Curve*: Intelligence, Family Background, and Schooling. In *Meritocracy and Society*, ed. Kenneth Arrow, Samuel Bowles, and Steve Durlauf, 137–78. Princeton, NJ: Princeton University Press.

Kotkin, Joel. 2000. *The New Geography: How the Digital Revolution Is Reshaping the American Landscape*. New York: Random House.

Kotlowitz, Alex. 1991. *There Are No Children Here: The Story of Two Boys Growing Up in the Other America*. New York: Anchor Books.

Kozol, Jonathan. 1991. *Savage Inequalities*. New York: Crown.

Krans, C. 1988. Forty-two Catholic Churches without a Prayer. *New York Times*, August 14, A 35.

Kristol, Irving. 1970. The Cities: A Tale of Two Classes. *Fortune* 81: 197–98.

————. 1972a. An Urban Civilization without Cities? *Horizon* 14 (Autumn): 36–41.

————. 1972b. *On the Democratic Idea in America*. New York: Harper and Row.

Krivo, Lauren, and Ruth Peterson. 1996. Extremely Disadvantaged Neighborhoods and Urban Crime. *Social Forces* 75, no. 2 (December): 619–50.

Krutnik, Frank. 1997. Something More than Night: Tales of the *Noir* City. In *The Cinematic City*, ed. David Clarke, 83–109. London: Routledge.

Kunstler, James Howard. 1993. *The Geography of Nowhere: The Rise and Decline of America's Man-Made Landscape*. New York: Simon and Schuster.

Kushner, David. 2000. Stop Thief! You've Got Mail. *New York Times*, March 9, G1.

Lacayo, Richard. 1993. Los Angeles: Unhealed Wounds. *Time*, April 19, 26–31.

Lane, Chuck. 1985. The Manhattan Project. *The New Republic*, March 25, 14–16.

Lasch, Christopher. 1995. *The Revolt of the Elites*. New York: W. W. Norton.

Law, Robin M., and Jennifer R. Wolch. 1993. Social Reproduction in the City: Restructuring in Time and Space. In *The Restless Urban Landscape*, ed. Paul Knox, 165–206. Englewood Cliffs, NJ: Prentice Hall.

Lazare, Daniel. 2001. *America's Undeclared War: What's Killing Our Cities and How We Can Stop It*. New York: Harcourt.

Leiss, William, Stephen Kline, and Sut Jhally. 1997. *Social Communication in Advertising*. 2nd Edition, Revised. New York: Routledge.

Lemann, Nicholas. 1986a. The Origin of the Underclass (Part 1). *Atlantic*, June, 31–64.

———. 1986b. The Origin of the Underclass (Part 2). *Atlantic*, July, 54–68.

Leo, John. 1993. When Cities Give Up Their Streets. *U.S. News and World Report*, July 26, 20.

———. 1995. Punished for the Sins of the Children. *U.S. News and World Report*, June 12, 18.

———. 1997. *Two Steps Ahead of the Thought Police*. New York: Simon and Schuster.

Lewis, Oscar. 1968. The Culture of Poverty. In *On Understanding Poverty*, ed. Danial P. Moynihan, 187–200. New York: Basic Books.

Lewontin, R. C. 1992. *Biology As Ideology*. New York: Harper Collins.

Lieberman, Trudy. 2000. *Slanting the Story: The Forces That Shape the News*. New York: The New Press.

Lipsitz, George. 1998. *The Possessive Investment in Whiteness: How White People Profit from Identity Politics*. Philadelphia: Temple University Press.

Liska, A. E., and W. Baccaglini. 1990. Feeling Safe by Comparison: Crime in the Newspapers. *Social Problems* 37: 360–65.

Lofland, Lyn H. 1998. *The Public Realm*. New York: Aldine.

Logan, John. 2001. *The New Ethnic Enclaves in America's Suburbs*. Albany, NY: Lewis Mumford Center for Comparative Urban and Regional Research.

———. 2002. *The Suburban Advantage*. Albany, NY: Lewis Mumford Center for Comparative Urban and Regional Research.

Los Angeles Times to Double Weekday Newsstand Price to 50. 2001. *Los Angeles Times*, February 21, C2.

Lusane, Clarence. 1994. Congratulations, It's a Crime, Bill. *Covert Action Information Bulletin*, no. 50 (Fall): 14–22.

MacDonald, Heather. 2000. *The Burden of Bad Ideas: How Modern Intellectuals Misshape Our Society*. Chicago: Ivan Dee.

Macek, Steve. 1999. Places of Horror: Fincher's *Seven* and Fear of the City in Recent Hollywood Film. *College Literature* 26, no. 1 (Winter): 80–97.

———. 2000. The Mall of America. In *St. James Encyclopedia of Popular Culture*, ed. Tom Pendergast and Sara Pendergast, 3:245-46. Detroit: St. James Press.

Magner, Mike. 1996. Fear of Crime Is Paying Off for Nation's Security, Alarm Companies. *The Cleveland Plain Dealer*, December 26, 3C.

Magnet, Myron. 1993. *The Dream and the Nightmare: The Sixties' Legacy to the Underclass*. New York: William Morrow.

————, ed. 2000. *The Millennial City: A New Urban Paradigm for 21ˢᵗ-Century America*. Chicago: Ivan Dee.

Mahoney, Elisabeth. 1997. "The People in Parenthesis": Space Under Pressure in the Postmodern City. In *The Cinematic City*, ed. David Clarke, 168–85. London: Routledge.

Males, Mike. 1995. Poor Logic. *In These Times*, January 9, 12–15.

————. 1996. *The Scapegoat Generation: America's War on Adolescents*. Monroe, ME: Common Courage Press.

Marchand, Roland. 1985. *Advertising the American Dream: Making Way for Modernity, 1920–1940*. Berkeley and Los Angeles: University of California Press.

Marx, Karl, and Fredrick Engels. 1978. *The German Ideology*. New York: International Publishers. (Orig. pub. 1932.)

————. 1998. *The Communist Manifesto*. New York: Verso Books. (Orig. pub. 1848.)

Massey, Douglas, and Nancy A. Denton. 1993. *American Apartheid: Segregation and the Making of the Underclass*. Cambridge, MA: Harvard University Press.

Massig, Michael. 1995. Ghetto Blasting. *The New Yorker*, January 15, 32–38.

————. 1998. *The Fix*. Berkeley and Los Angeles: University of California Press.

Massood, Paula J. 1996. Mapping the Hood: The Genealogy of City Space in *Boyz N the Hood* and *Menace II Society*. *Cinema Journal* 35, no. 2 (Winter): 85–95.

————. 2003. *Black City Cinema*. Philadelphia: Temple University Press.

Mattson, Kevin. 2003. The Perils of Michael Moore: Political Criticism in an Age of Entertainment. *Dissent* 50, no. 2 (Spring): 75–80.

Mauer, Marc, and the Sentencing Project. 1999. *Race to Incarcerate*. New York: The New Press.

Mayne, Alan. 1993. *The Imagined Slum: Newspaper Representation in Three Cities 1870–1914*. Leicester and London: Leicester University Press.

McArdle, Andrea. 2001. Introduction. In *Zero Tolerance: Quality of Life and the New Police Brutality in New York City*, ed. Andrea McArdle and Tanya Erzen, 1–16. New York: New York University Press.

McCarthy, Cameron, Alicia P. Rodriguez, Ed Buendia, Shuaib Meachem, Stephen David, Heriberto Godina, K. E. Supriya, and Carrie Wilson-Brown. 1997. Danger in the Safety Zone: Notes on Race, Resentment, and the Discourse of Crime, Violence, and Suburban Security. *Cultural Studies* 11, no. 2: 274–95.

McChesney, Robert. 1999. *Rich Media, Poor Democracy: Communication Politics in Dubious Times.* Urbana: University of Illinois Press.

McGowan, William. 1995. A New Paradigm for Race Relations? *The Wall Street Journal,* September 21, A20.

McKenzie, Evan. 1994. *Privatopia: Homeowner Associations and the Rise of Residential Private Government.* New Haven, CT: Yale University Press.

McNamara, Kevin. 1996. *Urban Verbs: Arts and Discourses of American Cities.* Stanford, CA: Stanford University Press.

Mead, Lawrence. 1985. *Beyond Entitlement: The Social Obligation of Citizenship.* New York: Basic Books.

———, ed. 1997. *The New Paternalism: Supervisory Approaches to Poverty.* Washington, DC: Brookings Institution Press.

Mearns, Andrew. 1883. *The Bitter Cry of Outcast London: An Inquiry into the Condition of the Abject Poor.* London: James Clarke.

Meckler, Laura. 1999. Welfare Rolls Decrease Least in Major Cities, Study Finds. *The St. Paul Pioneer Press,* February 19, A1.

Merrifield, Andy. 2002. *Dialectical Urbanism: Social Struggles in the Capitalist City.* New York: Monthly Review Press.

Metro Futures: A High-Wage, Low-Waste, Democratic Development Strategy for America's Cities and Inner Suburbs. 1996. New York and Madison, WI: Sustainable America and the Center on Wisconsin Strategy.

Meyerson, Harold. 1993. The Death of Urban Liberalism? *In These Times,* June 28, 25–27.

Mickey, Kaus. 1992. *The End of Equality.* New York: Basic Books.

Miethe, Terance D. 1995. Fear and Withdrawal from Urban Life. *The Annals of the American Academy of Political and Social Science* 539 (May): 14–27.

Mills, Nicolaus. 1997. *The Triumph of Meanness: America's War Against Its Better Self.* New York: Houghton Mifflin.

Mishel, Lawrence, Jared Bernstein, and John Schmitt. 1999. *The State of Working America, 1998–99.* Ithaca, NY: Cornell University Press.

Mitchell, Alison. 2000. Bush Draws Campaign Theme from More Than "Heart." *New York Times,* June 12, A1.

Mitchell, Don. 1995. The End of Public Space? People's Park, Definitions of the Public, and Democracy. *Annals of the Association of American Geographers* 85: 108–33.

Montgomery, Lori. 1996. Crime at a Distance: That's the Top Concern. *Austin-American-Statesman,* February 4, D6.

Moore, Micki. 1999. Future Shock. *Toronto Sun*, January 17, 46.

Morganthau, Tom, and John McCormick. 1991. Are Cities Obsolete? *Newsweek*, September 9, 42–45.

Morris, Lydia. 1994. *Dangerous Classes: The Underclass and Social Citizenship*. London: Routledge.

Morris, Michael. 1996. Culture, Structure, and the Underclass. In *Myths about the Powerless*, ed. M. Brinton Lykes, Ali Banuazizi, Ramsay Liem, and Michael Morris, 34–49. Philadelphia: Temple University Press.

Morse, Margaret. 1986. The Television News Personality and Credibility: Reflections on the News in Transition. In *Studies in Entertainment: Critical Approaches to Mass Culture*, ed. Tania Modleski, 55–79. Bloomington and Indianapolis: Indiana University Press.

———. 1990. An Ontology of Everyday Distraction: The Freeway, the Mall and Television. In *Logics of Television: Essays in Cultural Criticism*, ed. Patricia Mellencamp, 193–221. Bloomington and Indianapolis: Indiana University Press.

Muharrar, Mikal. 1998. Criminal Communities: "Racial Dualism" Puts White Supremacy in the Media Crime Frame. *Extra!* January/February, 15–16.

Murray, Charles. 1984. *Losing Ground: American Social Policy, 1965–1980*. New York: Basic Books.

———. 1990. Here's the Bad News on the Underclass. *Wall Street Journal*, March 8, A14.

———. 1992. The Legacy of the 60's. *Commentary* 94, no. 1 (July): 23–30.

———. 1993. The Coming White Underclass. *Wall Street Journal*, October 29, A14.

———. 1994a. Race, Pathology and IQ. *Wall Street Journal*, October 10, A12.

———. 1994b. The Real "Bell Curve." *Wall Street Journal*, December 2, A14.

———. 1995. Welfare Hysteria. *New York Times*, November 14, 25A.

———. 1999. And Now for the Bad News. *Wall Street Journal*, February 2, A22.

———, and Herrnstein, Richard J. 1994. *The Bell Curve: Intelligence and Class Structure in American Life*. New York: The Free Press.

Muzzio, Douglas. 1996. "Decent People Shouldn't Live Here": The American City in Cinema. *Journal of Urban Affairs* 18, no. 2: 189–215.

Nadel, Alan. 1997. *Flatlining on the Field of Dreams: Cultural Narratives in the Films of President Reagan's America*. New Brunswick, NJ: Rutgers University Press.

Nasaw, David. 1993. *Going Out: The Rise and Fall of Public Amusements*. New York: Harper Collins.

National Crime Prevention Council Press Release. 1995. Attorney General's Remarks. October 6.

Natter, Wolfgang, and John Paul Jones III. 1993. Pets or Meat: Class, Ideology, and Space in *Roger and Me*. *Antipode* 25, no. 2: 140–58.

Naureckas, Jim. 1995. Racism Resurgent: How the Media Let *The Bell Curve's* Pseudo-Science Define the Agenda on Race. *Extra!* January/February, 12–15.

New York City in Crisis. 1965. *New York Herald Tribune*, February 5.

Newfield, Jack. 2002. *The Full Rudy: The Man, the Myth, the Mania*. New York: Thunder's Mouth Press.

Norquist, John. 1999. *The Wealth of Cities*. New York: Perseus Books.

O'Connor, Alice. 2001. *Poverty Knowledge: Social Science, Social Policy, and the Poor in Twentieth-Century U.S. History*. Princeton, NJ: Princeton University Press.

O'Keefe, Garrett J., and Kathaleen Reid-Nash. 1987. Crime News and Real-World Blues. *Communication Research* 14, no.2 (April): 147–63.

Olasky, Marvin. 1993. *The Tragedy of American Compassion*. Washington, DC: Regency.

———. 1996. Don't Look to Government. *USA Today*, May 23, 14A.

Omi, Michael, and Howard Winant. 1993. The Los Angeles "Race Riot" and Contemporary U.S. Politics. In *Reading Rodney King, Reading Urban Uprising*, ed. Robert Gooding-Williams, 97–114. New York: Routledge.

Orfield, Myron. 1997. *Metropolitics: A Regional Agenda for Community Stability*. Washington, DC: Brookings Institution Press.

Orwell, Miles. 1994/1995. Documentary Film and the Power of Interrogation. *Film Quarterly* 48, no. 2 (Winter): 10–18.

Osborn, Barbara Bliss. 1996. What's Happening in the City of Angels? Don't Count on the *L.A. Times* to Tell You. *Extra!* September/October, 24.

Paget, Karen. 1998. Can Cities Escape Political Isolation? *The American Prospect* 9, no. 36 (January/February): 54–62.

Parenti, Christian. 1999. *Lockdown America: Police and Prison in the Age of Crisis*. New York: Verso Books.

Parenti, Michael. 1986. *Inventing Reality*. New York: St. Martin's Press.

Parisi, Peter. 1998. A Sort of Compassion: The *Washington Post* Explains the "Crisis in Urban America." *The Howard Journal of Communications* 9: 187–203.

Pattillo-McCoy, Mary. 1999. *Black Picket Fences: Privilege and Peril Among the Black Middle Class*. Chicago: The University of Chicago Press.

Peck, Keenen. 1983. Ad Nauseam. *The Progressive*, May, 43–48.

Perkinson, Robert. 1994. Clinton's Politics of Punishment. *Z Magazine*, October, 12–14.

Pew Research Center for the People and the Press. 2000. *Survey Report: Internet Sapping Broadcast News Audience.* June 11. Available at http://www.people-press.org.

Pierce, Neal. 1994. Violent Filmmaking Impacts Public's Crime View. *Nation's Cities Weekly*, April 11, 5.

Piven, Frances Fox, and Richard A. Cloward. 1971. *Regulating the Poor: The Functions of Public Welfare.* New York: Vintage Books.

———. 1996. Welfare Reform and the New Class War. In *Myths about the Powerless*, ed. M. Brinton Lykes, Ali Banuazizi, Ramsay Liem, and Michael Morris, 72–86. Philadelphia: Temple University Press.

Platt, Anthony. 1995. The Politics of Law and Order. *Social Justice* 21, no. 3: 3–13.

Platt, Larry. 1999. Armageddon—Live at 6! In *Impact of Mass Media*, ed. Ray Eldon Hiebert, 242–48. New York: Longman.

Puttnam, David. 1986. Puttnam's New Mission. *American Film*, March, 45.

Quart, Leonard. 1996. Spike Lee's *Clockers*: A Lament for the Urban Ghetto. *Cineaste* 22 no. 1: 9–11.

Quigely, William. 1995. The Minimum Wage and the Working Poor. *America*, June 3, 6–7.

Rainer, Peter. 1993. *Falling Down* Trips Over Its Own Hate. *Los Angeles Times*, March 15, F7.

Rainwater, Lee, and William L. Yancey. 1967. *The Moynihan Report and the Politics of Controversy.* Cambridge, MA: MIT Press.

Reardon, Patrick. 1993. Fear, Anger and Regret: Ex-Chicagoans Speak Out. *Chicago Tribune*, November 29, A1.

Reed, Adolph, Jr. 1990. The Underclass as Myth and Symbol. *Radical America* 24, no. 1: 21–42.

———. 1994. Intellectual Brown Shirts. *The Progressive*, December, 15–17.

Reeves, Jimmie. 1999. Re-Covering the Homeless: Hindsights on the Joyce Brown Story. In *Reading the Homeless*, ed. Eungjun Min, 45–63. Westport, CT: Praeger.

———, and Richard Campbell. 1989. Covering the Homeless: The Joyce Brown Story. *Critical Studies in Mass Communication* 6: 21–42.

———. 1994. *Cracked Coverage: Television News, the Anti-Cocaine Crusade, and the Reagan Legacy.* Durham, NC: Duke University Press.

Ridgeway, James. 1997. Heritage on the Hill. *The Nation*, December 22, 11–18.

Riis, Jacob. 1890. *How the Other Half Lives*. Repr., New York: Dover, 1971.

Rivers, Caryl. 1996. *Slick Spins and Fractured Facts: How Cultural Myths Distort the News*. New York: Columbia University Press.

Roberts, Sam. 1994. Gap Between Rich and Poor in New York City Grows Wider. *New York Times*, December 25, 33.

Rogers, Everett M., William B. Hart, and James Dearing. 1997. A Paradigmatic History of Agenda-Setting Research. In *Do the Media Govern? Politicians, Voters, and Reporters in America*, ed. Shanto Iyengar and Richard Reeves, 225–36. Thousand Oaks, CA: Sage Publications.

Rogers, Joel, and Daniel D. Luria. 1999. *Metro Futures: Economic Solutions for the Cities and Their Suburbs*. Boston: Beacon Press.

RoperASW. 2002. *National Geographic—RoperASW 2002 Global Geographic Literacy Survey*. November. Available at http://news.nationalgeographic.com/news/2002/11/1120_021120_GeoRoperSurvey.html.

Rorty, Richard. 1995. Color-Blind in the Marketplace. *New York Times Book Review*, September 24, 9.

Rosenberg, Charles. 1992. *Explaining Epidemics*. Cambridge: Cambridge University Press.

Ross, Andrew. 1990. Ballots, Bullets or Batman: Can Cultural Studies Do the Right Thing? *Screen* 31, no. 1 (Spring): 26–44.

———. 1994. *The Chicago Gangster Theory of Life*. New York: Verso Books.

Ross, Loretta. 1995. White Supremacy in the 1990s. In *Eyes Right! Challenging the Right Wing Backlash*, ed. Chip Berlet, 166–81. Boston: South End Press.

Rotella, Carlo. 1998. *October Cities*. Berkeley and Los Angeles: University of California Press.

Rothenberg, Julia, and Andreas Heinz. 1998. Meddling with Monkey Metaphors—Capitalism and the Threat of Impulsive Desires. *Social Forces* 25, no. 2: 44–64.

Rowse, Arthur. 2000. *Drive-by Journalism*. Monroe, ME: Common Courage Press.

Ruben, Matthew. 2001. Suburbanization and Urban Poverty under Neoliberalism. In *New Poverty Studies: The Ethnography of Power, Politics, and Impoverished People in the United States*, ed. Judith Goode and Jeff Maskovsky, 435–69. New York: New York University Press.

Ryan, William. 1971. *Blaming the Victim*. New York: Pantheon.

Rybczynski, Witold. 1995. *City Life*. New York: Simon and Schuster.

Sacco, Vincent F. 1995. Media Constructions of Crime. *The Annals of the American Academy of Political and Social Science* 539 (May): 141–54.

Sanborn, F. B. 1886. Migration and Immigration. *Proceedings, National Conference of Charities and Correction* 13.

Sassen, Saskia. 2000. *Cities in a World Economy.* Thousand Oaks, CA: Pine Forge Press.

Sawhill, Isabel. 1989. The Underclass: An Overview. *Public Interest*, no. 96 (Summer): 2–15.

Schiller, Herbert I. 1989. *Culture Inc.: The Corporate Takeover of Public Expression.* New York: Oxford University Press.

Schiraldi, Vincent. 2000. Americans Overreact to Youth Crime. *Milwaukee Journal Sentinel*, December 20, 19A.

Schneider, William. 1992. The Suburban Century Begins. *The Atlantic Monthly*, July, 33–44.

Schudson, Michael. 1997. The Sociology of News Production. In *Social Meanings of News*, ed. Dan Berkowitz, 7–23. Thousand Oaks, CA: Sage Publications.

Schwartz, John, and Thomas Volgy. 1993. Working Poor. *The Nation*, February 15, 191–92.

Scott, Janny. 1997. Turning Intellect into Influence. *New York Times*, May 12, B1.

Sennett, Richard. 1970. *The Uses of Disorder.* New York: Vintage Press.

———. 1978. *The Fall of Public Man.* New York: Vintage Press.

———. 1990. *The Conscience of the Eye.* New York: W. W. Norton.

Sharpe, William, and Leonard Wallock. 1994. Bold New City or Built-Up 'Burb? Redefining Contemporary Suburbia. *American Quarterly* 46, no. 1. (March): 1–30.

Sharrett, Christopher. 1993a. The American Apocalypse: Martin Scorsese's *Taxi Driver*. In *Crisis Cinema*, ed. Christopher Sharrett, 221–35. Washington, DC: Maisonneuve Press.

———. 1993b. The Horror Film in Neo-Conservative Culture. *Journal of Popular Film and Television* 21, no. 3 (Fall): 100–110.

———, and William Luhr. 2003. *Bowling for Columbine. Cineaste* 28, no. 2, 36–38.

Siegel, Fred. 1997. *The Future Once Happened Here.* New York: The Free Press.

Silverstone, Roger. 1994. *Television and Everyday Life.* New York: Routledge.

Simmons, Patrick, and Robert E. Lang. 2001. The Urban Turnaround: A Decade-by-Decade Report Card on Postwar Population Change in Older Industrial Cities. *Fannie Mae Foundation Census Note 01.*

Simon, Roger, and Angie Cannon. 2001. Who We Were, Who We Are. *U.S. News and World Report*, August 2, 11–18.

Simpson, Philip L. 1999. The Politics of Apocalypse in the Cinema of Serial Murder. In *Mythologies of Violence in Postmodern Media*, ed. Christopher Sharrett, 119–44. Detroit: Wayne State University Press.

Sklar, Holly. 1993. Mothers in the 'Hood. *Z Magazine*, March, 28–33.

———. 1995. *Chaos or Community? Seeking Solutions, Not Scapegoats for Bad Economics*. Boston: South End Press.

Smith, Neil. 1997. Social Justice and the New American Urbanism: The Revanchist City. In *The Urbanization of Injustice*, ed. Andy Merrifield and Erik Swyngedouw. New York: New York University Press.

———. 1998. The Revanchist 1990s. *Social Text*, no. 57 (Winter): 1–9.

Smith, Ruth L. 1990. Order and Disorder: The Naturalization of Poverty. *Cultural Critique* 14: 209–29.

Soley, Lawrence. 1992. *The News Shapers: The Sources Who Explain the News*. New York: Praeger.

Solomon, Norman. 1998. Writers of the Right Unite. *Extra!* March/April, 14–16.

———, and Martin A. Lee. 1990. *Unreliable Sources: A Guide to Detecting Bias in News Media*. New York: Lyle Stuart.

Sparrow, Bartholomew. 1999. *Uncertain Guardians: The News Media as a Political Institution*. Baltimore: The Johns Hopkins University Press.

Stacey, Judith. 1995. Scents, Scholars, and Stigmas: The Revisionist Campaign for Family Values. *Social Text*, no. 40 (Fall): 51–75.

Stack, Carol. 1974. *All Our Kin: Strategies for Survival in a Black Community*. New York: Harper and Row.

Stallybrass, Peter, and Allon White. 1986. *The Politics and Poetics of Transgression*. Ithaca, NY: Cornell University Press.

Stam, Robert. 1983. Television News and Its Spectator. In *Regarding Television*, ed. E. Ann Kaplan, 23–43. Frederick, MD: The American Film Institute.

Stark, Andrew. 1998. America, the Gated? *Wilson Quarterly* (Winter): 58–79.

Stefancic, Jean, and Richard Delgado. 1996. *No Mercy: How Conservative Think Tanks and Foundations Changed America's Social Agenda*. Philadelphia: Temple University Press.

Stolberg, Sherly Gay. 1998. U.S. Awakes to Epidemic of Sexual Diseases. *New York Times*, March 9, A1.

Strong, Josiah. 1885. *Our Country: Its Possible Future and Its Present*. New York. Repr. Cambridge, MA: Harvard University Press, 1963.

Sugrue, Thomas J. 1996. *The Origins of the Urban Crisis: Race and Inequality in Postwar Detroit*. Princeton, NJ: Princeton University Press.

Surrette, Ray. 1998. *Media, Crime, and Criminal Justice.* Belmont, CA: Wadsworth Publishing Company.

Taubin, Amy. 1996. The Allure of Decay. *Sight and Sound* 6, no. 1 (January): 23–24.

Teaford, Jon. 1986. *The Twentieth-Century American City: Problem, Promise, and Reality.* Baltimore: The Johns Hopkins University Press.

———. 1997. *Post-Suburbia: Government and Politics in the Edge Cities.* Baltimore: The Johns Hopkins University Press.

Thernstrom, Stephan, and Abigail Thernstrom. 1997. *America in Black and White.* New York: Simon and Schuster.

Thomas, G. Scott. 1998. *The United States of Suburbia.* New York: Prometheus Books.

Thompson, Kenneth. 1998. *Moral Panics.* London: Routledge.

Toffler, Alvin. 1980. *The Third Wave.* London: Pan Books.

Toler, Deborah. 1999. The Right's "Race Desk." *Extra!* March/April, 13–15.

Tuan, Yi-Fu. 1979. *Landscapes of Fear.* Minneapolis: University of Minnesota Press.

Turner, Graeme. 1988. *Film as Social Practice.* New York: Routledge.

U.S. Bureau of the Census. 1975. *Censuses of Population 1950–1970.* Washington, DC: Government Printing Office.

———. 1995. Detailed Poverty Tables, Table 19. *U.S. Bureau of the Census Website.* Available at: www.census.gov/hhes/www/poverty.html.

———. 2000. *Statistical Abstract of the United States.* Washington, DC: Government Printing Office.

———. 2002. Poverty Tables and Historical Poverty Tables. *U.S. Bureau of the Census Website.* Available at: www.census.gov/hhes/www/poverty.html.

U.S. Conference of Mayors. 1997. *A Status Report on Hunger and Homelessness in America's Cities: A 29-City Survey.* Washington DC: The United States Conference of Mayors.

Ward, David. 1989. *Poverty, Ethnicity, and the American City, 1840–1925.* Cambridge: Cambridge University Press.

Watney, Simon. 1987. *Policing Desire: Pornography, AIDS, and the Media.* London: Methuen.

Westphal, David. 1999. Youth Crime Plunge Shoots Down Scare. *Pittsburgh Post-Gazette,* December 13, A-13.

Whang, Insung, and Eungjun Min. 1999a. Blaming the Homeless: The Populist Aspect of Network TV News. In *Reading the Homeless,* ed. Eungjun Min, 121–33. Westport, CT: Praeger.

———. 1999b. Discourse Analysis of Television News on Public Antagonism against the Homeless. In *Reading the Homeless*, ed. Eungjun Min, 95–107. Westport, CT: Praeger.

White, Morton, and Lucia White. 1962. *The Intellectual versus the City*. New York: Mentor.

Will, George. 1991. Nature and the Male Sex. *Newsweek*, June 17, 70.

———. 1990. America's Slide into the Sewer. *Newsweek*, July 30, 64.

———. 1994a. "187": In-Your-Face Look at a Society Run Amok. *The Chicago Sun-Times*, August 10, 34.

———. 1994b. "Street" values true oppressors of inner-city Americans. *Saint Paul Pioneer Press*, September 15, 11A.

———. 1994c. About those "Orphanages." *Newsweek*, December 12, 88.

———. 1997. What's Causing the Nation's Welfare State to Unravel. *The Times-Picayune*, August 21, B7.

Williams, Raymond. 1975. *Television: Technology and Cultural Form*. New York: Schocken Books.

Wilson, James Q. 1968. Urban Problems in Perspective. In *The Metropolitan Enigma*, ed. James Q. Wilson, 386–409. Garden City, NY: Anchor Books.

———. 1975. *Thinking About Crime*. New York: Basic Books. Revised edition, 1983. New York: Random House.

———. 1997. Crime and American Culture. In *The Eighties: A Reader*, ed. Gilbert T. Sewell, 61–69. Reading, MA: Addison-Wesley.

Wilson, William Julius. 1987. *The Truly Disadvantaged: The Inner City, the Underclass, and Public Policy*. Chicago: The University of Chicago Press.

———. 1996. *When Work Disappears: The World of the New Urban Poor*. New York: Alfred A. Knopf.

Wimsatt, William Upski. 1998. The Fear Economy. *Adbusters*, Spring, 31–33.

Withorn, Ann. 1998. Fulfilling Fears and Fantasies: The Role of Welfare in Right-Wing Social Thought and Strategy. In *Unraveling the Right: The New Conservatism in American Thought and Politics*, ed. Amy Ansell, 126–47. Boulder, CO: Westview Press.

Wood, Robin. 1985. An Introduction to the American Horror Film. In *Movies and Methods II*, ed. Bill Nichols, 195–220. Berkeley and Los Angeles: University of California Press.

Woodyard, Chris. 1997. Selling Fear Marketers Tap Boomers' Feelings of Insecurity. *USA Today*, August 6, 1B.

Wright, Gwendolyn. 1981. *Building the Dream: A Social History of Housing in America*. Cambridge, MA: MIT Press.

Yanich, Danilo. 2001. Location, Location, Location: Urban and Suburban Crime on Local TV News. *Journal of Urban Affairs* 23, no. 3–4: 221–41.

Zbar, Jeffery D. 1994. Fear! It's Everywhere You Want to Be. *Advertising Age*, November 14, 18–19.

Zukin, Sharon. 1991a. *Landscapes of Power: From Detroit to Disney World*. Berkeley and Los Angeles: University of California Press.

———. 1991b. The Hollow Center: U.S. Cities in the Global Era. In *America at Century's End*, ed. Alan Wolfe, 245–61. Berkeley and Los Angeles: University of California Press.

Filmography

187. 1997. Directed by Kevin Reynolds.

A Touch of Evil. 1958. Directed by Orson Welles.

After Hours. 1985. Directed by Martin Scorsese.

Armageddon. 1998. Directed by Michael Bay.

Bad Influence. 1991. Directed by Curtis Hanson.

Batman. 1989. Directed by Tim Burton.

Blue Steel. 1990. Directed by Kathryn Bigelow.

Bonfire of the Vanities. 1990. Directed by Brian De Palma.

Bowling for Columbine. 2002. Directed by Michael Moore.

Boyz in the Hood. 1991. Directed by John Singleton.

Clockers. 1995. Directed by Spike Lee.

Colors. 1988. Directed by Dennis Hopper.

Dangerous Minds. 1996. Directed by John Smith.

Darkman. 1990. Directed by Sam Rami.

Death Wish. 1974. Directed by Michael Winner.

Deep Impact. 1998. Directed by Mimi Leder.

Desperately Seeking Susan. 1985. Directed by Susan Seidelman.

Die Hard: With a Vengeance. 1995. Directed by John McTiernan

Die Hard 2. 1990. Directed by Renny Harlin.

Dirty Harry. 1971. Directed by Don Siegel.

Escape from L.A. 1996. Directed by John Carpenter.

Escape from New York. 1981. Directed by John Carpenter.

Eye for an Eye. 1996. Directed by John Schlesinger.

Falling Down. 1993. Directed by Joel Schumacher.

Fatal Attraction. 1987. Directed by Adrian Lyne.

From Hell. 2001. Directed by Allen and Albert Hughes.

Godzilla. 1998. Directed by Roland Emmerich.

Grand Canyon. 1991. Directed by Lawrence Kasdan.

Home Alone. 1990. Directed by Chris Columbus.

Independence Day. 1996. Directed by Roland Emmerich.

It Could Happen to You. 1994. Directed by Andrew Bergman.

Johnny Mnemonic. 1995. Directed by Robert Longo.

Judgment Night. 1993. Directed by Stephen Hopkins.

Kiss Me Deadly. 1955. Directed by Robert Aldrich.

Lean on Me. 1988. Directed by John G. Avidson.

Little Caesar. 1930. Directed by Mervyn LeRoy.

Menace II Society. 1993. Directed by Allen and Albert Hughes.

Mimic. 1997. Directed by Guillermo del Toro.

Money Train. 1995. Directed by Joseph Ruben.

New Jack City. 1991. Directed by Mario Van Peebles.

Pacific Heights. 1990. Directed by John Schlesinger.

Predator. 1987. Directed by John McTierman.

Predator 2. 1990. Directed by Stephen Hopkins.

Public Enemy. 1931. Directed by William Wellman.

Ransom. 1996. Directed by Ron Howard.

Scarlet Street. 1946. Directed by Fritz Lang.

Seven. 1995. Directed by David Fincher.

Sleepless in Seattle. 1993. Directed by Nora Ephron.

Something Wild. 1986. Directed by Jonathan Demme.

Speed. 1994. Directed by Jan De Bont.

Street Justice. 1989. Directed by Richard Sarafian.

Sugar Hill. 1993. Directed by Leon Ichaso.

Taxi Driver. 1976. Directed by Martin Scorsese.

The Big Chill. 1983. Directed by Lawrence Kasdan.

The Big Sleep. 1946. Directed by Howard Hawks.

The Crow. 1994. Directed by Alex Proyas.

The Devil's Advocate. 1997. Directed by Taylor Hackford.

The Hand That Rocks the Cradle. 1992. Directed by Curtis Hanson.

The Substitute. 1996. Directed by Robert Mandel.

The Warriors. 1979. Directed by Walter Hill.

The Woman in the Window. 1945. Directed by Fritz Lang.

T-Men. 1947. Directed by Anthony Mann.

Touch of Evil. 1958. Directed by Orson Welles.

Trespass. 1992. Directed by Walter Hill.

Unlawful Entry. 1992. Directed by Jonathan Kaplan.

You've Got Mail. 1998. Directed by Nora Ephron.

Volcano. 1997. Directed by Mick Jackson.

Index

ABC World News Tonight, 145, 182; on crack, 163, 164; on Edge Cities, 196; on the graffiti problem, 169, 171; on the homeless, 172–73; on relocating the disadvantaged, 196; on urban crime and violence, 165, 168; on the urban crisis in New York City, 191, 194. *See also* news media; television

Abraham, Spencer, 118

ACLU, 116, 124, 125

ACORN, 294

Ad Council, The, 283–90

ADT, 265, 269, 283, 285

Advertising Age, 259

advertising, xvi, xix, xx; and the Ad Council, 283–90; and anxiety about street crime, 278–83; and city as exotic, 323n1; as cultural bellwethers, 262–63; and fear appeals, 260–62, 263–65; and the image of the besieged family, 265–68; and the image of the postindustrial

city, 257–60, 276; and the promise of freedom, 276–78; and the promise of safety, 273–76; and the protective father, 268–69; targeted at women, 270–71

AFDC, 49, 76, 77, 79, 96, 130, 175, 178, 181

African Americans: conservatives, 91, 160; and coverage of poverty, 182–83; coverage of the crisis in the black family, 174–75; and drug abuse, 135; Dinesh D'Souza on, 90–92; economic status of, 24; family structure, 59–60, 160; filmmakers, 220–24; Great Migrations of, 3, 12–14, 79; impact of economic restructuring on, 25–26; said to be victimized by liberal paternalism, 113; suburbanization of, 17; as victims and perpetrators of violence on TV news, 165. *See also* civil rights movement; ghetto; race; segregation

Steve Macek teaches speech communication and media studies at North Central College in Naperville, Illinois. His articles and reviews have been published in *College Literature*, *Bad Subjects*, *Quarterly Review of Film and Video*, and the *St. Louis Journalism Review*, as well as many newspapers and popular magazines.